URBAN MASS TRANSPORTATION:
A Dozen Years of Federal Policy

URBAN MASS TRANSPORTATION
A Dozen Years of Federal Policy

George M. Smerk

INDIANA UNIVERSITY PRESS
Bloomington & London

Published in Canada by Fitzhenry & Whiteside Limited,
Don Mills, Ontario
Manufactured in the United States of America

Library of Congress Cataloging in Publication data

Smerk, George M
  Urban mass transportation; a dozen years of federal policy.

  Bibliography
  1. Urban transportation policy—United States.
I. Title.
HE308.S53   1974   388.4'0973   73-21242
ISBN 0-253-36170-2

Dedicated to the memory of my good friend
JOHN RONALD ZALKE 1934–1956
who would have made great contributions
to this world had he not been called
so soon to a better one.

Acknowledgments

In preparing this manuscript I was most fortunate to have the advice and commentary of good friends and colleagues. I was also aided by the comments, insights, and suggestions gathered over the years from friends and acquaintances in government and in the transit industry. The completion of this work was made possible through the encouragement of my wife, Mary Ann. I am grateful, too, for the advice and wise counsel of Chester E. Colby, Director of Transportation; Professor William R. Black, Department of Geography; and Professors James E. Suelflow and L. L. Waters of the Transportation Department of the Graduate School of Business, all of Indiana University at Bloomington. My special thanks, also, to Professor John C. Spychalski of the Pennsylvania State University at State College, Pennsylvania, for his many helpful suggestions and comments on the manuscript.

BLOOMINGTON, INDIANA
INSTITUTE FOR URBAN TRANSPORTATION
GRADUATE SCHOOL OF BUSINESS
INDIANA UNIVERSITY
MARCH, 1974

URBANT CRISIS .

Defining →

A. Evolutional → UC

B. CAUSES & CONSEQUENCE

C. IS THERE A SOLUTION :

  IS IT FEASIBLE, REASON

WHAT IS THE^UT "CRISIS"?
CAUSES OF UTC? & SOME
SOL

CONTENTS

x   Contents

xii   Contents

List of Figures

List of Tables

URBAN MASS TRANSPORTATION
A Dozen Years of Federal Policy

INTRODUCTION

Back in 1955 I was searching for a thesis topic as part of the requirement for a master's degree. I had long been interested in urban mass transportation and proposed to my academic advisor that I do something along that line. With much good will he suggested that mass transit was a dead issue in the United States and that railway electrification would probably be a much more interesting and valuable topic. So I didn't write a thesis on urban mass transportation. At the time, the advisor was quite correct: to have even suggested in 1955 that not so many years in the future the federal government would be parcelling out money to cities for mass transportation improvement would have been cause to doubt my sanity.

Things have changed! On the very day that I typed the original draft of this introduction, I received from the Urban Mass Transportation Administration (an agency undreamed of in 1955) a computer printout three-eighths of an inch thick listing the projects that have been supported with federal money since the mass transportation programs got under way in 1961.

Which brings me to the reason behind this volume: some years ago I wrote a book* that set forth the role of the federal govern-

---

* *Urban Transportation: The Federal Role* (Bloomington: Indiana University Press, 1965).

1

ment in urban transportation, and in it covered the first four years of the nation's experience with federal programs to aid urban mass transportation. Since then so much has happened—most of that three-eighths of an inch printout—that it is time to bring matters up to date.

The objective of this book is, essentially, to recount what has happened over a little more than a decade of federal participation in urban mass transportation. The events of this period are important in the history of mass transportation. Although far from what it might be, the general public awareness of the role that mass transit can and should play in urban areas has greatly increased. Today no faculty advisor would suggest that mass transportation is a dead issue in the United States. Much of the substantial rise in interest in the subject has been kindled by funds from the federal government. Concern with the ecology of our environment has drawn attention to the impact of the automobile and the highways and other facilities that serve the auto. Mass transportation, as an alternate and perhaps less damaging means of urban mobility, has enjoyed strong support from the environmentalists. There has also been a growing realization that the mobility needs of the urban residents probably could not be met by continuation of the strong and singular emphasis on the automobile for urban transportation. It is probably fair to say that a large proportion of U.S. citizens who are concerned about urban transportation feel that improved mass transportation is a "good thing" for their city or town.

Another factor arose in 1972: suddenly the public was warned of possible shortages of home heating oil and natural gas. Early in 1973 notice was given that there might be spot shortages of gasoline during the summer travel months. Magazines and newspapers began to print articles on the energy crisis. In almost the same breath came calls for greater use of mass transportation as a means of conserving scarce energy resources.

As it turned out, the winter of 1973–1974 was one of real fuel shortages in many parts of the United States. The price of gasoline rose sharply, long lines formed at filling stations, speed limits were cut back nationwide to 55 miles per hour, thermostats were cut back to save heating fuel, and the nation got a taste of what promises to be a long-term shortage of energy.

The rise in federal interest in mass transportation has produced a tidal wave of material on the subject. Indeed, so much material is available on urban transportation that it is impossible for a nonprofessional in the field to comprehend it all, even if there were time available to read it.

This book is not aimed at the professionals; it is mainly addressed to interested laymen and students. The notes and references lead the reader to other sources of information as well as providing documentation. In short, this book might best be viewed as the narrative version of a survey course in federal urban mass transportation policy. Moreover, it is not intended to be a sophisticated analysis of the subject. The author was not an insider in the formulation of mass transit policy. Much of the story could be told only by persons privy to much of what went on within the various agencies. Perhaps someone will be inspired by this volume to prepare a definitive work.

Unlike the Marine sergeant who leaves no tone unsterned, in evaluating the success of federal projects I have sought to look not only at what has happened but also at why federal action did not always produce salutary effects. One point that I hope is crystal clear in the pages that follow is that improving mass transportation is an extraordinarily difficult undertaking—a truly Herculean task. Moreover, the fond hope that improving mass transportation will provide spillover benefits that will greatly improve the quality of urban life must be modified with a dash of reality. More inviting, safer, and economically and socially robust cities are not the inevitable output of an investment in better mass transportation. Many other investments must be made to accomplish a true urban revivification, including investments of that rare commodity, common sense.

This book begins with a review of the development of federal policy and goes on to discuss some of the pros and cons regarding transit. There is a brief examination of the transit industry and the federal agency responsible for the execution of the national government's transit policy. A few chapters follow devoted to some of the findings, successes, and failures of federal policy, including an examination of some of the very basic causes lurking behind the failures. Finally, there are some suggestions for long-run and short-run policy and procedural changes that might lead to improvement in urban mass transportation. Since it is expected that many readers will be interested in some specific parts of the text, rather than in the work as a whole, an effort has been made to compose chapters and sections of chapters so that they are as self-contained as possible. The price of this effort is some repetition from chapter to chapter.

A fair amount of stress is placed upon marketing in the pages that follow. In the use of the term I do not mean the blatant tub-thumping that many people mistake for marketing. Marketing, as it is used in this work, means a creative attempt to meet a consumer's needs by finding out what those needs are, shaping a product or service to meet the needs, and then through promotional effort bringing the product or service to the consumer's attention. Pricing must enter into this process, of course, along with feedback on the success of the product or service in meeting the consumer need as originally perceived, with necessary modifications made as required. In its ideal sense, marketing is, therefore, much more than mere huckstering. Good information in a constant stream is needed, along with a concern for the consumer.

Those involved in mass transportation, taken as a whole, virtually ignore the art of marketing. Yet, barring some means of coercion not common to the United States insofar as personal travel is concerned, real marketing is necessary to shape transit service to play an acceptable role for more people in U.S. urban areas, and thus enlarge patronage.

In this book I have attempted to adhere to the definitions for the main subject matter put forth by Wilfred Owen:

> The terms "transit" or "mass transportation" are synonymous and include surface street car, bus, or trolley bus in local urban service as well as rail rapid transit operating on exclusive rights-of-way, generally subway or elevated. The term "public transportation" includes transit or mass transportation plus rail commuter services and taxis.[1]

CHAPTER ONE

The Urban Transportation
Crisis and the Growing
Role of Federal Government

Introduction

Federal policy toward urban mass transportation has experienced a twisting and checkered career. Initiated as a none-too-popular reaction to a crisis and emerging a dozen years later as an issue with enormous support within the Congress, transit policy has come full circle. This change of heart is one of the aspects of the federal role in mass transportation that makes it so interesting.

To the casual observer, federal policy on any topic, and the legislation which gives it life, may just seem to happen. But over time many forces are at work that affect the shape and scope of policy, not the least of which is the political pressure brought to bear on the Congress by the various interest groups affected by certain policy or legislation. Opposing forces, or at least a lack of agreement on substantive issues, may hinder policy development. Eventually, consensus may be found when several interest groups agree, perhaps for different reasons, on a given piece of legislation. When action is finally taken, it may precipitate a crescendo of legislative and operational activity.

This chapter traces the threads of the federal mass transit policy and weaves them together into a case history of policy and legislative development.

The Urbanization of America

The background to federal mass transit policy begins with important changes in American life. Within the past half century the United States has become predominantly an urbanized nation. As a result, the focus of national interest, concern for the national well-being, and the physical site of national problems has become increasingly urban.

The process of urbanization has come about rather rapidly; indeed, in 1900 only 40 per cent of the population was considered to be urbanized by the Census Bureau. By 1920, the 50-per-cent mark of urbanized proportion of the population was passed. In the 1940 census, persons living in urban areas amounted to some 56.5 per cent of total population. The relatively slow rate of urban growth in the 1920-to-1940 period was largely the result of the massive dampening effect of the Great Depression. In the 1960 nose count, there were almost 180 million Americans, and over 67 per cent of them lived in urban areas. By 1970, of 203,166,000 in the population, 149,279,000, or 73.5 per cent, resided in urban areas. The rapid growth in population and in urbanization is expected to continue; predictions have it that by 1980 the population of the country should exceed 225 million and the degree of urbanization should be in the neighborhood of 80 per cent.

It is more to the point, perhaps, that much of the total population counted in the 1970 census—139,374,000, to be exact—was to be found in 243 Standard Metropolitan Statistical Areas (SMSA) of the 50 states. (There are also four SMSA's in Puerto Rico.) This was an increase in the number of SMSA's from 212 in the 1960 census. The Standard Metropolitan Statistical Area is defined as

> . . . an integrated economic and social unit with a recognized large population nucleus. . . . Thus, each standard metropolitan statistical area must contain at least one city of at least 50,000 inhabitants . . . [and will] include the county of such a central city and adjacent counties that are found to be metropolitan in character and economically and socially integrated with the county of the central city. . . .[1]

Most of the population growth between 1960 and 1970 occurred in the metropolitan areas: of a population increase approximating close to 25 million, places considered urban accounted for all population growth. The rural population declined from 30.1 per cent of the population in 1960 to 26.5 per cent in 1970. Within the SMSA's the bulk of the growth has been in that portion of the area outside the central city.

The urbanization of America was a fact long before its meaning was recognized and dealt with by institutions within our society. Unfortunately, urban government in most places has continued in its nineteenth-century form and manner. Although on every hand there was the reality of the central city surrounded by expanding rings of suburban development—closely related to the central city socially, culturally, and economically, but not politically—there was no large-scale movement toward metropolitan government to match the movement of population and its relationship to various political subdivisions. The political institutions established for a thinly populated, relatively uncomplicated agrarian society continued to be used.

The failure to grasp the full impact of urbanization is not confined to political institutions. Organized religion, while it had performed admirably in bringing the gospel and hope for salvation to the people under difficult American frontier conditions, has, for the most part, achieved an undistinguished record in making religion meaningful under conditions of extreme industrialization, urbanization, and metropolitanization. Colleges and universities, with the possible exception of the work of some sociologists, historians, architects, and city planners, made but slight effort to study the process of urbanization or ponder its effects. It appears that even those most affected by the problems of urbanization—the urban population itself—did not understand the full consequences of its rapid growth in terms of crowded schools, overcrowded recreational areas, air and water pollution, and physical crowding and traffic congestion.

It was not until the late 1950's that the people of the United States finally woke up to what had been going on for a long time. So subtly had the changes come that the people had adapted themselves to the process almost unquestioningly; nevertheless, serious difficulties were mounting almost unchecked. As a nation we have always had problems of health, education, housing, lawlessness, human and civil rights, poverty, and the waste or pollution of valuable resources. But as the United States prepared to enter the decade of the 1960's, these problems had become predominantly and overwhelmingly focused in our cities. The concentration of difficulties seemed to make solutions harder to find. Regardless of how great the desire to keep one's head buried in the sand, some problems eventually become so burdensome that action must be taken to lighten the load. Yet, at the same time, by the late '50's and early '60's it was clear that urban burdens and infelicities are particularly difficult to either uproot or solve. Indeed, experience indicates that coping with the myriad problems of urbanization is likely to be the greatest challenge that the nation faces in the next 50 years.

Traffic Congestion, Mobility, and the Urban Transport Problem

One of the primary symptoms of the problems of rapid urbanization is congestion in transportation, particularly notable in the crush of automotive traffic at certain times of day. Traffic jams are perhaps the most obvious signs of what are really mobility problems. Life is tolerable, even if population density is relatively high, if personal physical movement and access to economic, cultural, and social activities is relatively easy and low in time, effort, and money cost. However, the jamup of cars in a city is a sign of thwarted mobility. Breaking the jam by construction of expensive highways may relieve congestion and restore mobility to those with cars, but in reflecting on other uses for the resources devoted to the building of the highway, the mobility may have been purchased at a very high cost, especially in forgone opportunities.

Other less obvious forms of immobility may be even more insidious to urban well-being than the traffic jam. In most American cities, public mass transportation service may charitably be described as fifth rate. It typically offers a poor alternative to the automobile, in terms of frequency, convenience, and general access to the activity and opportunity of the community as a whole. Those who do not have access to an automobile—the very young, the elderly, the poor, the handicapped, and the suburban housewife in a one-car family—are isolated from opportunity and virtual prisoners of a narrow geographic area. Unemployment, underemployment, frustration, enforced idleness, and loneliness are likely products of such immobility. Such burdens on the human spirit are probably far more serious barriers to the good life and a decent civilization than the traffic jam, but they are subtle factors and, therefore, much less visible to the bulk of the American population. Automobile congestion and its attendant frustrations gave the alarm that all was not well concerning transportation in U.S. cities. It was to the symptom of congestion, therefore, rather than to the real problem of mobility, that attention was initially directed.

Congestion as a hindrance to mobility is, of course, not new to cities—Rome, for example, had awesome traffic problems during the period of the Empire, and London suffered from jamups in the nineteenth century.[2] Nor was it new to American cities: in the last half of the nineteenth century, downtown streets in New York, Philadelphia, Chicago, and other major urban areas were plagued with congestion of horsedrawn vehicles that rivaled modern automobile jams.

In the past, however, advancing technology seemed to save the day at the critical moment, much like the timely arrival of the cavalry in the last reel of a western movie. The horsedrawn streetcar, which could move more people faster than the omnibus, helped alleviate the clotting of omnibus traffic in larger cities. In turn, the cablecar and the electric streetcar were capable of moving even more people with considerably greater dispatch than the horsecars. In certain great cities, elevated and underground railroads provided a private right-of-way for high capacity rapid transit trains at a time when street traffic threatened to grind to a halt. The developments in public transport managed, however inelegantly, to make relatively intensive use of limited urban space and provide mobility within the city at a comparatively low cost to the bulk of the population.

At the present time, however, automotive congestion seems much more difficult to eradicate or decrease to any appreciable extent at a reasonable cost. Large sums of money have been spent to improve highways in urban areas since the end of the Second World War. At best, these new roads have provided temporary relief from congestion. At worst, they have added to traffic woes by enticing more cars into already congested areas. Added to this, lack of provision for adequate parking space in conjunction with highway construction has often led to extreme parking problems.

Congestion is costly, not only in terms of the time, effort, and money lost in delay and that which is spent in traffic control devices, traffic engineering, policing, and the construction, administration, and maintenance of urban streets and roads, but also because congestion is a thief that robs the city of its vitality. Overcrowding and slowdowns make it difficult to get about and thus encourage separation and lack of personal confrontation, thwarting the realization of the essence of a desirable urban society even by those who have access to automobiles. Congestion—and, indeed, some of its remedies and their side effects—robs the city of its beauty and amenities. A park as well as a slum may become the site of a superhighway, ugly parking lots dot the city, and residential streets are spoiled by the cluttered chaos of curbside parking.

Automotive congestion helps rob the city of its pure air, by concentrating exhaust fumes and, in many places, polluting the atmosphere to dangerous levels. It robs the traveler of time: it takes longer to reach destinations; the number of stops a delivery truck may make during the working day is seriously reduced; fire, police, and sanitation departments are greatly impeded in their work. Indeed, in some places, traffic and travel conditions are so bad that the zest of going places has been extracted from urban life, to be replaced by tension and fatigue.

In short, by losing vitality, amenity, pure air, and time, cities become less attractive and more costly places in which to live or do business. Traffic congestion is, therefore, a force that weakens and debilitates the city. It is a truism that in an urbanized society like the United States, whatever weakens the city weakens the economy and the society as a whole. Ridding American cities of congestion is thus a matter of great concern and importance. Yet, even so, it is only one part of the whole mobility problem. Providing mobility—transportation—for those in the population without regular access to the automobile is the only way such persons can participate fully in American life and enjoy the benefits, rights, and privileges of citizenship.

The Causes of the Urban Transport Problem

The urban transport problem of congestion is often blamed solely upon the automobile. A closer evaluation of the situation reveals a more complex chain of factors and events.

One of the most critical elements has been the increasing tendency of urban residents to locate away from the core area of the city and in a less concentrated manner. Suburbia is principally the site of single family homes on relatively large building lots. As a consequence, despite an apparent recent trend toward an increasing number of multiple-family dwellings in the suburbs, density per square mile tends to be quite low in comparison with the older parts of the central city.

Decentralization, or suburbanization, or metropolitanization—whatever name one wishes to give it—is pretty much a worldwide phenomenon. The desire for more spacious living seems to be a rather universal trait. Federal mortgage guarantees, a product of the mid-1930's, made it possible for many families to enjoy the suburban dream. Affluence and the automobile help make it possible to live in such a decentralized manner. Indeed, the automobile is often cited as the cause for decentralization but it is probably more accurate to consider it only as one of several means to that end.

Whatever the cause, the move outward from the city into the suburban or outer ring portion of the metropolitan areas has been largely on rubber tires and life must perforce be geared to the automobile. This in and of itself would not be critical except that the shift of population to the outlying areas has reached tidal wave proportions. This shift is shown in Table 1–1, which shows the pop-

TABLE 1-1
Population, by Residence: 1950 to 1970
(in thousands, as of April)

Residence	Population				Percent Increase	
			1970		1950-	1960-
	1950	1960	Total	Percent	1960	1970
TOTAL	151,326	179,323	203,184	100.0	18.5	13.3
Standard metropolitan statistical areas	94,579	119,595	139,387	68.6	26.4	16.5
Central cities	53,817	59,964	63,816	31.4	11.4	6.4
Outside central cities	40,762	59,631	75,570	37.2	46.3	26.7
Nonmetropolitan areas	56,747	59,728	63,798	31.4	5.3	6.8

Source: Adapted from *Statistical Abstract of the United States, 1971*. 92d ed. (U.S., Bureau of the Census), p. 16.

ulation of the United States in 1950, 1960, and 1970 according to the Bureau of the Census. From the table it is clear that the population of the country, while expanding on all fronts, is increasingly located in the urban places outside the central cities. As this portion of the population is the most rapidly increasing and mainly an auto-using group, the possibilities for congestion and other traffic and

transport problems become quite clear. When there is a mass movement of this population in a relatively constrained time period and
within a relatively small space—such as the downtown core of a
metropolitan area—a jamup is the inevitable product.

Moreover, that portion of the metropolitan population living in
the outer fringe area is difficult to serve with any form of transportation other than the automobile. For example, population density
is so thin, relative to the older, central part of the city, that under
conventional mass transit operating procedures it is difficult to locate a bus line that provides decent and acceptable service at reasonable fares and still makes a profit for the operator. Consequently,
in the outer part of most metropolitan areas, if there is any public
transportation service offered at all, it is often confined to just a
few trips per day offered only at peak hours.[3] People are obliged
to use automobiles because there is no reasonable alternative.

Another major cause of transport problems, even in the central
part of urban areas, is the decline of public transport as a major
force for the movement of people and therefore an effective alternative to the use of the automobile. The declining fortunes of the
mass transit industry are not of recent vintage. Despite increasing
ridership trends, the troubles of the transit industry began toward
the end of the nineteenth century, primarily as a result of financial
chicanery which seriously weakened the industry. Street railways,
like the intercity steam railways, were often greatly overcapitalized
to begin with; the mergers and amalgamations that were part of the
unification of all transit firms in a given city were usually accompanied by further injections of water into the capital, often in the form
of bonds. Overcapitalization meant there was little relationship
between the outstanding capital and the asset value—hence, earning
power—of a transit property. The promoters of these transit firms
unloaded vast amounts of stock on gullible persons who were anxious to invest in a monopoly of passenger transport in a given city.

Added to the burden of excess capitalization were obligations
imposed on the street railways by the communities in which they operated. A franchise was usually required for the use of the public
streets. Among the normal provisions of the franchise were requirements for street and bridge maintenance, sprinkling the streets
against dust in the summer, and clearing the streets of snow in the

winter. Most burdensome in the long run, perhaps, was the fact that many franchises set the maximum fare at a nickel.

Neither the franchise requirements nor the relatively high debt capitalization were overly troublesome during most of the period of declining prices between the end of the Civil War and the turn of the century. However, around 1900 prices began to trend upward. At the same time, as noted earlier, the pyramiding of separate transit companies into citywide monopolies greatly inflated the debt capital. The five-cent fare then began to pinch as high debt costs and rising operating costs had to be met. Therefore, even before the automobile arrived on the scene, many public transit firms were in shaky financial condition, and bankruptcy was common during World War I.

The automobile came on the scene as a practical alternative for urban transportation around the time of the First World War. During the 1920's, with money from all levels of government spent on the construction and improvement of highways, the competition from automobiles became increasingly severe. The Depression spelled lean days or financial ruin for many transit firms. Replacement of streetcars with buses lightened the burden of fixed costs for transit firms. However, so weakened were most transit firms by the events of the past that they were unable to provide either the equipment or a service that was really attractive to the increasingly substantial number of Americans who could afford to own and drive a car.

Another factor aiding and abetting the demise of mass transport was the calibre of management. For a variety of reasons, transit management is, typically, operations oriented. In other words, most transit managers and the transit properties under their direction lacked the vital spark of marketing, in the sense of understanding consumer needs and meeting those needs. The thrust of management efforts is often marked by a relatively indifferent, unrealistic, or impractical attitude toward maintaining or boosting demand. As a result, if revenues decline or profit margins shrink, the usual reaction of management is to cut costs, often by reducing service, and at the same time to raise fares to boost revenues. Needless to say, neither of these ploys encourages ridership. Indeed, such policies carried on for very long almost guarantee that a transit company will eventually move only those persons unable to drive a car. In brief, up to the 1960's efforts to increase demand for mass transportation had been sporadic at best, and nothing was really accomplished that helped reverse the downward trend of patronage.[4]

The factors behind the commuter railroads' tale of woe are slightly different, but the result has been almost the same. Most rail commuter operations started many years ago as byproducts of through passenger service offered at specially reduced or commuted fares. Over the years, however, as demand for such service rose with the expansion of the city, suburban operations grew to the extent that they were often handled as a completely separate operation from through train service. The low fares continued, however, and often many years went by before any really substantial increase in fares was permitted to bring revenue into some practical relationship with cost. With increasing automotive competition the commuter railways and the local transit companies were both faced with a sharply peaked demand for their services at the rush hours with little demand at other times. Expensive specialized equipment and plant—as well as manpower—were fully utilized for only about four or five hours a day. As was the case with transit, many commuter railways cut back their service drastically to shave costs. New equipment was often out of the question. In Philadelphia, for example, commuters on Penn Central suburban lines utilize the same equipment their grandparents knew; the cars are 50 to 60 years old.

Although the tire-gas-auto shortage days of the Second World War revived the patronage of all modes of public transport, the resurgence of demand was to last only until automobiles became plentiful once again. Then the decline in all but peak traffic continued. By the middle fifties the service on most mass transport operations was poor, the equipment often abominable, the conveniences minimal, and the customers were staying away in droves.[5]

So decrepit and deplorable was the state of mass transit and commuter railroad service and the quality of the equipment that it could truly be said that for people who could afford a choice, there was no suitable alternative to the use of the automobile in most U.S. cities. Only in some of the very largest population centers—such as New York, Philadelphia, and Chicago—was mass transportation used by a majority of persons entering the downtown area. Even in these cities, of all trips made on the average day throughout the metropolitan area, only a fraction were by public transportation.

As the decade of the 1950's wore on, and congestion grew worse, it became clear to some observers that the almost complete dependence on the automobile for urban transportation was, to say the least, unwise. Most especially for trips to and from areas of high population concentration, such as the downtown core of a metropolitan area, less use of private automobiles and increased use of mass transportation made a great deal of sense. A free choice of the public in the direction of transit utilization required improvement in the quality of rolling stock and facilities. Such improvements were unlikely, however, as long as aid from the federal government was available for the construction of highways only. In the 1950's only Cleveland made a major improvement in mass transport by finally completing a rapid transit line that had been initiated just before the Wall Street crash of 1929.

Since the inception of its programs of highway aid, the federal government has provided both considerable leadership and cash for the improvement of roads for the use of motor vehicles. Beginning in 1916, aid has been available to the states for the construction of highways. Intercity roadbuilding went on apace during the 1920's. By the end of the 1930's, remarkable progress had been made in knitting the country together with good roads. Up to 1944, however, urban areas had been specifically omitted from federal highway aid. In the earliest federal-aid programs it was felt, with considerable justification, that rural areas were in greater need of highway improvement than were the cities. During the Depression, federal aid for urban highway work was made available as part of the general program of relief measures undertaken by the government, but no regular program of federal highway aid was available for cities.

As the 1930's came to a close, however, it was becoming abundantly clear that cities were in need of highway improvement to meet the needs of the increasingly auto-borne urban population. War preparations and the war itself deflected federal attention from such programs. Nevertheless, in 1944 Congress enacted a federal-aid highway act—to become effective after hostilities ceased—which specifically made funds available for urban areas. At war's end urban places took advantage of the federal money, as well as funds from other sources, to undertake substantial improvement and expansion of urban highway facilities.[6]

But, as no federal aid was available for public transportation, its relative position became worse. As the cities groaned under a rising tide of automobile traffic, despite the efforts to provide highways adequate to meet all transport needs, public transport became shabbier, less attractive, and generally unable to generate revenues sufficient even to buy new buses.

Solutions to Urban Problems

By the middle of the 1950's the evolving form of urban development had become quite clear. The metropolitan pattern of a relatively compact and densely settled core city surrounded by the thin wash of dispersed suburban population was apparently the wave of the present and the foreseeable future. Urban population was mounting rapidly, but primarily on the suburban fringe. The number and use of cars, made almost mandatory in the dispersed city form, expanded rapidly.

And as the city spread, congestion spread with it. The American penchant for lack of comprehensive urban planning practically guaranteed that the rosy postwar dream of door-to-door travel convenience upon congestion-free highways would not materialize. The only practical answer in a society whose transport was dominated by the private automobile seemed to lie in the construction of more, bigger, and better highways. But, build and spend as the nation might, real solutions to traffic congestion in the United States proved to be most elusive.

Indeed, for ease of solution, problems could find no worse place to focus than in U.S. metropolitan areas. It was becoming painfully obvious that as the problems grew more complex and distributed throughout an urbanized area, there was no effective unit of governmental authority on the local level that could handle metropolitan problems.[7]

The jurisdictional and fiscal fragmentation in metropolitan areas lies at the heart of many urban and metropolitan problems. As suburban development in areas surrounding established central cities began to mount in the period between the two world wars, the tendency was for each of the suburban areas to maintain its political and fiscal individuality, although close social and economic ties with the central city remained. The situation continued at a more rapid rate in the post-World War II period when the great migration to the suburbs began in earnest. Impetus to this movement was given by the influx of nonwhites to Northern cities during the war, and in the postwar period, stimulated by better job opportunities in most major urban centers. Smaller suburban communities, populated by a relatively homogeneous socioeconomic group, could find the cohesion necessary to keep the invaders out. In the postwar era central cities became increasingly the haven of the poor and black while suburbs grew richer and predominantly white.

Further enforcing the pattern of fragmentation, state laws frequently prevented the central city from annexing adjacent areas without the assent of all parties involved. Most suburbs, whose residents were anxious to escape the problems of the central city, fiercely resisted any overtures from the central city for union. If annexation did occur, it was typically the end-product of a long and bitter legal battle.

The result of this attitude was the establishment in any given metropolitan area of a number of political subdivisions with differing financial needs and resources, many of which could supply residents with governmental services of only the most limited nature. Consequently, when a problem such as transportation, which affects the whole of the metropolitan community without respect to artificial political boundaries, became serious, it was difficult to marshal any broad metropolitan approach to its solution.

Adding to the common difficulty of the disparity of needs and resources of the segmented communities within a given metropolitan area, each segment fears that it will pay more than it will benefit from any proposed metropolitan plan. Moreover, there is a general feeling on the part of the suburban units that the central city is the only real beneficiary of metropolitan-wide programs and should jolly well solve its own problems.

The fact that all fragments of a metropolitan area will eventually suffer from adverse effects upon the social or economic health of one segment is often obscured by problems of a strictly local nature within a fragment.[8] In effect, therefore, a political void exists on the metropolitan level in regard to meeting metropolitan problems. In such a situation outside help—either from the state or federal government—is the only course of action tolerable to the metropolitan community as a whole. The unwillingness or inability of state governments to take effective action eventually makes the search for solutions of many metropolitan problems the responsibility of the federal level of government.[9]

The Federal Role in Urban Transport

If the mantle of leadership in urban mass transport rests on the shoulders of the federal government, it should not be supposed that the adoption of this role happened quickly, that it was the desired objective of a well-thought-out plan, or that it was greeted by wide public acclaim. Furthermore, the laws now on the books and the part played by government are all a product of the slow process of practical politics; any idealism or do-goodism has been well tinctured with reality.

What exists, as regards transit policy, is but a beginning, a product of compromise and half-way measures. As a result, there have been no great changes in the urban transport picture. A decade ago American cities were sadly belabored and blighted by traffic jams: they remain so today. A decade ago urban mass transportation was in a sorry plight: for the most part this is still true. What has occurred in the past dozen years, however, is proof that the situation is not hopeless.

Federal Action: A Need for Crisis and Support

Before investigating briefly the events leading up to federal participation in programs benefiting urban mass transport, it would be wise to begin with a broad overview of some of the factors that were instrumental in shaping the mass transport legislation. It should be recognized, of course, that many of these factors are not unique to the passage of legislation to aid urban transport, but are common problems faced by any new program of federal action.

In even a cursory view of the history of federal participation in urban mass transportation, one of the major items of note is the relative lack of grass-roots support in the early efforts to take action against this urban sea of troubles. The other factor was the initial strength of the opposition within the Congress for action to solve what many view as a purely local problem that should be handled strictly on the local level.

It has been said of Americans—and other democracies as well—that only in the case of a crisis, such as a war with some threatening foreign power, is any strong popular unity of purpose discernibly aimed toward any particular goal. In the crisis of wartime there is a clear-cut national perception of a very obvious problem and the course of action that must, in general, be followed. Other problems, particularly those that develop slowly, and with which the public lives every day, are often not treated—perhaps not even noted by any large segment of the public—until a crisis develops. By that stage of the game, solutions may be both costly and difficult. Even then, unless the problem strikes a majority of the population in the same way, there is likely to be little agreement as to the course of action that should be followed.

Air pollution is an example of little or no action until a crisis situation becomes painfully obvious. Not until suffocating smog began to descend regularly upon a fairly large number of otherwise somnolent communities was there very strong public pressure to stop the befouling of the atmosphere. Barring, then, some critical event or chain of events, new causes or courses of action for the federal government have a rocky road to travel between conception and realization.

A new idea for federal action may come from one or more of several sources, most of them—with the clear exception of outright disaster like a flood or earthquake—involved one way or another with the business of politics. Consequently, one of the most common ways for a new idea for federal action to be generated is when a given program will meet the needs of a particular political constituency. Depending upon the nature of the problem and the form of succor required, chances of any action on a new program are slim, unless, of course, similar problems are faced in a good many of the constituencies of the members of the House and Senate. Congressional support for mass transportation was limited at first because it seemed mainly a problem of the large cities.

Another initiating force would be federal action to meet the needs of a pressure group. Again, unless the problem is widely perceived and appreciated, or the political advantage of most of the Congress or other pressure groups met–or at least not injured—necessary support for any sort of action will be difficult to muster. The larger and better financed the pressure group, the easier it will be; nevertheless, acquiescence will not come without difficulty. Typically, a number of groups must bring their influence to bear before anything is done.[10]

A call for federal action may come from a politician or group of politicians who see a political opportunity. This opportunity may have considerable payoff even if federal action is never forthcoming, for if the cards are played right, the proponents can gain recognition nationally as well as in their own constituency. On the other side of the coin, there are those politicians and nonpoliticians who see some plan for federal action as a genuine opportunity to serve the public in a selfless manner. Included in this group would be those idealistic enough to see a need to remake at least part of the world in the pattern of how it should be according to some notion of decency, justice, or welfare.

Doubtless, most of the above mentioned motives are to be found behind proposals for any governmental activity.

Recognizing a problem and successfully finding means for the federal government to take action are thwarted, at least for a time, by another set of factors. Public apathy is perhaps one of the strongest forces. The difficulty here is that the problem may be perceived as such by only a very small or narrow group, a group that is insufficient, either in numbers or the base of their appeal, to get the broad sort of support necessary to win the legislative day in the Congress. Often the problem may be of such a nature that, if some governmental action is undertaken, no matter how modest, it will help bring the matter to wider public attention and thus gain the broader support necessary for strong remedial action. On the other hand, if the group trying for new federal activity is likely to become troublesome, or if there is a genuine and reasonable doubt as to the merits of the suggested action, a program or study may be initiated that will serve to gain better understanding of the difficulty. Upon completion of the study, or examination of project results, proposals for a larger scale of activity may win wider political support, or the whole scheme may be dropped as impractical. Again, the limited activity may be merely of a delaying nature to quell certain unrest that might otherwise get out of hand, and thereby serve to cool the fires of discontent. A classic ploy is to conduct a study of the problems in the hope that the difficulty will go away or be forgotten.

Opposition to new federal activities may come from pressure

groups who see a threat to their own interests or, perhaps, to the interests of the country as they perceive them. The highway interests, as an example, have bitterly fought use of the Highway Trust Fund for any purpose other than building more highways. Finally, opposition may come from individuals, the Congress, the administration or some member of the public who is powerful enough to be troublesome. Vested interests are never happy with the threat of being unvested.

Overriding any attempt to enlarge the scope of activities carried on by the federal level of government is a strong core of hostility and opposition to increase or extension of federal activity. Such attitudes are likely to be particularly strong when federal action is called for on a matter of local or state interest, as noted earlier. The abiding philosophy is that local problems should be solved by local or state governments. On the surface such an idea makes considerable sense. In reality, however, particularly in the case of governmentally fragmented metropolitan areas, local action on some problems is often practically impossible. The rules of the game will only fit when there is some local unit of government that has the jurisdiction and the financial ability to act. As noted in earlier pages, such is rarely the case in the majority of American metropolitan areas, especially the larger ones.

The fear of federal involvement has a number of historical roots. It may be based on a general fear that each additional activity undertaken by the national government is but another step along the road to socialism. In the United States, socialism has, in general, been uncritically tarred with the brush of Communism; in any event, a loss of freedom in the long run is seen as the outcome of steps to meet today's problems with federal action. It should also be noted that the history of major federal involvement in the lives of the American people dates back only to the early 1930's.

Simple fear of change is another reason for opposition. There is is a certain comfort in the past, and it is easy to feel that the methods and nostrums that were effective in a far simpler, less urbanized, less industrialized society will still work. When such a fear is at work, it makes little real difference what level of government is called upon; it still amounts to change and is per se wrong.

Individuals with some degree of power on the local or state level may fear that this power will be seriously eroded if there is federal intervention. In short, a man may cut considerable ice in a local pond; he is afraid he will be lost and impotent in the federal ocean.

A more legitimate concern is that programs will be administered by unfeeling and unknowledgeable bureaucrats in Washington, with little control in local hands. If such is the case, it seems likely to many persons that action will be capricious or arbitrary. In particular, there is concern that the attitudes and feeling of the local people will not be taken into account. Moreover, there is a tendency for all bureaucracies to establish means to assure that all participants are treated fairly and equally. This is a noble sentiment and a desirable practice. However, it usually means that more safeguards, in the shape of red tape, are developed by the bureaucracy.

Finally, there is the fear and dislike of paying out a sum greater than the value of the benefits received. Tax money collected by the federal government to help defend the nation against attack is one matter; federal tax money used to solve a problem somewhere else —particularly one that is not felt strongly in the immediate local area—is likely to cause local hackles to rise in righteous indignation. It is small wonder, then, that federal or state programs of aid to urban areas are often rebuffed by rural legislators and rural population.

The charge is often levied that the federal government is only too anxious to invade the bailiwick of the state and local governments. While there are doubtless members of Washington officialdom who would be happy to expand their sway unilaterally, the truth is that federal programs to provide aid on the state and local levels are initiated largely at the behest of those lower levels of government. Particularly in the case of cities and metropolitan areas, the federal government has usually moved into areas where a political vacuum exists. Obviously, the best way to prevent federal encroachment is to make those necessary changes on the state and local level that will guarantee the ability of those levels of government to solve their own problems. Fifty years ago, had state and local government geared itself to the growing problems and necessities of the twentieth century, there would probably be far less need for federal action today. Federal revenue sharing, initiated in 1972, is an attempt to push federal tax monies down to lower levels of government with few strings attached, so that lower levels of government can decide for themselves how best to spend the funds. With little evidence to go by at the time of this writing, it is not possible to state whether this policy is good government in action or an adventure into fiscal irresponsibility on a monumental scale.

Perhaps a more valid criticism of federal activity is that, as a product of compromise, it is not always able to provide the relief needed. There are too many halfway measures, such as the use of the mass transportation demonstration program device in the first stages of federal urban mass transport activity. Such programs might offer some proof of what could be done. If they failed, little was lost; if they succeeded, greater public interest and political support could be aroused. In short, too often federal programs are nothing more than cautious probes, the result of the political necessity of agreeing to do little.

The Crisis of 1958

Federal activity on behalf of urban mass transportation was the re-sult of a crisis situation that came to a head in 1958. It should not be thought, however, that before that time cities showed absolutely no interest in the problems of congestion and deteriorating mass transportation. Some tried to take steps toward a solution.[11]

In the early 1950's the winds of reform swept into Philadelphia. After interminable years of complacency and decrepitude under a Republican machine, newly-elected Democrats, as a party of reform and reinvigoration, began programs that would at long last bring the Quaker City into the twentieth century. One of the major items for consideration was transportation. Philadelphia was fortunate in having an excellent base of high capacity public transportation facil-ities, but over the years there had been little modernization of either the facilities or the equipment and patronage had been slipping.[12]

The problem was particularly acute for the commuter railroads. Both the Reading and Pennsylvania railroads were suffering from serious financial losses on their commuter service, and their attitude was becoming increasingly one of withdrawal from this service on the idea that private enterprise could no longer make a go of it. Since these two carriers moved approximately 100,000 people daily within the region, the loss of service and a shift of the patrons to private automobiles would be a disaster in Philadelphia's narrow streets.

The first step was taken in 1953 by Mayor Joseph S. Clark when he created the Urban Traffic and Transportation Board to investigate the city's transport problems. The members of this group represented a cross-section of road and rail transport, downtown interest groups, and labor and civic leaders. The board reported late in 1955 and recommended a coordinated road and rail program, with emphasis on upgrading the service on existing rail facilities as well as extending them more widely throughout the Philadelphia area. This mix appeared more attractive to the group than relying upon highways alone, particularly in light of the high cost per mile for freeways and the gruesome traffic and parking problem that would ensue in Philadelphia's compact central city area if an auto-dominant program were undertaken. It was estimated that about $25 million would be required for the necessary mass transport work within the city limits, while somewhere in the neighborhood of $65 to $80 million would be needed to modernize mass transport within the whole region. Inflation since 1955 makes these cost figures seem modest. However, at the time, this appeared to be a very expensive undertaking indeed, because the City of Philadelphia had neither the money nor the jurisdiction to do the whole job necessary to provide the needed calibre of transport. Not unexpectedly, the suburban counties and communities were financially unwilling to go along, and the rurally dominated Pennsylvania state legislature of the middle 1950's made help from that quarter out of the question.[13]

Since federal funds were in use in Philadelphia's urban renewal program, it was not too much of a jump to suggest that federal aid be provided for mass transportation. Richardson Dilworth, who succeeded Clark as mayor, worked to get some of the federal highway money diverted to mass transportation in 1956 and 1957. He very soon ran into the strong opposition of highway groups. Dilworth then proposed an alternate plan in which highway funds would be used only for the planning and engineering work in designing mass transit systems. To provide the capital funds needed for construction he suggested a federal lending agency modeled on the Federal National Mortgage Association. The bill providing for such legislation was introduced in the U. S. House of Representatives by Congressman William Green of Philadelphia in 1957. The Green bill was never permitted to reach the floor of the House; it expired quietly in committee without attracting much notice. Other efforts of Philadelphia to interest Congress and the U. S. Department of Commerce—nonregulatory matters in transportation were housed in the Commerce Department at that time—in aiding mass transportation were equally abortive.

Another major city which showed concern over the mass transportation situation in the 1950's was San Francisco. Because of its geography, the San Francisco Bay Area has had to rely on ferries and expensive bridges to link it together. Rapid population growth and the automotive explosion after the Second World War made an already troublesome transport problem more abrasive than ever. The counties affected prevailed upon the California legislature to create the San Francisco Bay Area Rapid Transit Commission in 1951. Three-quarters of a million dollars was granted to the counties by the state in order to study the problem. In 1957, again at the request of the Bay Area counties, the state created the San Francisco Bay Area Rapid Transit District to do developmental and planning work. However, no push for federal funds was evident at that time.[14]

Some other cities had made spasmodic attempts to cope with rising urban transportation problems. In general, these did not go much beyond the generation of primarily highway-oriented plans, which was to be expected as transportation had come to mean highway transportation in most places. Even the elaborate volumes of the Chicago Area Transportation Study and the Pittsburgh Area Transportation Study paid relatively minor attention to mass transportation. Those conducting the studies can hardly be blamed. It was simply unimaginable that mass transportation, in its then derelict state, could ever hope to attract an increasing share of patronage. In some ways the assumptions upon which these and other transport studies of the 1950's and early 1960's were based were similar to those of the Federal Electric Railway Commission in 1920. In the immediate post-World War I period, it was inconceivable that urban transportation in the future would not be based on the electric streetcar. In the post-World War II era, few could imagine urban transportation progress in terms other than those of the private automobile operating upon publicly provided highways.

There was no power or pressure group representing the mass transportation viewpoint. In the main, American cities had no particular position on what should be done about mass transportation. As individual entities their actions had often done more to hinder effective mass transportation service than to help it.[15] Also uninterested or unable to take any sort of concerted position on transit—often because all concern was focused on the highway development program—were planners, downtown business interests, labor, civic interest groups, and academics who were interested in urban affairs. Among carriers, the railroads had a rather definite position on commuter service; they wanted to cut their passenger service losses, usually through discontinuation of money-losing services. As commuter services typically produce substantial deficits, they were prime subjects for pruning. However, this problem was one of many in the railroads' package of woe and for most of the postwar period their pleas for relief had been ignored by Congress. As for the transit industry, its trade organization, the American Transit Association, was primarily a statistical and information service for its members rather than a lobbying instrument. The industry did not have a strong power position of the sort that gets important measures through Congress.

It is safe to say, then, that by the end of 1957 little had been done to interest the federal government in aiding mass transportation, with the exception of Philadelphia's futile effort. If there was any opinion on the matter in Washington, it was that urban mass transportation problems were strictly a local affair and should be handled on the local level.

Then in 1958 came the kind of crisis which seems necessary to force various groups together to gain action. Oddly enough, the whole process got under way inadvertently as Congress strove, finally, to provide some legislative relief for the nation's railroads.

The Depression of the 1930's had hurt the railroads as it had most business, but wartime traffic had greatly stimulated revenues and profits. After the vicissitudes of the preceding fifteen years, the attitude of the American railroads as a whole on their entrance into the postwar world seemed one of optimism. Expectations appeared sanguine even in the passenger business, which had been generally unprofitable since the mid-twenties, when the federally aided intercity highway system and easy availability of automobiles on credit began to siphon traffic away from the rails. Wartime passenger traffic was, of course, both heavy and profitable as rationing of gasoline and tires curtailed automobile use. Even though it was soon clear that more federal money, as well as state and local funds, would be expended on highways, airways, and airports, the railways invested very heavily in new passenger equipment and made a bid for the expected expansion of travel.

By the early 1950's it was quite evident that there was indeed a great rise in travel, but not by rail. Increasing numbers of people traveled by automobile and the air transportation business began an almost explosive period of growth, but the passenger traffic trend for the railroads was obviously downward. Freight transportation profits had always permitted the railways to maintain their passenger operations even though they might lose money. However, even freight revenues began to languish against the severe inroads of competing modes of transport, particularly highway trucks. The spasmodic prosperity of the fifties also hurt rail earnings because when business in general is bad, it is usually very bad for the railroads. The fitful behavior of the economy and shrinking revenues and profits spurred the railroads to seek legislative relief in the hope of gaining a more equal footing with their competition. One of the prime needs, from the railroads' viewpoint, was relief from the obligation to carry passengers. In 1957 alone the railroads had considerable reason to grieve about passenger service. The losses from this service, according to the ICC, totaled $723.7 million.[16]

Congress finally provided some relief from this distress in the Transportation Act of 1958.[17] One of its several parts dealt with the problems faced by the railroads in attempting to relieve themselves of the burdens of unremunerative passenger transportation. Before the passage of this act, the discontinuance of a passenger train was a matter for the action of state regulatory commissions; ICC jurisdiction involved only the complete abandonment of a line. From long experience the railroads had learned that gaining permission from state bodies was typically a very drawn-out and expensive affair. Sections 13a (1) and (2) of the 1958 Act were aimed at remedying the situation. In its seventy-fifth Annual Report the Interstate Commerce Commission explained this portion of the law as follows:

> Under section 13a (1), enacted in 1958, railroads desiring to discontinue or change the operation or service of any train operating between points in two or more States, but whose right to do so is governed by State laws, may elect to file a notice with the Commission of their intent to make the discontinuance or change, and 30 days thereafter, put it into effect regardless of State laws or decisions to the contrary, unless, within that time, the Commission enters upon an investigation of the proposal. If it does

so, it may order the operation or service continued for not exceeding 4 months pending a decision in the investigation, at which time, provided it makes the required statutory findings, the Commission may require continuance (or restoration) of the service for not more than 1 year thereafter. If it decided not to enter upon an investigation, or if the Commission fails to decide the case within the 4-month period, the carrier may discontinue or change the service as proposed. Under section 13a (2), where the proposed discontinuance or change in service of a train operated wholly within a single State is prohibited by the constitution or statutes of that State, or where the State authority having jurisdiction has denied an application or petition or has not acted finally on such application or petition within 120 days from their presentation, the carrier may file an application with the Commission for authority to effect the discontinuance or change. The Commission may authorize it only after notice and hearing and upon prescribed findings.[18]

Under the terms of the new law, interstate passenger service could be withdrawn quickly after the proper notice was given, unless, of course, the ICC investigated and required the service continued. In most cases, where there has been some delay, the desired discontinuance in such situations has, at most, taken only a few years. To discontinue passenger service of an intrastate nature requires that the carriers seek relief from state agencies first; after that course of action has been exhausted under the 1958 Act, the Interstate Commerce Commission can be petitioned by the carrier. All in all, after passage of the 1958 Act, the railroads were in a much better position than before to remove the passenger millstone from their necks.[19] The National Railway Passenger Corporation—called AMTRAK—which began life in May 1971, has further lightened the burden. Only the Southern Railway; the Chicago, Rock Island and Pacific; and the Denver and Rio Grande Western still operate passenger trains on their own account.

As noted earlier, among the prime contenders for the financial millstone title is commuter railway service, which has almost without exception proved to be a losing operation for the railroads. Discontinuation of commuter service was therefore high on the list of priorities for carriers concerned. All commuter service was, of course, vulnerable under the 1958 Act, most especially that of the New York City region, which was interstate in nature. The Transportation Act of 1958 was signed into law by President Eisenhower on August 12, 1958; on that very day the New York Central Railroad posted notices announcing that it would discontinue its West Shore Ferry Service (linking Manhattan with the New York Central's commuter railway operation on the west side of the Hudson River). The Erie Railroad followed suit shortly. The ICC did not investigate the action proposed by the New York Central, and thirty days later the ferry boats stopped running.

Throughout the autumn of 1958, the New York area commuter railroads made ominous noises and announced whopping deficits. At the beginning of December the Lehigh Valley and the Delaware, Lackawanna & Western railroads announced plans for abandonment of commuter service, and the Pennsylvania stated it would discontinue most off-peak commuter service to Manhattan. Railroads in other parts of the country made similar threats. It soon became clear that the legislation that had been aimed at helping the railroads had suddenly become the vehicle by which the urban mass transportation problem in the large cities served by commuter railroads had reached a critical stage.[20]

The threat to commuter service brought alarm and a reaction from the older and larger cities. In the New York area attempts were made to join with New Jersey and Connecticut to find some way to retain the railway service. In Philadelphia, the city formed a nonprofit corporation, the Passenger Service Improvement Corporation, to lease improved service at reduced fares from the Reading and Pennsylvania railroads.[21]

Gradually it became clear to the worried big cities that they must take the same kind of steps to solve their mass transportation problems as had been taken to meet the critical difficulties of the Depression period. At that time, the cities had been unable to help themselves and state governments had proved unable to act effectively. In short, the federal government, which had inadvertently touched off the urban transportation crisis, appeared to be the best place to look for solutions.

Even so, the atmosphere in Washington could hardly have been more hostile to any enlargement of federal functions in metropolitan areas. President Eisenhower wished to keep federal involvement in cities and local areas as low as possible, and mass transportation seemed particularly local in nature. Moreover, the administration was fully committed to the highway program—indeed, it had initiated the Interstate Highway System program—and it was most likely that the powerful highway interest groups would take a dim view of any mass transport programs, especially if it appeared that highway money might be diverted for this purpose.

Although it is getting ahead of the story a little bit, the position of the Eisenhower administration in regard to urban transportation problems was perhaps most clearly set out in *Federal Transportation Policy and Program,* issued by the Commerce Department in March 1960:

> Metropolitan areas are increasingly congested with mass highway transportation, and are afflicted by rush-hour jams, parking area deficiencies, and commuter and rapid-transit losses.
>
> This is primarily a local problem but the Federal Government contributes toward the problem with its huge highway program. It also has a deep concern in the railroad commutation passenger losses because of their effects upon the health of the railroad system and upon the extent to which the Nation can secure the benefit of the railroads' capability for mass long-distance transport of freight. Ways and means must also be found to encourage tax relief by local and State jurisdictions in helping solve the problems of commuter or local passenger deficits.
>
> The Federal Government should encourage communities to make broad land-use plans with transportation as an essential part. It should consider as a long-run problem means by which such forward planning can be encouraged. It should also consider possible community charges on highway gateways and parking areas to help reduce the highway congestion and help finance the over-all transportation plan. Jointly with communities, the Federal authorities should consider the total urban transport situation so that Federal participation may contribute to the efficiency with which urban transport as a whole is performed.[22]

Beneath the federalese it is clear that the administration did not feel that the federal government should touch the urban transport problem directly, even with the proverbial ten-foot pole. This particular position on urban transportation—as well as many others embodied in the report—did not jibe with the thinking of some of the staff who had performed the background work. Ernest W. Williams, the director of the transportation study, and David W. Bluestone, a member of the staff, issued an Appendix to the Commerce Department's policy statement to help set the record straight.[23] Their position on urban transportation is of considerable interest:

> . . . Downtown areas were not designed to handle the traffic load which results from . . . [population] dispersion and the accompanying reliance

upon the private automobile. The two major past and continuing trends are the resulting decline in business activity in the heart of the central city, and a sharp reduction in the use of public transportation facilities.

From the standpoint of total cost, serious problems are raised by these trends. Mass transportation is clearly much less expensive per passenger-mile than total costs of the private automobile with an average of less than two occupants. From the standpoint of efficiency, there is little doubt that per passenger . . . transit vehicles are far more efficient in terms of space occupied. . . . Rail lines are similarly much better space users.

The present highway program has provided substantial sums for improving access to our major metropolitan areas. However, the present program does not require any test to determine the most efficient use of these funds in terms of passenger movement. Merely adding highways which will attract more automobiles which will in turn require more highways is no solution to the problems of urban development.

. . . Since our essential purpose is to move people rather than vehicles and since the objective of moving people is to facilitate the purchase and provision of services in our downtown areas, it is becoming increasingly apparent that a new look must be taken at long-range transportation planning in our cities.

. . . In all cities, one thing is clear: while continued highway development is essential, it is being viewed increasingly as only one part of the total transportation problem. . . .

The conclusion is clear that urban planning must allow for increased use or at least maintenance of existing rail transit facilities. In the long run, it will be false economy for the nation to devote public funds exclusively to the highway program without encouraging the cities to develop long-range plans to ensure the most efficient use of money, material and manpower in the handling of urban transportation. As a minimum, the Federal Government must provide incentives to encourage such planning in our cities. . . .

Our highway program should be re-examined with respect to urban transportation. The emphasis should be on appraising total transportation supply and requirements in our cities, in close coordination with other municipal planning. Highway expenditures should be based on integrated plans. Our cities must be encouraged to look at total economics as well.

This means that tax or other adjustments for private companies hauling passengers by rail or bus must be considered as alternatives to increased expenditures on widened streets or reduced tax ratables due to declining business activity in the central business district. The net cost to the area as a whole must be considered in arriving at sound transport solutions. . . .

Some of the funds in the highway program and possibly in the urban renewal program may be usable in connection with such planning. Because the problem of commutation by rail is especially acute in some areas where service is rapidly being curtailed, Federal or State loans to municipalities or metropolitan authorities may need to be considered, especially where localities may acquire commuter rail facilities and equipment and lease them to the carriers.[24]

In addition to the attitude of the administration in the late 1950's, Washington was not set up to investigate or administer a program to aid mass transport for urban areas. Responsibility was scattered among various agencies and departments. It appeared that the federal government was ill adapted organizationally to handle the problems of urban transportation through policies and programs. Of course, it was also abundantly clear to at least some observers that the federal level of government was not even very well arranged to formulate objectives and policies for nonurban transport.

Perhaps the greatest difficulty was that mass transportation problems, particularly as narrowly viewed in 1958 as mainly a commuter railway problem, had small appeal in Congress. Since commuter rail service on a substantial scale existed only in New York, Boston, Philadelphia, Chicago, and San Francisco, it seemed a problem affecting only a very limited number of larger cities. For Congress and the Executive Branch, there simply did not seem to be much political mileage in the issue.[25]

Reaction to the Crisis

Despite the infelicity of the atmosphere for federal action on the mass transportation issue in 1958, work was begun almost immediately to rectify the problems brimming on the horizon by the threatened discontinuation of commuter railway service. The support for action which eventually led to federal legislative programs in mass transportation came from the central cities, not the states or the suburban areas.

That the dominant force should be the central cities is not surprising. Suburban areas rimming the central city are principally occupied—indeed, preoccupied—with local problems; such communities are usually poorly equipped even to consider action that might include cooperation with bodies outside their own immediate jurisdiction. So suspicious are they of threatened loss of autonomy, or the need to spend without visible benefits for the cost involved, that the reaction to any proposal to band together with other suburban or central city governmental bodies is almost universally one of hostility. As for calling on or dealing with the federal government on some troublesome issue, suburban efforts tend to be sporadic, quite limited, and usually crisis-stimulated. Admittedly, from the rather narrow suburban viewpoint, it is difficult to see the whole of the problem here that might affect an entire metropolitan area. Such programs or federal aids as are envisioned would almost invariably be aimed at short-run solutions to very local aspects of a problem. As a result, outcries from suburban areas in danger of losing their commuter service were limited to pleas for the salvation of service on their particular line.

In Washington, pressures from suburban communities are still relatively weak; there is not yet any large, unified national suburban pressure group, although in recent years there is some evidence of the growth of what might be called a suburban bloc in the House of Representatives. In any case, the local congressman may be the only real voice a suburb has in the nation's capital. However, the disparity of pleas, plans, and programs the representative may be called upon to support are often contradictory. Thus the wise congressman is forced to serve his constituents by doing nothing on many issues. The slim political resources and lack of unity among suburbs of even the same metropolitan area—much less the nation as a whole—resulting from the fragmented nature of the genus suburbia have usually rendered the suburbs rather ineffectual in gaining administration support or congressional action.

However, on some issues that seem likely to affect all suburban communities in the same way—such as a federal policy of enforcing open housing or some federal program that is visualized as resulting in a power grab by central cities—there may be sufficient separate pressures of a similar nature put on congressmen throughout the country to have the same effect as would a single powerful pressure group.

The attitude of the states in regard to expanded federal programs in urban areas is often negative. This was especially true in the late 1950's. It is not unusual for the rural elements in the state legislature to harbor resentment and antipathy for the urbanites within their jurisdiction.[26] There is, moreover, considerable fear that any sort of regional authority or federally sponsored regional action may not only be harmful to state prestige and sovereignty, but may cause the state government to become financially entangled. One suspects that direct links between the city and the federal government are also resisted by state governments because they reflect upon the ability of the states to care for their own, damage a state's status, and render the states open to the threat of melting even further into the background on many of the vital issues which concern an urbanized society. In being bypassed as a level of government that does nothing useful in a given area or for a given problem, the states are in danger of fading into the limbo of archaic or unnecessary governmental institutions. Paradoxically, lack of state action—for whatever reason—pushes the cities ever closer to the federal level of government, exactly the opposite of what the states would wish to happen. In short, states view direct federal aid programs as a threat, and therefore give little or no support to plans for federal action in urban areas. This attitude may soften a bit if the state is given the role of an intermediary in parcelling out federal aid.

It is the central city, therefore, with its onerous burdens of slums, crime, eroding tax base, rape by highway, upper-class diaspora, and lower class in-migration, that carries the message to Washington. The political men of the central city, particularly those in the larger metropolitan areas, who have had to deal with the grim reality of opposition from state government and the adverse effects of decentralization of population, saw the handwriting on the wall. Although central cities did not come to grips with their problems soon enough to avoid most of them, when realization of the crisis came, they carried the day.

In undertaking the task of gaining federal support for urban programs, the big cities had available certain invaluable resources. Among these were prominent, powerful, and practical men of politics and business, buttressed by national urban lobbying groups, such as the American Municipal Association (now called the National League of Cities) and the United States Conference of Mayors. Another resource, not to be discounted lightly, was the large metropolitan newspapers, which often harbor nationally syndicated columnists on their staffs and can thus have some impact on national opinion. Added to these resources was the superior perspective granted to the central city as the focus of regional problems and strengths. While events or problems might be felt but subtly in the suburban ring, each tug of the metropolitan spider web was felt at the center.

Because of their superior resources and clearer and more realistic point of view, the central cities could and did carry on a sustained effort to interest the federal government in broadening its responsibilities in urban areas, particularly in the post-World War II era. As urban problems mounted, a loose alliance of interest groups was formed. In the initial stages, it ordinarily consisted of Democratic politicians, the downtown economic interests, and some of the large metropolitan dailies. To this were soon added civic groups with a regional interest, some labor groups, planners, and college professors who saw the light outside their towers. On the urban transportation question the commuter railroads and, a bit later, the transit operators were added to this group.[27]

Every movement needs a champion. In the early stages of the development of a federal policy for urban mass transportation, that man was Richardson Dilworth, Democratic mayor of Philadelphia.

Not daunted by the earlier failure to gain federal aid, Dilworth and other representatives of the central cities and the railroads met in Chicago in January 1959 to assess the situation in the wake of the Transportation Act of 1958. At the conference were representatives of Allentown, Pa., Baltimore, Boston, Chicago, Cleveland, Detroit, Kansas City, Milwaukee, New York, Philadelphia, St. Louis, and Washington. The railroads represented were the Baltimore and Ohio, Boston & Maine, Burlington, Milwaukee Road, Chicago & North Western, Pennsylvania, New York Central, Jersey Central, Rock Island, Southern Pacific, Reading, Erie-Lackawanna, Long Island, Missouri Pacific, and New Haven.

Among the city representatives and the eastern commuter railroads there soon developed a consensus that the federal government had a role to play. The western commuter roads, especially those serving Chicago, perhaps less desperate than their eastern brethren, were coy about any federal intervention. The bugaboo of subsidy leading eventually to a federal takeover of the railroads was raised.[28] The meeting was not a failure, however, and a smaller working committee headed by Dilworth set about drawing up some plan or program that all could back.

The working committee met in Philadelphia in March 1959. In order to gain more time for agreement as well as to put together some factual basis for their case, a study was undertaken. The work was done by the Philadelphians and a report entitled *The Collapse of Commuter Service* was issued by the American Municipal Association toward the end of 1959. The report was based on a study of five cities with commuter rail or rapid transit systems: New York, Philadelphia, Boston, Cleveland, and Chicago. Among the findings the national alarm was raised with the following:

> The vast importance of the problem of mass transportation is indicated by the fact that more than 60% of the total U.S. population is contained in the Standard Metropolitan Areas, and by the end of the next decade, almost 80% of the U.S. population will be located in these areas.

The need for continuation of commuter rail and rapid transit service was sharply pointed out to the cost-conscious:

> If only twenty-five per cent of those now riding mass transportation lines were to be forced onto the highways . . . it would cost these five cities $4.4 billion to provide the highway capacity to move a comparable number of people. . . . If the commuter lines were to suspend operations completely, it would cost $17.4 billion to build highways to serve a comparable number of people in these five cities. This does not include the additional costs of constructing parking facilities, the loss in taxes or the cost of traffic engineering. . . .[29]

Also included was a suggestion that a federal lending corporation be set up to provide funds for urban transportation programs.[30]

The Collapse of Commuter Service and persistent efforts by Mayor Dilworth and the commuter rail people at the American Municipal Association Congress in Denver in December 1959 brought full AMA recognition of the problem. It adopted a resolution calling on Congress to estabish a policy that would promote coordinated transport on all levels. Congress was also asked to provide long-term, low-interest-rate loans to those communities where such aid was needed for the purchase of new equipment or upgrading of facilities. The issue of federal grants-in-aid was more touchy. A recommendation was made that a study of such a program be undertaken.[31]

Nevertheless, it was again difficult to muster a great deal of general enthusiasm in a program that was rather narrowly focused on rail commuter and rapid transit problems. The number of cities with such facilities and with concern over them was but a handful, even among the larger cities.[32] Nevertheless, the point had been made and an influential pressure group had had its attention drawn to the important issue of a federal role in urban transportation.

A firmer coalition had also been established between the central cities and the railroads, although many of the carriers still viewed federal participation with suspicion. Dilworth and James Symes, president of the Pennsylvania Railroad, worked together on drafting legislation to be presented to the Congress under the auspices of the American Municipal Association. Their aim was to meet immediate needs and at the same time evolve a legislative program agreeable to the AMA and the embattled commuter railroads.

As finally drawn up, the legislation was a rehash of the ill-fated Green Bill of 1958. It called for low-interest loans to be made by the Department of Commerce to states, local governments, and authorities for the acquisition, maintenance, and improvement of mass transport equipment and facilities.

Although it was expected that the legislation would not get a warm reception from the Eisenhower administration or the 86th Congress, it had been constructed to quell displeasure from potentially hostile pressure groups so that perhaps the next Congress would be more receptive. The mistake usually made by the railroads of trying, through legislation, to deny benefits of government largesse to other modes—for example, the railroads had dithered for years about the improvement of waterways with no user charges levied against the operators of barge lines—was avoided by the simple expedient of merely getting benefits for themselves.[33] No matter how much sense such denial might make on the grounds of justice in competition or economic rationality, it always aroused substantial and usually effective opposition from those whose vested interest was threatened. Moreover, the appeal of the proposed legislation was broadened by the provision of aid for urban mass transportation in general, not big city commuter railroads and rapid transit in particular. Thus, it was hoped that general support from traffic beleaguered cities throughout the country would be forthcoming.

The major error lay in putting the administration of the proposed bill in the hands of the highway-oriented Department of Commerce. As a matter of policy this department was opposed to any federal involvement in local transit problems. Its attitude mirrored that of the administration for the added reason that support of transit-oriented legislation might raise some doubts about the wisdom of the federal highway program, a program greatly expanded during the Eisenhower years, most notably by the Interstate Highway Act of 1956.

Therefore, when in February of 1960 a delegation of mayors and railroad representatives presented the case for the proposed legislation before the Secretary of Commerce, representatives of the Budget Bureau, congressional leaders, and representatives of the congressional committees that would consider the measure, the reception was noncommittal at best. On the brighter side, both Senate majority leader Lyndon Johnson and House Speaker Sam Rayburn, pledged their support for the proposed legislation, thus dispelling the frost a little.[34] Nevertheless, the situation on the whole continued to look very bleak indeed until Harrison Williams entered the scene.

If within their own ranks the city interests found a champion on the transit issue in Mayor Richardson Dilworth of Philadelphia, they found a much needed champion in the Congress in Senator Harrison Williams of New Jersey. Williams was a freshman in the Senate, and, like most new men in that august body, was seeking an issue or role he could play that would not be at odds with his New Jersey constituents, and yet would have relatively broad national interest. In effect, he needed a horse to ride. He found it in the mass transportation issue.

As a senator, Williams was in an excellent position to get action. The longer term of a senator permits more effort directed to important matters of legislation, rather than in the time-consuming biennial electioneering tour of speeches and mediocre dinners that is the sad lot of a representative. A senator is also blessed with greater resources for vital staff work. Since his constituency is statewide, his viewpoint is also broader; unlike a representative, a senator stands before the whole electorate of a state, including the whole of a metropolitan area or areas. At best, a representative from a metropolitan area can usually afford only a sub-regional outlook. Moreover, the Senate has been far more interested in needed innovations in government and more intent upon the federal government exercising its leadership function.[35] In this way the Senate, rather than the House, has generally been more representative of the changing needs of the increasingly urbanized American society in the period since the Depression.

Williams and his staff went to work to make needed changes in the legislative proposals drawn up by Dilworth and Symes. The first step was to shift the bill from the jurisdiction of the then largely hostile Department of Commerce by promoting the legislation more as a measure for urban areas than for transportation. The actions to be carried out would be under the jurisdiction of the Housing and Home Finance Agency, which at that time was the nearest thing to a Department of Urban Affairs within the federal framework. The change would also place consideration of the legislation in the hands of the Senate Committee on Banking and Currency, of which Williams was a member. This committee was likely to be far friendlier to the legislation than was the Commerce Committee, which would have handled the legislation as originally drafted. To add to the palatability, the original proposal for $500 million in loan authorizations was cut to $100 million. The proposed legislation was phrased in such a way as to emphasize even more carefully that it was intended to deal with all urban transport problems. The shift away from a railway-oriented bill designed to counteract the Transportation Act of 1958 and toward an urban mass transportation legislation program was in full motion. Backed by the American Municipal Association and the commuter railroad interests, Williams introduced his bill into the Senate on March 24, 1960.[36]

The Senate was friendly to the legislation and the Williams bill, S. 3278, was passed by the senior congressional body on June 27, 1960. It was not enough to win the day, however. In the House of Representatives the bill never got out of committee. As noted before, this was no particular surprise to Williams and the supporters of the transit program. However, with a national election coming up later in 1960, Democrats, and others with an urban stake, wished to go on record in support of an urban measure. Additional support was expected in the next session of Congress.

While the Democrats did not make any grand sweep of the Congress in the 1960 election, they did manage to elect a president who was firmly convinced of the importance of urban issues and the need for the federal government to play an increased role in coping with the staggering problems that faced U.S. metropolitan areas.

John Kennedy was the first man to run for the office of President of the United States with a major thrust of his campaign aimed at the problems of urban areas. In contrast, his opponent, Richard Nixon, virtually ignored the urban issue. Whether or not this was vital in winning the close election for Kennedy is debatable, but Kennedy's stand on the problems of urban areas is certain.

Moreover, his election marks a critical turning point in the attitude of the national government toward urban problems. When campaigning for the nomination to the Presidency, Kennedy spoke to the 1959 American Municipal Congress in Denver. In his speech he said:

> ... Our national defense posture, our Federal budget, our schools, highways, interest rates, race relations, reclamation, juvenile delinquency and the steel strike will be great issues in the 1960 election. But I would like to stress perhaps the greatest issue in a sense but the issue which is going to be talked about probably the least based on my own experience of traveling around the United States in the past year. I am asked what I think on the subject of birth control for India and what we should do in outer space, but hardly ever am I asked what we should do about the cities of the United States. I would say this is the greatest unspoken issue in the 1960 election and I think therefore we should address ourselves to it.[37]

The Rationale of Federal Urban Transport Policy

As 1961 dawned and the Kennedy administration took office, the way seemed relatively clear for federal participation in urban mass transportation programs. The original rationale for a federal role in urban transportation had as its origin a simple reaction to the Transportation Act of 1958. Through evolution the narrowly based railroad approach, which could affect only the largest cities, was broadened into a mass transportation approach. By fostering legislation for mass transportation in general, the large city-commuter railroad coalition provided a base of appeal to cities and communities of all sizes throughout the nation. But except for some highly vocal concern expressed in the early stages of worry about loss of commuter service immediately after the passage of the Transportation Act of 1958, no substantial pressure came from any major segment of the public.

As a happier note, no major opposition group outside the Congress had formed on this issue. A coalition of highway interests— including motor car manufacturers, petroleum companies, tire manufacturers, highway construction firms, and an assemblage of state, local and federal personages who saw some threat to highway programs—might have aroused themselves into opposition. This group, in league with the American Automobile Association and other associations of automobile users, had been the major force behind the 1956 enactment of the program getting the Interstate Highway System under way, and was considered one of the strongest lobbying groups ever to put pressure on Congress. It appears, however, at that time the highway interests were unworried about the programs for urban mass transportation. Dilworth, Williams, and other promulgators of mass transportation legislation had been careful to avoid an either/or approach. The mass transport legislation was promoted in terms of both highways *and* mass transport.[38]

The opposition which did develop against the program came from those whose disfavor stemmed from their over-all attitude toward further federal involvement in local affairs, regardless of whether proposed legislation was for urban transportation, urban housing, or anything else. The opponents of increased federal urban action were still a strong force in Congress, although by no means a majority. Their effectiveness lay in being able to get others to join them as part of the political log-rolling in which Congress indulges. In all honesty, since the proposed mass transit program had no loud murmur of grassroots public support in 1961, it appeared to have little political appeal. In contrast with, say, the push for civil rights legislation, with its vast public outcry pro and con, urban mass transportation legislation seemed a picayune matter, indeed. Even to many persons in Washington who were not adverse to federal action, it still seemed as if urban transportation were very much a local issue to be handled on the local level.

Nevertheless, Washington was in the process of re-evaluating the federal approach to many urban problems. Even prior to the election of John Kennedy, there had been a rising dismay in many parts of the country over the rapidly deteriorating urban situation. It was obvious, too, that however high the hopes for it had been, urban highway policy as carried out by the federal government in the decade of the 1950's was not a solution to all urban transport problems. Despite the vital need for urban highways and the tremendous increase in highway construction expenditures in the postwar era, the visible blight of congestion continued to expand. Since the nation's poor were not to be rediscovered until the mid-sixties, the issue of transit was rarely bandied about as a means of providing mobility to those who did not have access to the automobile.

The new, more urban-oriented administration which took office at the beginning of 1961 showed evidence of an over-all concern for the urban situation. Transport, of course, was only one element of a new broader attack to be made on urban problems. Housing, civil rights, education, redevelopment, and race relations were also matters of vital interest, and, frankly, items that attracted more public and administration interest than did transport.

Whatever the federal government might do in the urban transport field, it is unlikely to be revolutionary. The federal government had first undertaken a direct role in urban affairs during the early days of the New Deal through the exercise of its legitimate, but largely unused, welfare powers. Where once such interference would have been condemned by many as exceeding the constitutional and traditional rights of the federal government, the emergency conditions of the Great Depression permitted the federal government to take action hitherto undreamed of.[39] The initial broad programs undertaken in the first Roosevelt administration were knocked down with monotonous regularity by a conservative Supreme Court that reflected a Jeffersonian bias in its conception of the proper role of the federal government. With caution bred of desperation, from the late '30's on, the federal government had usually taken a role of leadership, and as a provider of funds, but had generally left the day-to-day operations of federal programs to local officials or to private enterprise.[40] Caution fostered by New Deal setbacks had often been translated into a lack of imagination in programs undertaken. This, along with a not unnatural fear of risk by administrators on all levels of government, had almost guaranteed that federal urban programs would be less than satisfactory.

The failure of federal programs over the past thirty years to improve urban areas and urban life throughout the nation results in part from suburban attitudes. Many suburban political officials, probably supported by most suburban dwellers, regard the central city as something to be milked, not fed. As has been noted elsewhere, this attitude stems from the fear of becoming entangled—financially if not otherwise—in some of the ghastly problems that plagued the big cities. There also arose a genuine fear of the minority groups—usually nonwhite—that were taking over increasing proportions of the central city area. Whatever limited political strength the suburban areas muster in Washington was generally joined to the strategically powerful Southern conservative group and big business pressure group to achieve certain ends through the process of political compromise. Thus it was assured that what would be done in urban areas by the federal government would definitely benefit private interests and the suburbs—although it would not necessarily meet any of the higher ends for which programs had been initiated. Such a result can be almost automatic. Legislation for various kinds of federal action may have enthusiastic support in the time leading up to its consideration by the Congress. But all too often, when the legislation becomes law the enthusiasm dies. To many members of the public, the problem is solved when a bill is passed; the vital implementation phase is largely anticlimatic, and the public usually shows little interest in making sure a law accomplishes its stated objective.

Even though many federal programs had been aimed at helping cities, honest men could say in 1961 that federal programs had actually aided in the devitalization of the city. For example, beyond their stated functions, the FHA and VA loan programs were the guardian angels of ticky-tacky suburban developments. Urban renewal projects had displaced many people, usually low-income groups, forcing them to double up in already overcrowded neighborhoods, while the renewal project itself provided housing for medium- and upper-income groups. The highway program did not relieve congestion; indeed, in many instances it probably made it worse by encouraging greater use of the automobile.

Thus the homogenized dullness, lack of amenities, and enervating congestion which are typical of American cities are, in part, sins which may be laid at the doorstep of the federal government. No matter how good the intentions may be, there are many slips between the legislative cup and the public lip.

The Aims of Federal Policy

The objectives of federal urban transportation policy were shaped by both the shorter run needs of big cities in danger of losing vital commuter railway and mass transit services and the longer run needs of providing for less chaotic development in rapidly growing metropolitan areas. Where the big-city mayors had looked toward the federal government to help preserve existing transportation services as reasonable alternatives for the private automobile, the general policy of the federal government has been to treat mass transport as an integral part of urban development.

Federal policy aims were perhaps most clearly stated in President Kennedy's Transportation Message of 1962:

> To conserve and enhance values in existing urban areas is essential. But at least as important are steps to promote economic efficiency and livability in areas of future development. In less than 20 years we can expect well over half of our expanded population to be living in 40 great urban complexes. Many smaller places will also experience phenomenal growth. The ways that people and goods can be moved in these areas will have a major influence on their structure, on the efficiency of their economy, and on the availability for social and cultural opportunities they can offer their citizens. Our national welfare therefore requires the provision of good urban transportation, with the properly balanced use of private vehicles and modern mass transport to help shape as well as serve urban growth.[41]

Put differently, the broad goals were three in number: (1) preserve and enhance urban values, (2) serve population at lowest cost, (3) help shape cities. This was to be accomplished in a coordinated manner achieving a balance between the use of private and public vehicles. The objectives are interesting in that they treat the urban mass transportation issue in a far broader perspective than had hitherto been the case. While the old "save the commuter trains" notion can be seen within these three objectives, nevertheless, something larger and of a higher spirit is envisioned. The thought is tied to the reality of facing up to the challenge of an urbanized society in great need of reinvigorating the tarnished promise of past urban development in order to insure a livable future.

Looking behind the goal of preservation and enhancement of urban values, one sees an understanding that in our increasingly urbanized and metropolitanized civilization the central city was too often little more than a rotting core. There was considerable truth in the wry comment that the metropolian area could be compared with the doughnut—nothing in the middle and the dough all around the edges. Statistics, and the moans of public officials, indicated that central cities were growing financially weaker yet becoming increasingly overburdened by social problems. As the century waxed on, the older center cities were becoming increasingly unattractive, either for visits or investment. The city had become a place to work in and to get away from.

As an objective, preservation of the city was, of course, not a completely unselfish motive. Continuing deterioration endangered the values of property located in the central city. Various federal renewal programs, coupled with transportation programs for easier access to central business district property and central city property in general, were therefore most appealing. Retail establishments also recognized that improved access to downtown shopping districts would boost sales.

The values to be preserved and enhanced in the urban areas were, of course, not merely economic values. Social interests and needs were also to be met by the urban transportation program. If improved mass transportation would help reduce congestion and make circulation in metropolitan areas easier, communications between people and places could be greatly enhanced. Ease of movement through at least partial removal of the congestion barrier could make city life more interesting and vital. Sociologists and urban planners could see improved mass transportation as a means of injecting greater heterogeneity into the lives of urban dwellers. It was expected that improved transportation might even be able to dispel the intellectual and cultural void of the suburbs. Perhaps this was asking too much. In any event, to many people the social effects of improved mass transportation could be no worse and probably much better than the appalling results of large-scale highway construction in urban areas.

From the perspective of the early 1970's, what seems missing is a lack of concern over the social and economic costs of automobile accidents and air pollution that might be reduced through greater use of mass transportation. Other arguments might have been made on the issue of preserving and improving U.S. cities' sparse aesthetic appeal.

In having the shaping of cities as a goal for mass transportation policy one can see an attempt to regain some of the lost opportunities of the New Deal 1930's. Then, failure of effective control and bold action by the federal government had encouraged sprawling metropolitan development and resultant fragmentation. Proper urban transportation planning, including both highways and mass transportation, and greater emphasis on comprehensive planning could act to help prevent further suburban sprawl. There was an obvious need for shaping, reshaping, and rationalizing development on the urban scene, and properly geared mass transportation policy could help in such programs.

The goal of serving urban populations at lowest cost had significant attraction. First, it had a shorter-range appeal: savings in highway investment. Looking ahead ten to twenty years it seemed obvious that attractive and well-planned mass transportation systems might take pressure off all levels of government for increased expenditures for highways.

On a longer-run basis the appeal of mass transportation was even greater. In the early 1960's estimates of future urban populations were, to say the least, most frightening. Projecting ahead to the end of the twentieth century, even the most unsophisticated observer could note that almost exclusive dependence upon the automobile for the transportation of people in urban areas was unthinkable; there would be too many people, too many cars, and too little room.

The initial factors which conditioned federal urban transport policies were, first of all, the need for a broad attack on urban problems; a key factor of this attack was the improvement of urban transportation. Second, the policy should seek to redress at least some of the imbalance caused by the highways-only program under the Highway Act of 1944—a policy which had continued unabated from war's end until 1961—by providing reasonable alternatives to the use of the private automobile.

Overriding, and possibly having a far greater role in shaping urban transport policy than is generally realized, is an unpublicized shift in attitude at the Bureau of the Budget. (Under President Nixon the Bureau of the Budget became the Office of Management and Budget.) A change of heart is, of course, not unthinkable when administrations change. What matters is that the subtle but increasing power of the Budget Bureau pervades the policy of all federal departments and agencies. The budget people appear increasingly unwilling to put all of the federal government's financial power behind any one program in a given field. A mix of alternatives is usually sought. Much of recent federal transport policy seems to reflect this position. To date, the Budget Bureau has not publicly questioned the sanctity of road building in the United States. Yet neither does one hear unstinted praise of highway building as the highest and most valuable function of the federal government. During the Nixon administration, the Office of Management and Budget did question the wisdom of trust funds, such as the Highway Trust Fund. Money so inflexibly committed hampered administration efforts to dampen the rise of inflation, or use alternative spending policies to provide a boost for the economy when needed. In any event, as the 1960's wore on it was increasingly clear that the policy of highway construction was no longer to have a monopoly of federal funds in urban transportation.

Perhaps, too, in many official and unofficial circles since 1955 there has been a serious questioning of the wisdom of uncritically gearing American life to the automobile. Ransoming one's heritage and future to a mechanical contrivance seems odd indeed in a democratic society which supposedly prides itself on its care and concern for the individual.

Housing Act of 1961

The advent of the new Kennedy administration seemed to bring with it almost immediate promise of the fulfillment of the aims of Senator Williams and the central city–railroad interests that had started the push toward a federal role in urban mass transportation back in 1958. Adding to the air of hope were two reports which took a favorable view of federal aid to mass transportation. James Landis, in his report on the federal regulatory agencies, had recommended to President Kennedy that the federal government guarantee loans for the commuter railroads.[42] The "Doyle Report," a study carried on for the Senate Commerce Commitee, was concerned with federal policy toward railways—and transport in general—and had grown out of the senatorial investigations of 1958 which led up to the passage of the Transportation Act of 1958. The panicky reaction of the Eastern commuter roads had caused a section on urban mass transportation to be included in this report. As a means of solving the commuter problem, the Doyle report suggested a loan program to be administered by the Interstate Commerce Commission.[43]

Senator Williams' Urban Mass Transportation Bill of 1961, introduced shortly before the inauguration of President Kennedy, called for a program of loan authorization and demonstration grants. The demonstration grant idea, of which more shortly, was a new wrinkle that had been added to the legislative package by Senator Williams and his chief legislative assistant, ArDee Ames.

To the dismay of the principal supporters of the legislation, the reception from the administration was not at all warm. In retrospect, this should not have been surprising. The new president was burdened with many other problems; transit, at the time, seemed a minor issue among the many that confronted his administration. The Bay of Pigs disaster had made the administration reluctant to put its prestige behind legislation that might not fare well in Congress. Legislative victories were a must to bolster the morale and image of the administration. Moreover, the president was advised by some of his closest aides that he should wait for a complete study of the urban mass transportation situation before taking an administration position on the issue.

Williams and other central city–railroad–mass transportation interests rallied around and both sides eventually compromised. The administration remained largely neutral on the issue at that time; a stronger and most definite position—the one outlined earlier—was taken when urban mass transportation was given a position of considerable importance in the President's Transportation Message of April 5, 1962. However, in early 1961 it was clear that an urban mass transportation act would stand virtually no chance of passage by itself. Accordingly, the urban transportation program was eventually included as a part of the omnibus housing act of 1961, and was passed into law on June 30.[44]

There were three provisions in the Housing Act of 1961 relative to urban mass transportation. First of all, $25 million was authorized for mass transportation demonstration projects. This was to prove the most notable and important part of the act. Secondly, the Act of 1961 specified that mass transportation planning should be included as an integral part of comprehensive urban planning under the Section 701 program of planning grants.

Finally, loans were authorized under the Act of 1961. Noting that it was difficult for many mass transport undertakings to raise money at reasonable interest rates, the Housing and Home Finance Agency was authorized to loan funds at low interest in circumstances where repayment was reasonably certain.[45] While a total of $50 million was authorized for the loan purpose, this portion of the act and subsequent loan programs included in mass transport legislation have been but little used. Logically, many local governments and agencies held out on the hope of eventually getting grants that would not need to be repaid. Then, too, the idea that many transit operations would be able to pay off a loan was undoubtedly rather optimistic.

The urban mass transportation provisions contained in the Housing Act of 1961 are modest indeed, especially when compared to the aims of programs initially pushed by the central city–railroad group. All told, only $42.5 million was appropriated for loans and demonstrations. It was, in short, a limited program, a foot-in-the-door approach to the problem. Since it was largely a demonstration program, the 1961 Act has some of the flavor of many governmental actions which are the fruits of compromise; that is, it is a matter of "doing something, but not too much." Of course, the legislation—however modest—was a victory for the mass transportation interests, although no direct aid was available for impoverished transit operations about to go down for the third time in a sea of fiscal difficulties. Yet, if no life-preserver was thrown to the drowning, it appeared at long last that there might be help coming with a life-boat.

Despite the limited funds devoted to it, the program was one that would draw attention to itself. The transit demonstrations that would be conducted—something novel, indeed, in the field of public mass transportation—would be more likely to interest newspapers and other mass media than would the same small sum spent on capital investment efforts. Probably there was no other way a similar amount of money could have helped arouse increased interest in mass transportation on a broad national scale.

The Act of 1961 in and of itself did little to help the sagging fortunes of urban commuter railways or mass transit systems. However, it did help to answer the question of whether or not people will ride transit if it is improved to some degree. Up to this time, the opposition to federal transit aid had not dwelled upon this question. Richardson Dilworth had given the affirmative side at the hearings on mass transportation legislation introduced before the Congress. He could point with great pride to the success of Philadelphia's Passenger Service Improvement Corporation and its city-sponsored commuter railroad experiments within Philadelphia. Experience in the Quaker City showed that patrons could indeed be wooed back to mass transportation.[46]

As for the wisdom of initiating a program—albeit a truncated program from that which had initially been attempted—of mass transport aid with demonstrations, successful results from a number of demonstration studies would be powerful ammunition in getting the federal government to play a greater role in solving urban mass transportation problems. Successful demonstrations would ward off the inevitable criticism that investing funds in mass transportation was pouring money down a rat hole—criticism that was bound to arise when urban transport interests once again besieged the Congress for an expanded program of federal aid.

Highway Act of 1962

The Highway Act of 1962, at first blush, may not seem a part of an urban mass transportation program. Yet it is a vital part of the necessary over-all package of legislation required for an intelligent approach to the urban transportation problem. The aim of the legislation was to plug a gap in planning which had existed for many years. It grew out of a realization on the part of the federal government of the enormous impact that highway construction had had on cities. The effect had not always been a happy one. The idea that highway construction was not enough and that alternative forms of transportation should be considered, had obviously made its point with the Kennedy administration. The Highway Act of 1962 and its planning provision may therefore also be viewed as examples of federal efforts, however belated, to rationalize past programs which had inadvertently gone astray, or which had produced unforeseen developments.

The problems of noncomprehensive planning could be solved by tying strings on federal money. Under the terms of Section 9 of the Highway Act of 1962, approval of funds for federal aid to highway programs in any urban area with a population of 50,000 or more would be forthcoming only upon the finding of the secretary of commerce that proposed highway projects were based on a comprehensive and continuing planning process, carried on in cooperation with the state and other local levels of government. This imperative was to take effect July 1, 1965.[47] In requiring comprehensive and continuing planning, the Highway Act of 1962 guarantees that urban areas will at least have given consideration to transport alternatives other than highways. As might have been expected, cities were hard pressed to find sufficient talent to get their planning done within the deadline time, and the Bureau of Public Roads was equally hard pressed to find qualified people to evaluate the planning programs submitted by municipalities.[48]

Whether or not high standards of planning, and truly comprehensive planning, have been the outcome of this legislation is questionable. However, the long-run benefits of such a program are undeniable. In that sense the Highway Act of 1962 permits the federal government to resolve the mistakes made through misinterpretation of model planning legislation passed in the late 1920's. Herbert Hoover, then secretary of commerce, appointed a nine-man committee to prepare the Standard City Planning Enabling Act of 1928. His aim was to insure more orderly urban development, and the 1928 Act became the model adopted by most municipalities throughout the United States. "The 1928 Act specifies as the principal duty of the City Planning Commission the preparation, adoption, and maintenance of a long-range comprehensive, general plan for the physical development of a city."[49]

There were many weaknesses in the Standard Act, none perhaps more glaring than that—as the act was interpreted—planning commissions might adopt the urban general plan as a whole or adopt it in separate parts. Frequently, therefore, plans were developed in a noncomprehensive and piecemeal fashion, which acted more to obstruct the planning process than to aid it. Eventually, planning and planners became bogged down to the point of quibbling over zoning and other micro-aspects of city planning rather than devoting time and talent to over-all comprehensive planning. Hardly surprising, therefore, is the thumping failure of cities to understand just how highways could carve up a city, the proper role for urban mass transportation, or how urban sprawl and suburban blight could be prevented.[50]

The Highway Act of 1962 also belatedly put some muscle behind federal pressures for intelligent planning that could well have occurred almost thirty years earlier, had the federal government followed through on some New Deal programs. Had such action been taken in the middle '30's, a good bit of the regional sprawl and proliferation of fragmentized local government might have been prevented.[51]

Urban Mass Transportation Act of 1964

Some sort of follow-up was definitely needed to complement the legislation already on the book fostering alternative modes of transportation and more intelligent, comprehensive planning. In short, capital funds were needed to provide a financial transfusion for urban mass transportation. Of course, such funds were available through the loan provisions of the 1961 Act, but this approach was usually foreclosed to the neediest cases, who could not hope to pay back the money borrowed, regardless of the low rate of interest.

Moreover, in its provisions for demonstration grants the Housing Act of 1961 had been most specific in stating that the money not be used for capital projects.[52] This point was noted by the HHFA assistant administrator in charge of the Office of Transportation:

> . . . the prohibition of the use of demonstration grants for "major long-term capital improvement" has been conscientiously applied because the principal and sometimes sole objective of some proposals was the construction of a permanent transit facility for which regular financing had proved impossible. Rentals and other recognized charges for the use of capital equipment or facilities during the term of a demonstration was, however, recognized as a proper use of funds insofar as the particular items could be shown to be essential for the attainment of project objectives. Provision for crediting the project with any remaining capital value at its conclusion has been a mandatory requirement in these cases.[53]

All was not to be roses in furthering the cause of improved urban mass transportation and any sanguinary hopes that new legislation would shortly be passed providing for capital grants were soon to wither away. The congressional hurdle was, in the main, located in the House of Representatives. The House, with its strong rural, non-urban, conservative predilections, was to be the main factor causing the urban mass transportation program to run aground in the three years after 1961. Even though growing support was discernible on the part of smaller cities and suburban areas,[54] House opposition, plus the lack of strong grass-roots support from the public and the absence of continuing applications of pressure on the Congress from a well-organized power group, enabled opponents of the program to stall it.

Nevertheless, in the early months of 1962 it looked as if new and far more comprehensive mass transportation legislation would soon be forthcoming. In a major section of his transportation message President Kennedy recommended

> . . . that the Congress authorize the first installment of a long-range program of Federal aid to our urban regions for the revitalization and needed expansion of public mass transportation . . . [through] a capital grant authorization of $500 million to be made available over a 3-year period, with $100 million to be made available in fiscal 1963. . . .[55]

Continuation of the demonstration and loan provision of the Act of 1961 was also recommended. The president's message also focused considerable attention on the need for comprehensive planning, calling for the provision in highway legislation that was soon to be such a critical part of the Highway Act of 1962, as discussed earlier. Thus, in one message, the president had given a tremendous boost to the profession of land-use planning, and had come out for a far stronger and larger capital grant program than supporters of mass transportation had hoped.[56] The ground seemed well laid for quick passage of a mass transport bill.

Immediately following the president's message, Senator Williams introduced legislation containing a capital grant program. Hearings were soon held in both the House and Senate. These were generally successful in pointing up the need for federal aid and gave evidence of strong support for the measure from various urban interest groups. Against the tide of support the strongest opposition came from the Chamber of Commerce of the United States and the American Farm Bureau Federation. Both of these groups recited the litany of free enterprise and no enlargement of government spending. For its part labor gave cautious support to the proposed legislation, but evinced some concern over the possible loss of jobs that might result from improved and more efficient transport systems and the loss of the right to strike if the bill fostered an increase in municipal ownership of transit companies. Automotive interests were also cautious in their approval, taking care to point out that mass transportation and the private automobile were complementary to one another and that there was a laudable and necessary, though limited, role for mass transportation. They were firm in resisting any diversion of highway user charge revenues for the support of mass transportation programs.[57]

Both the House and Senate Banking Committees reported favorably on the legislation. Senator Lausche of Ohio, a major foe of the mass transportation program, insisted that since some commuters cross state lines the Senate Commerce Committee should also hold a hearing. In September, the Senator held a one-day hearing that was generally hostile—one might even say grumpy—in tone and the Commerce Committee reported the bill without recommendation.[58] Regardless of the action of the Senate, where favorable action was expected, it soon became clear that the House Rules Committee was not going to let the bill reach the House floor. Becalmed in the Rules Committee, the Urban Mass Transportation Act of 1962 died a lingering death as the 87th Congress passed into history. Despite this setback, Congress did pass a bill extending a 1961 Act for six months beyond its scheduled expiration date.[59]

The defeat of the 1962 Urban Mass Transportation Bill in the supposedly liberalized House Rules Committee came as a surprise, particularly after President Kennedy's strong support for a program of greater aid to urban transit. Not daunted, Senator Williams submitted a 1963 Urban Mass Transportation Bill on January 9, 1963, early in the first session of the 88th Congress. Opposition developed from Senator Lausche and others on the Surface Transportation Subcommittee. In spite of this, the Williams bill, largely intact, passed the Senate by a 52–41 vote on April 4.[60]

Even with passage of the Senate bill, it appeared as if an enlarged federal mass transport program would never make it through the House of Representatives. It was fully expected that the legislation would die in committee as a casualty of the "anti-urban revolt of Southern Democrats in retaliation for the Administration's civil rights program."[61]

The House version of the bill remained in committee for more than a year, but the House Rules Committee was not, in the main, responsible for the delay. The bill, in actuality, was held in the Rules Committee at the behest of House Speaker John McCormack, who felt that if the bill did come up for a vote in the House, it stood a good chance of being defeated.

There was a considerable amount of political wisdom in the Speaker's action. After President Kennedy had been murdered, President Johnson had supported the programs of his predecessor, including the mass transportation legislation. But of first importance on the Johnson administration's list of priority legislation were civil rights matters. Speaker McCormack did not wish to jeopardize the administration's reputation for legislative success at that point in time by bringing the urban mass transportation bill to the floor of the House only to have it defeated.

In April of 1964, the mass transportation bill was not on the White House list of "must" legislation. This precipitated an unusual train of events. To fully appreciate what happened one must go back to 1963. At that time there was a proposal before the House of Representatives for the construction of a rapid transit system in the District of Columbia. Labor lobbyists in Washington were persuaded to bring pressure against Congress to defeat the bill as an anti-labor measure. Organized labor was worried about the loss of bargaining rights and concerned that the proposed subway system would put bus drivers out of work. Too late, labor leaders realized their mistake in thinking small; defeat of the bill would actually cut down job opportunities. Unfortunately, it was too late to make the change of heart known to Congress and the bill was defeated in the House. Out of this, however, supporters of metropolitan mass transportation were quick to see the point. To get desired action, particularly in the House of Representatives, a strong, coordinated lobbying approach was necessary.

A pressure group was formed to push the fortunes of the bill by the time-honored process of lobbying. Called the Urban Passenger Transportation Association (UPTA), it represented the central city interests, the transit industry, the railroads, and organized labor— now firmly in the camp of transit as long as there was a quid pro quo in the legislation that protected jobs. Labor's active interest and membership in this group was made known to the president and by May 1964 the mass transportation bill had found its way onto the "must" list of legislation.[62]

The problem then became one of persuading Speaker McCormack to bring the matter to the floor of the House and persuading enough congressmen to vote in favor of it to assure passage. The Speaker had to be shown there were sufficient Republican votes from Northern urban centers to offset the predicted loss of Southern Democrats. The UPTA reported that thirty-five to forty Republicans would vote for the bill. McCormack finally moved the bill out of committee, but was still reluctant to schedule it for a House vote.

Again, he could hardly be blamed. Late in May the House Republican Policy Committee took a firm party stand of direct and unalterable opposition to the mass transit bill. Rarely does the Policy Committee take a stand when it fears defections from Republican ranks. However, the Urban Passenger Transportation Association had been busy lining up Republican support and felt it had enough to get passage. Getting McCormack to move was the problem.

Finally, Representative William Widnall of New Jersey, a most effective supporter of mass transit legislation, threatened to embarrass both Speaker McCormack and the White House. Widnall promised he would call a press conference to indicate Republican support sufficient to pass the bill and at the same time denounce the Speaker and the White House for obstruction of the legislative procedures.

McCormack set the vote for June 25. The House passed the bill 212 to 189. The Senate accepted the House changes on June 30, and on July 9, 1964, President Johnson signed into law the Urban Mass Transportation Act of 1964.[63]

Senator Mansfield is reported to have called the Urban Mass Transportation Act of 1964 a legislative miracle; never in memory had so many Republicans deserted the party line set by the Republican Policy Committee. Miracle or not, the Act of 1964 was a decided step forward in the over-all federal program of mass transportation encouragement and support.

The aim of the 1964 Act, which is the cornerstone of the federal transit program, is not only to provide aid for the improvement and development of mass transportation systems, but also to encourage the planning and establishment of areawide coordinated transport. Hand in hand with the planning provision of the Highway Act of 1962, powerful incentive is given to plan and develop a rational and integrated urban transport system combining both the private automobile and mass transportation.

There are three major parts of the 1964 Act. One of these continues the program of demonstrations originated under the Housing Act of 1961. However, under the 1964 legislation the HHFA administrator (under the present organization structure, it is the administrator of the Urban Mass Transportation Administration) was given the authority to initiate demonstrations on an independent basis, as well as by contract with sponsors initiating demonstrations from the local level. Furthermore, matching funds from the local area are not mandatory, although it is assumed that as a matter of policy the two-thirds federal, one-third local contributions followed under the 1961 Act would be continued. (As time has passed, the federal contribution in the demonstration programs has often been more than two-thirds. This will be discussed more completely in later chapters.)

The program of low interest rate loans begun under the 1961 Act is also continued under the 1964 legislation.

The part of greatest interest to most persons concerned with mass transportation was that involving grants of capital. The act provided for a long-run program of aid and a short-run, or emergency, program. Under the long-run program, if a city can satisfy the administrator of the program that "the facilities and equipment for which the assistance is sought are needed for carrying out a program . . . for a unified or officially coordinated urban transportation system as a part of a comprehensive and continuing program of planned development, capital will be made available up to two-thirds of the net project cost of a capital project.[64] The funds may be used for almost any transit-related capital project except the construction of public highways.

The short-run program was predicated on the need to keep a jeopardized transport operation running under emergency conditions. That is, where the planning for the development of a unified or coordinated transport system is under way, but not yet completed, a federal grant of up to fifty per cent of the net project cost may be made. If the planning is completed within three years of the execution of the grant agreement, an additional sum will be granted to bring the federal contribution up to the full two-thirds of the net project cost. Thus, planning is encouraged but not at the cost of permitting a transport system to cease operations.[65]

There are some other important provisions. Persons displaced by capital improvement projects receiving grants from the federal government are able to receive payments of up to $200 for purposes of relocation. Displaced business firms can receive displacement aid up to $3,000. Job protection is also provided for labor, including continuation of the rights of collective bargaining, wage security, and retraining of affected personnel where necessary. While all grants or loans were to be made to public bodies, private enterprise is to receive every encouragement to participate in conjunction with and through public agencies. Finally, no state may receive more than 12½ per cent of the total funds disbursed in any given year.

The act authorized the expenditure of $75 million for the fiscal year of 1965, and $150 million each year for the fiscal years 1966 and 1967. Up to $10 million of this sum was to be available for demonstration grants the first year of the act; this was to be increased to $20 million on July 1, 1965, and $30 million on July 1, 1966.[66]

Amendments of 1966

Federal programs—particularly those in their embryonic stages— are rarely left to rest for very long. Changes are always sought by both supporters and opponents. Urban mass transportation legislation was no exception. With the addition of the capital grant program and the planning requirements of the Urban Mass Transportation Act of 1964, federal programs of aid and encouragement to mass transport had moved well beyond the small first step of the Act of 1961. Much remained to be done, however, for if the mass transport program was out of its infancy, it still had to navigate through the awkwardness of adolescence.

(Moreover, there would soon be a new agency responsible for handling urban mass transportation responsibilities. In December 1966 the HHFA was merged into the newly formed Department of Housing and Urban Development.)

One of the most conspicuous gaps in the federal mass transit program was that concerning money. Despite the importance of the Urban Mass Transportation Act of 1964 as a legislative milestone, the programs were small in comparison with other federal expenditures for transportation. Between the passage of the Housing Act of 1961 and the last quarter of 1966, the government spent $375 million for programs under the acts of 1961 and 1964; during the same period it spent about $24 billion on highways, airways, and waterways.[67] Much had been achieved toward awakening public interest, but the fact that relatively little capital had been invested in public transportation in the previous forty years left a great deal of work to be done before any substantial improvement in urban mass transport and the quality of urban life was to be realized.

For example, although only New York, Philadelphia, Boston,

Cleveland, and Chicago at present have rapid transit systems (at the time of this writing only about ninety per cent of the system in San Francisco was in revenue service) all of them have expanded their systems since 1964, or are in relatively advanced stages of planning or construction. A number of cities are currently in the process of constructing entirely new systems. San Francisco is nearing completion of the Bay Area Rapid Transit District's system, and Washington, D. C., and Baltimore have started digging on their subway systems. Atlanta and Los Angeles are in the planning stages, and Buffalo and Pittsburgh are very likely to be candidates for rapid transit construction work in the near future. It is not news that construction of such facilities is most costly.

In addition to expansion of facilities and upgrading of equipment for rapid transit, the commuter railway operations serving Boston, New York, and Philadelphia need considerable renovation. Many of the cars are well over the brink of mechanical senility and more fit for museums than for hauling the public. Chicago and San Francisco commuter services are generally not in such bad shape physically; nevertheless, some improvements will be needed in the near future. Furthermore, certain cities not currently served by such means may find commuter rail service desirable in the near future.[68]

In addition to the needs of the expansion or improvement of rapid transit or commuter railway services, there is an obvious need for more modest, but still expensive, projects. Merely replacing an aging bus fleet will require expenditures of no piddling magnitude. Other financial demands will be created by the necessity for construction of garages, maintenance facilities, and terminal facilities. Some cities may be interested in constructing systems based upon transport modes not currently in vogue, particularly where demand exists that is too great for buses to handle readily and yet not large enough to warrant full-scale rapid transit.[69] All in all, it was as clear after the passage of the Act of 1964 as it is today that significant sums of money are necessary to make mass transport a reasonable alternative to the private automobile.[70]

In many cities, of course, capital expenditures alone would not be enough. Operating deficits, on systems large and small, plagued the meager financial resources of many municipalities. Even federal aid under the 1964 Act could not guarantee any solution to that problem. Indeed, so fiscally strapped were some cities, they could not match federal grants for demonstration or capital purposes, even after projects were approved by the Department of Housing and Urban Development (HUD).[71]

Another financial problem that grew out of the Act of 1964 was the need to provide plans and cost estimates of the sort necessary to qualify for a grant of capital. A city seeking funds just to buy some new buses as replacement for old ones might not run into much difficulty with engineering expense; however, planning a new bus transit system or trying to make improvements on an existing service requires great effort and expense. A large-scale project, especially one concerning rapid transit or a commuter railway, requires hundreds of thousands of dollars for the engineering and planning studies needed to qualify for a capital grant. No federal aid was available for such purposes under the 1964 Act, and local money was in short supply.

At the time, these local financial problems pointed up the organizational difficulties of local government in the United States. As noted earlier, the need for federal aid sprang in large part from governmental fragmentation on the local level, particularly in the larger metropolitan areas. The Act of 1964 and the Highway Act of 1962 certainly gave encouragement to coordinated efforts in transportation on the local level. However, neither provided sufficient incentives to all metropolitan area fragments to give up petty animosities and unite their efforts and financial capabilities.

There was also a need for more mass transportation research in the mid–1960's. Although the demonstration program had provided a valuable boost in knowledge about mass transport, it could hardly be considered as a systematic research program. Nothing approaching a complete "package" of high-calibre mass transport equipment, practices, or systems had been developed. Over all, considerable attention seemed needed in developing new methods of transporting people and—with the interest in reducing urban air pollution—improved, fume-free propulsion systems, as well as looking into economic, psychological, and sociological factors behind the demand for various modes of transport. Apart from some statistics published regularly by the American Transit Association, data on mass transportation in the United States were sparse. There was virtually no knowledge of mass transportation methods and research carried on abroad, save for the work done in Canada. Indeed, even many of the top-flight professional research firms that did much of the transit planning (apart from engineering) in the United States, in the mid-sixties and after, lacked real knowledge, experience, and wisdom in the field of mass transportation.

Another appalling gap in the American transport system had become painfully clear at about the same time the urban transportation crisis came to a head. As intercity business and personal travel expanded rapidly in the post-World War II period, what is often called the American transportation system was found to be no system at all, but rather a hodge-podge of competing and uncoordinated private and public carriers. Interchange between bus, plane, and train services was more often than not time-consuming, and frequently an exercise that could, with charity, only be described as one that separated the men from the boys. Typically, the coordination between the intraurban and interurban public transport systems was totally inadequate. In many cases, so difficult was it to get to and utilize public transport, that the traveler had no rational choice other than to use his own automobile.[72]

Another shortcoming lay in the calibre of management of mass transport systems. One of the major mass transportation problems—and one to be harped on in subsequent chapters—revolved around the need to sell mass transport service to the public. The mass transportation industry was neither consumer nor marketing oriented, yet, barring mandates prohibiting the use of automobiles, if mass transportation was to play a larger role in urban areas, the service offered would have to be effectively marketed to the public. The many years of decline in the industry had not made it attractive to talented and experienced business managers; nor, for that matter, to bright, young, college-trained persons. Real professional management, with the broad base of skills needed to operate a business successfully in the mid-twentieth century, was sorely lacking in transit. The core group of engineers who held management positions in many of the larger mass transportation firms were hardly versed in the managerial skills needed to sell mass transport services in the face of automotive competition.

Some means of upgrading the proficiency of those currently in the various echelons of transit management was needed. In addition, provision had to be made to provide for a continuing supply of talent that would find its way into transport management and related fields if the forthcoming new and improved systems were to operate smoothly in the future. It was not enough to spend money for equipment and facilities alone: men had to be educated to manipulate these resources in the most efficient, effective, and appealing manner.

The year for mending the gaps was 1966, when the authorization of funds under the Act of 1964 ran out. Interest in urban transportation had been stirred on several issues early in the second session of the 89th Congress. For example, on January 20, 1965, Senator Harrison Williams introduced

> S. 2804, a Bill to amend the Urban Mass Transportation Act of 1964 to authorize certain grants to assure adequate commuter service in urban areas. . . .

which was aimed at providing federal funds to defray 50 per cent of the cost of deficit operations. At the same time, he also introduced

> S. 2805, a Bill to amend section 13a of the Interstate Commerce Act, relating to the discontinuance or change of certain operations or services of common carriers by rail, in order to require the Interstate Commerce Commission to give full consideration to all financial assistance available before permitting any such discontinuance or change.

These particular bills were of special interest in the senator's home state of New Jersey. The commuter railways in the New York metropolitan area of the Garden State were growing increasingly morbid, and were making ever louder noises about either severe cuts in service or getting out of the business entirely.

Another bill, introduced by Senator Joseph Tydings of Maryland, concentrated on the need for more research and development work. The gist of this proposed legislation was that

> the Administrator [at the time the bill was introduced, the Administrator of HHFA. Upon the formation of a new cabinet level department for urban affairs it was to be the Secretary of the Department of Housing and Urban Development] shall undertake a program of research designed to achieve a technological breakthrough in the development of new kinds of public intraurban transportation systems which can transport persons in metropolitan areas from place to place within such areas quickly, safely, and economically, without polluting the air, and in such a way as to meet the real needs of the people and at the same time contribute to good city planning.[73]

The bill would have authorized $10 million annually from the federal coffers to develop new urban transport technology.

The major changes finally adopted in 1966 were introduced by Senator Williams and reported out of the Committee on Banking and Currency on August 8, 1966, as S. 3700, with a recommendation from the committee for passage. As reported, this bill called for an increase in the amount of money made available each year from $150 million to $225 million. It also called for aid for the planning, engineering, and designing of urban mass transport systems; training programs to help upgrade transport management; and grants to college and other nonprofit institutions for research purposes. It directed the secretary of housing and urban development to conduct research on new transport systems. The committee killed a measure introduced by Senator Williams to allow the federal government to cover up to 50 per cent of the operating deficits of transport agencies.[74]

In the House, the Committee on Banking and Currency reported favorably on H.R. 14810. This bill was in many ways similar to the legislation in the Senate except that it had no provisions for management training programs and called for expenditures of only $175 million annually for mass transportation.[75]

However, the recommended House bill went well beyond the Senate version in one important financial matter. It provided that beginning with fiscal 1968, $175 million would be authorized "for each fiscal year thereafter," thus making the federal mass transportation activity a permanently funded program of the federal government.[76] The certainty of continuation of the federal mass transport assistance programs would give stability to the efforts of the Department of Housing and Urban Development. It would relieve them of the need to return periodically to the Congress to justify the continuance of the program, and it would "give assurance that a locality starting on . . . expensive, long-term commitments for new or improved transit systems can count on continuing Federal assistance."[77]

In committee, Representative Fino of New York had fought vainly for a provision that would allow federal funds to be used to pay the interest on local bond issues sold for the purchase of mass transport equipment or the construction of facilities. Also abortive was Fino's attempt to strike out the provision of the 1964 Act limiting any given state to no more than 12½ per cent of the annual allotment of funds, and to change the matching provisions for grants to a minimum of two-thirds and a maximum 90 per cent from the federal side.

In an individual statement appended to the committee report from the House, Congressman Fino spoke up for his defeated amendments and worried over the diminutive scale of fund authorizations in light of the enormous job that is necessary in urban transportation.

> These amendments would be a great boon to mass transit in cities like New York, Philadelphia, Chicago, Los Angeles, and so forth. The present mass transportation program is not of sufficient scale to have a meaningful impact on the mass transit needs of the developed core areas of the megalopolis. Because of the 12½ per cent limitation on the share of the yearly mass transit program outlay that can go to any one State, New York City is not going to get much benefit even from the new enlarged, permanent program embodied in this legislation. Assuming a $175 million a year program, 12½ per cent of this—and that is the maximum New York State share, not New York City's share—is less than $22 million. The New York City subway operating deficit last year was almost four times this figure. Sliced any way you will, the Mass Transportation Act program is still "small potatoes."
>
> I especially regret the noninclusion of my proposal that Mass Transportation Act funds be made available for the payment of interest costs on local bond issues floated to pay for transportation projects which are of a type that would qualify for regular Mass Transportation Act grants. Instead of subjecting the city of New York to the slow dole of funds mandated by the 12½ per cent of $175 million (statewide) limitation, payment of interest costs would enable the city to float a quarter of a billion dollar bond issue and pay the interest costs with the Federal aid. On a 25-year bond issue carrying 4 per cent interest, the interest costs would equal the principal to be amortized and paid off, so that in effect the Federal grant share would be one-half. Of course, it would be one-half at the beginning, enabling the marshaling of a large sum of money, instead of a slow dole which does not encourage any large-scale local financial undertaking. Federal payment of interest costs would stimulate local borrowing on a large scale, whereas the slow dole, subject to the overall dollar and State percentage limitation, will never mobilize any large-scale change in mass transit patterns.[78]

The debate on the legislation that took place in both houses of the Congress was fairly extensive, but it is noteworthy, in comparison with past debate on the issue, that the major items for discussion centered around the amount of money to be spent rather than the issue of whether or not the federal government had a role to play in urban transportation. This change in attitude was to have important implications in the years following 1966.

In the Senate, Senator Tower pushed for economy and introduced an amendment to cut spending from the $225 million recommended by the Committee on Banking and Currency to $150 million per annum. The cost of the war in Vietnam and the urging of President Johnson that government keep its spending down were the factors most invoked.[79] Not surprisingly, Senator Lausche of Ohio voiced disapproval of the entire aid program, saying:

> I respectfully submit to the committee that all of the demands for increased money come from the profligate management of the railway systems on the east coast—New York, New Jersey—and in that area in which they are trying to run a railroad system by charging practically nothing at all for the carriage of passengers.[80]

He was rebutted by several senators. Senator Javits struck a note on the great importance of the city in American life and the vital need for ease of movement in urban places. He said at one point:

> The cities are fighting. This exemplifies the fact that they are fighting for a place in the sun which will recognize what they amount to, because they are, today, what the country was a hundred years ago; namely, they are the repository of the essential population of this country. Nothing typifies it more than mass transit.[81]

The Senate voted in favor of the bill 47 to 34. Senator Tower won the day for the economy minded, however, and the authorization for expenditures was reduced to $150 million per annum for the next two fiscal years, thus continuing the practice of very low budgets for mass transportation. In all other ways the bill went through unscathed.

There was remarkably little opposition to the version of the bill that was debated in the House of Representatives. Many rose to support the legislation, although Representative Fino was unsuccessful in getting all the federal funds he wanted to pay interest on bonds or relaxation of the 12½ per cent limit of funds to any given state. The big defeat came in authorizing funds for the program. Far from providing $175 million on an annual basis, the bill was amended to provide $175 million for one year only. The amended bill passed the House by 235 to 127, and was sent on to a joint Senate-House conference committee to iron out the differences.[82] The Senate agreed to the conference report on August 25, and the House concurred on August 26. President Johnson signed the measure into law on September 8, 1966.

The act authorized $150 million for each of the fiscal years 1967, 1968, and 1969, and provided for increased sums of money to be devoted to the demonstration grant program: $40 million for the fiscal year commencing July 1, 1967, and $50 million for the next fiscal year.

In addition, funds were made available for the planning, engineering, and designing of urban mass transportation projects. Section 9 of the amended Urban Mass Transportation Act read, in part, as follows:

> Activities assisted under this section may include (1) studies related to management, operations, capital requirements, and economic feasibility; (2) preparation of engineering and architectural surveys, plans, and specifications; and (3) other similar or related activities preliminary and in preparation for the construction, acquisition, or improved operation of mass transportation system, facilities, and equipment.[83]

In addition to the engineering money made available in section 10, funds of up to $1,500,000 per year were authorized for management training purposes. This was to be awarded in a maximum of 100 fellowships annually, not exceeding $12,000 each. Like so many of the mass transport programs, management training was a much needed undertaking, but the sum of money involved was not in line with the need.

Another new program was established under section 11, whereby $3,000,000 a year was made available in grants to public and private nonprofit institutions of higher learning to conduct comprehensive research involving the problems of urban transportation. Not only was research to be carried out, but persons could also be trained for further research or managerial activities with operating companies.

A final provision of the 1966 amendments directed the secretary of housing and urban development—the agency administering the urban mass transportation program—to consult with the secretary of commerce and thereafter undertake a project to study and prepare, develop and demonstrate new systems of urban transportation.

Encouragement was given in this section to investigate the more exotic forms of transportation. Thus was the New Systems Research Program born.

The New Systems program was fostered by Congressman Henry Reuss of Wisconsin, who felt that the demonstration grants provided for in the 1964 Act did not really meet the needs of the urban transportation problem. While he felt that the demonstrations had been useful, he did not believe they had fully plumbed the broad range of technical solutions to urban transit problems.[84] The Johnson administration was neither for nor against such a program of research, nor did representatives of urban transportation interest groups at first see any need for federal leadership for encouraging research of a more sophisticated nature.[85] Congressman Reuss introduced the New Systems idea as an amendment to the administration's transportation bill while the bill was under consideration in an executive session of the House Banking and Currency Committee. The Reuss amendment gained support and was included in the final version of the bill as it emerged from committee. In the Senate, Senator Joseph Tydings and nine other senators introduced similar legislation.[86]

HUD was not prepared to take on the New Systems Research Program; HUD had almost no staff to devote to the activity, and since it knew of the program only three months before the bill passed, it had made no plans on how to carry out the work. It fell, then, to Assistant Secretary for Metropolitan Development Charles Haar to devise a way to conduct the study.

> Haar's philosophy on how to affect innovation was to acquire a good number of bright people, give each of them a problem to solve, keep them isolated from each other, and then evaluate the many forthcoming solutions.[87]

Haar felt that aerospace, engineering, and consulting firms had the proper expertise to conduct the work. Requests for proposals were sent to interested industrial firms, universities, research institutes, and other potential performers, and seventeen contractors were finally selected early in 1967.[88] Because of Haar's personal bias, most of the firms chosen had a definite hardware orientation. Nevertheless, many of the contractors, in their final reports, recognized the institutional problems involved.[89]

The New Systems program made 1967 an eventful year for mass transportation. For the first time, the Urban Transportation Administration (UTA) undertook some research projects of a future-oriented nature for the purpose of determining what sort of transportation systems were either possible or needed. The research focused on three periods: the immediate future—that is, up to three years; the more distant future—fifteen to twenty years in the future; and, finally, the period up to the turn of the century.[90]

In all frankness, while the calibre of research work was very high in some cases, as well as imaginative, the projects tackled had relatively little value for cities faced with transit and mobility problems in the here and now; indeed, this problem continues to plague research in urban mass transportation. The immediate problem of most of the hard-pressed cities was money, and the anemic state of the budget for mass transit provided little encouragement. To many observers, including some in Congress, it appeared as if the cart had been set before the horse. It seemed foolish to study future systems when there were insufficient funds to provide a decent level of aid for existing systems.[91]

The New Systems project was a policy failure, as well. Its long-range purpose was to help establish a comprehensive urban transport research program, but it ran afoul of impediments blocking the way into the policy system. That system was unresponsive to the New Systems report, in large part because it gave little mandate for legislation. Assistant Secretary Haar had desired and anticipated rather exotic and visible hardware solutions to urban problems; he was disappointed that the recommendations were only partially hardware oriented. Apparently, no technical gimmick was seen as solving the mass transportation problem.

As a result of Haar's disillusionment, the findings and recommendations of the New Systems contractors and the report *Tomorrow's Transportation: New Systems for the Urban Future* did not find their way into the administration's legislative program. It was too late, in any event; the Johnson administration by mid-1968 was a lame duck, and the shift of the mass transportation programs from HUD to the Department of Transportation was a certainty. There was simply no one willing to take action.[92]

Another event of 1967 had more portent for the future of mass transportation programs. On April 1 the new Department of Transportation (DOT) became a Cabinet-level agency of the federal government. In passing the act establishing the Department of Transportation (Public Law 89–670), Congress ordered the secretaries of HUD and DOT to study the question of whether or not the mass transportation program should be moved into DOT. Getting the new department organized took some time, but by early 1968 it was clear that DOT was interested in taking the urban mass transportation programs under its roof. This gave rise to serious questions on the part of some observers as to whether such programs were more urban than they were transportation and if the transit program's constituency would be best served by a switch in departments.

Within the federal establishment, there was some disillusionment with HUD's handling of the mass transportation program. The Bureau of the Budget was apparently disappointed at the relatively slow progress that was being made, not only in carrying out substantial improvements in mass transportation, but also in working deftly and diplomatically with the Congress to gain more funds for the mass transportation programs. Among mass transportation advocates, particularly the big city interests, unhappiness and concern arose over the fact that no major advance had been made in the funding for capital programs. Part of the problem was undoubtedly that HUD was closely identified with the Great Society programs of the Johnson administration, and these programs had fallen on hard times—something akin to the sawdust running out of a doll. The mass transit programs could hardly avoid being tarred with the same brush as the rest of HUD.

Organizationally, the great difficulty with the mass transit program in HUD was that it lay buried within the structure of that department, coming under the Office of Metropolitan Development. High-level administrators in HUD appeared far more interested and concerned with the larger problems of that particular section of the agency—that is, metropolitan development. It was felt by many parties with an interest in mass transportation that relatively short shrift was given to the transit programs. Unfortunately, Charles Haar, who headed up the metropolitan development section in HUD, had difficulties in building and maintaining a strong and sound relationship with the Congress, a relationship that was critical in getting the necessary funding for any of the programs. Haar was accused, perhaps unjustly, of offending some key congressmen. Whatever the problem, the sad fact was that the Urban Transportation Administration was poorly funded as well as dreadfully understaffed. As an example, travel money for those administering the demonstration program in January 1968 ran out six months before the new fiscal year would bring in more administrative funds. For six months, surveillance of programs and projects could be carried out only by letter or telephone. At the same time, the staff consisted of only two people.

On the other hand, as a new department DOT was not in any hot water regarding Great Society programs or the general debacle of the latter part of the Johnson administration. Indeed, for the first year or so, it is fair to say that DOT was in the honeymoon period where experimentation and flexibility were still possible. This was not true with HUD, which in its formation had inherited many agencies which had been in existence for a rather long time, had acquired the bureaucratic barnacles of red tape, and had lost much glamour in the eyes of a Congress becoming increasingly cynical about the effectiveness of what HUD tried to do.

Alan Boyd, the first secretary of DOT, indicated to a House committee that if transit programs were shifted to DOT, the urban transportation agency would be placed on a much higher level within the DOT organization. Indeed, it would be on an equal footing with the Federal Highway Administration, the Federal Railway Administration, and the FAA, and would thus move up a number of steps in the pecking order for both the ear and the influence of the secretary.

Rather quietly, President Johnson announced in early 1968 that unless there were objections, the Urban Transportation Administration would be switched out of HUD into DOT.[93] Shortly thereafter the report of the study conducted by the secretaries of HUD and DOT practically clinched the matter, stating:

> We therefore recommend that there be transferred to the Secretary of Transportation such functions and authorities as he may need to provide effective leadership in urban transportation matters. We also recommend that the Department of Housing and Urban Development intensify its efforts in promoting comprehensive planning, including comprehensive transportation planning, and that the two Departments work closely together in developing the standards, criteria, rules, regulations, or procedures that are needed to assure that transportation will be fully related to urban development goals.[94]

The Senate did not even hold hearings on this question. In the House hearings there was much assurance from Alan Boyd and HUD representatives that the two departments would, indeed, work very closely together, albeit recognizing the difficulties of coordinating efforts between two federal departments.[95] The major question before the House committee was whether or not DOT would give full care to the role that transportation plays in urban development. In all honesty, because of its over-all mandate, HUD could be expected to be far more sensitive to the issues of urban development than DOT. Some brilliant lobbying went on behind the scenes within the administration so that key senators and congressmen were convinced that DOT was a better place for the mass transportation programs than HUD. Given a top-notch lobbying job by HUD, the results might have been different. But, despite its interest in retaining the transit programs, HUD simply did not apply effective lobbying muscle.

Vague assurances were given, both at the hearings and in a memorandum of agreement between the secretary of transportation and secretary of housing and urban development, that the two departments would work together. Between the lines, it was clear that interested and influential members of Congress had sincere intentions that the mass transportation program was not to become overwhelmed by the DOT highway people, who would build highways in the future with as little thought as they had given in the past. HUD was to continue to be involved in some parts of some programs—particularly the research and demonstration programs; the capital grant program was to move over completely to DOT; however, the approval of the required comprehensive planning remained in the hands of HUD.[96]

The final result was that after 1968 HUD went quietly out of the transit business, and the programs came into the province of DOT's Urban Mass Transportation Administration (UMTA). For a time HUD retained oversight of a few projects which had been started under its jurisdiction. However, by 1972, UMTA had its own in-house planning review staff, and the active role of HUD in the transit programs became virtually nil.

In the meantime, because of the uncertainty of where they would be located, the mass transportation programs bogged down for awhile. Administrators were reluctant to make important decisions until the switchover was accomplished and a new pecking order established. The announcement by President Johnson that he would not run in 1968 also raised the spectre of a possible sharp change in the administration, which, again, would be highly upsetting and perhaps embarrassing in regard to some decisions which might be made in the interregnum. Added to the upset was an actual physical move into the new Department of Transportation building, which was finally ready for occupancy in September 1968. Finally, the election of Richard Nixon made lame ducks of the remnants of the Johnson administration and, under the circumstances, no major action was taken. It is fair to say that 1968 was a period of slowdown and almost total stoppage while the people involved in mass transportation programs tried to figure out what was going on.

Act of 1970

Within a few months of taking office, the Nixon administration had a chance to evaluate what it had inherited. In the area of transportation it was apparent immediately that UMTA was conspicuously undermanned. For example, although it was placed on the same organizational level in DOT as the FAA, which had 40,000 employees, UMTA had only 58 staff people. There was little question that most of the staff were highly dedicated and individually and collectively burned much midnight oil in attempting to carry out their assigned task. There were just not enough people to go around to administer effectively even the programs and projects UMTA had in hand. Even though the level of expenditures by UMTA was not high in comparison to other federal agencies, on a per man basis it averaged out to one of the highest ratios of money to manpower in the federal government. The ordinary routine of paper shuffling and riding herd on projects already in hand made it difficult to evaluate the new proposals which came flooding in. There was an obvious need to rethink and regroup some of the parts of the organization in order to better meet urban transport needs.

Some other things were clear in early 1969 as the Nixon administration began to pick up the reins. There seemed to be no strong lobbying voice for the mass transportation program. What may be thought of as the main constituency of the UMTA programs—that is, the urban transportation industry itself—was relatively ineffective as a lobbying group with the Congress. Part of the problem was a dichotomy within the industry. Those interested in rail commuter and rapid transit operation had relatively little to do with the "bus transportation" people, who made up the majority of the members of the American Transit Association. Indeed, there had been some concern earlier that the ATA did not fully meet the needs of the major cities that contained rail mass transportation; as a result, a decade earlier the rail transit group had split off to form the Institute for Rapid Transit (IRT).

Moreover, within the IRT itself some of the commuter railroad members seemed to feel little community of interest with rapid transit operators, preferring to work through the Association of American Railroads. All groups attempted to carry out some lobbying activities, but they were relatively ineffective separately. Adding to the problem, city officials had become used to working with HUD and its predecessor agencies over the years on a variety of urban problems; they had to learn to work with a new department.

Even though the situation appeared a bit unsettled during and just after the changeover in administrations, a most encouraging position was taken by President Nixon on the mass transportation issue. Both the president and Secretary of Transportation John Volpe took a strong stand on giving priority treatment to urban mass transportation problems in the first session of Congress under the new administration. What made such a position encouraging was the fact that the mass transportation program was often viewed as very much a child of the Democratic Party. The promise of support from a Republican president and his secretary of transportation gave hope to increased bi-partisan effort in behalf of the mass transportation program.

Advocates of mass transportation faced some inherent difficulties, in addition to those cited earlier, in garnering congressional support. In the minds of many, particularly Republican legislators and more conservative Democrats, the mass transportation activities of the federal government were still tarnished by the Great Society program failure. The federal mass transportation programs had never been wildly popular in the Congress. Early in 1969 they appeared to lack glamour and had not provided the sort of nationwide example of success and general acceptability that would allow almost any legislator to back them without suffering within his own constituency. An observer in early 1969 would be accurate in stating that mass transit was a "safe" issue only for a senator from a state with one or more major urban centers, or to a representative from a congressional district in a large urban area.

Counteracting the image of mass transit as primarily a big-city affair was the slow but steady failure of private mass transit firms. The growing inflation of the late 1960's was a severe blow to an industry that was relatively labor intensive. Labor costs rose sharply as new contracts with the transit workers unions were hammered out. The cost of equipment and supplies also rose sharply. Marginal private operators all over the nation began to go under. An increasing number of cities—large, medium, and small—found that they would have to get into the transit business themselves if service was to continue. Pressure began to mount on the Congress to augment the mass transit programs.

Perhaps the most serious problem for cities was that the funding of the mass transportation program was uncertain. Capital projects in particular had rough sledding on the local level because there was no certainty that Congress would appropriate funds for capital grants in the future or that the funds would be sufficient in magnitude even if granted. Consequently, it was very difficult for a city to consider a major project or issue bonds without some certainty that the federal portion of the money would be there when it was needed for construction purposes. By 1969 a number of urban places that had received technical studies grants in order to carry out the more detailed planning of mass transportation systems were ready to give serious consideration to the construction or extension of rapid transit systems or to major improvements in their bus transit systems. Yet, without the certainty of the capital grants some years in the future —particularly for the rapid transit systems, which involved long lead times—it was impossible to move ahead.

A means of remedying the problems of long-range financing of the transit program was contained in bills that were introduced into the Congress in mid-February and early March of 1969. The bill in the Senate was introduced by Senator Harrison Williams, and bills in the House were put forth by Representatives Patman and Barrett, Koch, and Moorhead. All of these bills called for the use of trust fund financing, similar to the Highway Trust Fund, in order to provide sustained support for transit programs. The beauty of the trust fund approach is that Congress does not have to make annual appropriations; the money flows in regularly and may be doled out just as regularly with no need for the Congress to tap the general fund for appropriations. Suggested as a source of trust fund money was the excise tax on new automobiles. This money did not go into the Highway Trust Fund, and utilizing it did not seem likely to raise the blood pressure of the highway interests who guarded the Highway Trust Fund against diversion to other than highway purposes with the same fierceness as a mother bear her cubs.[97]

In his speeches and in much of his commentary on mass transportation in the spring and early summer of 1969, Secretary Volpe apparently felt he was voicing the thoughts of the administration as he discussed and supported the use of a trust fund to help place money in the federal transit coffers. Highway interests greeted this with some dismay at first, but talk of using the excise tax on automobiles, rather than tapping the money of the Highway Trust Fund, allayed their anxiety. The future began to look rosy for a greatly expanded federal mass transportation program.

A setback came in August 1969 when President Nixon proposed a ten-billion dollar program in mass transportation to extend over a twelve-year period, but to Secretary Volpe's apparent surprise, the president made clear that he had no intention of having the transit programs financed through a trust fund, at least in the near future. The Bureau of the Budget had taken a dim view of the transit trust fund approach and the idea had been squelched.[98]

At about this time, a coalition of interest groups began to form. The catalytic force was the combination of the U.S. Conference of Mayors and the National League of Cities. The Mayors' Conference and the League of Cities began to assemble a new mass transportation coalition, with Fred Burke, a highly skilled and effective lobbyist, employed to guide the work on the transit legislative program. The coalition was based initially on the NLC/USCM, the Institute for Rapid Transit, the American Transit Association, and the railroads.

But that was just the start! In the early fall of 1969, the urban transportation interest group made it very clear to the highway interests that they, too, had an important stake in supporting a well-financed transit program. The critical point of attraction to the highway interests was the fact that the Highway Trust Fund was to come up for reevaluation by the Congress in 1972. Big-city mayors let it be known through NLC/USCM that they would take a highly jaundiced view of continuation of both the Highway Trust Fund in its existing form and the steady flow of money to the highway interests—if those highway interests did not back the mass transportation program. Seeing the handwriting on the wall, and assured that the Highway Trust Fund would not be tampered with for transit purposes, the highway interests jumped on the transit bandwagon.

The highway men were wise in giving a little to get support in the future. Many mayors and public officials had become disillusioned with the highway program. Moreover, citizens in urban areas were voicing much displeasure with the practice of ramming highways through residential areas or places of historic interest. Equally unpleasant for highway supporters, of course, was the unconcealed attitude of the Office of Management and Budget (OMB) toward trust funds. The OMB felt that the Highway Trust Fund should be abolished or at least altered to follow the funds collected to be used more broadly. This attitude was echoed, in part, by some members of Congress who were unhappy at the relative loss of control over money, which was their fate when the trust fund method was used. This was a serious problem as regards a future trust fund for mass transit, but it was even more worrisome to the highway interests, who had much to lose if the Highway Trust Fund were tampered with. In short, seeing a fight ahead on the extension of their trust fund, the highway people wanted the support of the constituency of the NLC/USCM.[99]

The thorny problem of guaranteed funding of some sort remained, even though general support for mass transit was building. The Nixon program called for authorization of $3.1 billion to begin with, but this, of course, did not mean that there would be a binding obligation. Congress still would have to make annual appropriations. The long-range projects would still suffer from uncertainty.[100]

The breakthrough came when Senator Harrison Williams introduced an amendment, inspired by Fred Burke of the NLC/USCM, to overcome the objections to the short-term nature of the annual appropriations process and yet not depart too far from the administration's program.[101]

The gist of the Williams amendment is the following:

To finance the programs and activities, including administrative costs, under this act, the Secretary is authorized to incur obligations in the form of grant agreements or otherwise in amounts aggregating not to exceed $3,100,000,000.

This amount shall become available for obligation upon the effective date of this subsection and shall remain available until obligated.

There are authorized to be appropriated for liquidation of the obligations incurred under this subsection not to exceed $80,000,000 prior to July 1, 1971, which amount may be increased to not to exceed an aggregate of $310,000,000 prior to July 1, 1972; not to exceed an aggregate of $710,000,000 prior to July 1, 1973; not to exceed an aggregate of $1,260,000,000 prior to July 1, 1974; not to exceed an aggregate of $3,100,000,000 thereafter.[102]

Although much work still remained to be done in maintaining the support of the Nixon administration and in getting the new mass transportation legislation through the Congress, the Williams amendment was the hole in the dike. After that, it was a matter of strengthening the coalition, carefully dealing with key senators and congressmen, and carefully putting together effective testimony to be heard by the committees under whose jurisdiction the transit bill would pass.

Some slight difficulties arose in the fall and winter of 1969, when the committee jurisdiction of the bills was questioned. Transit legislation had always fallen to the House and Senate committees on Banking and Currency. These are the committees which traditionally deal with HUD matters. Although the mass transportation programs had been shifted to DOT, the Banking and Currency committees maintained that they still had jurisdiction. When the House Interstate and Foreign Commerce Committee and the Senate Commerce Committee—which have jurisdiction on DOT legislation—insisted that they should handle the transit programs, there was some worry on the part of mass transport advocates. Both Banking and Currency committees held many firm supporters of transit legislation; to lose their support on transit matters would raise serious difficulties, since members of the DOT jurisdiction committees were considered to be unknown quantities. For the time being, at least, the committee jurisdiction was not changed.[103] (Subsequently, early in 1973, an Urban Mass Transportation Subcommittee was formed as part of the House Banking and Currency Committee.)[104]

Meanwhile, the coalition built by the NLC/USMC was doing its work. At the NLC Congress of Cities in San Diego in December of 1969, Fred Burke noted that the panel discussion on transportation was crowded with mayors from cities of all sizes from all parts of the nation. Most of them had just inherited (or were about to inherit) a transit system as the result of a public takeover forced by the failure of a private transit firm. The mayors wanted help; Burke, seeing the opportunity to get a choir of grass-roots political voices, suggested strongly that they contact their congressmen to let the House members know just how important the transit legislation was back home. A flood of letters from a broad constituency deluged Capitol Hill. Here was the nationwide support for mass transit that was so badly needed to carry the day in the Congress![105]

The grass-roots political effort of the NLC/USCM coalition began to pay off. It began to pull aboard even very conservative legislators without big-city constituencies. Lobby effort and committee testimony made it clear that the mass transportation programs benefited not only a few large cities but also the small towns and cities in states with large nonurban populations. To back this up there was strong evidence available from UMTA of the dispersion of funds through the capital grant program. While the demonstration grants had, indeed, tended to be concentrated in the larger cities on the East Coast and West Coast, the capital grants—and the technical study grants as well—had been well distributed around the country.

Furthermore, the transit program came to be seen as not only generally beneficial but one which rather neatly filled certain welfare needs. For instance, a congressman could claim to a part of his constituents that by backing the mass transportation programs, he was going to be taking important steps to relieve highway congestion so that his constituents with automobiles could drive more easily. On the other hand, he could also claim to low-income and minority groups in his district that improvements in mass transportation would be highly beneficial to them by providing the mobility necessary to reach jobs, places of medical care, and so on. The failure of much of the Great Society effort had made many outright welfare programs decidedly unpopular. In a very real sense, however, backing transit could be construed as being all things to all people.[106]

The work of the coalition began to pay off. The Senate passed the Williams bill by an 83 to 4 vote on February 3, 1970. The effort of the transit lobby was then directed toward the House. The spring and summer of 1970 saw a concerted drive on the House of Representatives. On September 29, 1970, the House backed the transit bill by a vote of 327 to 16, and President Nixon signed the transit aid bill into law on October 15, 1970. Without doubt, a major victory—one that had seemed virtually impossible a year earlier—had been achieved for the cause of urban mass transportation.[107]

Some of the speeches made in the House on the occasion of the passage of the bill reflect the attitudes of the Congress and the support developed as the federal government's mass transportation programs came of age.

Representative Wright Patman of Texas— . . . The transit industry has been the victim of the American desire for the automobile so that public transportation has not received much new capital and is now operating with old equipment, old ideas, and, all too often, uninspired management operating on the premise that their primary goal is to minimize losses. . . .

In view of the apparent local nature of the problem, some people might wonder why the Federal Government should undertake the vast responsibility of assisting communities in the development of their public transportation service. The first and most significant reason is the Federal interest in keeping the cities of this country healthy . . . it is not only fair but essential that we assist the cities in financing needed public transportation service.

A second and perhaps less obvious reason is the fundamental federal interest in building up this local transportation link which will enable other transportation modes to work more effectively. . . .[108]

Representative William Widnall of New Jersey— . . . The Urban Mass Transportation Assistance Act of 1970 . . . has been reported favorably and unanimously by the Banking and Currency Committee. A very similar bill, S. 3154, passed the Senate by the overwhelming majority of 83 to 4.

I think these actions, and the degree of unanimity with which they were undertaken are significant barometers of a sense of urgency, not only within the House and the other body, but in the hearts and minds of the public in every part of our Nation. The problems of mobility within our urban and metropolitan areas, not only for the affluent who can afford cars but also for the poor, the young, the old and the physically handicapped, must be solved—now. The problems of strangulation of our cities' streets and the wasteful use of valuable urban land for freeways and parking facilities by an ever increasing flood of automobiles, trucks, and buses must be solved—now. The problems of pollution of the very air we breathe by the exhaust emissions from millions upon millions of internal combustion engines must be solved—now.[109]

Representative Gerald Ford of Michigan, House minority leader—I en-
dorse the Urban Mass Transportation Assistance Act of 1970 as recommended by President Nixon. The need for this legislation is beyond
question.[110]

Clearly, in one of the strange twists of politics, mass transportation had become a safe issue. Supporting transit helped the poor and
the not-so-poor in cities large and small. Plain people and influential
people around the country, carrying all shades of political opinion
and in both political parties, at last came to realize the importance
of aid to mass transportation in the urban twentieth-century United
States. Interests usually considered as competing with transit, such
as the highway lobby, came to realize that their bread, too, was but-
tered in part with the mass transportation issue and that they had to
lend their support or lose the vital backing of powerful, big-city
politicians—and even small-city politicians—in getting the highway
trust fund renewed in 1972.

After almost ten years, the mass transportation programs of the
United States government finally received a start toward the kind of
funding necessary to do a decent job. The sums involved were still
small, considering the magnitude of the task, which meant that the
work of the coalition was far from over.

Highway Act of 1973

Intense lobbying effort was mounted by the mass transportation
coalition beginning in 1971. There were two goals for this effort.
The first was to gain support for legislation that would provide federal operating subsidies for mass transportation. This move was
strongly opposed by the Nixon administration. The administration's
stated position was that operating subsidies were financially unsound
and lacked the necessary incentives to push transit management to
do a better job of serving the public without massive, bureaucratic
butting-in on the local level by the Urban Mass Transportation Administration. The principal unspoken reason for opposition was concern that organized transit labor would make off with most of the
subsidy by means of high wage demands.

The second goal, the campaign for which was launched in early
1972, was to split off some of the Highway Trust Fund money for
mass transportation purposes. The Nixon administration gave very
strong support to this aim. Both Secretary Volpe and, later, Secre-

tary Brinegar spoke out on this issue at every opportunity, as did the president.[111]

In the Congress the issue of the Trust Fund was a difficult one, so much so that the Congress was unable to pass a highway bill at all in 1972. The pro-highway and pro-transit lobbies were about equally balanced, and it was undoubtedly a tender issue in an election year. With the start of the first session of the 93rd Congress, intense efforts were once again made to enact the trust-busting legislation.[112] The Senate was first to pass such legislation, but the House bill, while similar in many ways to the Senate bill, did not open the Trust Fund.[113] There was a certain element of desperation involved. Many states were almost out of federal highway money as the mid-point of 1973 was reached—and passed. Unhappily for the highway lobby, the mass transit lobby was strong enough to block passage of a highway act; compromise was imperative to get the federal highway funds rolling again, even if it meant opening the Highway Trust Fund to mass transportation purposes. In the heat of the summer of 1973, a conference committee of both houses worked to hammer out an accord. They were successful in reaching a compromise on July 20, 1973. The Senate quickly ratified the much-amended legislation.[114]

On August 3, 1973, the House voted 382 to 34 in favor of the conference report on the 1973 Federal Aid Highway Act. The president signed the act into law on August 13, as Public Law 93–87. Another major step had been taken to provide increased aid for mass transportation. The urban transportation priorities of the federal government had taken another decisive shift away from the highway orientation that so marked the period after the Second World War. Indeed, some observers noted that mass transit aid was the fastest growing of all federal programs.

The Highway Act of 1973 is certainly not a trumpet blast announcing the arrival of the transit millenium, but it is an indication of strong support for mass transportation improvement in the United States. Despite its deceptive title, it is not just a highway act in the sense of providing passenger transportation by means of the private automobile; it might better be dubbed a transportation act because of its broad mobility implications in both rural and urban areas. The act also gives the local levels of government much more of a say to determining what sort of transportation system they really wish to have; no longer will local government have to opt for a major highway effort simply because highway funds are available rather than developing mass transit.

The act has vital implications for transport improvements. President Nixon put it well in the signing ceremony:

> This Act is not only a highway act. One of its most significant features is that it allows the Highway Trust Fund to be used for mass transit capital improvements. Under this Act, for the first time, states and localities will have the flexibility they need to set their own transportation priorities. The law will enable them to relieve congestion and pollution problems by developing more balanced transportation systems where that is appropriate rather than locking them into new highway expenditures which can sometimes make such problems even worse.[115]

The Highway Act of 1973 actually continues the process of allowing the Highway Trust Fund to be opened up for purposes other than the construction of highways. The 1970 Highway Act contained a modest provision that permitted monies earmarked for the Interstate, Urban System, and Urban Extension funds to be used in the construction of transit support facilities. Under the 1970 Act such items as exclusive or preferential bus lanes, traffic control devices, bus passenger loading areas and facilities, shelters, fringe area parking, and transportation corridor parking facilities could be built to serve bus and other public transportation passengers. However, the value of this provision was limited in that the funds expended for mass transportation purposes could not exceed those that would have been spent in conventionally providing highway capacity. Under the 1973 Act this restriction no longer applies, and all apportioned highway funds for the various systems can be used for the transit related purposes outlined above, even if the cost of such installations would exceed that of a conventional highway.

There are other transit-oriented features of the 1973 Act that help make it much more than just highway legislation. Besides opening the Highway Trust Fund, the 1973 Act provides another $3 billion in contract authority for mass transportation under the provisions of the 1970 Act; these funds are, of course, in addition to any transit money from the Highway Trust Fund. The 1973 Act also brought about an increase in the proportion of federal aid from two-thirds of the net project cost of a mass transportation capital grant project up to a mandatory 80 per cent for all projects administratively reserved after July 1, 1973. Furthermore, at the direction of the secretary of transportation, transit planning may receive federal funding up to 100 per cent of the project cost.

The gradual opening of the Highway Trust Fund to transit use is the obvious product of compromise; the highway interests have by no means had the rug pulled out from under them in an unseemly manner. Indeed, the more ardent transit supporters can fault the 1973 Act as proceeding too slowly in using the Trust Fund for non-highway purposes; such is probably the inevitable judgment on all compromises.

In any event, in fiscal year 1974 cities may choose to use their share of the Highway Trust Fund's $800 million Urban Systems' road apportionment for the construction of fixed mass transit facilities or the purchase of buses or equipment for rail transit. However, in fiscal 1974 the money will come from the general fund of the United States, and an offsetting amount will be kept in the Highway Trust Fund for highway use. For example, if local officials choose to invest in a mass transit improvement in place of a highway project, after approval of the secretary of transportation, 70 per cent of the cost of the transit project will be paid from federal general funds. Urban System highway funds apportioned to the particular state would be reduced by an amount equal to the federal expenditure on the transit project.

The situation changes in fiscal year 1975, when up to $200 million—one quarter of the amount of the Trust Fund money earmarked for urban highway systems—may be used for mass transit purposes. However, in that year the Trust Fund money can be used only for bus-related projects. The use of the Trust Fund is broadened in fiscal year 1976, when cities will have the freedom, if they so choose, to tap the Trust Fund for the whole of the $800 million Urban Systems fund for mass transportation purposes and may use the bonds for rail as well as bus-related capital projects.

The decision to use Highway Trust Fund money for mass transportation is in the hands of local officials. They may use money as they choose within certain broad limits. It must be recognized that the 1973 Act does not require that expenditures be made for mass transportation purposes; it merely permits the action. Possibly no more than $50 to $100 million of the potential $800 million available in fiscal 1976 is likely to be spent for transit purposes at the option of local government. Urban highway construction is not stopped.

Cities, working together with their state governments, are also allowed to trade money from the Highway Trust Fund earmarked for construction of Interstate Highway System segments in large urban areas for an equal amount of general fund money for mass transit. In order to accomplish this switch, the governor of a state and local government officials must make a joint request to the secretary of transportation for approval of the deletion. The secretary can withdraw his approval of a portion of the Interstate, if the segment is not to be replaced by a toll road in the same corridor or if the segment is not essential to the integrity of the over-all interstate system. Local officials may then give notice to the state highway department that local needs require, in place of the Interstate segment, construction of a rail transit line or the purchase of bus or rail equipment. If the state highway department determines that the transit project fits in with the comprehensive transportation plan for the urban area, it may then be submitted once again to the secretary of transportation for approval. Approval by the secretary obligates the federal government to pay to the local area a sum not above the expected cost of the withdrawn Interstate highway segment. The federal share for the transit project will be at a maximum of 80 per cent of the net project cost. The mileage withdrawn from an urban segment of the Interstate in one state may be applied to modification of the Interstate System in any other state. Interstate funds equal to the amount apportioned for the withdrawn segment are deducted from the withdrawing state's apportionment of Interstate Highway money.

The 1973 Act contains other facets that strengthen the role of the cities in the realm of urban transportation. States are required to allocate a portion of the Urban Systems highway funds authorization among urban areas of 200,000 population or more, thus assuring all cities of some size of at least a modest chunk of the money. Previously, each state government had total discretion on the allocation of road money within its borders. Furthermore, highway funds may be allocated directly to metropolitan planning agencies for transportation planning, without going through the state. These funds are over and above the planning and research funds already available to cities before the passage of the 1973 Act.

Many interests were taken care of in the Highway Act of 1973 as it wore its way to a final compromise. Rural areas and intercity transportation needs were not ignored; $12 billion was assured in the act in the 1974–1976 period for the Interstate System and rural primary and secondary roads. Bicycle transportation was given some significant aid. Up to $40 million per year may be utilized from highway funds to aid in the construction of bicycle paths in conjunction with highway projects. These pathways need not be constructed in the highway right-of-way. Pedestrian walkways may also be constructed; the funds for both bikeways and pedestrian ways are to come from money apportioned for the urban and rural Primary Systems and the Urban System.

The Highway Act of 1973 takes action to augment rural mobility beyond merely providing roadways. Rural transit demonstration programs are encouraged as a means of increasing the mobility of persons in rural areas who do not have access to private automobiles. Funds amounting to $30 million in fiscal 1975 and $20 million in fiscal 1976 are to be taken from the Highway Trust Fund for the purpose of highway transit service demonstration in rural areas. Funds may be used for capital purposes, both equipment and facilities, in support of these demonstrations, as well as to cover the demonstration research and operating costs.

The act also includes some provisions that restrict mass transit operating agencies. All equipment purchased for capital or other project purposes must meet the standards for emissions and noise under the Clean Air Act and the Noise Control Act. Furthermore, federal capital aid for buses will not be provided without an agreement on the part of the local public transit agency that it will not engage in charter operation in competition with private bus operators outside the area in which a given local public transportation agency provides regularly scheduled transit service. Local public transit agencies must also agree not to operate school bus service in competition with private school bus operators. This provision does not apply if private operators are unable to offer adequate, safe transportation of school children at reasonable cost. School children may, of course, be carried as a part of regular transit operation, either at regular or specially reduced fares. To put real incentive behind these regulations to protect private enterprise, failure to comply with these rules means that a transit agency will not be eligible for future federal funds. This regulation does not apply if a transit agency has been operating charter or school services in the twelve months prior to the passage of the 1973 Act.

A new requirement for mass transportation under the 1973 Act may cause transit operating agencies some grief. If federal assistance is requested for mass transit, the secretary of transportation must be assured that transit projects receiving federal financial aid can be effectively used by elderly and handicapped persons. No one quite knows what this provision really means. Does it mean that such persons are to be given precisely the same access to transit service as the general public, or does it mean that they may be served by some sort of auxiliary service such as dial-a-bus or some other form of demand-responsive system? Providing such service, regardless of whether it is through the entire system or by means of special services, is likely to be highly expensive. This is evident in relation to the new rapid transit system being constructed in the Washington, D.C., metropolitan area by the Washington Metropolitan Area Transportation Authority (WMATA). Under the Highway Act, WMATA must provide access to all Washington Metro rapid transit stations for the handicapped and the aged. This means, for the most part, that elevators must be included in all rapid transit stations. Under the provisions of the Highway Act, the federal share of this installation is to be $65 million. What the long-run cost of such services would be across the nation is probably not calculable at this time, especially if it means that all transit facilities and vehicles must be equipped to meet the special needs of the aged and handicapped. The implications are worrisome, if, for example, all buses had to be accessible for persons in wheelchairs; no standard bus now made could comply—the doors and aisles are too narrow. Many rapid transit cars now in use might also fail to comply.

The idea of a transit trust fund is not quashed by the passage of the Highway Act, despite its opening of the Highway Trust Fund for transit use. Indeed, the Highway Act raises the funding issue again. The act instructs the secretary of transportation to cooperate with the governor of each state, as well as with local officials, in making an evaluation of the mass transit element of the 1972 National Transportation Report based on the Transportation Needs Study conducted in 1971. The mass transport requirements are to be reviewed carefully and a program developed to meet the transit needs existing in each urban area. The capital investment requirements and the operating and maintenance costs for the mass transit system programs are to be determined along with an appraisal of the financial resources available for transit on all levels of government.

The secretary of transportation must then study various revenue mechanisms, such as a tax on fuels used in mass transit service, or an additional gasoline tax imposed in urban areas that might be used to finance mass transportation activities. The magnitude of the potential sources of user tax revenues is to be investigated along with the rates at which such taxes could be levied. The various mechanisms for collection of taxes and the potential impact on transit usage caused by such taxes are also to be subject to study. The secretary is obliged to report on this matter to the Congress no later than 180 days after enactment of the Highway Act. This means that a recommendation for a transit trust fund or at least some other major source of revenue for public mass transportation is not at all unlikely in 1974.[116]

The authorizations under the 1973 Highway Act from which the various sums for mass transportation as well as highway related purposes will be withdrawn are shown in Table 1–2:[117]

TABLE 1-2
Authorizations—1973 Highway Act
($ in millions)

	FY 74	FY 75	FY 76
Federal Aid Highways			
Interstate	2,650	3,050	3,050
Rural Primary	697	715	715
Rural Secondary	390	400	400
Urban System	780	800	800
Urban Extensions	290	300	300
Subtotal	4,807	5,265	5,265
Other DOT Programs	466	493.5	613.5
Safety—Title II	461	763	801.5
Other Agency Programs	315	330	330
TOTAL	6,049	6,851.5	7,010

The new UMTA contract authority for fiscal years 1974 to 1976 is $3 billion. The Department of Transportation appropriations bill for fiscal year 1974 included almost a billion dollars for mass transportation. The breakdown is as follows: Capital Facilities grants,

$872,000,000; Technical Studies, $37,600,000; Research, Development and Demonstrations, $68,950,000; Administrative Expense, $7,000,000; total, $985,550,000.[118]

Just how much the Highway Act of 1973 will do to affect the fortunes of mass transportation is difficult to say. It is certainly no great financial bonanza as regards tapping the Highway Trust Fund. At the moment, only a fraction of the $1 billion of Trust Fund money that might be used for transit in fiscal years 1975 and 1976 is likely to be utilized. As things stand now, the substitution of transit for urban segments of the Interstate system is apt to be a more fruitful source of new transit money. The important thing is that the Highway Trust Fund as a sacred cow is no more. The mechanism that inevitably assured highway construction, whether or not it was the most desirable approach to the solution of mobility problems, has been dismantled and an opening wedge for transit purposes in the future. It is certainly good, considering the need, that more money for transit is to be available. More responsibility for the use of the funds is thrust upon the cities, since it is at their option—given the cooperation of the states—that money can be diverted from highway use to transit purposes. There is, of course, no guarantee that the funds will be used wisely. The 1973 Act is complicated, and interpretation is still uncertain; the pathway to implementation of a transit project is likely to be strewn with red tape.

The Highway Act contains no provision for federal operating subsidies for mass transit. Ever since the issue was raised, both DOT and UMTA were firm in their opposition to such a program. However, with the energy shortage of the winter of 1973–1974, the Nixon administration reevaluated its position and began a push for what amounted to an urban transportation revenue sharing program that would give cities an option on spending block grants of federal money for capital or operating purposes. No action had been taken at the time of this writing. In the longer run, the requirement of the 1973 Act that the DOT secretary investigate alternate sources of funding for transit on all levels of government may serve to solve this need, which arises at present because of local jurisdictional and revenue problems.[119]

The heyday of the private automobile is far from over, but the notion of the desirability of improvement of mass transportation in the cities is now firmly entrenched in the United States. The idea of publicly owned and subsidized mass transport is no longer foreign. By all signs the nation is on the brink of major transit activity. Making real progress will depend to a great extent upon the vigor and dedication of local government armed with the will to make mass transportation a useful servant of the community.

CHAPTER TWO

Mass Transportation:
Pro and Con

Introduction

The previous chapter has outlined the growth of federal policy toward urban mass transportation. Before examining the institutions involved and reviewing the effects of the federal mass transportation programs, it appears wise to devote some attention to a basic question: Will people use mass transportation? In other words, the federal approach, albeit limited until recently by microscopic budgets (from 1961 through 1970, $1 billion for transit, $41 billion for highways), is by typical federal standards based mainly on the notion that improvements in mass transportation will attract riders to transit and help solve some of the problems of urban life in the United States.

A question not asked frequently until recent years is "Do people need mass transportation?" This, in part, reflects the rediscovery of the poor in the mid-1960s and the finding that not all Americans had regular access to an automobile. As the reader will recall, the original rationale for mass transit improvement centered mainly on the problems of traffic congestion and the use of transit to shift people out of their cars as a means of providing relief from traffic jams. The "shifting" rationale is associated more with the quality of transit than anything else. In other words, only transit service of quality approaching or surpassing the automobile would be effective in at-

90

tracting patrons. The "need" argument is more closely related to provision of mass transportation service for those without an alternative means of mobility.

It is obvious that bringing about any major improvements in mass transportation is a formidable task, given the history of industry decline stretching back the better part of a half century. One perceptive British writer summed up the United States situation as follows:

1. Unless distances are long, transit speeds and service frequencies high, car speeds low and parking difficulties considerable, it is difficult to attract car commuters to public transport.
2. Because of this, public transport users tend to be people who have no car available, whether or not the family owns one.
3. Service frequency is more important than lower fare levels or proximity to public transport routes in attracting people to public transport.
4. The discovery of successful public transport systems involves considerable risk, costs and controversy, particularly when fixed costs are high and the capital irretrievably sunk.[1]

Regardless of whether mass transport is to solve the vexations of affluence or of poverty, many concerned persons feel strongly that more and better mass transport will cure many ills, or at least must be included as a critical part of the prescription for urban health. In a broad sense, improvement in the quality of urban life, which means the life of most Americans, is the desired end result of federally fostered transit improvement.

Over the years since 1961 there is no doubt that the vocal positions of various administrations in power in Washington have been for a strong commitment to mass transportation. Under Presidents Kennedy and Johnson this commitment was not matched with the necessary money to do the job at hand. While the Nixon administration has not always followed through on its positions on transit, the over-all thrust of the administration has been for increasingly larger expenditures for mass transportation.[2] Gone, too, at least for the moment, are the days of even token opposition to the notion of federal aid to mass transit. As noted in Chapter 1, whatever opposition there is to mass transportation comes from the highway lobby, which is not so much opposed to aid for transit as it was to the use of Highway Trust Fund money for nonhighway purposes.[3]

Even though the battle of general attitudes toward transit seems won in Washington for the present, there are still arguments against mass transportation or against certain forms of transit. For the sake of completeness, both sides of the matter should be discussed. Therefore, some of the arguments both for and against mass transport will be held up for inspection.

Heat, Light, and the Mass Transit Issue

At first blush there is, to be sure, a certain challenge in being pro-mass transport. As a mass transit advocate, one has the somewhat masochistic pleasure of supporting what has been for many years the underdog. In some circles it has even become fashionable to downgrade private transportation by means of the automobile and see almost incredible virtue in the stoic rider of mass transportation. Considering the quality of mass transportation in most United States cities, virtue may be its own reward. Nevertheless, it is indeed quite legitimate to question whether or not it is a waste of time to attempt to resuscitate mass transport.

The critic of the pro-mass transport position can ask some sticky questions. Might time and resources be better spent on providing improved private transportation through highway betterments or, perhaps, increasing the supply of parking in downtown areas? Perhaps the resources being allocated toward improving mass transportation might be better spent on automotive safety programs, increasing expenditures for education, improving mental health, aiding mentally retarded children, or a host of other worthy projects? These questions cannot be answered objectively because of the difficulty of valuing the output of the various programs.

Perhaps an even thornier question is, "Why try to beat the dead horse of mass transit back into life; hasn't the public already voted strongly in favor of the private automobile?" Admittedly, the public glee at the unveiling of new auto models goes on practically unabashed, somewhat akin to the feeling of little boys in times past when they were presented with the Lionel Train catalog just before Christmas. There is widespread agreement that new highways are good things, although many may quibble over site and amenities. Likewise, few people are made glum over the thought of more parking space. In short, the automobile and its accoutrements have a generally happy position in the public favor.

Recently the auto-highway euphoria has somewhat dimmed, primarily as a result of the interest and concern over air pollution caused by the internal combustion engine, the prospect of a long-term shortage of energy resources, and the dismaying results of trying to build major chunks of the Interstate System through highly populated urban areas. The realization that many citizens without cars are marooned in immobility is another recent phenomenon. For instance, who would have dreamed even as late as the mid-1960's that a governor of Massachusetts—in this case Francis W. Sargent —would describe the expressway system in the Boston area as chains to imprison the city and would propose a freeze on the number of parking spaces in downtown Boston to encourage the use of mass transit? Likewise, across the border in Canada, William Davis, premier of the Province of Ontario, has been the leader of a government that has scotched the Spadina Expressway in Toronto on the ground that it and other major highways precluded a human scale of life. The government of the province is pushing for great expansion of mass transit systems within Ontario,[4] rather than continued expansion of and reliance upon the highway system. Even so, there is little doubt, despite its shortcomings, that the automobile delivers a very high quality level of services.[5]

More pointed is the question: "Can mass transit do the job it is supposed to?" This gets back to the issue raised earlier as to whether or not people will use mass transportation if it is provided. Indeed, will mass transportation effectively relieve urban traffic congestion, make urban life better, preserve amenities, provide the needed mobility so that the ghetto poor may find employment, strengthen downtown, and a host of other things which are often claimed for it?

Furthermore, when inspecting the idea of mass transportation on a pro and con basis, the observer is apt to run into intense and conflicting arguments between pro-automobile and pro-mass transit advocates. Unfortunately, far more heat than light is usually generated by these debates. Any attempt to put the pro and con arguments in perspective will probably not do much to lower the temperature of the arguments. More than likely, those holding positions either for or against mass transit will only have their attitudes strengthened by reading on. One point should be made, however. The decision to improve mass transportation, or to make major investment or provide operating subsidies for transit, is essentially a local matter. If a given urban public, through its elected officials, expresses the wish that money be spent and improvements be made, then the desires of the public have to be carried out as a part of the political process. Criticism from outside the given city and even sophisticated economic theory and analysis would have to provide ironclad, irrefutable opposing arguments in such a situation, once the public has expressed its will.

The arguments pro and con mass transit are too often viewed as an "either-or" situation of limited transportation alternatives rather than as an attempt to increase the traveler's choice. Overly staunch advocates of mass transit often take a position as follows: "Instead of wasting X number of dollars on highways that don't solve anything, we will invest that same sum in new buses or rail rapid transit and bring an end to all the chaos and confusion and congestion which results from unbridled use of the private automobile." Highway hyper-advocates will take the stand that: "The automobile is the most desirable means of urban transport the world over; to attempt to foster other modes of urban transport is not only a waste of good money but it flies in the face of public opinion and is in direct opposition to what the public really wants and needs. Every available dollar should be pumped into provision for the needs of the private automobile." In such headbutting, the only public result is a headache.

Often the heat is generated in the clash between highway and rail mass transit advocates rather than from those advocating improvements in mass transport in general. The highway forces, realizing that rail construction is a matter involving large sums of money, have been threatened at seeing the federal Highway Trust Fund tapped to pay for new or improved rail facilities. Congress passed legislation to that effect in 1973. As a result, road advocates usually pull out all the stops of ridicule, invective, and outrage in attempting to defeat what promises to be inroads on the highway exchequer. Rail advocates, on the other hand, often make an argument too strongly in their favor in order to downgrade the possible effectiveness of highways; clearly, they hope to shift considerable sums into their rail bailiwick. In truth, even if there are as many as thirty or forty cities that can justify and use rail mass transit—and this is a matter of some reasonable doubt in the foreseeable future—there are hundreds of urban areas that will need improved mass transportation by means other than rail. To state the argument only in terms of rail versus highway is therefore to narrow it unduly and obscure the broad issue of enhancing mobility in urban areas by a variety of means.[6]

Perhaps the best question to ask regarding mass transportation is whether or not, given some encouragement and substantial improvement in service, it will be possible to increase the mobility of the population (or at least keep present standards of mobility from declining) and to perform this chore, in league with the private automobile, at a reasonable cost? At the heart of the urban transport issue is the nubby problem of mobility and what must be sacrificed to keep American society moving.

Closely associated is the matter of those modifications of urban form resulting from the means of transportation investment chosen. It is a matter of either continuing the pattern of highway-oriented sprawl which symbolizes most American urban places today, or preserving—or increasing—a certain amount of urban clustering supported and served by mass transit, if such clustering is more economic or otherwise more desirable than other alternatives. Pandora's box is opened wide when this issue is raised because honest men can and have debated hotly on whether or not the sprawled or clustered city is best.[7]

Perhaps the real focus should be on what may best be called affordable mobility. That is, the means for any citizen to move about easily in an urban area should be available to him at a cost reasonable both to the traveler and to society. Again, the ground is touchy; "reasonable" cost and "move about easily" must be defined.

To carry this point a bit further, the concept of affordable mobility may be a wise approach since it links cost with mobility. From our beginnings as a nation the issue of mobility in the United States has been solved in a manner typical to our society: private interest and private profit have always had priority over the public interest. It is hardly news that this system has worked well in that many persons in our society have prospered; the great bulk of the United States population has a high *private* standard of living. Nevertheless, our public living standard is low—witness the standards of health, education, housing, mental care, transportation, to name a few, when it is *public* health, *public* education, *public* housing, *public* mental care, or *public* transportation. The issue—and the contrast—is sharpened when one relates the standards of public services to our vast national wealth and finds disturbing extremes. It is further sharpened today because the majority of the nation's population resides in urban places. In such close quarters and such tight focus, the problems become overwhelming.

Only when something of a public nature is of great and obvious benefit to private individuals on a regular basis will it be supplied in anything even approaching adequate quantity and quality. Highways, principally benefiting the *private* motorist, are a case in point. Because they meet a private need, they are publicly provided on a sufficient scale to come close to meeting that private demand. The roads are made available by charges levied on users and nonusers and in a private sense the mobility is affordable for most Americans who can buy gas, pay taxes, and keep up their car payments. However, the idea is beginning to dawn on the nation that, although a given private individual can afford to drive his car, the public— society as a whole and urban society in particular—may not be able to afford the trip in terms of what that car may do to the city. It is simply a matter of considering all the costs—pecuniary and nonpecuniary—and finding that perhaps we cannot afford a transportation system that is so one-sided in favoring private good at public loss.[8]

Affordable mobility in the complete sense would involve both planning and renewal to arrange dwelling and work locations so as to reduce the demand for urban transportation.[9] It is only wise to design or redesign an urban area so as to allow citizens freedom in location of housing and work, yet at the same time not require the population to travel long distances or devote a large share of their income to travel. This is especially true when the absence of such careful planning may impose intolerable public burdens such as extensive use of automobiles with resulting air pollution. The concept of affordable mobility would also involve thinking on those forms of transport that are less costly for society to build, tolerate, and use. It is in this latter sense that the federal government and other levels of government have fostered the notion that mass transport must be resuscitated because we cannot do otherwise. On this issue is largely built the case for mass transportation.

The Case for Mass Transportation

The general case for mass transportation, set out in some detail in the pages that follow, is not a bad one at all. Moreover, it has been

strengthened in recent years by adding to the argument two important related points: increased choice of travel means and more equal
physical mobility for all members of American society.

The argument for mass transport, in its primeval form, ran along
lines somewhat as follows: "Automobile congestion is intolerable
and expensive; if we can get people out of their cars and into mass
transit, we can reduce congestion at lower cost to the taxpayer than
building new highways." Such thinking is, of course, oriented to
the middle class and is couched in terms of transit as a substitute for
the automobile to be used by those who had a car. It reflected the
fears of city fathers that our cities would be inundated and finally
choked by automotive traffic. However, this argument neglects those
too old, too young, or too poor to afford an automobile or to drive
an automobile safely. It also ignores those who could not afford a
second automobile (or perhaps even a third and fourth) needed to
provide mobility for all members of the family in areas unserved by
mass transportation.[10] The recent interest in civil rights and social
justice and increasing public awareness of the spectrum of unmet
needs have focused attention on social objectives for transit. This
awareness was heightened in the late 1960's by the sharp counter-
point of riots and other disasters in our cities: many people otherwise blind to minority problems have come to see that mass transportation has value beyond mitigating urban traffic jams.

Special emphasis has been given in recent years to the needs of
elderly and handicapped persons who often cannot use an automobile even if it is available. Studies have pointed up the serious lack
of mobility suffered by these unfortunate citizens. The Urban Mass
Transportation Administration has adopted a policy of providing
funds for demonstrations of special services and equipment for the
old and the handicapped. Moreover, the federally aided transit technical study projects require that consideration be given to these
groups, and equipment development projects have been funded to
provide transit hardware to meet the needs of the not-so-spry; particular attention is also being paid to provisions for the nonambula-
tory.[11] As mentioned in Chapter 1, the Highway Act of 1973 requires the transit needs of the elderly and handicapped to be met.

In general, the case for mass transportation has been made on
the basis of its potential passenger capacity, the possibility of conserving valuable space, preservation of social and economic values,

and in the cost savings possible through increased use of mass transportation. Let us take these up one at a time.

Capacity

A major point made by advocates of mass transportation is that a principal problem in urban transport is the limited carrying capacity of streets and highways as used by the private automobile. The superior capability of a given space devoted to transit—either by bus or by rail—in providing increased passenger carrying capacity is indeed an important facet of mass transport. Figures typically somewhat similar to those shown in Table 2–1 usually reveal that, at worst, highways range from around 750 passengers per lane per hour on city streets and about 2,500 on freeways up to a happier figure of about 1,200 on city streets and 4,000 on freeways, depending upon the average number of passengers per vehicle. Buses, on the low side of their capacity, range from 2,250 up to 4,500 persons when used only on regular city streets, and from 9,000 to 18,000 when used on freeways. Various sorts of rail rapid transit capacities range from 12,000 to 21,600 where six-car trains are used on a three-minute headway (headway is the scheduled time span between vehicles) all the way up to 40,000 to 72,000 per hour where ten-car trains operating on a ninety-second headway are provided. There is little to argue with in terms of sheer capacity; mass transit has it all over private transportation when it comes to effective utilization of space.

The successful functioning of the nation's very large cities, such as New York, Chicago, Boston, or Philadelphia, where considerable demands are placed on travel arteries, cries out for means of transportation possessing substantial capacity; mass transportation fits these needs. Moreover, these are the cities which could not survive without rail rapid transit and commuter railway service.

Table 2–2 shows data for some selected cities and indicates the number of persons entering downtown areas during an average day, and the type of transport mode for peak-hour inbound and outbound flows. As would be expected, the larger cities attract sizable numbers of persons and a considerable number of these are carried by mass transport; this fact is especially true during the hours of peak movement. The rapid transit and commuter railway services account for the bulk of persons moved by mass transit during peak periods in

TABLE 2-1
Passenger Capacities per Lane or Track*

Facility	Vehicles per Lane per Hour	Effective Capacity at Various Passengers per Vehicle			
		1.25	1.50	1.75	2.00
Private Automobile					
City Street, Design Flow Rate	600	750	900	1,050	1,200
City Street, Capacity	800	1,000	1,200	1,400	1,600
Freeway, Design Flow Rate	1,500	1,875	2,250	2,625	3,000
Freeway, Capacity	2,000	2,500	3,000	3,500	4,000

Facility	Vehicles per Lane per Hour	Headway (min.)	Effective Passenger Capacity for Various Loading Ratios			
			75%	100%	125%	150%
Transit Bus (50 seats)						
City Street	60	1.00	2,250	3,000	3,750	4,500
City Street	90	0.67	3,375	4,500	5,625	6,750
City Street or Freeway	120**	0.50	4,500	6,000	7,500	9,000
Freeway	180**	0.33	6,750	9,000	11,250	13,500
Freeway	240**	0.25	9,000	12,000	15,000	18,000

Type of Train	Trains per Track per Hour	Headway (min.)	Effective Passenger Capacity Passengers per Car			
			100	120	150	180
Rail Rapid Transit Train						
6-Car Train	20	3.00	12,000	14,400	18,000	21,600
	30	2.00	18,000	21,600	27,000	32,400
	40	1.50	24,000	28,800	36,000	43,200
10-Car Train	20	3.00	20,000	24,000	30,000	36,000
	30	2.00	30,000	36,000	45,000	54,000
	40	1.50	40,000	48,000	60,000	72,000

*This table provides the elements necessary to determine the number of persons that may be accommodated per facility. Example of the number of persons carried in the peak direction on representative facilities are: 8-lane freeway—7,500 to 16,000 persons per hour; 2-track rail rapid transit with 6 car trains—12,000 to 43,000 persons per hour. This table considers capacity only. A more complete comparison must consider demand and level of service, which reflect convenience, flexibility of use, comfort, and many other factors.

** Capacity would be limited by design of bus turn outs and type of operation.

Source: "Capacities and Limitations of Urban Transportation Modes, Washington, D.C. Institute of Traffic Engineers, May 1965, p.20.

TABLE 2-2
Persons Entering Selected Central Business Districts Daily and Entering and Leaving During A.M. and P.M. Peaks by Mode of Travel

	Cities With Rapid Transit and Rail Commuter Service					Cities Without Rapid Transit and Rail Commuter Service			
	Boston	Chicago	New York	Phila-delphia	Baltimore	Dallas	Los Angeles	Louisville	St. Louis
Year of Cordon Count	1954	1961	1960	1955	1955	1958	1960	1953*	1957
Total Number Entering CBD	839,738	863,771	3,349,000	900,389	385,431	354,190	678,977	283,369	347,574
By Automobile									
Number	407,216	354,392	954,000	425,935	266,684	281,746	506,798	205,690	255,519
Percent	48.5	41.0	28.5	47.3	69.2	79.6	74.6	72.6	73.5
By Public Transportation									
Number	380,272	509,379	2,395,000	474,454	118,747	72,444	172,179	59,445	92,055
Percent	45.3	59.0	71.5	52.7	30.8	20.4	25.4	21.0	26.5
Entering—A.M. Peak Hour									
TOTAL	141,112	205,773	848,000	154,513	53,623	59,704	76,880	35,431	55,607
Private Transportation									
Number	41,750	40,704	86,000	40,874	26,960	42,543	48,384	24,753	34,268
Percent	29.5	19.8	10.2	26.4	50.2	71.2	62.9	69.8	61.6
Public Transportation									
Number	99,362	165,069	762,000	113,639	26,663	17,161	28,496	10,678	21,339
Percent	70.5	80.2	89.8	73.6	49.8	28.8	37.1	30.2	38.4
Surface Transit (Bus–Streetcar)									
Number	7,189	31,226	63,000	28,000	26,663	17,161	—	10,678	21,339
Percent	5.1	15.2	7.4	18.1	49.8	28.8	—	30.2	38.4
Rapid Transit Subway–Elevated									
Number	63,836	72,443	608,000	64,022	—	—	—	—	—
Percent	45.3	35.2	71.7	41.4	—	—	—	—	—
Commuter–Railroad									
Number	28,337	61,400	91,000	21,617	—	—	—	—	—
Percent	20.1	29.8	10.7	14.0	—	—	—	—	—

100

Subtotal Rapid Transit									
Number	92,173	133,843	699,000	85,639	—	—	—	—	—
Percent	65.4	65.0	82.4	55.4	—	—	—	—	—
Subtotal Non-Rapid Transit									
Number	48,939	71,930	149,000	68,874	53,623	59,704	76,880	35,431	55,607
Percent	34.6	35.0	17.6	44.6	100.0	100.0	100.0	100.0	100.0
Leaving P.M. Peak Hour									
TOTAL	152,245	223,106	—	176,902	67,062	64,883	121,255	49,124	61,749
Private Transportation									
Number	46,821	43,326	—	50,310	37,751	43,672	71,985	34,177	35,644
Percent	30.8	19.4	—	28.5	56.2	67.3	59.4	69.5	57.7
Public Transportation									
Number	105,424	179,780	—	126,592	29,311	21,211	49,270	14,947	26,105
Percent	69.2	80.6	—	71.5	43.8	32.7	40.6	30.5	42.3
Surface Transit (Bus-Streetcar)									
Number	6,916	32,182	—	32,091	29,311	21,211	49,270	14,947	26,105
Percent	4.5	14.4	—	18.8	43.8	32.7	40.6	30.5	42.3
Rapid Transit									
Subway-Elevated									
Number	70,812	83,233	—	72,569	—	—	—	—	—
Percent	46.5	37.4	—	41.0	—	—	—	—	—
Commuter-Railroad									
Number	27,696	64,365	—	21,912	—	—	—	—	—
Percent	18.2	28.8	—	12.4	—	—	—	—	—
Subtotal Rapid Transit									
Number	98,508	147,598	—	94,501	—	—	—	—	—
Percent	64.7	66.2	—	53.4	—	—	—	—	—
Subtotal Non-Rapid Transit									
Number	53,737	75,508	—	82,401	—	—	—	—	—
Percent	35.3	33.8	—	46.6	—	—	—	—	—

* The data for persons entering and leaving the CBD during peak hours in Louisville was gathered in 1957.

Note: Figures in particular categories may not agree with total shown because of pedestrian traffic.

Source: Adapted from *Transportation and Parking for Tomorrow's Cities* (New Haven, Conn.: Wilbur Smith & Associates, 1966), tables B-22 and B-23, pp.320-323.

those cities possessing such services. Moreover, even cities without rapid transit show a fairly high percentage of mass transit use during hours of peak travel.

Admittedly, however, if mass transportation is to alleviate congestion and augment mobility, the important point is not the capacity of the mode involved, but whether or not the mode or service offered will incite utilization. In other words, if traffic is jammed up on existing highways, the provision of a new rapid transit line that will move 21,600 passengers per hour will not necessarily do much to alleviate the traffic jam if the new line is not located in a place where potential patrons have convenient access. Even given convenient access at both origin and destination point, will the other features of mass rapid transit be sufficiently attractive to entice people to leave their cars at home? Furthermore, is the service such that it substantially expands the real level of mobility throughout the community?

The matter of prime importance is, therefore, the capacity that will actually be used to help alleviate congestion and to increase the mobility of the population. This is mostly a marketing question, assuming no coercion or deception is used to shift auto users to mass transportation. Unfortunately, as noted before, the industry lacks good marketing procedures. Proper location of routes, service quality, pricing, and understanding of the attitudes and needs of the transit consumer, or potential consumer, are necessary to gain better utilization of capacity.

Conservation of Space

A second argument in favor of mass transport is that it helps conserve scarce urban space. This argument is obviously a corollary of the first. Space conservation is an important factor in cities if one considers the congestion of various "facilities" competing for limited space—particularly in downtown parts of metropolitan areas. Buildings are built up rather than out, as everyone knows, because downtown land is expensive. It is strictly a matter of using a given space more intensively.

Downtown property values have fluctuated considerably over the years. According to some experts, the generalization can probably be made that—allowing for inflation—values are lower now than they were 50 to 70 years ago. This is due not only to competition for use from suburban areas, but also because in many cities land values were raised to undue heights in the late nineteenth and early twentieth centuries by uninhibited speculation. Values are now coming to reflect more realistic considerations of worth.[12] Even so, downtown property values tend to be the highest in any given city.

One striking feature of downtown districts is their small size relative to the city they serve. One research effort indicates that when a city grows 70 times—say, from a population of 7,500 to 550,000—the Central Business District will grow only five times in size, from 0.1 to 0.5 square miles.[13]

The size of the central business districts of a number of American cities is shown in Table 2–3. Only a few have central business districts as large as one mile square. Not shown on the list is New York City, which shares with London the distinction of possessing a central business district of more than nine square miles.[14] Despite the small area involved, in many central business districts it appears that somewhere between 40 and 50 per cent of the area is devoted to streets and parking.[15]

TABLE 2-3
Land Areas of Selected Central Business Districts in Square Miles
(in declining order of population)

Los Angeles	0.63	Dallas	
Chicago	1.06	(core area)	0.54
Philadelphia	1.90	Kansas City	0.90
Detroit	1.08	Columbus	0.79
Boston	1.37	Phoenix	0.70
Washington	1.70	Sacramento	0.55
Pittsburgh	0.50	Hartford	0.54
Cleveland	1.03	Nashville	0.58
St. Louis	0.85	Tucson	0.20
Baltimore	0.76	Charlotte	0.74
Minneapolis	0.91	Chattanooga	0.38
St. Paul	0.75	Winston-Salem	0.52
Cincinnati	0.52	Houston	0.90

Source: Adapted from *Transportation and Parking for Tomorrow's Cities,* New Haven, Conn.; Wilbur Smith and Associates, 1966, table B-16, p. 314.

With land values relatively high and space limited, it seems sensible to use land as efficiently as possible; undue amounts of space should not be used for transport and vehicle storage, if the best use is to be made of valuable land. Mass transit is a means to fill the bill. For instance, a good argument can be made for using buses on an improved type of highway—not necessarily a freeway, perhaps nothing more than reserved bus lanes on a conventional street—as a way of getting more use out of existing space. As can be noted from Table 2–1, even a modest number of buses operating only at fair frequency can move a substantially higher number of people per highway lane than can private automobiles.[16] Rapid transit, with its greater capacity, is even more economical in terms of space needed to handle large numbers. Moreover, transit vehicles need not be stored in scarce downtown space.

One way of viewing the space-conserving capabilities of transit is to translate peak-hour mass transit patronage into automobile passengers and then calculate the number of extra lanes of highway necessary to handle the traffic. This is done in Table 2–4, which utilizes and combines some of the information from 2–1 and 2–2. The number of peak-hour transit patrons in the non-rapid-transit cities of Baltimore, Dallas, Los Angeles, Louisville, and St. Louis is a key factor. It is assumed that, in the absence of a mass transit alternative, present transit patrons would continue to journey into the central business district, but would travel by automobile at a density of 1.5 persons per car. The number of cars needed to handle this demand and the number of lanes required—depending upon the type of highway—are indicated in the table. In essence, Table 2–4 shows that without transit, Baltimore, for example, would have to find room for from fifteen to twenty more lanes of ordinary streets, or from six to eight lanes of freeway; St. Louis would need twelve to sixteen more lanes of street or five to six more freeway lanes, and so on. Part of the cost of a loss of transit patronage would be a sharp increase in space needed for roads, not only downtown, but on the approaches to the central business district as well. Private property needed to expand the roadway system would be removed from the tax rolls, of course.

If more persons out of a given number entering the downtown center used mass transit and thus reduced the peak load on the streets, it is unlikely that there would be any sudden, dramatic increase in the amount of space devoted to nontransport use in the central business district. Indeed, while reduced need for street capacity to move traffic might lead to the eventual construction of pedestrian shopping malls or other bits of beautification and rejuvenation, it is more likely that, over time, the lessened demand for

TABLE 2-4
Highway Lane Equivalents to Carry Transit Passengers in Private Automobiles into Central Business Districts

City	peak hour inbound transit riders	autos required if transit riders used autos at a rate of 1.5 persons per car	extra lanes of city street needed at design flow rate	extra lanes of city street needed at capacity	extra lanes of freeway needed at design flow rate	extra lanes of freeway needed at capacity
Baltimore	26,663	17,775	20	15	8	6
Dallas	17,161	11,440	13	10	5	4
Los Angeles	28,496	18,997	21	16	8	6
Louisville	10,678	7,119	8	6	3	2
St. Louis	21,339	14,226	16	12	6	5

Source: Number of peak hour transit passengers entering CBD from
Table 2. Lane capacity of different types of streets from Table 2-1.

parking might be the more potent force at work, and parking lots might be converted to new uses.

No doubt the chief immediate beneficiaries of increased space would be the motorists facing reduced congestion. Of course, if fixed transit facilities, such as a rapid transit system, are installed, there is likely to be substantial new construction in the vicinity of the stations. The real estate involved would be more valuable and would yield greater tax revenues to the municipality. The relatively new subway in Toronto sparked a building boom along its route that is alleged to put more into the public coffers in taxes than was spent on construction. In the United States, a billion dollar construction boom along Market Street in San Francisco was touched off by the building of the Bay Area Rapid Transit System.[17]

A related argument is that parking space may be located away from the central business district or other concentrated activity areas if improved mass transportation is available for the remainder of the journey. An individual who leaves his car at home and takes the bus or train to work is providing parking space outside the central business district. Driving to the end of a commuter railway line or express bus line and depositing a car at that location rather than taking it downtown is another example. In either case, lower value land is utilized for automobile storage.

Another aspect of space conservation is the argument often made that if people would use mass transit, there would be less need for expensive public facilities—such as highways or public parking garages—that remove property from the tax rolls. This is a good point because if a highway is built in a high value area, as it must be in order to reach the downtown, the typical overstrained tax base of the city will suffer from attrition and a greater tax burden will be placed upon remaining property owners. Public parking garages located downtown have also removed some highly valuable land from the tax rolls, although one can argue that the increased access to nearby buildings given by location of public parking facilities increases or maintains the value of that property and thereby maintains or perhaps increases the downtown taxables. Even where downtown parking space is not publicly owned, parking is generally considered a lower value use of property than is a conventional building. The land so used is usually taxed at a lower rate, although this situation may change. Obviously, in this age of rising costs, cities are vitally concerned with getting every dollar of taxes that they can muster out of property within their borders. This is one of the compelling factors that has apparently helped to persuade city fathers that improved mass transit is not a quaint nineteenth-century idea.

Preservation of Values

This is an argument that is often closely connected with the preceding section. It hinges on the idea that mass transit may be much less intrusive in an aesthetic sense than a ten-lane superhighway. This is a particular favorite with planners trained as architects who are aghast to see the already paltry aesthetics of American cities swept away by what many see to be grotesque ribbons of freeways. Moreover, the sensitivities of the planners are not the only ones touched by the shattering visual and physical impact of a large highway development in a highly urbanized area. The objection of the general public to massive road development in San Francisco and New Orleans is well known. Indeed, the San Francisco Board of Supervisors is unequivocal in its position that no new freeways will be built in that city until the rather ghastly Embarcadero Freeway—which cuts off the view of the historic Ferry Building from Market Street—is torn down.[18]

More to the point, and perhaps the real reason for the growing discontent with the highway program in a nation not generally known for its interest in things aesthetic, is the realization that the highways have not done one of the important things they were supposed to do—reduce congestion—and are therefore legitimately open to scorn on several levels. At the least, increased use of mass transportation—although there is sometimes a tendency to put it on an either-or basis in relation to highways—provides hope for a less messy way out of traffic jams than the addition of still more roads.

Moreover, beyond the problems of aesthetic blight ecologists are dismayed at the impact of the private automobile on the biosphere. Automotive exhaust emissions are perhaps the most serious single cause of pollution associated with transportation, but noise pollution from large-scale highways is another serious matter. There is even concern over the runoff of salt and other chemicals used for control of ice and snow on highways in cold climates. The National Environmental Policy Act of 1969,[19] which became effective on January 1, 1970, is a federal response to some of these problems. Given proper enforcement, this act might help develop major improvement in the environment. There is evidence, however, that highway interests are mounting a strong campaign to weaken portions of the act.[20] Apparently, to the devout highway man, nothing must stand in the way of building more roads.

It can be argued that improved highways have indeed provided some relief.[21] Travel times are generally less today in many cities than they were in the days before the superhighway. Moreover, commuting in the private automobile is almost always faster than by transit. Indeed, as noted earlier, one of the major reasons for a program of transit improvement is to reduce travel time and thus make it a more attractive and useful alternative to urban travelers.

Despite some debate and carping on visual values and the success of the highway program, they are somewhat peripheral issues; it will be remembered that the goal of preservation of economic and social values is about as close as we come at present to some stated objectives of national mass transport policy. There is apparently little real doubt the preservation of economic and social values can be aided by improvements in mass transportation; at the very least, such values will not be impaired by transit improvements. For example, downtown property values are relatively high because the center city is at the focal point of the whole urban transport system, regardless of mode, and usually enjoys a high degree of access. In recent years, with the rapid move to the suburbs, downtown business and real estate interests have become increasingly aware of the threat to the values of their property and have often become strong advocates of improved mass transport systems—particularly one of the forms of rapid transit—in order to help reinforce the position of the downtown and preserve economic values. This is a typical response of business interests. In his interesting and highly perceptive book, *The Private City,* Warner points out how downtown business interests in Philadelphia worked diligently in the 1920's for the construction of massive public works, principally new subway lines, to improve access to the central business district.[22] In the late forties and fifties the downtown interests supported freeway building as giving promise of improved access; more recently it has been transit once again. Whatever the device, the purpose is plainly to find means to keep values up, and certainly there is no sin in this unless the funds expended on the transport improvements might have been better spent elsewhere or the costs are excessive for the value received.[23]

There is, also, the issue of whether or not it is good to take action that promotes greater concentration in the CBD. In other words, more people in a limited space may have short-run benefits to property owners, downtown business and service organizations, and the tax receipts of the city, but such congestion may continue to erode the quality of urban life. This problem has no easy answer, since no one seems clear on the "goodness" or "badness" of various levels of concentration. Again, congestion and overcrowding are a function of whether or not areas of high concentration are designed carefully along with associated residential development and redevelopment; another factor is design of intra-downtown (or concentration center) mobility systems tying building and other facilities together in a way that minimizes interpersonal friction.[24]

Improved mass transportation is often discussed in terms of its power in preserving social values. It is true that any form of transport which aids in social intercourse and involvement in the community can be beneficial in helping to preserve a spirit of community, a factor critical in what Lawrence Haworth calls "the Good City." The interactive life is the one that can support the spirit and make life worth living through enhancement of the spirit of community; however, the institutional structure of a community, including the transportation system, may be such that real interaction or community is difficult or impossible.[25] Improved transportation of all types can help maintain the value of interaction and community, and the availability of mass transportation as a good travel alternative for those without automobiles will help reverse the process of social fracture that is so widely mourned in the United States today.[26]

Nevertheless, it is certainly too much to expect revivified mass transit to preserve economic and social values all by itself: people may stop shopping downtown not only because it takes too long to get there on the bus—or parking is too difficult—but because unperceptive merchants with wretched stores are trying to foist sleazy merchandise on their customers; social fragmentation may be more closely related to class differences, desires, and "natural" stratification, rather than to physical travel barriers.[27] There are probably no simple answers to such complex human values and social problems.

Cost Savings

Mass transportation advocates generally argue that transit is more economical than use of the private auto. Insofar as individuals are concerned, on the basis of strict pecuniary cost (that is, without calculation of social costs and benefits), there are a number of estimates as to what it costs the passenger to travel by means of the various modes of mass transportation and what it may cost him to drive his own automobile. Table 2–5 gives one estimate of the costs. In a somewhat later study

> The Federal Highway Administration has a persuasive argument for traveling by bus. It calculates that it costs the average motorist 13.55 cents for every mile he drives his standard sized automobile, as compared with the average bus fare of 3.81 cents a mile.[28]

Certain failings with this sort of presentation are obvious: the person must be traveling a greater distance than one mile to enjoy the savings shown; there may be an element of subsidy in both the public and private modes; and there is the ever-present problem of averaging anything.

TABLE 2-5
Average Cost for One Person to Travel One Mile
(in cents)

	Out-of-Pocket Cost	Full Cost*
Commuter Rail Coach	2.6	
Subway or Elevated	3.2	
Bus	3.2	
Auto		
One rider	3.5-4	10-11
Two riders	1.8-2	5-5.5
Three riders	1.2-1.3	3.3-3.7

* Full cost includes depreciation, insurance, etc., but not downtown parking.
Source: "Tide Turns for Transit," *Business Week,* October 20, 1962, p.88, citing Senate Committee on Interstate and Foreign Commerce.

Regardless of the source of the information, cost comparisons are always suspect because of the pitfalls of averaging; this is a theme, and a caveat, that will recur subsequently. To harp a bit on Table 2–5, for example, automobile operating costs vary widely as differences arise in the age and condition of the car, taxes, fees, terrain, and other operating conditions such as speed, road design, and degree of congestion. Furthermore, the purchase price of new cars varies widely, affecting depreciation cost. The possibility of used-car purchase and depreciation introduces more variation. Except where a car is specifically purchased and used for purposes competitive with a mode of mass transportation, such as commuting to work, a typical family car is used for many different reasons and only out-of-pocket costs can be specifically assigned to a given trip. These costs may be lower than the cost-per-mile of transit use, or may be perceived as less by the motorist. Moreover, the labor costs of driving a car are often ignored; even when the "wages" of the driver of a car are calculated, they are associated only with the time of actual travel. On the other hand, transit costs must include a large burden of operatives' wages paid when no actual work is performed because of labor agreements calling for a full day's pay when much less than a full eight-hour day is worked. The peaked nature of the demand for urban mass transportation makes such labor cost burdens almost inescapable in mass transportation.[29]

The average cost to the patron of public transportation can differ widely, depending upon the distance involved and whether charges are assessed on a flat-fare, zone, or mileage basis. Traveling a long distance under a flat-fare system produces a low average cost per mile, while the cost per mile for a short trip might be very high indeed. On the other hand, distance-based fares, such as are commonly used in commuter railway services, may appear on the surface to be more uniform on a per-mile basis and thus more easily susceptible to generalization and comparative analysis; yet even here there are wide variations possible if fares are tapered—that is, if the fare per mile is less as distance increases. Such tapering is a common feature of railway fares. Moreover, discounts are generally given to patrons buying multiple ride and commuter tickets. In the author's personal experience as a railroad commuter on the Illinois Central in Chicago from Bryn Mawr (71st and Jeffrey) to the Loop, the fare pattern shown in Table 2–6 was in effect in the late 1950's. Depending upon the type of ticket purchased, the average fare per ride between a pair of commuter stations on the Illinois Central varied from 29 cents to 40 cents and the average fare cost per mile from 2.64 cents to 3.63 cents. Which of them is *the* average fare cost? The same situation could be found between many points on many railroads.

Cost estimating, like cost comparisons, is another game filled with snares, pitfalls, and stumbling blocks. Some idea of the variation possible in cost estimating was discovered by John Leavens in his highly interesting study *The Cost of Commuter Transportation*.[30] Table 2–7 shows the cost per mile variations, with 1.5 passengers per car based on a number of cost studies. Out-of-pocket costs vary from 1.75 cents to 3 cents per passenger mile; total costs range from 4.67 cents to 8.84 cents per passenger mile.

TABLE 2-6
Comparison of Average Fares and Different Types of Tickets
Between the Same Station Pairs

	One-Way Single Fare	Multiple Ride Fares		Commutation Fares		
		10 Rides Limit 1 Year	25 Rides Limit 1 Year	12 Ride Individual Weekly	46 Ride Individual Monthly	54 Ride Individual Monthly
Cost per Ticket	$ .40	$ 3.77	$ 9.16	$ 3.94	$14.15	$15.73
Cost per Ride	.40	.377	.366	.328	.307	.291
Cost per Mile (11 miles)	.0363	.0342	.0333	.0298	.0279	.0264

Source: Illinois Central Railroad Electric Suburban Schedules, No. 402—in effect October 25, 1959, p.1. Distance calculated from Illinois Central Railroad List of Stations, No. 4, April 1, 1956, pp.26, 27.

Leavens picks what appear to be the most reasonable figures and goes on to show the comparative costs of commuting into Manhattan from New Jersey by automobile, bus, and commuter railroad. The rail and bus costs to the traveler are based on actual fares and distances. For the various distances involved, as shown in Figure 2–1, he finds that when calculating total costs to the traveler, including highway, bridge or tunnel tolls, and parking, on either the out-of-pocket cost or total cost basis, the automobile is by far the most expensive means of travel. On the other hand, if only out-of-pocket costs are considered and the various tolls and parking fees are ignored, the automobile is almost always the cheapest means of travel.

Leavens' work is considerably more valuable than many such studies. He confines his effort to the specific area of New York City; he does not attempt to generalize to any great extent. He therefore avoids being absurd. In short, to be as logical and consistent as possible, one must investigate a specific situation to determine whether or not one means of travel is less costly than another.

TABLE 2-7
Automobile Operating Costs in Cents per Passenger Mile[1]

Source	AAA (1961)[2]	AAA (1962)[2]	AAA (1965)[3]	AAA (1966)[3]	ALA[4]	ALA[5]	M.K.W.[6]	Botzow[7]	Smith[8]
Factor									
Variable									
Gasoline	1.79¢	1.79¢	1.72¢	1.72¢	–	–	0.70¢	1.78¢	1.43¢
Oil	–	–	–	–	1.84	1.08	0.07	–	0.13
Tires	0.33	0.33	0.29	0.29	–	–	1.10	0.27	0.12
Maintenance	0.53	0.53	0.45	0.45	0.67	0.67	1.13	0.55	1.32
Sub-total	2.65¢	2.65	2.46	2.46	2.51	1.75	2.00	2.60	3.00
Fixed									
Insurance	0.93	0.46	1.05	0.52	1.08	0.90	–	0.53	0.86
Registration	0.15	0.07	0.16	0.08	0.19	0.09	2.67	.07	0.13
Depreciation	4.30	2.25	4.18	2.09	5.06	3.20	–	1.67	1.69
Sub-total	5.38¢	2.78	5.39	2.69	6.33	4.19	2.67	2.27	2.68
Total Variable & Fixed	8.03¢	5.43	7.85	5.15	8.84	5.94	4.67	4.87	5.68
Miles Per Year	10,000	20,000	10,000	20,000	10,000	10,000	5,000	20,540	10,000
Annual Cost	$803	$1086	$785	$1030	$884	$594	$234	$1013	$568

[1] Based on 1.5 passengers per car (Botzow, p.17).

[2] American Automobile Association, Your Driving Costs, 1961–62 ed. Based on a 4-door V8 sedan.

[3] American Automobile Association, Your Driving Costs, 1965–66 ed. Based on a 4-door V8 sedan.

[4] Automobile Legal Association, "Cost of Car Operation," The Automobilist, June 1963, pp.12–13. Based on a 4-door V8 sedan in Morristown, N.J.

[5] Ibid. Based on a 1963 compact in Morristown, N.J.

[6] J. R. Meyer, J. F. Kain, M. Wohl, The Urban Transportation Problem (Cambridge, Mass.: Harvard University Press, 1965), p.218. Based on the cheapest operation possible.

[7] Botzow, table 1. Based on an average of automobiles crossing the Hudson River.

[8] Future Highways and Urban Growth (New Haven, Conn.: Wilbur Smith and Associates, 1961), p.280. Based on a medium-priced four-door sedan. Source: Hermann Botzow, "An Empirical Method for Estimating Auto Computing Costs," paper presented at the annual meeting of the Highway Research Board, January 1967, p.17.

113

Figure 2–1   Auto, Bus, and Rail Commutation Charges Per Passenger Mile, New Jersey to Manhattan

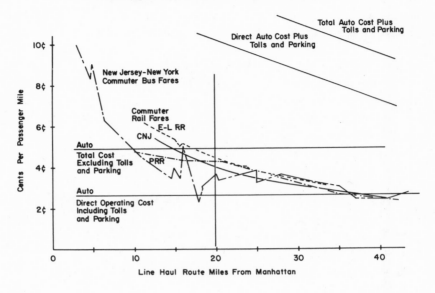

The matter of straightforward cost finding and cost comparison is not helped at all when analysts attempt to reflect social benefits and costs. This involves a whole spectrum of factors that should be weighed in any private or public decision, but factors which are difficult to pin down. For example, the gasoline engine of an automobile produces pollutants that poison the atmosphere; there is a cost involved, but how much is it and how can it be assessed? Diesel-powered buses and trucks do not emit the same poisonous vapors, but they do produce considerable smoke and a harmless but unpleasant stench; how is the cost of smoke and smell to be figured? Public means of transportation are considerably safer—in terms of accidents, injuries, and fatalities—than is the private automobile, but most comparative calculations ignore a cost factor that hinges on the dubious calculus of placing a monetary evaluation on life itself. New highways are often partially justified on the basis of the improvements in safety in terms of reduced slaughter compared to existing roads; again, the matter hinges on arbitrarily placing value on human life in dollars and cents. Moreover, such roadways often induce more travel so that the accident level in the absolute may stay the same, or even rise, while the proportion of accidents to vehicle miles, or some other standard, falls. The point of all this is, very simply, that what may be the most important cost factors of all tend to be ignored, or massaged to prove a pet conclusion, because they are so difficult to grapple with.[31]

Perhaps the most intensive and complete attempt to determine the comparative cost per passenger (not the fare paid by the passenger, but the cost per passenger of providing the service) of the various modes of urban transportation is the analysis undertaken by Meyer, Kain, and Wohl.[32] (To sum up the results of their work in a paragraph or two is an unavoidable injustice; the book should be carefully read by persons interested in urban transport.) For the line-haul portion of the trip, calculated on a series of comparisons based on a roadway and rail system of radial configuration, it was felt that the automobile was the least costly of the modes as long as distances were short and volumes relatively low; either bus or rail systems are comparable at higher volumes and longer distances.

Express bus systems sharing rights-of-way with automobiles on freeways are, not surprisingly, less costly than rail because the costs of the highway facilities may be shared with the other vehicles using them. Buses sharing freeways may, of course, suffer from the same jams that plague automobiles and thus the service may lose much of its attractiveness. Where volume of bus traffic (or freeway congestion) makes freeway sharing undesirable, the cost of completely separate highways for buses is at least comparable to that of rail. Since a busway may require a somewhat wider right-of-way than a rail facility, where land acquisition costs are high the expense of constructing a busway may exceed rail construction costs for the fixed way. Rail costs appear to be much more favorable in those situations where rights-of-way are already in place and a relatively modest amount of replacement or new work needs to be done.[33]

Turning to comparisons of complete systems, including pick-up and delivery in residential areas, the line-haul, and delivery and pick-up in downtown centers, the integrated bus system (pick-up, line-haul, and delivery by the same vehicle with some express running on the line-haul over exclusive rights-of-way) seems to have the cost edge. Where volumes in any particular corridor are in the range of 5,000 to 10,000 or below, the automobile seems to have a cost advantage. Only where passenger volumes are high in a given corridor does rail transit appear to offer any cost advantage, and then under conditions where it is operated in conjunction with feeder buses at the residential pick-up and delivery end and with a subway for downtown distribution. Again, an additional edge is given rail when basic facilities, whether utilized for transit service or not, are already in existence.[34] This can be—and often is—interpreted as concluding that only a very few of the largest cities, or those with facilities already in place, can justify rail rapid transit.

It is not surprising that those directly interested in favoring rail rapid transit, as well as others with less reason for bias, have been unhappy with the Meyer, Kain, and Wohl analysis. Indeed, an earlier study by the same authors, which is largely re-presented in *The Urban Transportation Problem,* drew a sharp reaction and a serious questioning of the veracity of the authors.[35] Even more cutting was the commentary of a critic who fumed:

> Not only does this study fail to deal with matters of primary human significance in the domain of urban transportation; it exhibits a partiality toward the bus-automobile mode, as opposed to that of rail mass-transit, so evident and consistent that the reader is slightly embarrassed to note that this very long, one cannot say substantial work, was financed by the Ford Foundation. One would have been happier had it been the Ford Motor Company.[36]

One great and obvious fact lacking in the Meyer, Kain, and Wohl analysis is its failure to come to grips with the costs of accidents and air pollution that are so closely associated with automotive-related transportation systems and which have loomed large in recent public discussion. Criticism may also be levelled at the unrealistically low pecuniary cost of automobile operations presented. For example, in his study, Leavens notes the small portion of costs Meyer, Kain, and Wohl allocated to gasoline:

> A brief calculation will show that a gasoline allowance of 0.70 cents per passenger mile for a car carrying one and one-half passengers and using gasoline costing 33 cents per gallon calls for a car capable of 31.5 miles per gallon. A Volkswagen may be able to do this, but not the stripped compact or used car of which Meyer, Kain, and Wohl are speaking. Moreover, their assumption of a "utilitarian vehicle" for commuting purposes is certainly not reflected in the types of automobiles seen on the highways during the morning rush.[37]

On the matter of automotive costs Entwistle, also, takes exception:

> In calculating the comparative cost of commuting by automobile, which
> is after all the foundation on which this entire work is erected, the ex-
> traordinary assumption is made, and made almost parenthetically, that
> ownership costs (the largest single component in automobile transit),
> will be reduced to 4 cents a vehicle-mile by one of the following expe-
> dients. One will buy a second car specially developed for commuting
> needs to cost $1,600 and last 12 *years* in continuous use. Alternatively,
> one will buy a used car for $200 and drive it continuously for three and
> a half years: No evidence is advanced to suggest that the driving public
> is likely to accept such vehicles for the cause of urban economics, and
> the tenor of all Detroit advertising strongly suggests that the public would
> not, even if these proposals were feasible.[38]

Meyer, Kain, and Wohl are not presenting deliberate falsifica-
tions; rather they are trying to generalize on the basis of certain
assumptions and averages.[39] Any generalization contains considerable truth and considerable inaccuracy. One need only consider the
grotesque *average* physical makeup of a group of fifty men and fifty
women. In any case, the methodology of the study appears im-
peccable. If it is indeed so, then it should be used in given, real-
life situations with whatever slight modifications are necessary to
make it more realistic. In short, no generalization of comparative
costs can point the true way for all cities at all times under all
circumstances.

Is mass transit less costly than the private automobile? The only
fair answer is that it all depends. The important point is that—
brushing aside the inevitable "rail-transit-versus-something-else"
arguments—mass transportation does indeed have a place that can
be justified by cost analysis. The problem still remains whether or
not people will use transit if it is provided.

Even more important than cost comparisons for the individual
user of transport is whether or not mass transportation is less costly
than the private automobile to society as a whole in given metropolitan areas. Objective measures are not available. Yet, in the
larger urban areas at least, there is a growing feeling that the
automobile cannot continue to be the dominant mode of transport.
Public officials—not a bad barometer of public feeling—are coming
to believe that the costs to society of the private automobile are
beginning to outweigh its benefits. Much of the thinking at the
Urban Mass Transportation Administration reflects this position.[40]

The Case Against Mass Transit

A fairly strong case against mass transit can be made on a number of grounds. Many persons contend that mass transportation is unattractive, inflexible, too expensive, and utterly incapable of handling the kind of spread-out population that is now common in United States urban areas. One of the best summaries of the skeptical position on mass transportation is found in a paper by James M. Hunnicutt, Jr., the Chief of the Bureau of Public Parking in Montgomery County, Maryland:

> Another favorite topic when parking is mentioned is how mass transit or rapid transit is going to make downtown parking unnecessary. Of all the strange concepts now being held, this is probably the winner. Believe me, the average American is going to give up downtown long before he gives up his automobile. The idea that great numbers of new people are going to come to town on transit is plain silly until that method of competing transportation can beat the automobile at its own game. This is going to be some job, and we now know it. The automobile is the most convenient method of transportation yet devised. The car is ready to go when its owner wants and where its owner wants and operates strictly on the owner's schedule. On the other hand, transit leaves when it wants, and goes where it wants, and runs on its schedule and the rider has to re-mold his trip to meet that pre-determined by the bus or train. The automobile is considerably faster than transit in most cases. Exclusive of rail transit, the bus averages between 9 and 11 miles per hour on its overall trip. The automobile averages between 15 and 20 miles per hour. The bus takes twice as long to get there, not including transfers. The idea that transit is cheaper also doesn't hold water. From Silver Spring to downtown Washington is a distance of about 9 miles. The one way transit fare is 47 cents. If there are two people involved, this makes a total fare of about $2.00 a day for riding transit. Assuming that most people are going to have a car anyway, the fixed costs of insurance and depreciation are going to go on regardless of whether that car sits in the driveway or is rolling. The only additional cost is gasoline, tires and oil. Assuming that parking can be had near governmental offices for $1.00 to $1.50 per day, and gasoline is 30 cents a gallon, it is immediately evident that the automobile is cheaper than transit, and a whole lot more convenient and comfortable.
>
> Another argument to try to get people to use transit is that the average citizen should want to see the downtown remain in a good state of health so their tax situation will stay on an even keel as downtown pays most of the taxes. The average citizen could not care less about the downtown merchants' problems of traffic, parking, taxes, or what have you. He has his hands full with his wife, mortgage, and crab grass. He is going to give

the average retail merchant no two minutes of his time, or care what happens to him because he is quite sure the merchant is not staying up at night worrying about his problems either.[41]

Lamentably, this sort of argument often breaks down into a fight against mass transit by rail rather than transit in general, with the resultant danger of throwing out both baby and bath.[42]

In any case, the arguments against mass transit should be carefully evaluated.

Unattractiveness

The case for the unattractiveness of mass transportation almost makes itself. At the most obvious level, the cosmetic virtues of most transit facilities are so sparse as to be nonexistent. In terms of aesthetic pleasure which may be derived from the equipment used, much of it has seen better days; too often, in the case of rail equipment, those better days were from twenty to fifty years ago. The federal-aid programs are slowly changing the reality in many places, but the image lingers.

Many transit buses in regular use today first saw the light of day fifteen or twenty years ago. Since the average economic life of a bus is estimated at ten to twelve years, these old coaches are living on borrowed time. The scratches, rattles, and discomfort—often because of lack of modern suspension and air conditioning—rate them considerably below even the roughest foreign compact car in amenities. The amount of space per passenger is skimpy in most buses, even the newest models. In the typical seating arrangement, there is little room for the knees of taller riders. The narrowness of the seats often leaves the posterior of aisle passengers partially hanging in mid-air, and open to unceremonious scuffing by passengers passing up and down the narrow aisle. Moreover, being thrown together with a bunch of strangers may be in and of itself most uncomfortable.[43]

The meanness of the dimensions of the ordinary motor bus is related to its having to share public streets with other vehicles. It would be difficult to make buses much larger. Only by cutting down on the number of seats could more comfortable seating be provided for the passengers. It is possible that large articulated or double-deck buses could maintain high seating capacity yet offer greater comfort and room.[44]

Admittedly, even at best a vehicle designed for the mass transportation of many people must inevitably have a long way to go to match the aesthetic desires of any one of them. If, on top of this, equipment is marred by its age, it is small wonder that mass transport is viewed by much of the public as an inferior good.[45] Some railway equipment is still so unbelievably ancient that one gets the impression that the only concession to modernity is the electric light and the removal of the posters encouraging young men to join the Army and help General Pershing rid Europe of the Kaiser.

In some situations the equipment may not be so bad but the mass transit facilities may be quite ancient and most unattractive. In other cases it is the lack of facilities, such as the absence of bus shelters at even major stops, that makes the use of the bus uncomfortable and unattractive. On the other hand, users of rail transit, particularly the subways, often enjoy the use of facilities of remarkably low standards, a presentiment of which may have inspired Dante. The New York City subway system, for example, is often cited as possessing possibly the most wretched "standard of living" in the world.

Most subway stations in the United States were designed not by architects but by engineers who thought mainly in terms of structural strength and cost saving rather than aesthetics. Design which is dominated by engineers is often infelicitous at best, unless it is impossible for them to avoid aesthetic competence as in the case of a large cantilever or suspension bridge. From the start, such facilities could not be attractive; to improve them is often an enormously costly business. Modern standards of lighting alone would improve many subway stations and might even make them safer. Perhaps, as residents of a generally affluent nation, we place undue emphasis on surface gloss. Nevertheless, the fact remains that to attract more patronage, mass transport must be made visually and physically more attractive.[46]

Unpleasant facilities are not endemic to mass transit. In San Francisco the Bay Area Rapid Transit District has taken considerable pains to assure the attractiveness of all of the station facilities and linear parks have been contructed under some of the elevated segments of the system. Similar care is being taken in construction of the new rapid transit systems in Washington, D.C., and in the renovation work being carried out in Boston.[47]

Not to paint the picture too darkly, modern bus and rail equipment is considerably more comfortable and attractive than mass transit hardware of the past generation. Atlanta, Chicago, Philadelphia, Dallas, Cleveland, New York, and Boston—to name only a few—have purchased substantial numbers of new buses and rail cars. The federal capital grant program has helped to provide these tools for better mass transportation. Over the horizon is the promise of a greatly improved bus design. The rapid transit equipment in present use in San Francisco not only gives passengers a fast and comfortable ride, but also appeals to them visually. Equipment of equally high standards is slated for Washington. The problem is, of course, that there is still so much decrepit or poorly designed or overage equipment in use today that it blemishes the image of all mass transportation undertakings.

Another, related, factor is that many white Americans do not wish to ride in the same vehicle with minority groups—particularly Blacks and Puerto Ricans. The reverse may be true as well. Solid, middle-class citizens may also fear to use public transportation at night because of robberies and other violence. Indeed, apart from danger to passengers, the situation for the bus drivers—who usually carried a hundred dollars or more in change—reached a crisis point in 1968. After a number of murders and shootings in connection with robberies, many systems refused to allow drivers to make change, and patrons were forced to have the exact fare or to purchase tokens in advance.[48] If the drivers are fearful, is it any wonder that the patrons shy away from transit?[49]

For whatever reason, there is very clear evidence that people have been staying away in large numbers from mass transportation. Total passengers moved by transit fell from 17.2 billion in 1950 to 6.8 billion in 1971. In a little over twenty years patronage had fallen off by a little more than 60 per cent. Patronage declines will be discussed in greater detail later in this book but the defection of riders is evidence of dissatisfaction with transit among those who have a choice in utilizing the service.[50]

Various factors are cited for the use of the automobile instead of mass transport. Analysts have developed lists of determinants that affect the use of mass transportation, including such things as city age, population age, race, housing conditions, family income, automobile ownership, population density, and CBD density, to mention just a few. There seems to be fairly conclusive evidence that automobile ownership is the key variable; if a person owns a car, he is going to use it as a better alternative than mass transit.[51]

Another obvious element affecting the great fall off in comparative attractiveness of mass transportation is the fact that government highway construction policy has encouraged the use of the automobile. This, coupled with a policy of government mortgage insurance encouraging suburban development, means that many people can only be served effectively by private automobiles and highways. In short, building highways causes a demand for more highways because the type of living carried on can have its transport demands met only by highway-oriented private transportation.[52]

Inflexibility

It is often charged that mass transportation is inflexible, meaning usually that a transport line cannot be altered to meet changing needs of the population over time. It is sometimes claimed that transit can handle only the journey-to-work with any degree of effectiveness. This allegation is usually associated with rail transportation, where, in all truth, it has a certain validity.

Flexibility, however, has several dimensions. First of all, it is the ability to perform several alternative tasks at any given time; secondly, it is the ability to meet changing conditions over time. A highway is rather flexible as an investment in that it can handle not only the private automobile carrying a breadwinner to work but it can also carry the family downtown for a show or out of town on a vacation. Trucks and buses can also use it for a variety of purposes. Highways *are not* flexible, however, in accommodating demand increases over time; lax planning also permits encroachment of residential and business uses that may greatly overtax the capacity of a given highway or network.

Rail is usually held to be the least flexible mode of mass transportation, one that cannot meet the changing needs of the public as well as the other modes of transport. A rapid transit line built to serve portions of a city in the 1910–1920 period, when most people did not have an automobile and jobs were concentrated downtown, cannot meet today's needs of the more affluent and widely distributed population which work at jobs scattered broadly about the urban area. This conception of rail transport focuses mainly on the obvious difficulty of physically moving a rail facility.

Some new thinking has been generated in the provision of rail transit facilities, particularly in regard to improved pickup and delivery. New rail lines under construction and some already in existence have recently focused attention on the provision of parking space at stations. The Cleveland Transit System has taken the lead in providing a considerable amount of space at stations toward the ends of the rapid transit line. The new San Francisco Bay Area Rapid Transit system has large parking areas at its outlying stations. The Washington Metro, now under construction in the nation's capital, has also made provision for massive car parking at the stations outside the downtown area. Cleveland, San Francisco, and Washington, then, are good examples of rapid transit designed to act as an interceptor of automobile traffic from outlying areas. There are a number of recent moves—some sponsored by federal grants—to do a better job of planning the feed-in of passengers by bus as well as automobile to rail transit lines; this approach is becoming standard in rapid transit design.[53]

Bus inflexibility is one of the more peculiar facets of this issue because it has nothing at all to do with the capabilities of the mode of transportation itself but, rather, on how it is operated. Improvement in the flexibility of service in meeting new needs is possible with astute management. However, the rigidity of public officials who refuse to allow bus route changes and the equally short-sightedness of management, who, too often, can see no reason for any change other than cutting back service, has provided the ludicrous spectacle of buses continuing religiously to follow trails blazed by the streetcar three-quarters of a century ago. (As an example of governmental rigidity, Indiana's mass transit law prohibits non-fixed route services, as the Greater Lafayette Public Transportation Corporation learned when it wished to offer dial-a-bus service.) How often today will bus route 14 follow the route of the old 14 streetcar line, regardless of how conditions have changed? When asked why this situation is so, management usually replies politely that it has always operated the 14 line there, and they couldn't get permission from the city or the Public Utilities Commission to change it if they so wished. Sometimes one gets the impression that

Moses brought much of the United States transit route structure down from Sinai, etched indelibly on stone tablets.

The bus probably offers the most golden opportunities for fast transit improvement with relative ease and lack of expense. Service to new areas, express running, and downtown shuttle service can be implemented quickly, since major public works are not needed. Reserve lanes on existing highways or newly constructed busways can overcome the problem of slowness in bus transit; however, the busways may add to the line-haul inflexibility, in terms of being able to switch the routing site as need demands, by giving the bus a private pathway that would have the same virtues and problems of the rail right-of-way. Really, major gains in attractiveness—especially speed—may therefore be purchased only by giving up on some of the bus's strong points in flexibility.

Nevertheless, many means may be used to increase flexibility and usefulness of the bus. Some of these are the result of federal programs, to be discussed at length in subsequent chapters. Outstanding among these are the subscription bus service operations, in which passengers contract in advance for door-to-door bus service. In effect, the bus chases after the people instead of the other way around. Dial-a-bus can also be worked out so that smaller buses can be used somewhat in the manner of taxicabs by use of the telephone and two-way radio communications.[54]

In summary, flexibility is a problem in mass transport, but one that can be mitigated, if not completely overcome, by astute management, open-minded city fathers, and willingness of both parties to try operational innovations.

Expense

It is charged that transit is not a low-cost solution to the problem of mobility. This has been discussed at length earlier, with the conclusion that it depends upon circumstances.

Population Distribution

One of the most serious arguments raised against mass transportation and attempts at its resuscitation is that urban population in the United States has become so thinly distributed—and is apparently growing more so—that it simply cannot be handled effectively by mass transportation. Certainly, the trend of the last fifty years has been toward urban dispersion just as it has been to metropolitaniza-tion.[55] The single family home on a spacious lot in the suburbs is still thought to be the dream of most Americans. It is equally true that such areas are extremely difficult to serve with mass transportation. This is especially so if density is conceived of solely in terms of persons living close enough to a transit artery to walk to it.

If for many years the trend has been toward dispersal and low density, one of the greatest mistakes one can make is to depend upon the projection of past events for an accurate clue to the future. For example, the Federal Electric Railway Commission in its delibera-tions in 1919, basing much of its thinking on the past trends toward increasing use of the streetcar, could not envision how the city would ever get along without the electric trolley.[56] Looking at the trends, it simply could not be imagined that in the future the automobile would become the dominant means of transportation in most cities. Perhaps the single family home and increasingly dispersed living are the inevitable and inescapable trend of the foreseeable future. How-ever, the rapid rise in the number of apartments being constructed in both urban and suburban areas indicates that many Americans are willing to put up with considerably more density in their housing than has been suspected. In any event, as powerful as the decentral-izing force has been, there is no reason to believe that it is inevitable and unchangeable.[57]

Another factor to consider is that certain forms of mass transpor-tation will serve as a population centralizer. New investment in rapid transit and commuter railways—investment which has only rarely been made in the United States in the half-century of the auto age—could sharply affect future densities. A city which has invested heavily in mass transit facilities, such as Stockholm in Sweden, may find that either because they planned it that way, or through private but not inadvertent decisions, a considerable number of people are attracted to concentrated locations along the right-of-way of the rapid transit lines rather than scattering thinly over a considerably wider area.[58] The Swedish experience is interesting in that the coun-try has a level of auto ownership about equal to that of the United States.

Another element often neglected by critics is that people can supply, in effect, their own pickup and delivery service in connec-tion with mass transportation. A rail line projecting out into the suburbs equipped with large parking lots at its stations need not pass through an area of great population density to secure ridership as long as there is reasonably good access to the stations. Even the superhighway or freeway running out into a suburban area acts merely as a line-haul agent, very much like a railway. Most such highways deliberately avoid passing through high-density areas. The thinly distributed suburban population taking advantage of modern superhighways in a very real sense performs pickup and delivery service in getting to and from the freeway through the use of conventional streets. It is, in many ways, like a feeder bus connection to a commuter railway line. Clearly the role of mass transit in a dispersed community is a matter that needs considerable thought and analysis, but the notion that rapid transit or commuter rail service depends strictly on massive numbers of people highly concentrated in very small areas immediately adjacent to the transit line is no longer necessarily true.

Mass Transport in the Decentralized Metropolis

The trend toward decentralization of population is difficult to evaluate in relation to the pros and cons of mass transit. Really, one immediately gets to the tough and value-laden question of "what should a city be like?" This again raises the economic and social issue of affordable mobility. Mobility costs the individual time, money, and effort (or energy, including stress). So far, the question of mobility has been given only middle-class answers primarily through increasing the supply of automobile-oriented facilities to satisfy the wants of the automobile-owning class. This approach seems to affect the time cost dimension of mobility, with perhaps some reduction in effort.

Inadequate transportation looms as one of many factors in prolonging the vicious cycle of apartheid and poverty faced by ghetto dwellers, many of whom have rural origins and are ignorant of city ways. Jobs are one of the primary keys to breaking the ghetto cycle and ending the cold civil war in the United States. The problem is that many jobs—particularly in the sort of heavy industry that still has a place for persons of marginal skill—have been moved out of the central cities and scattered in the suburbs.

Public transport is often not available at all to suburban locations, or is even more execrable than the mass transit service oriented to the city core. A dependable car is necessary to get and hold a job, yet the cost of a dependable car is often beyond the means of the poor. Providing mobility for those without cars is a vital role for mass transport. The provision of transportation alone is obviously not a cure-all for the problems of poverty or the ghettos; but mobility, along with such items as health, education, legal assistance—and even babysitting services—is part of a bundle of activities necessary to help break people out of the ghetto cycle.

Another factor often neglected has been the cost of poor public transportation to poor people. The erosion of traffic from mass transportation modes, often as a result of the highway policy of the federal and other levels of government, has usually resulted in a substantial decline in the quality of service and a rise in the fares charged by public transit companies. The service decline as much as the fare boost is a substantial cost to the poor as well as to the community as a whole. Failure to account for such costs to captive riders of public transport is one of the many gaps in our thinking in regard to the true cost of highways that encourage greater automobile use. The decline in the quality of mass transit service is as much a cost of highways as is the concrete that goes to build them.

Such federal urban transportation policy as can be discovered has indicated that its intent is the preservation and enhancement of central city values; the hope is expressed that mass transit service, along with highways, can help shape as well as serve cities. However, as long as mass transit expenditures are so small—$175 million a year at most up until the early 1970's—it is doubtful that much shaping will be done. Much more than just spending money is involved, of course. The will to solve our urban problems must be found, and that has proved to be an elusive quest.[59] Until a change comes, the United States must suffer from the burdens of dispersion, poverty, blight, and staggering mobility problems.

Transportation as a Status Symbol

In any list of pros and cons of mass transportation versus the automobile one inevitably runs into the problem of the automobile as a status symbol. It is easy to conclude that the average American is so goofy about his automobile—in large part because it enhances his standing in the community—that it is hopeless to try to get him to shift to mass transport.

It is easy—too easy—to conclude that the joys of ownership do not also include the pains of possession and use. Without doubt the automobile is a powerful symbol of both self and success. It is probably equally true, however, that there has been a considerable erosion of status power associated with the automobile among many social classes because automobiles have become so commonplace. It is far wiser, perhaps, to view status as just one of a whole group of factors that make the use of the automobile attractive. Still, there is no doubt that since most people are rational, even the most status conscious will be likely to use mass transportation if it is a better alternative than driving. The real problem is to provide that better alternative.[60] Another factor is to take appropriate action so that the negative connotations associated with mass transportation are eliminated and transit is given a more positive image.

Some Conclusions

One can safely conclude that mass transport has a definite role to play in the modern city and in modern life in the United States. By improving the quality and quantity of mass transit, the public can enjoy the advantages of added mobility through increased choice between transport means of relatively more comparable quality. Clearly, all our urban and domestic problems are not going to be solved by improving mass transportation any more than Prohibition solved domestic problems in that hectic decade of experiment in the 1920's.

It is also clear that many of the shortcomings of mass transit may be overcome. It can be made more attractive than it is, and as subsequent chapters will point out, it probably can offer a reasonable travel alternative to a fair number of people now attracted only to the automobile. Mass transport can certainly improve on its service to those people who have no alternatives. But public mass transportation is not going to meet everyone's needs; no one should expect it to do so.

The opposition to improved mass transportation generally views it as a threat to continued expansion of highways and highway-related activities and supply of equipment, not as an intrinsically bad thing. But the opposition generally pulls out the stops to make the strongest case possible against mass transit; they are aided and abetted by many federal, state, and local officials who cannot conceive of transportation other than highway transport. Moreover, the highway lobby is awesomely bankrolled. Thus the reasonable arguments for and against mass transportation, and the facts which can make it clear that improved mass transport of one form or another is, indeed, a wise policy in a given place, may be held back or even for a time overcome by the vested highway interests or by sheer ignorance.[61]

A thundering herd of interest groups ranging from the Automobile Manufacturers' Association to those who build highways and to the great petroleum companies all have a stake in the continued upward spiral of highway construction and the use of the automobile. There are good arguments on both sides of the transit issue, but the sheer economic power of the highway interests may—if they feel seriously threatened—overcome any good arguments that might be made in behalf of mass transit. It is no news that a well-organized interest group plays a far more important role in policy formulation and action on the part of all levels of government than the best interests of the public. The small sums traditionally spent by government for nonhighway transportation are enlightening evidence. Not so many years ago a national magazine stated:

> According to Department of Transportation experts, it would take a minimum of $37 billion over the next five years to make even a start on cleaning up the nation's transportation mess: $5 billion for corridor trains—Boston to Washington to New York; Chicago to Milwaukee and Detroit; San Francisco to Los Angeles—$4 billion for airports, $5 billion for airways (that is, for automated controls [sic] of flights), $8 billion for mass transit, the rest for establishing bus transit, fringe parking, automated roadways, and the like. That kind of money can only come from the U.S. Government—and justifiably so, since an efficient transportation system is vital to an efficient economy.
>
> But to quote [the nation's first Secretary of Transportation] Alan Boyd again: "Congress appropriated only $175 million for mass transit for 50 states. At best one city, after a couple of years of haggling, might get $900,000. Now what the hell good is that going to do against $1 billion available for highway projects?"[62]

For its part, mass transportation has developed its own lobbying group and, to some extent, there are more equal countervailing forces at work. As passage of the Highway Act of 1973 reveals, the situation has begun to change, though perhaps not as rapidly as one would like.

CHAPTER THREE

Urban Mass Transportation:
The Institutions

The principal institutional actors on the stage of mass transportation improvement are the mass transportation industry in the United States and the Urban Mass Transportation Administration (UMTA) of the U.S. Department of Transportation. A major role for the cities is the commitment to improvement of mass transportation and the provision—in conjunction with UMTA and the local transit operating agency—of the support needed to do the job. There are other more minor participants in the drama, of course—state and local government, planners, opposing forces—but they have many other roles to play.

Transit improvement, broadly defined, is the goal of federal programs; the delivery of this improvement to the public, whatever form it may take, is the province of the mass transportation industry. The improvement must come to grips with the urban mobility problem in its three major facets: (1) a lack of mobility for many citizens, (2) thwarted mobility for citizens who are victims of congestion, and (3) the purchase of mobility at high pecuniary and social costs. Put more simply, action has to be taken that will help provide mobility to all citizens who need it, and do the job with reasonable economy. If mass transportation is to be truly useful, it should have a broad appeal and should have reasonable value as an alternative to other means of transportation for those members of the public who can afford alternatives and who have regular access to them. It also means that the formulation and implementation of urban transportation policy should help make cities lower-cost and more beneficial places in which to live. In other words, barriers to mobility are an economic and social cost burden upon the urban public. Action that can lessen these costs will not only benefit urban dwellers, but all citizens who utilize goods and services produced in urban areas—goods and services whose ultimate costs must reflect the various costs of urban life, including transportation.

Much of what follows is a discussion of the transit industry. This is usually construed to mean those mass transportation firms and agencies that operate bus, rapid transit, street railway, and trolley bus services. The transit industry, as such, does not include taxicab companies nor operators of commuter railroads, even though they are clearly in the for-hire segment of urban transportation. The railroad industry is, of course, a thing unto itself, of which the commuter train operations are considered largely as an appendix. The railroads certainly don't consider themselves a part of the transit industry. Indeed, the reflections by members of the railway industry on the transit industry are hardly flattering and railroad interests tend to identify themselves on an institutional basis probably more strongly with the "regular" (meaning intercity freight) transportation industry. Mass transportation is often categorized by the railroads as "a bunch of crazy bus drivers." Whatever thoughts the transit industry may have about the railroad industry have not been vouchsafed.

Despite the fact that the taxicab industry in the United States moves about as many passengers as surface rail, rapid transit, trolley coach, and commuter rail, plus about half as many as those moved by bus, it is rarely considered in any discussion of urban transportation. If not properly a part of the mass transportation industry, taxicabs, along with transit and commuter rail, are public transportation. A happy exception to the usual omission of the taxicab is found in the book *Economic Characteristics of the Urban Public Transportation Industry*.[1] Despite this contribution, remarkably little is generally known about the taxicab industry.

All of which returns to the question of what is properly included in the mass transportation industry. Perhaps the best way to define an industry is to include within it all modes whose services are substitutes for one another. Speaking of the urban transportation industry in the broadest sense, one would have to include the private automobile, transit, commuter rail, and taxicab operations, since they are all substitutes for one another. A narrower view of the *mass* transportation industry would separate the for-hire, common carrier segment from the private automobile. What follows, therefore, involves the urban mass transportation industry, with emphasis on mass.

As noted above, the place of the taxicab in urban mass transportation is often ignored. Cabs, of course, are for-hire to particular individuals; however, there is nothing unusual about several passengers making separate journeys, but riding together, very much like a small bus. Cabs are certainly not private vehicles as far as their patrons are concerned, but not being entirely public either, have apparently been consigned to a kind of yellow-hued limbo. Taxis are excluded from the aid provided by the Urban Mass Transportation Administration and, as noted above, are pretty much ignored in urban transportation planning and in the hearts and minds of those involved in other segments of the mass transportation industry. For the sake of this work, the taxi will be included in the discussion of the transportation modes that deliver a service to the public.

An Overview of the Transit Industry

Chapter 1 gave a perspective on the setting for the development of federal urban transport policy and touched on the highlights of mass transit history. Here, the aim is more complete: to take a look at the transit industry as an institution, in order to see what gives it its particular tone and what factors are significant in affecting the industry's ability to deliver a useful and attractive public service.[2]

The typical way in which firms in an industry are organized often gives a clue to the effectiveness of that industry in providing goods or services. It is a fair assessment of the organization of the transit industry to say that it is geared to produce a service but most certainly not to sell it. If we review the various organizational charts presented in the book *Principles of Urban Transportation*[3] to see the organizational forms typifying different segments of the industry, the lack of a marketing function is most disturbing. Seven organizational charts are shown in *Principles,* some more or less idealized and others taken from those used by actual operating companies at the time the book was written. One of these, for a medium-sized firm, is reproduced in Figure 3-1, as being typical of the group. Not one of the charts in the *Principles* book includes marketing as a central line function of the firm. Even today, as one looks at some of the larger transit properties, a great deal of detail can be found in almost any organizational chart, or organizational structure beyond the charts, for the care and feeding of the equipment and the scheduling and utilization of manpower. But apart from some token public relations programs, little or nothing is done to find out what the public wants or to figure out how to deliver it in an appealing, marketing-oriented manner.

A recent unpublished study of forty small mass transit properties, conducted by the present writer, reveals that they, too, fail to include marketing as a formal part of the structure of the firm. The typical organizational form of the transit firm is derived from the days when the public transit companies had virtual monopolies on surface transportation, and there was no need to carry out any effort that approached a modern marketing program.

The virtue of a true marketing effort is that it provides information about customers and potential customers' needs and wants, and it helps to develop the means of providing the service to meet those needs and wants, in line with the objectives of the agency charged with the delivery of the service. The package of service, fare, and promotion can then be determined in an orderly, planned fashion. This whole effort requires constant monitoring of public attitudes and actions. Without the necessary information and the planned action oriented to the consumer, transit management's hands are tied. Whatever is done can only be a reaction based on limited knowledge and on tactical expediency.

If one assumes that demand—particularly increasing demand over time—is one good sign that transit is fulfilling its role in society, then an organizational structure that made marketing a central function of the organization would seem to be the wisest. This is undoubtedly not the case in the transit industry, where demand for service has eroded seriously since the end of the Second World War. Forces beyond the control of even the most enlightened marketing-oriented management have brought on this decline in patronage. In all likelihood, the declines were deeper and came more precipitously

Figure 3–1
Typical Organizational Chart of a Transit Firm

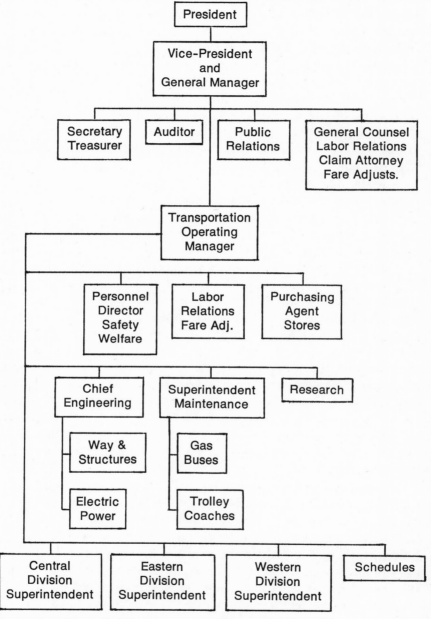

Source: Frank H. Mossman, *Principles of Urban Transportation*, p.80

because of the lack of true marketing effort. With a thorough marketing effort, one would expect that demand for mass transportation should be increased as a result of consumer needs being met by service that is useful and attractive. That is, transit becomes an increasingly better alternative relative to other means of transport, or to staying home for those citizens having no alternative means of mobility.

Some Industry Background

The present-day attitude and approach of the transit industry have developed over a long period of time. It is instructive to review these origins because they affect today's situation and provide some insight into the possibilities of change in the industry.

The transit industry developed in stages; in the beginning, a city often supported many independent transit firms. Each major street usually had its own street railway company, independent from those operating on other streets or sections of town. Toward the end of the nineteenth century these separate companies began to consolidate for the purpose of operating more profitably. Another reason was to increase the attractiveness of the firms for investment so that sufficient capital could be marshalled to convert animal-powered systems to electric traction. Consolidation made sense, not only for the managers seeking to improve their profit positions, but also for the public. Competition in transit is uneconomical for the operators and expensive and difficult for the public. Indeed, if there is any business that is a natural monopoly for a given urban area, it is the transit industry. With a merged and coordinated system, service could be improved and patrons could gain increased flexibility and mobility through transfer privileges between different lines of the united system.

Another reason for consolidation, and in many cases the dominant factor, was that financial manipulation of the securities of firms that were candidates for merger provided the possibility of substantial profit for insiders. As mergers proceeded in many cities, the Union Traction Company, or whatever it was called, came to have a near monopoly on surface transportation; it was not difficult to unload vast amounts of watered securities on an investing public greedy for a piece of an enterprise that monopolized an essential service.

The reason for making this point is that around the turn of the century a good bit of the public transit service in the United States was offered by companies not interested in making money from providing a good service to urban citizens. Rather, large profits were to be gained primarily through financial manipulation. This does not mean, of course, that all transit properties were engaged in financial hanky-panky or that service was necessarily poor; for an intraurban transportation monopoly, operation as well as manipulation was profitable. The problem was that the financial skullduggery burdened transit firms with a capital structure—much of it in bonded debt—that was far beyond the earning capacity of the property. In many cities, long before the advent of competition from the automobile, transit firms were in serious financial shape. Many such firms, their fares limited to a nickel by the franchise to operate in the public streets, went bankrupt when caught by the skyrocketing inflation of the First World War. This, despite rapidly increasing patronage as the nation geared itself for conflict.[4]

The situation changed as the twentieth century progressed and the plague of financial chicanery receded somewhat. The flavor of the mass transit industry changed in the first two decades of the twentieth century to one that was typified by a combination of transit operations and public utility service. When the street railway companies were electrified, many of them had excess electrical generating capacity; they sold some of this power to industrial and private users. Over time the electrical generating arm of what had originally been mainly a transit firm became larger and more profitable than the transit operation. By about 1920, electric utilities frequently had transit subsidiaries, rather than the other way around. Public utility holding companies were formed and began to expand in order to exploit the national thirst for electric power. Transit firms were usually gathered up as a part of the package. The success and continued growth of the electrical generating side of the combined transit-electrical utility made possible, in many cases, cross-subsidization of mass transportation services by the parent company. This cross-subsidy included not only a money subsidy from the power side to the transit side for capital improvements, but also a subsidy in the form of management talent. As the big utility firms grew larger, they could bid for the best executive talent, and some of the talent could be devoted to the mass transportation services. After the competition of the automobile made itself felt in the mid-1920's, and transit patronage began to decline, the industry needed all the talent it could get.[5]

In the '30's, in large part thanks to the financial shenanigans of utilities magnate Samuel Insull, the split-off of the transit industry from the public utility industry was begun under the Holding Company Act. Because the transit industry had already begun its decline, this necessity was not always viewed with gloom by the utilities. The spin-off tended to weaken seriously the newly independent transit firms. First of all, of course, there was no subsidy in the form of cash from the parent electrical utility to the transport undertaking; a source of ready internal capital thus dried up. The independent transit operation, standing alone, might have real trouble attracting funds in the capital market. In the darkness of the Depression, capital from any source was very hard to come by, and physical deterioration of the transit properties became serious. Secondly, and perhaps with more lasting and disastrous impact, the management subsidy which the utility companies had provided was pulled away. Indeed, at the time of divestiture the sharper transit managers were often taken up into the bosom of the public utility electrical generating firm, while the transit firms themselves were left with second best. Moreover, since transit is a local business, the opportunities for advancement are limited, especially in smaller cities. Talented transit management personnel tended to gravitate to the larger cities. Despite a lack of data to prove the point, the fact that the transit industry has been on a declining course for a half-century means that many talented individuals who might have made a significant contribution to quality management, and given the industry an infusion of fresh ideas, have sought careers elsewhere. There *are* talented transit management personnel, but they are not numerous and they are most likely to be concentrated in the larger urban places.

A new wrinkle in the transit industry developed during the '30's, as transit holding companies began to form. General Motors, seeing an economic opportunity for the wholesale replacement of the streetcar by the motor bus, through its subsidiary The Omnibus Corporation, entered into control of a good many of the formerly independent transit properties. General Motors, along with other equipment manufacturers and suppliers, was also behind National

City Lines, the largest of the transit holding companies as regards number of properties.[6]

Regardless of who the owners were, the transit holding companies apparently had as their major objective the profit potential of supplying buses and other equipment to their properties in the switchover from streetcar to bus operation. Certainly, in the 1930's there was still the chance of profitable operations for some years to come, but it is probably accurate to say that most of these firms were less interested in serving the public and building patronage as a means of profit than of making profit from sales of equipment and supplies.

In the postwar era it appeared that almost everybody—especially customers—had bailed out on the transit industry. There were declines across the board in patronage, which were soon reflected in declining revenues and earnings. For a long time it was difficult to find anybody who was really interested in taking effective action to ameliorate the situation. Stockholders did not seem to care to make improvements that would boost patronage and earnings; they were busy trying to get out of the transit business. Much of management effort was spent in cutting back service in order to shave costs while at the same time increasing fares. The regulators on the state level were not and are not now geared to the job of transit improvement even if they cared much about mass transportation. Besides, the regulatory rubric was based on public oversight of a monopoly; growing automobile ownership made such a concept totally irrelevant. In general, most U. S. cities appeared to be indifferent to the plight of the transit companies—not too surprising in that transit in the United States has traditionally been a private enterprise operating as a regulated monopoly. Usually the position of the city vis-à-vis the transit property operating within it was one of antagonism with mutual recrimination at times of service change or fare increase. To the local politician, savaging his city's transit firm was usually good sport and, in the short-term, good politics. The influential voting element of a city bought more cars and wanted something to operate them upon, so the politicos pushed for highways; constructive plans for mass transportation, or pleas for help, were ignored.

Most cities remained indifferent until their transit systems went broke. Many of the small and medium-sized cities continued to remain indifferent and, for this reason, over two hundred transit firms disappeared from the scene during the '50's and early '60's. In places where public pressure demanded continuation of service, the cities were not quite so indifferent, especially when they ended up inheriting a bankrupt transit property. As the '60's proceeded, public ownership became the only way most cities could continue to retain any sort of transit service. Another important factor in increasing the level of interest was, of course, the availability of federal money for mass transportation purposes.

While it is fair to say that in the 1970's many cities are far more directly interested in improving the quality of urban mass transportation than ever before, transit still provides a good whipping boy for politicians. A mayor wishing to find a scapegoat can always use the supposed ineptitude of the transit management as a place to deflect public attention. Newspapers looking for something to fill up the front page can usually find some lacklustre activity of the transit operator in the nearby vicinity to pounce upon. All this means that on the local level transit is likely to be observed with less objectivity than is desirable.

In any event, the complexion of the transit industry began to change markedly in the postwar era. As patronage plummeted, the possibility of profit from operations became to a large extent a forlorn hope. Even the lucrative possibilities of furnishing equipment and supplies began to erode as the changeover from streetcars to buses became almost complete. Declining patronage and revenues in the face of rising costs meant that the market for new buses was very small indeed after the spate of new equipment purchases for renewal and replacement in the immediate postwar period. The transit holding companies began to withdraw from the ownership and operation of mass transportation services and turn their attention to greener pastures.

One innovation that has grown increasingly popular in the transit industry is the transit management company. Usually based on one of the former holding companies, the management company will operate a transit property for a city at a fee. Often an incentive clause is built into the contract to encourage the management firm to boost patronage and/or revenues. It is too early to state definitely what the impact of such firms will be, but some of them have brought considerable skill to their work. Moreover, cities that have hired such firms have often made a strong commitment for transit improvement, aided, of course, by capital inputs from federal—and sometimes state—sources, and often with support from special local taxes. Many other cities have chosen to operate transit themselves or through some other governmental device, and have eschewed the services of a management firm.[7]

In this brief overview of the transit industry, it is obvious that management really didn't know what to do about the industry decline except to continue to utilize the old "reliable" ploys of a monopoly. All of the tradition of the industry pointed to such behavior. The apparently witless increases in fare and decreases in service, as a way of improving financial position, are not unintelligent actions from the viewpoint of a monopoly that faces a relatively large and inelastic demand for its services. While it seems whimsical and almost quaint today, thanks to 20-20 hindsight, there was a strong belief twenty years ago that one could pretty well hold all passengers if one reduced service from, say, a bus every ten minutes to a bus every twenty minutes. It was assumed, as monopolists—even mistaken ones—will assume, that half of the people using the dropped service would take an earlier bus and half would take a later bus. In reality, since the private auto spelled the end of anything resembling a transit monopoly, the reduction in service meant only that all the buses carried fewer people.

It is not unjust to say that any outside "help" except for money has certainly not been welcome by the transit industry. Any criticism, however relevant, was generally scorned. People trying to study the industry were often either discouraged or insulted. As with most industries in decline, transit turned inward. The meetings of most transit associations are often nothing much but a large-scale chewing of each other's cuds (not unlike the annual professional meetings of academics!). A golf tournament is often the big item. It is fair to say that the transit industry has been going to hell on a handcar but the handcar has been upholstered so that the trip is pleasant. On the brighter side, the recent increase in public and governmental interest in mass transportation is improving the quality of of the proceedings, especially since 1966.

The point of this discussion is that transit management is a vital link in providing improved transit service and in fostering a more substantial role for transit in cities in the United States. Unfortunately, this link is a relatively weak one. Unless it is strengthened—and there is, lamentably, little in the transit industry tradition to suggest that it will be bolstered very quickly—there is small chance that the transit situation will really improve very rapidly.[8]

Structure and Vital Statistics

Those who identify the transit industry with the bus business are not far from wrong. As of 1972, the transit industry was composed of 1,045 firms. Of these 1,028 operated buses exclusively; only 15 operated rail or trolley coach vehicles in addition to buses. Some 769 of these transit systems were located in cities of under 50,000 population or were classified as suburban operations, a fair indication that the industry is made up of a large number of small firms along with about 30 very large undertakings, and about 250 medium-sized firms.

The publicly owned portion of the industry is by far the most important. Although accounting for only 160 of the operating transit systems in 1972—or 15 per cent of the industry total—the publicly owned firms gathered in 85 per cent of the industry revenue; operated 73 per cent of the vehicle-miles; hauled 86 per cent of the passengers; hired 86 per cent of the transit employees; and owned 70 per cent of the passenger vehicles, including 63 per cent of the buses, 100 per cent of the rapid transit equipment, 96 per cent of the streetcars, and 100 per cent of the trolley coaches.[9]

The impact of the public sector in transit in 1972 is in marked contrast to the industry as recently as 1948. At that time there were only 36 public systems, accounting for only about 25 per cent of the operating revenues for the industry. Of major cities only Seattle, Detroit, New York, Chicago, Boston, San Francisco, and Cleveland had publicly owned properties.[10] This movement toward public ownership has, of course, come as a matter of necessity and has caused relatively little fuss of a doctrinaire kind. At one time, in the first two decades of this century, the issue of public ownership of transit would have initiated a battle of ferocious headlines, usually couched in terms of free-enterprise capitalism pitted against socialism. When it became clear that the only way to preserve transit is public ownership, and federal money was available to acquire the typically sagging private firm, often the only controversial issue on the local scene was the form of the public ownership and the source of local funds to support transit. In any case, the move toward public ownership has also meant a substantial influx of subsidy money to mass transit, mostly—though not exclusively—to public systems. American Transit Association figures for 1971 show that $528,836,905 was provided to mass transit for capital improvement purposes by federal, state, county, transit district, and city sources. In the same year funds to subsidize operating expense from the same sources totaled $238,131,875. School fare and senior citizen fare reimbursement to transit was $52,409,967. The total transit subsidy in 1971 was $819,378,747.[11]

The decline in patronage is perhaps the most glaring statistic of the industry. The accompanying tables and charts show the decline in transit since 1950. Tables 3-1 through 3-4 present figures on patronage, employment, revenues, mileage operated, equipment owned, et cetera, with 1950 used as the base year and an index number derived for each subsequent year. These indices are then utilized in the construction of the graphs shown in Figures 3-2 through 3-5. The base year chosen was 1950 because by that time the widespread and intensive use of transit that was artifically induced by wartime restrictions on gasoline, tires, and new cars, may be considered to have withered away.

Reviewing the statistics shown in the tables and looking at the graphic presentation shown in the figures, there is no doubt that transit usage has plummeted since 1950; bad as that is, the situation would look far worse, of course, if the all-time peak year of 1946 had been used as a base year. In any case, as shown in Figure 3–2, the decline in transit patronage was particularly sharp in the 1950's. Indeed, between 1950 and 1955, as seen in Table 3–1, the transit industry lost a third of its patrons. This fall in ridership leveled off somewhat in the early 1960's after an especially sharp decline of 512 million annual patrons in 1961 as compared with 1960. For reasons that are obscure (but often related to the federal interest in mass transportation that began in 1961 and the concurrent rise in public takeover of properties at about the same time), annual losses in patronage were relatively modest through 1969. Indeed, 1967 showed an annual increase of 89 million total annual passengers over 1966, bringing some hope that the trend in transit patronage had turned a corner. (The definite cause of the patronage increase is unknown; one reason might be that high levels of employment in that year brought many persons into the labor market who did not own automobiles. Another possibility is that patronage was below

**Figure 3–2   Urban Mass Transportation: Total Patronage; Operating
Revenue; Operating Expenses Including Depreciation; Net Revenue;
Operating Revenue; Average Operating Expense per Passenger,
1950–1971**

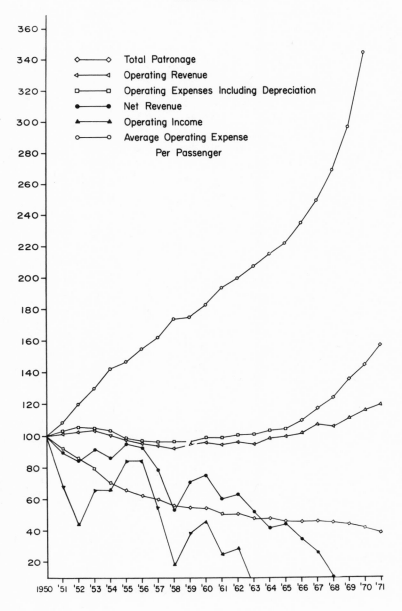

Figure 3–3   Urban Mass Transportation: Total Patronage; Average Number of Employees; Total Payroll; Average Annual Earnings per Employee; Average Passengers per Employee; Average Cost Per Passenger per Employee, 1950–1971

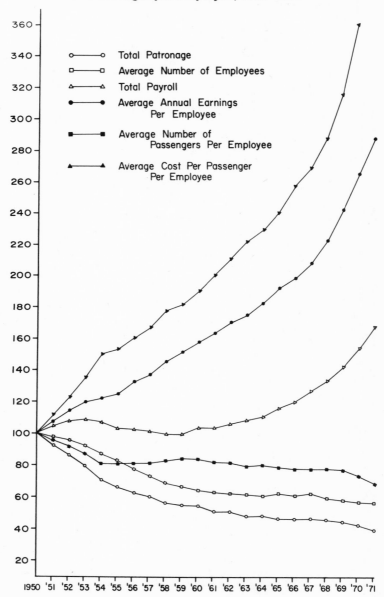

Figure 3–4   Urban Mass Transportation: Patronage of Rapid Transit by Population Size of Urban Area, 1950–1971

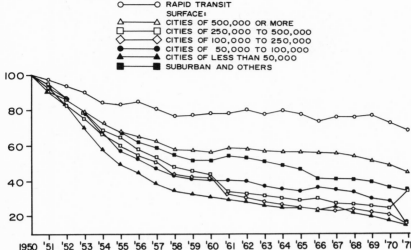

its "normal" rate of decline in 1966 because of a lengthy transit strike in New York.)

Unfortunately, the bottom really fell out of things in 1970, when 471,000,000 fewer patrons used transit than had done so in 1969. If that wasn't bad enough, the year 1971 was even more of a disaster, as 485,000,000 fewer patrons presented themselves as transit customers than had done so in 1970. The year 1972 was not quite so bad, as total ridership was down only 280 million annual patrons from 6.847 billion to 6.567 billion patrons. The annual losses of better than 5 per cent are the highest since the late 1950's.

There is some reason to believe that the decline in transit patronage may be nearing its end. Preliminary statistics gathered by the American Transit Association for 1973 show relatively modest losses over-all, and some cities such as Atlanta and San Diego are showing marked increases in patronage, immediately traceable to significant cuts in fares. Perhaps, too, there have been enough service and equipment improvements spread throughout the country to improve the quality of transit enough to slow passenger defection to

TABLE 3-1

Urban Mass Transit: Total Patronage; Operating Revenue; Operating Expense, including Depreciation; Net Revenue; Operating Income; and Average Operating Expense Per Passenger, 1950–1972

Year	Passengers	Index	Total Passenger Revenue	Index	Operating Revenue	Index	Operating Expense including Depreciation	Index
1950	17,246	100.00	$1,386.8	100.00	$1,452.1	100.00	$1,296.6	100.00
1951	16,125	93.49	1,411.6	101.78	1,472.7	101.41	1,331.2	102.66
1952	15,119	87.66	1,438.1	103.69	1,501.3	103.38	1,369.5	105.61
1953	13,902	80.60	1,448.6	104.45	1,513.1	104.20	1,370.7	105.70
1954	13,392	71.85	1,410.0	101.67	1,471.8	101.35	1,337.2	103.12
1955	11,529	66.85	1,358.9	97.98	1,426.4	98.23	1,277.3	98.51
1956	10,941	63.44	1,351.1	97.42	1,416.1	97.52	1,271.3	98.04
1957	10,389	60.24	1,319.8	95.16	1,385.6	95.42	1,261.5	97.29
1958	9,732	56.43	1,282.2	92.45	1,349.5	92.93	1,265.8	97.62
1959	9,557	55.41	1,308.3	94.33	1,376.4	94.78	1,266.0	97.63
1960	9,395	54.47	1,334.9	96.25	1,407.2	96.90	1,289.8	99.47
1961	8,883	51.50	1,320.9	95.24	1,389.7	95.70	1,295.7	99.92
1962	8,695	50.41	1,330.2	95.91	1,403.5	96.65	1,306.0	100.71
1963	8,400	48.70	1,316.3	94.91	1,390.6	95.76	1,312.5	101.22
1964	8,328	48.28	1,326.0	95.61	1,408.1	96.96	1,342.5	103.53
1965	8,253	47.85	1,340.1	96.63	1,443.8	99.42	1,373.7	105.94
1966	8,083	46.86	1,385.4	99.89	1,478.5	101.81	1,423.7	109.79
1967	8,172	47.38	1,457.4	105.09	1,556.0	107.15	1,530.8	118.05
1968	8,019	46.94	1,470.2	106.01	1,562.7	107.61	1,625.3	125.34
1969	7,803	45.24	1,554.7	112.10	1,625.6	111.95	1,744.9	134.57
1970	7,332	42.51	1,639.1	118.19	1,707.4	117.58	1,891.7	145.89
1971	6,847	39.71	1,661.9	119.83	1,740.7	119.87	2,040.4	157.35
1972	6,567	38.07	1,650.7	119.03	1,728.5	119.03	2,128.2	164.14

146

TABLE 3-1 (continued)

Year	Net Revenue	Index	Operating Income	Index	Average Operating Expense/ Passenger	Index
1950	$155,410	100.00	$ 66,370	100.00	.075	100.0
1951	141,430	91.00	46,090	'69.44	.082	109.3
1952	131,740	84.76	29,750	44.82	.090	120.2
1953	142,400	91.62	45,050	67.87	.098	130.6
1954	134,540	86.57	44,840	67.56	.107	142.6
1955	149,030	95.89	55,710	83.93	.110	146.6
1956	144,740	93.13	55,690	83.90	.116	154.6
1957	124,040	79.81	36,610	55.16	.121	161.3
1958	83,650	53.82	6,590	9.92	.130	173.3
1959	110,320	70.98	25,620	38.60	.132	176.0
1960	117,350	75.50	30,690	46.24	.137	182.6
1961	93,930	60.44	16,730	25.20	.145	193.3
1962	97,500	62.73	19,700	29.68	.150	200.0
1963	78,040	50.21	(D) 880	−1.33	.156	208.0
1964	65,520	42.15	(D) 12,390	−18.67	.161	214.6
1965	70,040	45.06	(D) 10,610	−15.99	.166	221.3
1966	54,740	35.22	(D) 37,030	−55.79	.176	234.6
1967	25,136	16.17	(D) 66,568	−100.30	.187	249.3
1968	(D) 62,525	− 40.23	(D)161,072	−242.69	.202	269.3
1969	(D)119,356	− 76.80	(D)220,512	−332.25	.223	297.3
1970	(D)184,325	−118.61	(D)288,212	−434.25	.258	344.0
1971	(D)299,753	−192.88	(D)411,400	−619.86	.298	397.3
1972	(D)399,693	−257.19	(D)513,126	−773.13	.324	432.0

Source: Adapted from American Transit Association *Transit Fact Books*, 1966 through 1972

147

TABLE 3-2

Urban Mass Transportation: Total Patronage; Average Number of Employees; Total Payroll; Average Annual Earnings per Employee; Average Number of Passengers per Employee; Average Cost per Passenger per Employee, 1950–1971

Year	Total Patronage	Index	Average Number of Employees	Index	Total Payroll	Index
1950	17,246	100.00	240,000	100.00	$ 835,000,000	100.00
1951	16,125	93.49	232,000	96.66	872,000,000	104.43
1952	15,119	87.66	227,000	94.58	903,000,000	108.14
1953	13,902	80.60	220,000	91.66	913,000,000	109.34
1954	13,392	71.85	211,000	87.91	895,000,000	107.18
1955	11,529	66.85	198,000	82.50	864,000,000	103.47
1956	10,941	63.44	186,000	77.50	852,000,000	102.03
1957	10,389	60.24	177,000	73.75	840,000,000	100.59
1958	9,732	56.43	165,000	68.75	831,000,000	99.52
1959	9,557	55.41	159,000	66.29	832,000,000	99.64
1960	9,395	54.47	156,400	65.16	857,300,000	102.67
1961	8,883	51.50	151,800	63.25	856,400,000	102.56
1962	8,695	50.41	149,100	62.12	878,100,000	105.16
1963	8,400	48.70	147,200	61.33	892,300,000	106.86
1964	8,328	48.28	144,800	60.33	916,900,000	109.80
1965	8,253	47.85	145,000	60.41	963,500,000	115.38
1966	8,083	46.86	144,300	60.12	994,900,000	119.14
1967	8,172	47.38	146,100	60.87	1,055,100,000	126.30
1968	8,019	46.94	143,590	59.82	1,109,500,000	132.80
1969	7,803	45.24	140,860	58.69	1,183,807,000	141.70
1970	7,332	42.51	138,040	57.51	1,274,109,000	152.50
1971	6,847	39.71	139,120	57.96	1,393,148,000	166.84
1972	6,567	38.07	138,420	57.67	1,455,486,000	174.30

148

TABLE 3-2 (continued)

Year	Average Annual Earnings/ Employee	Index	Average Number of Passengers/ Employee	Index	Average Cost/ Passenger/ Employee	Index
1950	$ 3,479	100.00	71,858	100.0	.048	100.0
1951	3,760	108.07	69,504	96.7	.054	112.5
1952	3,978	114.34	66,603	92.6	.059	122.9
1953	4,150	119.28	63,190	87.9	.065	135.4
1954	4,242	121.93	58,729	81.7	.072	150.0
1955	4,304	125.43	58,227	81.0	.074	154.1
1956	4,581	131.67	58,822	81.8	.077	160.4
1957	4,746	136.41	58,694	81.6	.080	166.6
1958	5,036	144.75	58,981	82.0	.085	177.0
1959	5,229	150.30	60,106	83.6	.087	181.2
1960	5,481	157.40	60,070	83.5	.091	189.5
1961	4,642	162.17	58,517	81.4	.096	200.0
1962	5,889	169.27	58,316	81.1	.101	210.4
1963	6,062	174.24	57,065	79.4	.106	220.8
1964	6,332	182.00	57,513	80.0	.110	229.1
1965	6,645	191.00	56,917	79.2	.116	241.6
1966	6,845	198.18	56,015	77.9	.123	256.2
1967	7,222	207.58	55,934	77.8	.129	268.7
1968	7,727	222.10	55,846	77.7	.138	287.5
1969	8,404	241.56	55,395	77.0	.151	314.5
1970	9,230	265.30	53,115	73.9	.173	360.4
1971	10,014	287.84	49,216	68.4	.203	422.9
1972	10,515	302.24	47,442	66.0	.221	460.4

Source: Adapted from American Transit Association *Transit Fact Books*, 1966 through 1972.

TABLE 3-3
Urban Mass Transportation: Patronage of Rapid Transit by Population Size of Urban Area, 1950–1971

Year	Total Revenue Passengers	Index	Rapid Transit Passengers (in millions)	Index	Proportion of Total Revenue Passengers	Surface Lines 500,000 Population and Over (in millions)	Index	Proportion of Total Revenue Passengers
1950	13,845	100.00	2,113	100.00	15.26	5,207	100.00	37.60
1951	12,881	93.04	2,041	96.59	15.84	4,739	91.01	36.79
1952	12,022	86.83	1,982	93.80	16.48	4,448	85.42	36.49
1953	11,036	79.71	1,903	90.06	17.24	4,102	78.77	37.16
1954	9,858	71.20	1,781	84.28	18.06	3,694	70.94	37.47
1955	9,189	66.37	1,741	82.39	18.94	3,478	66.79	37.84
1956	8,756	63.24	1,749	82.77	19.97	3,368	64.68	38.46
1957	8,338	60.22	1,706	80.73	20.46	3,274	62.87	39.26
1958	7,778	56.17	1,635	77.37	21.02	3,095	59.43	39.79
1959	7,650	55.25	1,647	77.94	21.52	3,057	58.70	39.96
1960	7,521	54.32	1,670	79.03	22.20	2,997	57.55	39.84
1961	7,242	52.30	1,680	79.50	23.19	3,089	59.32	42.65
1962	7,122	51.44	1,704	80.64	23.92	3,029	58.17	42.53
1963	6,915	44.94	1,661	78.60	24.02	2,990	57.42	43.23
1964	6,854	49.50	1,698	80.35	24.77	2,991	57.44	43.63
1965	6,798	49.10	1,678	79.41	24.68	3,000	57.61	44.13
1966	6,671	48.18	1,584	74.96	23.74	3,003	57.67	45.01
1967	6,616	47.78	1,632	77.23	24.66	2,945	56.55	44.51
1968	6,491	46.88	1,627	76.99	25.06	2,886	55.42	44.46
1969	6,310	45.57	1,656	78.37	26.24	2,787	53.52	44.16
1970	5,932	42.84	1,574	74.49	26.53	2,610	50.12	43.99
1971	5,497	39.70	1,494	70.70	27.17	2,399	46.07	43.64
1972	5,271	38.07	1,454	68.81	27.58	2,335	44.84	

TABLE 3-3 (continued)

Year	Rapid Transit and Surface Lines in Cities of 500,000 Population and Over (in millions)	Index	Proportion of Total Revenue Passengers	Surface Lines 250-500,000 Population (in millions)	Index	Proportion of Total Revenue Passengers	Surface Lines 100-250,000 Population (in millions)	Index	Proportion of Total Revenue Passengers
1950	7,320	100.00	52.87	2,007	100.00	14.49	1,585	100.00	11.44
1951	6,780	92.62	52.63	1,893	94.31	14.69	1,476	93.12	11.45
1952	6,430	87.84	53.48	1,745	86.94	14.51	1,322	83.40	10.99
1953	6,005	82.03	54.41	1,580	78.72	14.31	1,210	76.94	10.96
1954	5,475	74.79	55.53	1,400	69.75	14.20	1,053	66.43	10.68
1955	5,219	71.29	56.79	1,286	64.07	13.99	953	60.12	10.37
1956	5,117	69.90	58.43	1,179	58.74	13.46	866	54.63	9.89
1957	4,980	68.03	59.72	1,078	53.71	12.92	811	51.16	9.72
1958	4,730	64.61	60.81	984	49.02	12.65	720	45.42	9.25
1959	4,704	64.26	61.49	956	47.63	12.49	696	43.91	9.09
1960	4,667	63.75	62.05	911	45.39	12.11	691	43.59	9.18
1961	4,769	65.15	65.85	701	34.92	9.67	523	32.99	7.22
1962	4,733	64.65	66.45	680	33.88	9.54	496	31.29	6.96
1963	4,651	63.53	67.25	642	31.98	9.28	462	29.14	6.68
1964	4,689	64.05	68.41	612	30.49	8.92	432	27.25	6.30
1965	4,678	63.90	68.81	606	30.19	8.91	416	26.24	6.11
1966	4,587	62.66	68.76	608	30.29	9.11	413	26.05	6.19
1967	4,577	62.52	69.18	597	29.74	9.02	409	25.80	6.18
1968	4,513	61.65	69.52	581	28.95	8.95	396	24.98	6.10
1969	4,443	60.69	70.41	565	28.15	8.95	365	23.02	5.78
1970	4,184	57.15	70.53	529	26.35	8.91	342	21.57	5.76
1971	3,893	53.18	70.82	739	36.82	13.44	234	14.76	4.25
1972	3,789	51.76	71.88	685	34.13	12.99	220	13.88	4.17

TABLE 3-3 (continued)
Urban Mass Transportation: Patronage of Rapid Transit by Population Size of Urban Area, 1950–1971

Year	Surface Lines: 50-100,000 Population (in millions)	Index	Proportion of Total Revenue Passengers	Surface Lines Less Than 50,000 Population (in millions)	Index	Proportion of Total Revenue Passengers	Suburban and Other Carriers (in millions)	Index	Proportion of Total Revenue Passengers
1950	1,323	100.00	9.55	778	100.00	5.25	882	100.00	6.37
1951	1,235	93.34	9.58	667	91.62	5.17	830	94.10	6.44
1952	1,161	87.75	9.65	602	82.69	5.00	762	86.39	6.33
1953	1,038	78.45	9.40	509	69.91	4.61	694	78.68	6.28
1954	899	67.95	9.11	411	56.45	4.16	620	70.29	6.28
1955	786	59.41	8.55	360	49.45	3.91	585	66.32	6.36
1956	715	54.04	8.16	324	44.50	3.70	555	62.92	6.33
1957	655	49.50	7.85	285	39.14	3.41	529	59.97	6.34
1958	596	45.04	7.66	254	34.89	3.26	494	56.00	6.35
1959	582	43.99	7.60	240	32.96	3.13	472	53.51	6.16
1960	554	41.87	7.36	230	31.59	3.05	468	53.06	6.22
1961	554	41.87	7.64	217	29.80	2.99	478	54.19	6.60
1962	533	40.28	7.48	212	29.12	2.97	468	53.06	6.57
1963	504	38.09	7.28	205	28.15	2.96	451	51.13	6.52
1964	486	36.73	7.09	194	26.64	2.83	441	50.00	6.43
1965	474	35.82	6.97	192	26.37	2.82	432	48.97	6.35
1966	483	36.50	7.24	194	26.64	2.90	386	43.76	5.78
1967	469	35.44	7.08	190	26.09	2.87	374	42.40	5.65
1968	455	34.39	7.00	171	23.48	2.63	375	42.51	5.77
1969	422	31.89	6.68	150	20.60	2.37	365	41.38	5.78
1970	395	29.85	6.65	140	19.23	2.36	342	38.77	5.76
1971	196	14.81	3.56	107	14.69	1.94	328	37.18	5.96
1972	182	13.75	3.45	96	13.18	1.82	299	33.90	5.67

Source: Adapted from American Transit Association, *Transit Fact Books*, 1966 through 1972.

Figure 3–5   Urban Mass Transportation: Total Patronage; Mileage of Various Mass Transit Modes; Total Units of Equipment; Vehicle Miles Per Route Mile; Total New Equipment Delivered, 1950–1970

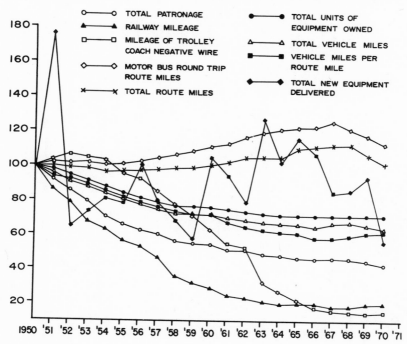

a trickle. New patronage has undoubtedly been attracted in some instances.[12]

It should be noted that the decline has not been uniform throughout the industry. As Table 3–3 and Figure 3–4 show, rapid transit ridership has declined only about 30 per cent since 1950, and surface transit ridership in cities of 500,000 population and over has fallen off by only a little more than half. This is in sharp contrast with that part of the industry located in medium and smaller cities, where ridership has fallen to a third or less of what it was in the base year.[13] Table 3–3 also shows that patronage of transit has come to be more and more concentrated in the largest urban places. The proportion of total revenue passengers moved by rapid transit—

TABLE 3-4
Urban Mass Transportation: Total Patronage
Mileage of Various Mass Transit Modes
Total Units of Equipment
Vehicle Miles per Route Mile
Total New Equipment Delivered, 1950–1970

Year	Total Passengers (in millions)	Index	Miles of Railway Track	Index	Miles of Trolley Coach Negative Wire	Index
1950	17,246	100.0	10,813	100.0	3,513	100.0
1951	16,125	93.49	9,457	87.45	3,678	104.69
1952	15,119	87.66	8,532	78.90	3,736	106.34
1953	13,902	80.60	7,352	67.99	3,663	104.26
1954	12,392	71.85	6,765	62.56	3,630	103.33
1955	11,529	66.85	6,197	57.31	3,428	97.58
1956	10,941	63.44	5,746	53.13	3,293	93.73
1957	10,389	60.24	5,019	46.41	3,007	85.59
1958	9,732	56.43	3,844	35.54	2,723	77.51
1959	9,557	55.41	3,445	31.85	2,491	70.90
1960	9,395	54.47	3,143	29.06	2,196	62.51
1961	8,883	51.50	2,601	24.05	2,017	57.41
1962	8,695	50.41	2,557	23.64	1,849	52.63
1963	8,400	48.70	2,236	20.67	1,119	31.85
1964	8,328	48.28	2,173	20.09	986	28.06
1965	8,253	47.85	2,173	20.09	766	21.80
1966	8,083	46.86	2,153	19.91	676	19.24
1967	8,172	47.38	2,049	18.94	616	17.53
1968	8,019	46.94	2,045	18.91	616	17.53
1969	7,803	45.24	2,081	19.24	563	16.02
1970	7,332	42.51	2,081	19.24	563	16.02
1971	6,847	39.71				
1972	6,567	38.07				

154

TABLE 3-4 (continued)

Year	Motor Bus Round Trip Route Miles	Index	Total Miles Operated	Index	Total Units of Equipment Owned	Index
1950	98,000	100.0	112,326	100.0	86,310	100.0
1951	99,700	101.73	112,835	100.45	85,335	98.87
1952	99,600	101.63	111,868	99.59	82,336	95.39
1953	100,000	102.04	110,955	98.77	78,875	91.38
1954	99,000	101.02	109,395	97.39	76,198	88.28
1955	99,800	101.83	109,425	97.41	73,084	84.68
1956	100,700	102.75	109,739	97.69	70,373	81.53
1957	102,400	104.48	110,426	98.30	68,971	79.91
1958	104,500	106.63	111,067	98.87	67,149	77.79
1959	106,300	108.46	112,236	99.91	65,780	76.21
1960	108,700	110.91	114,039	101.52	65,292	75.64
1961	111,500	113.77	116,118	103.37	64,012	74.16
1962	114,300	116.63	118,706	105.67	63,045	73.04
1963	117,400	119.74	120,755	107.50	62,189	72.05
1964	118,300	120.71	121,459	108.13	61,674	71.46
1965	120,900	123.36	123,839	110.24	61,717	71.50
1966	122,100	124.59	124,929	111.22	62,136	71.99
1967	123,600	126.12	126,265	112.40	62,069	71.91
1968	121,000	123.46	123,661	110.09	61,930	71.75
1969	117,300	119.69	119,944	106.78	61,347	71.07
1970	112,700	115.00	115,344	102.68	61,350	71.08

155

TABLE 3-4 (continued)

Year	Total Vehicle Miles Operated (in millions)	Index	Vehicle Miles per Route Miles Miles	Index	Total New Equipment Delivered	Index
1950	3,007.6	100.0	26,775	100.0	3,050	100.0
1951	2,913.4	96.86	25,820	96.0	5,348	175.34
1952	2,814.5	93.57	25,159	93.96	1,992	65.31
1953	2,695.5	89.59	24,293	90.00	2,246	73.63
1954	2,548.8	84.74	23,299	87.01	2,485	81.47
1955	2,447.5	81.37	22,366	83.53	2,429	79.63
1956	2,366.6	78.68	21,565	80.54	3,135	102.78
1957	2,289.5	76.12	20,733	77.43	2,415	79.18
1958	2,201.0	73.18	19,816	74.01	2,126	69.70
1959	2,158.9	71.78	19,235	71.83	1,747	57.27
1960	2,142.8	71.24	18,790	70.17	3,222	105.63
1961	2,077.1	69.06	17,887	66.80	2,883	94.52
1962	2,047.4	68.07	17,247	64.41	2,406	78.88
1963	2,021.7	67.21	16,742	62.52	3,858	126.49
1964	2,015.8	67.07	16,596	61.98	3,140	102.95
1965	2,008.2	66.77	16,216	60.56	3,580	117.37
1966	1,983.6	65.95	15,877	59.29	3,279	107.50
1967	1,996.8	66.39	15,814	59.06	2,585	84.75
1968	1,988.7	66.12	16,081	60.06	2,612	85.63
1969	1,966.7	65.39	16,396	61.23	2,880	94.42
1970	1,883.1	62.61	16,375	60.97	1,750	57.37
1971	1,846.3	61.38			2,764	90.62
1972	1,755.6	58.37			3,544	116.19

Source: Adapted from American Transit Association, *Transit Fact Books*, 1966 through 1972.

156

found only in large cities—rose steadily from a little more than 15 per cent in 1950 to better than 27.5 per cent in 1972; the proportion of surface line patrons in cities of 500,000 population and over rose from 37.6 per cent to 44.2 per cent of total revenue passengers between 1950 and 1972, having been at a high proportion of 45 per cent in 1966. Considering rapid transit together with surface lines in cities of over 500,000 population, the proportion of total revenue patronage in large cities rose from 52.87 per cent in 1950 to 71.88 per cent in 1972.

Figure 3–1 shows, in addition to the substantial falloff in ridership, the plunge and final disappearance of profitable operations on an industrywide basis. The growth in industry revenues, due entirely to fare increases, has simply not kept pace with the increase in expenses, especially as inflation mounted in the late '60's. The particularly sharp drops in patronage in 1970 and 1971 prevented revenues from keeping the same pace of increase as costs, despite fare increases. Over the entire period under discussion, the average operating expense per passenger has skyrocketed. Indeed, it increased almost four times since 1950; these costs doubled between 1950 and 1962 and doubled again by 1972. Worse yet, in 1970 and 1971 these expenses were increasing at a rate of better than 15 per cent per year.

Figure 3–3, which deals with statistics regarding labor, shows much of the reason for the sharp rise in cost. Except for rapid transit, the mass transit industry is labor intensive. That means that the lion's share of cost is labor cost—no great problem if labor productivity increases at the same or a faster rate than labor cost. Figure 3–3 shows that the average number of employees fell off at about the same rate as patronage, but total payroll costs, despite the cutback in the number of employees, have risen substantially in the same period, as the average annual wage per employee has risen steadily. A crude measure of employee productivity is shown in the average number of passengers moved per annum per employee. By this measure, productivity fell sharply in the early '50's and then remained remarkably even until 1970—a factor related to the steady cutback in the number of employees during the decade of the 1960's. However, in 1970 and 1971, while the number of employees stayed about the same, the number of passengers dropped very sharply; as a result, productivity also plummeted. At the same time, wages rose more sharply than ever. With the falloff in patrons in the face of escalating labor costs, the average cost per passenger per employee jumped skyward in 1970, 1971, and 1972.[14]

All of which means that the worst of all possible situations confronts the transit industry. Because of the labor intensive nature of the business, falling patronage can only mean rising costs per passenger, which has inevitably meant increased fares and, subsequently, fewer passengers. The average fare per revenue passenger rose from 10.02 cents in 1950 to 31.32 cents in 1972.[15] The industry was not blind to the fact that increasing fares was no solution to its problems. It began a lobbying campaign for a fare stabilization program, based primarily on a proposed change in the Urban Mass Transportation Act to permit a federal operating subsidy. As noted in Chapter 1, this legislation had failed to pass the Congress up to the time of this writing.[16]

If things are bad on the patronage side, they are equally dismal financially. The transit industry as a whole has not shown an after-tax profit since 1962. In 1972 the industry had an estimated before-tax deficit of slightly under $400 million and an estimated $513 million after-tax deficit. The rapid escalation of the deficit has, of course, been the basis for the rate hikes. The cycle of rising deficits, increased fares, service cuts, and passenger erosion continues with a vengeance. Labor cost increases have contributed mightily to this dismaying picture; average employee earnings per annum rose from $5,642 in 1961 to $10,515 in 1972. While the average annual number of employees in the transit industry dropped from 151,800 in 1961 to 138,420 in 1972, the erosion in patronage caused each employee to be less productive. Using total patronage figures, each employee moved 58,530 patrons in 1961 and only 47,442 in 1972.

In Figure 3–5, some comparisons on route mileage and vehicle miles operated are given. The mileage of motor bus routes has risen since 1950; to some extent this has been at the expense of streetcar and trolleybus route miles, which have declined substantially. Typically, trolleybuses and streetcars have been replaced by buses. Overall, route mileage has increased rather steadily since 1950, as shown in Figure 3–5, but began to decline somewhat after 1967. Total vehicle miles fell about 20 per cent between 1950 and 1957 and then continued to decline rather slowly in subsequent years. Vehicle miles per route mile, a very rough—perhaps hopelessly rough—measure of the over-all quality of service, have fallen off steadily, indicating that the amount of service per mile of transit route is less than it was in 1950. This measure, of course, tells nothing about convenience, comfort, reliability, or any other important factor.

There is apparently no particular pattern to the delivery of new equipment, as shown by the wild fluctuation of the line in Figure 3–5. Most of the deliveries are, of course, new buses. For years this fleet has ranged around 50,000 units; even the availability of federal money for new coaches has not increased this number. This market is estimated to be about 2,500 coaches a year, more if decisive action programs are undertaken to stimulate transit use.[17] The market for rapid transit equipment will follow a similar pattern, except as new rapid transit lines are opened needing new fleets of equipment. It is not unlikely that the streetcar and trolleybus may make a significant comeback in the years to come, and there may be a number of new installations. For the moment, however, it appears that new equipment will be purchased primarily to replace existing equipment.[18]

Commuter Railroads

At first blush the difference between the services offered by commuter railroads and rail rapid transit or transit in general would seem to be slight. Superficially, commuter railroad service is limited in its coverage to only five cities in the United States: Boston, New York, Philadelphia, Chicago, and San Francisco. Minor rail commuter services are offered in Washington, D.C., and in Pittsburgh, but these are insignificant relative to the other five. The equipment used in commuter rail service is usually larger and heavier than rapid transit equipment, and very similar to regular rail passenger cars with the major difference usually found in a larger number of seats in the commuter cars. The typical commuter railroad passenger travels a bit farther than the average transit passenger, and the great majority of them are suburbanites or exurbanites, whose income levels are somewhat higher than for the typical transit user. Commuter railroads usually serve areas far beyond the reach of the typical urban mass transit system operation. Indeed, connecting separate outlying places, even though they may fall within the metropolitan area of a given city, is the norm for a railroad commuter service. For example, many persons in Trenton, New Jersey, commute to work in either Philadelphia or New York City. Some residents of Providence, Rhode Island, commute to work in Boston.

Apart from the superficial differences, there are some major institutional differences. Commuter railroad service is performed by companies that are not solely in the business of moving passengers, as is the case with "regular" mass transit firms. While the commuter service may be the most publicly visible activity of a given rail carrier, it is usually only a tiny fraction of the business it handles. Put another way, railroads are principally interested in hauling freight; commuters are a sideline.[19] In providing the service, railroad operating practices are followed and employees are members of the various railroad brotherhoods rather than of one of the unions representing mass transit workers. Railroads, typically, do not feel themselves to be a part of the mass transit industry, nor do they participate to a great extent in meetings of even rail-oriented transit organizations, such as the Institute for Rapid Transit. On the other hand, considerable support for mass transit legislation on the federal level has been provided by individual railroads and by the railroad industry as a whole.

Despite their obvious and institutional differences, rail commuter service shares one strong bond with the transit industry: it loses money. The financial loss for 1970 was estimated to be over $41 million.[20]

If data are far from perfect for transit, they are particularly difficult to corral for commuter railroad services, because the information is intermixed with figures for other railroad operations. While the railroads do report passengers riding on commutation and multiple-ride tickets—which one would assume is the typical pasteboard purchased by the regular commuter—many others using commuter trains pay regular fares, which are therefore not included in the commuter totals.[21]

Total commuter patronage varied somewhat over the period from 1960 to 1970, as shown in Table 3–5, but was, on the whole, remarkably stable. While commuter operations in New York, Boston, and San Francisco did lose patrons, the number of patrons utilizing commuter service in Chicago and Philadelphia rose considerably. The substantial increase in Philadelphia is attributable to the subsidized operations on the Penn Central and Reading Company commuter lines; the tab for this service is picked up by the Southeastern

TABLE 3-5
Commuter Rail Passengers By City
(annual passengers in millions)

City	1960	1961	1962	1963	1964	1965	1966	1967	1968	1969	1970
New York	142	140	134	131	129	126	126	127	128	127	128
Chicago	62	62	60	60	61	62	64	67	70	72	68
Philadelphia	24	24	24	26	27	28	29	31	33	33	35
Boston	13	11	11	13	12	11	12	11	11	11	11
San Francisco	7	7	7	7	7	7	7	7	7	6	6
TOTAL	248	244	236	237	236	234	238	243	249	249	248

Source: Table 7.6, p.7-14, *Economic Characteristics of the Urban Public Transportation Industry.*

Pennsylvania Transportation Authority. Improved services and relatively low fares have been the prime cause for the increase of 11 million passengers on an annual basis on the Philadelphia commuter service between 1960 and 1970. In Chicago, the high quality services offered by the Milwaukee Road, Burlington Northern Railroad, and particularly by the Chicago & Northwestern Railroad are largely responsible for the growth in commuter traffic. Rapid suburban growth in the Chicago metropolitan area is clearly another factor. Another element favorable to both the Milwaukee Road and the North Western was the demise, in 1963, of the Chicago, North Shore and Milwaukee, one of the last of the interurban electric railroads, which in its last three decades was primarily a Chicago-oriented commuter line. Some of the patrons using the North Shore Line switched over to the other paralleling commuter railroads.

Despite the large numbers of persons moved in given cities, commuter railroad service with a 1970 total of 248 million patrons is small in comparison with the 7.332 billion moved in that year by mass transit. Even so, the importance of such service cannot be discounted merely because the annual patronage is not in the billions. The last thing in the world New York, Boston, Philadelphia, Chicago, or San Francisco need is more cars entering—or trying to enter—their central business districts. Commuter rails provide attractive, nonautomotive access to downtown areas at relatively modest public cost compared to providing highway and parking capacity. In a very real sense, commuter railroads help maintain the economic and commercial attractiveness and vitality of the five cities served.

Tables 3–6 through 3–9 show the commuter patrons on a city-by-city basis with the traffic on each carrier shown individually.

TABLE 3-6
New York City Commuter Rail Passengers By Railroad
(annual passengers in millions)

	1960	1961	1962	1963	1964	1965	1966	1967	1968	1969	1970
Central of New Jersey	6	6	6	6	6	6	6	6	6	6	6
Erie Lackawanna	16	16	15	15	14	14	13	13	14	15	16
Long Island	69	68	66	64	63	61	62	63	63	61	61
New York, New Haven & Hartford/Penn Central	21	21	19	19	19	18	18	18	18	18	18
New York Central/ Penn Central	22	22	21	20	20	20	20	20	20	20	20
Pensylvania/ Penn Central	8	7	7	7	7	7	7	7	7	7	7
TOTAL	142	140	134	131	129	126	126	127	128	127	128

Source: *Economic Characteristics of the Urban Public Transportation Industry*, Table 7.7, p.7–14.

TABLE 3-7
Chicago Commuter Rail Passengers by Railroad
(annual passengers in millions)

Railroad	1960	1961	1962	1963	1964	1965	1966	1967	1968	1969	1970
Chicago, Burlington & Quincy	9	9	9	9	9	9	9	9	10	10	10
Chicago, Milwaukee, St. Paul & Pacific	4	4	4	5	5	5	5	6	6	6	6
Chicago North Western	18	19	19	20	21	21	23	24	25	26	25
Chicago, Rock Island, and Pacific	7	7	7	6	6	6	6	6	6	7	6
Chicago, South Shore & South Bend	4	4	3	3	3	3	3	3	3	3	3
Illinois Central	20	19	18	17	17	18	18	19	20	20	18
TOTAL	62	62	60	60	61	62	64	67	70	72	68

Source: *Economic Characteristics of the Urban Public Transportation Industry*, Table 7.8, p.7–16.

Since San Francisco commuter service is provided only by the Southern Pacific, the figures in Table 3–5 are relevant. Tables 3–10 through 3–15 show the trends in revenues and costs.[22]

TABLE 3-8
Philadelphia Commuter Rail Passengers by Railroad
(annual passengers in millions)

Railroad	1960	1961	1962	1963	1964	1965	1966	1967	1968	1969	1970
Pennsylvania/ Penn Central	14	14	14	15	16	17	18	18	20	20	21
Reading	10	10	10	11	11	11	11	13	13	13	14
TOTAL	24	24	24	26	27	28	29	31	33	33	35

Source: *Economic Characteristics of the Urban Public Transportation Industry*, Table 7.9, p.7-16.

TABLE 3-9
Boston Commuter Rail Passengers by Railroad
(annual passengers in millions)

Railroad	1960	1961	1962	1963	1964	1965	1966	1967	1968	1969	1970
Boston & Maine	7	6	6	8	7	6	7	6	6	6	6
New York, New Haven, & Hartford/Penn Central	5	4	4	4	4	4	4	4	4	4	4
New York Central/ Penn Central	1	1	1	1	1	1	1	1	1	1	1
TOTAL	13	11	11	13	12	11	12	11	11	11	11

Source: *Economic Characteristics of the Urban Public Transportation Industry*, Table 7.10, p.7-17.

Considerable money has been provided by the government since 1964 for replacement of commuter rail facilities and the purchase of new rolling stock. (See the tables for capital grants in Appendix 1.) There is no doubt that capital was badly needed for refurbishment and renewal, since not too many years ago one study showed that 3,188 of the 4,693 commuter cars in use by U. S. commuter railroads were over thirty years of age. That amounted to 68 per cent of the total! Even at the time of this writing, despite large investment in new commuter equipment, the former Pennsylvania Railroad portion of the Penn Central is operating commuter cars in the Philadelphia and New York areas that were originally built when William Howard Taft was president. Ancient equipment and decaying stations have not helped the commuter railroad image and are probably part of the explanation for the decline in patronage on some lines in some areas.[23] The problem of equipment overly long

TABLE 3-10
Summary of Commuter Railroad Operations, by Railroad, 1970
(in thousands)

Railroad	Income				Expenses				Net Income	Commuter Passengers	Commuter Passenger Miles
	Total	Commuter Passenger Revenue	Revenue From State & Local Government	Other Income	Total	Operating Expenses	Interest on Equipment Obligations	Depreciation			
Boston and Maine	9,373	5,260	4,113	0	9,353	8,747	16	590	20	5,556	91,951
Burlington Northern	6,275	6,227	0	48	7,005	5,872	162	971	-730	9,726	173,654
Central of New Jersey	8,675	4,166	4,409	100	9,291	8,392	648	251	-616	6,516	123,758
Chicago, Milwaukee, St. Paul, and Pacific	4,968	4,956	0	12	5,955	5,194	218	543	-987	5,954	134,261
Chicago North Western	21,149	21,036	0	113	19,237	15,196	1,280	2,761	1,912	25,046	523,966
Chicago, Rock Island, and Pacific	4,289	4,264	0	25	5,824	5,132	283	409	-1,535	6,197	99,697
Chicago, South Shore, and South Bend	3,441	3,442	0	-1	5,238	5,092	0	146	-1,797	2,682	81,058
Erie Lackawanna	16,572	10,872	5,000	700	19,025	19,025	0	*	-2,453	15,839	325,217
Illinois Central	11,025	11,006	0	19	11,315	10,870	0	445	-290	18,785	310,241
Long Island	85,189	85,189	0	0	108,523	103,250	0	5,273	-23,334	70,069	1,760,614
Pittsburgh and Lake Erie	97	55	0	42	626	599	0	27	-529	69	1,497
Reading Company	13,716	9,016	4,700	0	16,473	15,183	717	573	-2,757	13,699	195,405
Southern Pacific	4,124	4,001	0	123	6,777	5,767	156	854	-2,653	5,826	144,429
Staten Island Rapid Transit	3,640	1,077	2,549	14	3,640	3,504	45	91	0	4,657	39,022
TOTAL, 14 RAILROADS	192,533	170,567	20,771	1,195	228,282	211,823	3,525	12,934	-35,749	190,621	4,004,770

* Equipment is being retired and replaced by the State of New Jersey.

Source: *Economic Characteristics of the Urban Public Transportation Industry*, Table 7.1, p. 7-6.

TABLE 3-11
Selected Revenue and Cost Ratios, by Railroad, 1970
(in dollars)

Railroad	Passenger Revenue per Passenger	Operating Cost per Passenger	Passenger Revenue per Passenger-Mile	Operating Cost per Passenger-Mile
Boston and Maine	.95	1.57	.0572	.0951
Burlington Northern	.64	.60	.0358	.0338
Central of New Jersey	.64	1.29	.0336	.0678
Chicago, Milwaukee, St. Paul, and Pacific	.83	.87	.0369	.0386
Chicago North Western	.84	.61	.0401	.0290
Chicago, Rock Island, and Pacific	.69	.83	.0427	.0514
Chicago, South Shore, and South Bend	1.28	1.90	.0424	.0628
Erie Lackawanna	.68	1.20	.0334	.0584
Illinois Central	.59	.58	.0354	.0350
Long Island	1.22	1.47	.0483	.0586
Pittsburgh and Lake Erie	.80	8.68	.0367	.4001
Reading Company	.66	1.11	.0461	.0777
Southern Pacific	.69	.99	.0277	.0399
Staten Island Rapid Transit	.23	.75	.0275	.0897
Average for 14 railroads	.89	1.11	.0425	.0528

Source: *Economic Characteristics of the Urban Public Transportation Industry*, Table 7.3, p.7-8.

in the tooth is in the process of being relieved, thanks mainly to infusion of federal money. Table 3–16 shows the situation in a recent year.

One great advantage that rail commuter services have over conventional transit by bus is, of course, better control over their operating environment. While the bus must share the street with other traffic, usually to its disadvantage, the commuter railroads have private rights-of-way. Many commuter railroads have extensive sections of line that are completely grade separated. It is no rash conclusion that one of the reasons that patronage has held up fairly well on the commuter railroads is that the quality of service is rather good in comparison with the automobile or mass transit. Indeed, studies conducted in Philadelphia reveal the importance of the quality of the service, as well as its quantity, as an attractive force. The status of commuter facilities, particularly inadequate parking at outlying stations, seems to be one of the biggest factors holding back even more substantial increases in commuter rail patronage than

TABLE 3-12
Average Trip Length per Commuter Rail Passenger
(miles)

Railroad	1964	1965	1966	1967	1968	1969	1970
Boston & Maine	18.5	16.8	17.4	17.1	17.0	17.1	17.1
Central of New Jersey	27.7	28.0	28.1	23.4	21.5	21.5	26.6
Chicago, Burlington, Quincy	17.0	17.2	17.2	17.2	17.2	17.4	17.6*
Chicago, Milwaukee, St. Paul, & Pacific	22.7	22.8	22.9	22.7	22.4	22.4	22.6
Chicago Northwestern	21.3	21.2	21.3	21.0	20.7	20.8	20.6
Chicago, Rock Island, & Pacific	15.1	15.1	15.2	15.4	15.4	15.5	16.1
Erie Lackawanna	24.7	19.9	20.3	20.5	20.5	20.6	21.0
Illinois Central	15.5	15.6	15.6	15.4	15.6	15.9	17.0
Long Island	24.9	25.1	25.1	25.3	25.5	25.9	25.9
New York, New Haven, & Hartford	25.9	26.4	26.7	26.7	26.9	—	—
New York Central	20.8	21.0	21.0	21.0*	—	—	—
Pennsylvania/ Penn Central	19.2	19.0	18.9	20.4	21.1	23.3	24.2
Reading Company	14.2	13.8	14.1	14.1	14.3	14.3	14.3
Southern Pacific	24.4	24.4	24.2	24.4	24.7	24.5	24.5
Weighted average, all railroads	21.7	21.4	21.5	21.6	21.6	21.9	22.3

*Estimated.
Source: *Economic Characteristics of the Urban Public Transportation Industry*, Table 7.14, p.7-22.

Philadelphia has enjoyed since its program to encourage use of commuter rail service began moving ahead in the late 1950's.[24]

The value of commuter railroad service to a metropolitan area is so great that there is likely to be a substantial increase in the investment in its improvements. Extensive planning has been carried out in the metropolitan areas of New York City, New Jersey, Philadelphia, and Chicago. Cities not now served by commuter rail service may find it to their advantage to make use of existing right-of-way and contract with railroads to supply the service.

Taxicabs

Taxicabs, when thought of at all, are usually conceptualized as a type of vehicle that disappears in wet weather. Despite the fact that it provides urban public transportation, the taxicab is rarely considered in discussion of urban transportation.[26] The taxi is, of course,

TABLE 3-13
Annual Commuter Rail Revenue Passenger-Miles
(millions)

Railroad	1964	1965	1966	1967	1968	1969	1970
Boston & Maine	85.2	65.5	63.2	66.4	64.1	62.2	64.3
Central of							
New Jersey	114.6	109.9	98.2	83.1	76.0	84.0	86.8
Chicago, Burlington,							
Quincy	156.4	150.7	157.3	161.9	165.0	168.4	171.8*
Chicago, Milwaukee,							
St. Paul, & Pacific	108.8	113.5	119.2	126.7	132.9	135.4	134.2
Chicago							
Northwestern	437.0	453.0	485.0	509.9	517.4	534.9	524.0
Chicago, Rock							
Island, & Pacific	90.3	86.1	87.9	95.1	99.4	103.1	99.6
Erie Lackawanna	275.2	215.3	212.0	205.3	228.4	247.1	261.9
Illinois Central	260.8	283.4	284.0	296.5	319.0	321.5	310.2
Long Island	1,368.8	1,349.3	1,379.4	1,411.5	1,406.7	1,379.4	1,383.2
New York, New							
Haven, & Hartford	355.1	347.2	349.3	351.8	352.6	–	–
New York Central	335.7	335.4	344.0	352.6*	–	–	–
Pennsylvania/							
Penn Central	365.2	358.1	362.7	382.5	770.7	1,260.1	1,308.1
Reading Company	82.1	79.0	76.3	80.4	85.2	87.1	88.1
Southern Pacific	143.6	144.6	142.5	141.0	134.0	132.1	126.6
TOTAL, ALL							
RAILROADS	4,178.8	4,091.0	4,161.0	4,264.7	4,350.4	4,515.2	4,558.8

*Estimated.
Source: *Economic Characteristics of the Urban Public Transportation Industry,* Table 7.13, p.7-22.

not a mass transportation vehicle in the usually accepted meaning of the term; nevertheless, taxis do haul a mass of people. In 1970, for example, the 2.378 billion taxi passengers far exceeded the number of patrons of commuter railroads and rail and trolley coach transit services. Cabs carried almost half as many passengers as motor buses in transit service. Obviously, the taxi is not a negligible factor in urban and suburban transportation.[27]

The taxi provides what some contend to be the best public transportation service available in the United States. Although dissimilar in many ways from the transit industry—demand for taxicab service has been relatively stable as opposed to the decline in demand for transit—the taxicab business in general joins with the transit industry in suffering from a profit squeeze. Indeed, a 1970 study indicated that in New York City total expenses for cab operations exceeded the income from fares by 4.5 per cent.[28] The taxi industry is not

TABLE 3-14
Commuter Rail Revenue per Passenger
(dollars)

Railroad	1964	1965	1966	1967	1968	1969	1970
Boston & Maine	.59	.61	.66	.67	.77	.83	.88
Central of New Jersey	.82	.81	.83	.68	.59	.59	.60
Chicago, Burlington, Quincy	.50	.55	.55	.55	.59	.61	.63*
Chicago, Milwaukee, St. Paul, & Pacific	.77	.78	.77	.77	.79	.83	.82
Chicago Northwestern	.71	.71	.71	.70	.74	.75	.79
Chicago, Rock Island, & Pacific	.60	.66	.66	.66	.67	.68	.68
Erie Lackawanna	.66	.67	.67	.68	.67	.68	.69
Illinois Central	.50	.49	.48	.49	.49	.50	.57
Long Island	.76	.81	.82	.83	.90	.94	1.05
New York, New Haven, & Hartford	.93	.95	.97	.98	1.01	—	—
New York Central	.76	.80	.81	.82*	—	—	—
Pennsylvania/ Penn Central	.60	.61	.61	.66	.75	.84	.88
Reading Company	.45	.45	.53	.54	.56	.59	.62
Southern Pacific	.48	.47	.48	.50	.57	.57	.60
Weighted average, all railroads	.69	.71	.71	.72	.75	.78	.83

*Estimated.

Source: *Economic Characteristics of the Urban Public Transportation Industry,* Table 7.15, p.7-23.

in the dire financial shape of mass transit, but neither is it prosperous.

The taxicab industry, like mass transportation, consists of a large number of small firms, along with a few large operations. Like the transit industry, its main competition comes from the private automobile; rental automobiles are another of its competitors.[29] There are approximately 7,200 fleet cab operations—fleet being defined as an operation with more than one vehicle. It is estimated that there are more individually owned and operated cabs than fleet operations. The taxicab companies operate about 170,000 vehicles and employ approximately 111,000 persons. Cabs provide transportation service in about 3,300 communities in the United States, and in many of them provide the only public transportation service. Some comparisons with the transit industry are provided in Table 3–16. It should be noted that not only do cabs haul a formidable

TABLE 3-15
Revenue per Commuter Rail Passenger-Mile
(dollars)

Railroad	1964	1965	1966	1967	1968	1969	1970
Boston & Maine	.032	.037	.038	.039	.045	.048	.051
Central of							
New Jersey	.030	.029	.030	.029	.028	.027	.028
Chicago, Burlington,							
Quincy	.029	.032	.032	.032	.035	.035	.035*
Chicago, Milwaukee,							
St. Paul, & Pacific	.034	.034	.034	.034	.035	.037	.037
Chicago							
North Western	.033	.034	.033	.034	.036	.036	.039
Chicago, Rock							
Island, & Pacific	.040	.044	.043	.043	.043	.044	.042
Erie Lackawanna	.027	.033	.033	.033	.033	.033	.033
Illinois Central	.032	.031	.031	.032	.031	.031	.034
Long Island	.031	.032	.033	.033	.035	.036	.041
New York, New							
Haven, & Hartford	.036	.036	.036	.037	.037	—	—
New York Central	.037	.038	.039	.039	—	—	—
Pennsylvania/							
Penn Central	.031	.032	.032	.032	.036	.036	.036
Reading Company	.032	.033	.038	.039	.039	.041	.043
Southern Pacific	.019	.019	.020	.021	.023	.023	.024
Weighted average,							
all railroads	.032	.033	.033	.033	.035	.036	.037

*Estimated.
Source: *Economic Characteristics of the Urban Public Transportation Industry*, Table 7.16, p.7-23.

TABLE 3-16
Rapid Transit and Commuter Railroad Car Deliveries and Orders
For U.S. Carriers

	Commuter Railroad Cars	Rapid Transit Cars	Street Cars	Total Cars
Cars delivered in 1971	376	340	—	716
Undelivered backlog	411	1,359	—	1,770
New car orders likely in 1973	295	328	230	853
Long-range (5-year) outlook	428	1,396	177	2,001

Source: Adapted from "Rail Transit/Commuter Car Market At a Glance," *Railway Age*, January 8, 1973, p.27.

number of passengers, they take in more revenue than transit and commuter railroad services combined.

In terms of supply, there is an average of about one taxi for each 2,000 persons in the population. Generally, the larger the city, the more cabs and the higher the proportion of cabs to each thousand in the population.[30]

In terms of organization, the relationship between the cab driver and his vehicle is the important factor. The cabs may be either owner operated or part of a fleet owned by a business organization such as proprietorship, partnership, or corporation. Generally, the fleet provides maintenance service, repair facilities, and dispatching service. On the other hand, these services may also be supplied to the fleet by an association of fleet and/or owner/operator cabs, or by a management company. Many so-called taxicab "companies" are really joined only by dispatching services via two-way radio, and what appears to be a single firm is nothing more than a group of owner/operators who utilize the common dispatching service and use a common name. The "company" may also deal with local government on the location of cab stands and provides advertising. Associations of owner/operators are also common in the industry. The major advantage of the association lies in the economies of large-scale purchase of insurance protection, materials and supplies, and maintenance service, along with dispatching. The association usually represents the owner/operators in negotiations and dealings with local government and regulatory agencies.[31]

Taxicab regulation is usually a function of local government. The number of cabs, the rate of fare, insurance requirements, driver licensing and the mode of operation are the typical points of regulation. While some cities—Washington, D.C., and Atlanta, Georgia, are perhaps the best examples—do not regulate the number of cabs, most do, based on the notion of public convenience and necessity that is so common in economic regulation of transportation. In a sense, then, the taxicab operator has some degree of monopoly power. The limitation in the number of cabs is a means of creating artificial values for the limited number of slots for vehicles that may be operated in a given city or jurisdiction. In New York City, for instance, the limited number of cab medallions—only a vehicle with a medallion is, legally, a cab—issued by the city initially for $100 each are now estimated to be worth $22,000 each.[32]

A fairly comprehensive view of the taxicab industry is shown in Table 3–17. In 1970 the average taxi trip produced about $2.00 in revenue, on the basis of receipts of 31 cents per mile on a total mileage basis, and 65 cents per paid mile. Approximately 44 per cent

TABLE 3-17
Medians of Selected Ratios Describing Taxicab Operations, by Month, 1970

Item No.	Ratio	Jan.	Feb.	Mar.	Apr.	May	June	July	Aug.	Sep.	Oct.	Nov.	Dec.	Range During Year
	Cab Receipts ($)													
02	per mile	.31	.31	.32	.31	.32	.31	.30	.31	.31	.32	.32	.31	.30– .32
03	per paid mile	.66	.66	.65	.65	.66	.65	.66	.65	.64	.64	.64	.64	.64– .66
04	per man hour-total	4.13	4.12	4.24	4.34	4.39	4.13	4.13	4.18	4.24	4.17	4.29	3.89	3.89– 4.39
05	driver commission	1.78	1.83	1.88	1.90	2.05	1.93	1.79	1.75	1.91	1.88	1.88	1.81	1.75– 2.05
	percent of total	43.10	44.42	44.34	43.78	46.70	46.73	43.34	41.87	45.05	45.08	43.82	46.53	41.87–46.73
06	per trip	1.97	1.90	1.86	1.98	1.95	1.95	1.95	1.94	2.04	2.06	2.06	1.99	1.86– 2.06
07	per shift	37.16	37.65	36.98	37.04	38.71	38.18	39.29	37.81	38.84	36.06	36.65	35.75	35.75–39.29
	Cab Mileage													
10	per cab owned per day	120.00	112.00	129.50	118.00	112.00	109.20	106.70	101.70	106.00	106.70	112.00	108.60	101.70–129.50
11	per man hour	11.70	11.80	12.30	12.05	12.10	12.10	12.05	12.30	12.20	12.30	12.10	12.10	11.70–12.30
12	per trip-total	5.90	5.70	5.62	5.90	5.70	5.90	5.85	5.90	5.90	5.80	6.00	6.10	5.62– 6.10
13	paid miles	2.90	2.90	3.00	2.95	3.00	3.00	2.95	3.00	3.00	3.00	3.00	3.20	2.90– 3.20
14	percent of total	52.00	50.85	51.00	52.00	51.00	50.00	49.45	49.00	50.60	51.50	50.00	46.70	46.70–52.00
15	per gallon of gas	10.35	10.30	10.60	10.60	11.20	11.50	11.45	11.35	11.20	11.15	10.70	10.60	10.30–11.50
	Trips													
16	per man hour	2.10	2.20	2.20	2.15	2.20	2.20	2.15	2.25	2.10	2.10	2.10	2.15	2.10– 2.25
17	percent from phone orders	87.50	83.10	82.00	82.50	84.00	84.00	88.15	88.00	82.90	87.00	83.20	90.00	82.00–90.00
18	passengers per trip	1.35	1.35	1.35	1.40	1.35	1.40	1.30	1.30	1.30	1.30	1.35	1.40	1.30– 1.40
	Other													
08	hours per shift	9.00	9.00	9.00	8.75	9.00	9.00	9.00	9.00	8.80	8.75	8.50	8.50	8.50– 9.00
09	phone orders per shift	15.20	15.00	15.55	15.15	16.50	15.95	16.45	16.30	15.60	15.40	14.85	15.10	14.85–16.50

Source: *Economic Characteristics of the Urban Public Transportation Industry*, Table 8.14, p.7-16.

171

of the revenue was paid to the drivers in the form of a commission—about $1.85 per man hour of commission to a total revenue per man hour of $4.10.[33] The typical cab carried about 14,000 persons in a year and traveled about 40,000 miles. In comparison, the average bus in transit service is operated about 30,000 miles each year. Each taxi is driven about 200,000 miles before it is replaced.

While only a few studies have been done on the nature of taxi riders, the preponderance appear to be housewives and white collar workers. The aged and infirm also make up a fairly large proportion of riders for obvious reasons. The majority of riders are white and are using a cab to go either to work or home. In noncentral areas —where mass transportation services are likely to be sparse or nonexistent—service and household workers may use cabs in large numbers along with other groups in the lower income levels who do not have access to automobiles.[34]

The cab can play a more important role in urban transportation than it does at present, particularly if group riding is permitted, so that each cab can be used more efficiently at times of peak demand. This practice is often outlawed by city regulation and cab operators are not enthusiastic about the practice if they cannot levy an additional charge for each person in the cab. For low-income persons suffering from limited mobility, the cab can provide a way to get about, if some means is found to reimburse the patron or the cab company for the cost of the service. Little is likely to be done, however, until the time when the cab is properly viewed as a part of the urban public transportation scene, and some research interest and money is devoted to the subject.[35]

The Role of Government

Apart from the transit industry and its associated components in the business of providing public transportation in urban areas—that is, rail commuter and taxicab service—the other major institutional participant is government.[36] The longest involvement of government with mass transportation has been through the state regulatory agencies. An unpublished study of these agencies conducted by the author in 1970 indicated that they are not particularly interested in urban mass transportation. As economic regulators dealing with entry, rates, and service, the regulatory bodies are not geared to do anything to help improve mass transportation. While the powers and interest of state regulatory agencies vary widely from state to state, what powers they do have are usually confined to changes in rates of fare and, sometimes, route location. Withdrawal or abandonment of service are issues that may also come before regulatory commissions. In sum, however, it is fair to say that the role of the commissions has been passive.

Equipment suppliers also have a role to play, but it is generally in response to what the transit industry or government desires. For three or four decades the transit industry has been fairly content with the products of the suppliers, and, lacking developmental capability itself, for many years the transit operators turned over whatever innovation there was in transit to the discretion of the suppliers. As the market is relatively limited, the degree of real innovation was very limited. Since the federal government emerged as a major participant in the field of urban mass transportation, it has tended to call more of the shots as the principal bankroller of innovative undertakings. Planning, as a profession, also has an institutional role to play. Most often, however, this has been in response to the needs or requirements of government. Individuals associated with planning and the writings of individual planners have helped provide stimulation for the transit movement and have articulated ideas that eventually worked their way into legislation and policy.

Many states have established state departments of transportation and often these contain an agency to handle issues involving mass transportation. The degree of state effort ranges from mere collection of information and some aid to local government in planning and in applying for federal grants to a state grant-in-aid program to help match federal monies. At the time of this writing, there are twenty-one departments of transportation.[37] Despite this rising interest in mass transportation on the state level, the primary input of interest and money on the part of governmental institutions has been from the federal level.

The Urban Mass Transportation Administration

The Urban Mass Transportation Administration is, as the reader will remember, the latest guise of the initially HHFA-based mass transit agency that dates back to 1961. UMTA has recently been reorganized to make it function more efficiently. Up until September 10, 1973, most UMTA activity was centered in two offices: the Office of Program Operations administered capital grants and the technical studies grants, the Office of Research, Development and Demonstration administered the RD&D programs. The Office of Program Operations had jurisdiction over about 90 per cent of the UMTA budget, with RD&D handling most of the remainder.

The new organization recognized the need to go beyond providing aid for planning and the execution of the capital element of a project. Many cities are now in a position where there is a decent transit product to be marketed and Frank Herringer, the new UMTA administrator, felt that it was time to have the organization fit the needs. There was also a felt need to have the span of administration narrowed so that closer attention could be paid to particular, related areas. Figure 3–6 is an organization chart of the new structure.[38]

Under the new organization the Office of Capital Assistance has jurisdiction over capital grants, capital loans, and loans for advance land acquisition. The Office of Program Planning oversees policy research, policy planning, and evaluation of projects. The Office of Research and Development supervises the research and development program as well as the program of university research and training. One of the new offices is that of Transit Planning; it will have jurisdiction over the technical studies grant program and the demonstration program. The other new office is the Office of Transit Management; it will work at providing aid in modernizing and improving transit operations and management, with emphasis on marketing and safety, as well as oversight of the managerial training fellowship projects. Staff functions are supervised by the Office of Administration, the Office of the Chief Counsel, the Office of Civil Rights, and the Office of Public Information. UMTA has ten field offices located in Boston, New York, Philadelphia, Atlanta, Chicago, Dallas-Fort Worth, Kansas City, Denver, San Francisco and Seattle.

Like most federal agencies, UMTA has broad objectives. These can probably best be summed up as "providing increased mobility to urban residents, relief of congestion, and improvement of the urban environment.[39] However desirable these objectives may be, of course, they are not the same as precise workable objectives. There are really no workable objectives for UMTA at the time of this writing. This is a major weakness—a point that will be be-

Figure 3-6
Organizational Chart of Urban Mass Transportation Administration

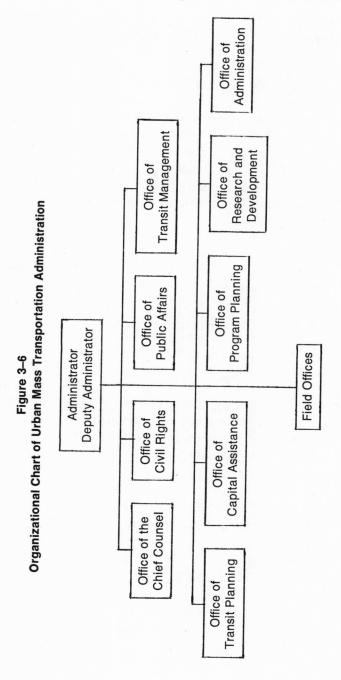

labored in a later chapter—because specific, workable objectives provide significant guidance for activities of an agency in both the long and short range. Without a statement of specific goals and backup data, there is no way to tell when or if the mobility of urban residents has been improved, congestion relieved, or the urban environment improved.

UMTA carried out its job through a series of programs and activities:

Activity No. 1[40] consists of the capital facilities grants administered by UMTA. The agency specifies three principal objectives for these grants: (1) provide mobility to those segments of the urban population which may not command the direct use of motor vehicles; (2) improve mobility: improvement in over-all traffic and reduction of time in travel about urban regions in peak hours of travel demand; (3) achievement of land use patterns and/or environmental conditions which effectively contribute to the physical, economic, and social well-being of the urban community.[41] In essence, the objectives of the capital facilities—or capital grant—program is the whole ball of wax as expressed in terms of the objectives for the agency's over-all activities.

In any case, these are all commendable objectives. Despite the fact that the first objective makes no mention of how mobility is to be defined or measured, it is pleasing to note that UMTA has moved to the position that mobility, rather than relief of congestion, is a prime reason for the existence of the agency. However, UMTA has made no attempt to measure what it is trying to provide or to establish data benchmarks to measure progress. The phrasing of the objective indicates that the major thrust of the activity is apparently directed at groups who are out of the mainstream of American life. This thinking perhaps indicates that UMTA itself regards mass transportation as something for the "losers" of our society, and it may have hampered progress, for, as long as this attitude prevails, it is unlikely that federal efforts would be bent toward the stimulation of robust programs of information gathering and marketing which are necessary to provide service that is useful and appealing to a broad general public.[42] The new organizational structure at UMTA is a healthy sign of a much more constructive position.

The mobility objective focuses on the number of people rather than vehicles moved through the system. However, concentrating on the peak seems unwise; there is a superabundance of overcapacity in off-peak periods in the public transit industry. In a sense this objective, or subobjective, if it means what it says, encourages the construction of facilities for fleeting use. This does not seem to be an optimum use of resources and reflects a very limited view of mass transportation's potential. If UMTA assumes that off-peak traffic will be handled by auto, it hurts the operating transit properties by saddling them with yet more capital that remains largely unproductive for much of the time. Without a strong incentive to maximize utilization of mass transportation capacity over an entire day or week, the transit industry, given its limited marketing prowess, is doomed to continue doing what it now does—handle peak loads at rush hour only, and then quietly starve for patrons in the off-peak.

On a more progressive note, the recent requirement that there should be attention to noncapital intensive options by local authorities to affect demand appears to be in the right direction. However, just what these actions might be remains in a state of fuzziness. It seems that UMTA is at least giving some thought to the pursuit of the grail, but, unfortunately, it has supplied no road map to the knights errant.[43] Again, the new organizational structure, especially the Office of Transit Management, may help clarify the activities.

Achievement of beneficial land-use patterns and environmental conditions centers around improving land use and reducing the need for transportation. Such goals are aimed at the entire population and, of course, are very long-term in nature. This thinking is in line with that of Wilfred Owen, who has long been an advocate of better planning to reduce the need for and cost of transportation, rather than throwing money at transportation in the hopes of solving what is essentially a problem of faulty land use.[44]

UMTA's priorities for the capital grant program are, first, to preserve existing services; second, to provide new services for those who would not otherwise have reasonable access to employment and social and economic opportunities; third, to provide aid that will improve service in line with whatever local priorities may happen to be for mass transportation. And, finally, the program priorities assume that the capital grants will complement research, development, and demonstration projects by making money available for installation or acquisition of technology proved out in RD&D projects.

To say the least, there have been some significant problems in attempting to carry out this program. Transit ridership keeps dropping. In appropriations hearings held in 1972 the UMTA administrator, speaking of the patronage decline, said that he "hoped it will bottom out in the next two or three years,"[45] but things may get worse before they get better. Even more dismal, perhaps, is the fact that despite the money that has been handed out, nobody knows what its impact has been, except that equipment has been purchased and facilities constructed. In the hearing for fiscal 1973 the UMTA administrator stated that he is "hopeful that next year we will have some information on the subject." In the same hearings Congressman Sidney R. Yates of Illinois expressed hope that something good would have happened after seven years of effort.[46] How long the Congress will continue to be patient is a matter of some concern. Some major victories are sorely needed.

There is no doubt that mass transportation can do a much bigger job in facilitating urban mobility than it has been doing up to now. According to the UMTA administrator in 1972, there was enough capacity in about 80 per cent of the cases—by which it is assumed he means cities—to handle about three times the present ridership of mass transportation. While the studies he discusses in the appropriations hearings are not documented, apparently only some slight increases of equipment would turn the trick even at the peak hour. Presumably, the remaining 20 per cent are the very large cities with enormous peak-hour demands that can barely be met now. So far, this capability remains largely untapped; if the potential is not soon utilized, critics of the transit program will have much grist for their mills. The problem can be especially serious if the transit programs come to be thought of as just another welfare program that doesn't work. There would be serious ramifications if the administration and/or the Congress begin to chip away at welfare programs that apparently don't produce very exciting results. Indeed, as a harbinger of what may come, after his re-election in 1972, President Nixon began a phase-out of many of the programs established in the Great Society days of President Lyndon Johnson.

Activity No. 2. Technical study grants make up the second major category of UMTA attention. The objectives of the technical studies programs are (1) to assist in studies of management and operations in communities faced with possible loss of all public transit; (2) to plan and improve existing transit systems, including better use of buses; (3) to aid major metropolitan areas in preparation of rapid transit plans and extensions of present rapid transit systems (including new systems in cities that currently do not have such services); and (4) coordinated transit system planning.[47]

The studies as carried out with UMTA help have generally fallen into four categories: first, studies aimed at developing organizational and financial plans for transit systems, particularly where public takeover is a matter at issue; second, studies aimed at setting out alternative approaches to local transportation goals; third, in-depth studies of large transit properties—a category of increasing interest; finally, regional transportation plans developed with technical studies aid. In addition to the one-shot technical studies carried out in smaller urban places, a regular coordinated and continuing program is under way in some of the larger cities in cooperation with the Federal Highway Administration, the Federal Aeronautics Administration, and the HUD 701 planning program.

The need to conduct transportation planning rather than modal planning was recognized in 1970. On a trial basis, the planning in the twenty-five largest metropolitan areas was conducted by Intermodal Planning Groups. This approach was considered sufficiently successful to institutionalize the procedures in March 1973. The goals of this type of planning are to work through a single recipient agency in each metropolitan area that is responsible for mass transit, highway, and airport planning. Unified transportation planning is to be carried on annually, with annual review. From this is to develop a five-year capital investment program, updated annually. The planning process is funded jointly by the various DOT agencies involved, which intentionally serves to blur the divisions between the agencies and the modes they represent.[48]

As in much of what UMTA does, one of the great mysteries and missing elements concerning the technical studies is a rundown of what the results of all the activity have been. According to the UMTA administrator, in 1973 the technical studies grants will at long last begin follow-up studies to see how things have panned out.[49]

In addition, under the technical studies grants environmental impact studies have been conducted, or at least aid for them provided. Some special studies have also been conducted concerning the needs of the elderly and handicapped, the impact of transit on the environment, downtown circulation, and transit in model cities areas.

Activity No. 3. Activity three in the UMTA household has been the Research, Development and Demonstration program. This will change under the new UMTA organization, but it is too early to note changes; the discussion here focuses on the RD&D program as it was carried out before September 10, 1973.

Any internally provided description of what the RD&D arm of UMTA is doing bristles with Space Age buzz words. Essentially, RD&D is trying to take a look at existing mass transportation systems and their needs, examine the current state of the transit art, and then develop new systems to meet unmet needs.

The stated objectives of RD&D are (1) to better the condition of the transit passenger through improved service, including greater availability of transit, less travel time, and more comfort; (2) to improve the condition of the transit operator through operating economies, including improved vehicles, engines, and operating and maintenance techniques; (3) to improve the condition of the transit vehicle manufacturer by developing a larger market for better vehicles; and (4) to improve the image of transit within the community by reducing congestion, air pollution, and urban disruption. RD&D has divided its activities by subdepartmentalizing on a modal basis, with bus, rail, and new system areas. Much of the thinking is technological and apparently relatively little attention has been paid to the management or marketing side of mass transportation.[50]

The gap in marketing research might be filled to a degree by means of a new marketing research program initiated by UMTA in spring 1973. The contractor selected to do the job was given nine months to dig into marketing literature as it relates to transit, develop general marketing concepts (including market research, transit service planning, fares and scheduling, and promotional methods and materials), develop modes for measuring transit marketing effectiveness, select and recommend a demonstration site, and develop plans for a marketing demonstration. After this gestation period, a second phase of thirteen months will include the implementation and evaluation of the marketing demonstration and the production of a marketing manual. Probably toward the end of the project, the contractor will conduct a two-day training session for personnel of transit operating agencies, both public and private, to discuss mass transportation marketing techniques.[51] It will be interesting to see how the program turns out; perhaps a modest continuing effort to develop some of the pertinent leads and a regular marketing conference will be a longer range result.

Activity No. 4. Activity four in UMTA is that concerning managerial training grants. The grants provide assistance to local transit properties in upgrading their management personnel. The local public body that is the potential management grantee's employer must pick up 25 per cent of the cost. In the case of a fellowship for graduate study by an individual, the sum from UMTA cannot exceed 75 per cent of annual income, with a maximum of $12,000 per fellow. The basic selection, using guidelines provided by UMTA, is made on the local level; UMTA merely verifies that a candidate is suitable. The candidate, of course, has to be employed in some facet of mass transportation and he must be accepted by the school conducting the training. To quote the official jargon, "He must have demonstrated ability in the past and offer potential for future contributions to the field of urban transportation, if given the fellowship."[52] Through 1971, 116 fellowships had been parcelled out; UMTA estimated that 100 fellowships per year would be given in 1972, 1973, and 1974.

Activity No. 5. UMTA's activity five is the university research and training grant program. These grants have two objectives; the first is usable results from research efforts and the second is to prepare students at the undergraduate level who will be suitable for employment in the urban transportation field. The grants can be used for course developments, student support, and research. Supposedly, the research is to be interdisciplinary in nature and have both theoretical and practical application. It should be noted that the theoretical nature of much of the work that was done in the past in this program has tended to shift UMTA's interest to programs that may yield results.[53]

Activity No. 6. A sixth activity also exists within UMTA: the capital facility loan program. This program was initially authorized by the Housing Act of 1961 and reinstigated in the Urban Mass Transportation Act of 1964 without a terminal date. At the present time under the Urban Mass Transportation Assistance Act in 1970, loans can be used for two purposes: (1) to aid in the acquisition, construction, reconstruction, and improvement of transit-related equipment facilities; (2) to aid in the acquisition of real property that will be used in the future for transit operations. Since grants are usually preferable to loans, the program has been used sparely.[54]

Considering the plight of transit in the United States, UMTA plainly has a very difficult job to carry out. How the federal programs have actually worked has been suggested in the preceding pages. A more detailed account of the accomplishments of the various programs is found in subsequent chapters.

Conclusion

A review of the two major institutional participants in the effort to upgrade mass transportation reveals that neither of them at present seem to possess the qualities from which victories are likely to be made. The mass transportation industry has been financially malnourished for years and peopled by managers whose skills are largely inappropriate for what must be a consumer-oriented task; even given large injections of government money, the industry possesses none of the managerial traditions or organizational structure to assure success in what must eventually come down to nothing more than a king-sized selling job. For its part, the Urban Mass Transportation Administration has striven valiantly to do a good job, despite the burdens of puny funding in the past and, until recently, a very small staff. UMTA also has the normal problems falling to any administrative agency that must face political pressure and political reality while attempting to treat its clientele on an equitable basis. UMTA seems to suffer from an overemphasis on technological solutions to problems that are often financial, organizational, and managerial in nature, and there is a danger of solving problems that are not important at the risk of neglecting those that are vital. The new organization structure may prove to be extremely helpful in allowing UMTA to do a much better job than in the past, but it is still too early to tell.

After examining the institutional participants in the mass transportation game, one of my students claimed they reminded him of Charlie Brown's All Stars: sincere losers. That may have, indeed, been true in the past; however, in time and with proper support and direction, it is likely that the institutional team will win a few victories, given a careful rethinking of many aspects of mass transportation and its relationship with the public.

CHAPTER FOUR

The Federal
Demonstration Programs

Of all the federal urban mass transport programs, probably the most interesting—and in some ways the most important—are the demonstration projects. For that reason, this chapter is devoted to a quick review of this program. Definitionally, the mass transport demonstrations are real-life experiments with the goal of proving some practical point in urban transport. They are not meant to be excursions in theory; theoretical research is the proper province of the research and development program carried out under the aegis of the Urban Mass Transportation Administration (UMTA). However, the demonstrations are closely related to the more esoteric R&D work.

The demonstrations cover a wide variety of project types: some involve testing new equipment or modes of tranportation; others carry out improvement or modification in operations and services with a goal of increasing transit patronage. Still other projects seek to improve management techniques, test devices that may increase managerial or supervisory effectiveness, or by means of electronic data processing cut the cost of transit operation.

Since the beginning of federal mass transportation policy, two distinct approaches to demonstrations are observable. Up to about 1970, much of the research carried out was in the form of unsolicited demonstration project ideas originating outside UMTA and its predecessor agencies. Since 1970 the thrust has been primarily toward demonstration projects generated internally at UMTA and farmed out on a contract basis. In this latter phase the projects tend to be predominantly technical in nature, although not exclusively so. Most of the demonstrations discussed here are those from the earlier period.

In order for an unsolicited proposal to qualify for a grant, the subject matter of the demonstration project must be generally applicable on a national basis if it should prove useful. The project must not be of such a narrow nature that it would apply only in a particular place. For example, a project involving the demonstration of an improved grip for cable cars would not qualify, since the only place in the nation still operating cable cars is San Francisco. Otherwise, there are relatively few restraints on the ingenuity of the demonstrator, given only that the demonstration be conducted as professionally as possible and that the findings be reported to the UMTA. In most cases, a final report of the project must be prepared presenting a detailed account of the demonstration, its purpose, procedures, and findings.

Under the 1961 mass transit legislation, all demonstration projects had to be initiated at the local level and, if acceptable, would receive a federal grant for two-thirds of the net project cost. However, the Urban Mass Transportation Act of 1964 gave the federal government the power to initiate demonstrations on its own, and no limit was established on the proportion of federal financial participation. For some years policy or tradition caused the funding share pattern of the 1961 Act to be closely followed. The research and development program was the child of the 1966 amendments to the Urban Mass Transportation Act. Unlike the earlier demonstrations, which were quickly mounted, the R&D approach was intended to be longer range.

An early change in the policy on initiative and cost sharing came in the aftermath of the Watts riot in Los Angeles. When the Mc-Cone Commission reported joblessness in Watts was very high compared to the rest of Los Angeles, this was largely attributed to a lower level of automobile ownership in Watts and a lack of alternative public transportation to areas where suitable employment was available. In response to this finding, HUD (which at that time had jurisdiction over the mass transportation program) initiated a project paying 100 per cent of the cost of a bus demonstration aimed at providing greater mobility to Watts residents. Several other demonstrations involving the question of poverty and mobility also enjoyed support at more than two-thirds of their cost, but most of these projects were not initiated by HUD itself.[1]

In late 1970 the policy on the proportion of the federal contribution was again modified. If the secretary of transportation finds a demonstration project to be sufficiently in the national interest, the federal government will pay 100 per cent of the net project cost. Since 1970 most demonstrations have been initiated at UMTA and have been 100 per cent federally funded.

The policy change toward initiation of projects primarily in-house was first manifested on September 11, 1970, when an invitation to bid on projects was published as a request for proposals in the *Commerce Business Daily*.[2] Under this rubric the UMTA deals only with the prime contractor who manages the particular chunk of research. The categories of project management included: (1) Bus Transportation: (a) Bus Technology, (b) Bus Traffic Systems Innovations, (c) Bus Transit Demand-Responsive Systems, (d) Bus Service Development and Evaluation; (2) Urban Rail Transportation: (a) Urban Rapid Rail Vehicles and Systems, (b) Urban Commuter Rail Vehicles and Systems, (c) Urban Light Rail Vehicles and Systems; (3) New Systems of Urban Transportation. Subcontractors may—and often do—carry out the individual projects within each category. The principal reason for this change in policy was the problem of administering a constantly increasing number of projects. Chronic shortages of staff personnel at UMTA had made evaluation of new proposals and surveillance of existing projects extremely difficult. The method adopted cuts down on the number of parties with which UMTA has to deal directly. It was hoped that more work could be carried out with greater efficiency and with better project management.

Unsolicited projects, once the backbone of the demonstration effort, have been few in number since 1970. This reflects, in part, an emphasis on demonstrations of a more highly technical or technological nature, rather than the operational demonstrations that predominated earlier. UMTA has tightened its review process of unsolicited demonstration proposals to include in-house review, and has also contracted with the National Bureau of Standards and the Naval Underwater Systems Center for review of both proposals and final report.[3] The documentation necessary to gain consideration of any demonstration proposal appears to have grown more formidable, and this may have discouraged some potential demonstrations.

The ramifications of this policy regarding demonstrations and research are twofold. The research, development, and demonstrations projects will be "neater" in the sense that they will fit more precisely within the framework of development UMTA wishes to promote. It does not, of course, guarantee that UMTA will move in the best of all possible directions, but certainly the work done can be better coordinated and may result in more efficient expenditure of public money.

The second effect has been to rule out operating demonstrations that hail from the local level and involve experiments with a functioning transit property. This is a mixed blessing. Unsolicited and often very practical demonstrations inevitably resulted in a hodgepodge of activity. Nevertheless, these projects were often quite interesting and of potentially great value. The loss of a certain spark of ingenuity flowing from ideas originating from many sources may be a result of relying mainly on internally generated projects and ideas. Moreover, simpler projects of a very practical nature may have more appeal and newsworthiness for the general public than those more complicated and highly technical.[4]

For those demonstration projects requiring matching funds, mainly those initiated locally, the matching sum must come from a local source, either government or private enterprise. The matching requirement means that federal funds can be stretched a bit further; the policy also insures sincere interest on the local level. On the other hand, the UMTA policy of 100-per-cent demonstration funding helps guarantee that projects with very limited local payoff but substantial national benefits will be undertaken. Indeed, projects as expensive as the demonstration of the personal rapid transit system in Morgantown, W. Va., would probably not have been undertaken at all if the local community had had to cough up a significant portion of the $63–$125 million price tag from its own resources.

The Demonstration Philosophy

An earlier chapter touched upon the fact that the federal role in transit began with the demonstration programs. This is a good place to explore the philosophy of beginning a new direction in public policy by such a device.

Of all ways to kick off a program of aid to urban areas and the transit industry, why demonstrations? Considering growing urban mobility problems and an industry that has been in ill health for the past half-century, one may think that both cities and mass transportation would have been better served if the money spent since 1961 on demonstrations—even though the sum is not terribly large—had been used to provide additional equipment and facilities. The necessity for capital funds is great, of course, but equally important is the pressing need for new ideas and departures from the status quo. Experimentation is a form of invigoration and rejuvenation. The demonstrations are, or can be, a means of overcoming the intellectual and, indeed, the spiritual bankruptcy of the mass transit industry. Practical demonstrations also provide a way of stimulating local officials whose job it is to make policy in regard to urban transportation.

The demonstration program, ostensibly designed to provide useful information and a shot of hope for a morbid industry that was sadly failing to meet public needs, also provided a hedge for Congress and the Kennedy administration. In other words, the program got the powers-that-be off the hook with but a modest involvement. A commitment to provide capital or operating subsidies smacks of deeper involvement than aid for practical experimentation. Even in 1961 there was no mystery over the fact that resuscitation of mass transit through physical improvements was bound to be an expensive venture, and it would—unfortunately, in the prevailing congressional view at the time—involve long-term commitments of capital. In the very nature of a capital program, the extensive lead-time and planning required for construction and renovation projects required legislation that would have to be in effect for a fairly long period of time. In short, to be worth anything at all, a capital grant program would have to be relatively long-lived and it would be difficult to turn off quickly, unless Congress were willing to put up with a barrage of flak from local governments that had had the rug pulled out from under them.

On the other hand, a demonstration grant program does not have the same connotations of longevity. It could be stopped in a relatively brief time without great difficulty. Even so, with the demonstration programs in the 1961 Act, Congress and the administration could point to visible action taken and hold out the carrot of "more to come" if the political climate was sufficiently warmed by the projects to warrant a greater federal commitment. As a happy dividend, the stock of knowledge about mass transportation could be enlarged.

In all fairness, Congress alone cannot be blamed for taking a somewhat dim view of the chances for a comeback of mass transportation, or even that such a revival might be of great importance to the nation. The state of the transit industry in the late fifties and early sixties left reasonable doubt the only prudent attitude to take. The wholesale deflection of transit patrons was the most visible sign that perhaps mass transportation might not deserve to be saved. There were substantial risks in depending upon mass transport to play a key role in both decongesting and boosting the level and quality of mobility within American cities. To both the Kennedy administration and the Congress there was no denying that mass transport was in many eyes a prime example of an inferior good. The demonstrations would either help to prove that a transit comeback was possible, or would show that transit improvement was useless.

In the final analysis, succeed or fail, the amount of money spent on short-term demonstrations would be relatively small. Therefore, the demonstration programs provided action to appease cities worried about the loss of mass transport, allowed needed information to be gathered, and, over time, would aid Congress and the administration in making future decisions with regard to federal transit involvement without the necessity for large, long-term financial commitments.[5] The growing list of federal mass transit programs, the $3.1 billion transit aid Act of 1970, and the Highway Act of 1973, are evidence that the demonstration program has achieved at least a part of its purpose.

In the years since the initiation of the demonstration program in mass transport, at least certain aspects of the philosophy outlined above were very evident in practice. For the first several years, when the programs were housed in HHFA, the projects got down to the key issue of efforts directly involved in moving people. Later, when the mass transportation programs were under the jurisdiction of HUD, projects with major social and poverty-fighting implications were funded, reflecting not only mental overspill of the Johnson administration's War on Poverty programs, but also the special interests of HUD as an agency involved in poverty and socioeconomic matters. The philosophy had changed from concentrating on moving people to moving people with special problems.

As noted earlier, only a few demonstrations of the "practical operational" variety have been undertaken during the Nixon years. The UMTA Office of Program Demonstrations has evidenced a strong interest in complete "packages" of research, development, and demonstration work, starting essentially from scratch with research on an idea, taking it through development, then demonstrating it in actual operations, and, finally, making capital grants available for broad implementation. The payoff from the research, development, and demonstration process is likely to take much longer to reach fruition than the simpler operational demonstration, but more may be learned. The personal rapid transit system project installed in Morgantown, W. Va., to be discussed later, is an excellent example of this new thrust. On the other hand, the Shirley Highway Express Bus and Haddonfield Dial-a-Bus projects are examples of the old familiar "practical operational" type.[6]

The Demonstration Projects

As quests for knowledge based on real-life experience, demonstrations involve the delight and stimulation of discovery. By nature they are of more intrinsic interest to the general reader, researchers, planners, and many aggressive transit operators, than are the capital grant or technical studies programs. On the other hand, there is no denying that the capital grant projects have been more important to given cities. Through grants of capital from the federal level, the money for needed investment has been provided, often for public acquisition of foundering, privately owned transit properties, so that service could be preserved.

Appendix 2 lists all the federal demonstration projects by state and by the serial number assigned by the U.S. Department of Transportation.[7] (Appendix 1 shows grants of capital, Appendix 3 lists Technical Studies Grants.)

Even a cursory examination of the projects listed in Appendix 2 will reveal, if nothing else, an interesting variety of undertakings. Improved service to help lure more patrons to mass transport is exemplified by the Shirley Highway Express Bus, INT-MID-23 (IT-06-0024); the Peoria contractual-fare subscription bus operation, ILL-MTD-3 (none given); suburban express bus operation in Baltimore, MD-MTD-1 (MD-06-0004); and bus service linking medical centers in Nashville, TENN-MTD-4 (TN-06-0002). WASH-MTD-1 (WA-06-0003) takes a look at the monorail built for the Seattle World's Fair; PA-MTD-2 (PA-06-0009), a study of the new mode of light rapid transit tested near Pittsburgh; CAL-MTD-13 (CA-06-0031) is a test of steam-powered (external combustion) buses; and NY-MTD-8 (NY-06-0011) is a test of the use of radio communication in the subway tunnels of New York. KANS-MTD-1 (KS-06-0001) and WVA-MTD-1 (WV-06-0001) both involve the use of computers for the time-consuming job of scheduling manpower and equipment to fit transit operating schedules, while INT-MTD-14 (IT-06-0013) is a study of the use of a computer in planning a bus system. Automatic fare collection is investigated in CAL-MTD-4 (CA-06-0023); INT-MTD-9 (IT-06-0012) studies the monthly pass as a patronage builder; CAL-MTD-10 (CA-06-0028) examines the sociological and economic impact of bus route restructuring; and NY-MTD-9 (NY-06-0012) mulls over the probable lasting effects of a strike on the New York City Transit Authority.

Is it, indeed, possible to evaluate the results of the demonstration and research programs? There is really no way to add up the precise payoff of the demonstrations because of the difficulty of placing objective values on the output. It may be possible for some of the more technical research studies dealing in easily quantifiable factors to be evaluated. Of course, a highly dedicated measurer might utilize some rough-and-ready form of benefit-cost analysis in order to compare projects with one another or against some norm. The method suggested by Professor Colin Buchanan may be useful in such a project. The pecuniary costs of the various projects are easily ascertained. A checklist may then be established for the benefit items, giving each benefit category a maximum point value and an earned point value. Of course, this technique is subject to the criticism that it amounts to nothing more or less than a listing and weighing of one's own values and prejudices.[8]

Furthermore, regardless of the technique that might be used, any over-all evaluation of a benefits-cost nature for the demonstration or research program as a whole is rendered especially difficult because of the wide variety of dissimilar factors involved. Put in another way, almost every project has a considerably different output from any other. The means of evaluation that could cope with such a wide variety of projects—some aimed at improving the quality of service, others testing the use of electronic data processing in driver job assignments, still others investigating the effect on patronage of the location of a new commuter railroad station, or tests of a completely new type of modal hardware—would probably have to be so generalized as to be useless.

In short, other than using some form of analysis that, at best, would involve a possibly spurious type of precision, only a very general evaluation is practical. The commentary that follows, therefore, is based on qualitative judgment grounded in some knowledge of the field of mass transportation and a review of the projects in light of types of information needed to fill the void in urban transport knowledge.

Taking a broad view of the demonstration and research program, the following points have been the salient, over-all achievements.

Demonstrations have helped generate awareness and have aroused renewed interest in mass transportation. This is probably the most important outcome of the demonstration programs since 1961. The projects have served to dramatize the entire federal effort in a unique way, especially the relatively straightforward operating demonstration. Getting a grant to buy some new buses—no matter how badly they may be needed—is not a particularly interesting event except to those transit enterprises and patrons who will benefit directly. It does not fan the imagination or bestir the thinking process as does a demonstration of a new mode of transport, a new technique of operation, or an interesting wrinkle in marketing.

In a more limited way, the research and development program has stimulated interest on the part of the RD&D "community." Ever since the research effort went beyond the practical operational demonstration stage, professional research and development organizations have been eager to get in line to do sponsored research. It has become especially helpful to some firms as defense-oriented research began to dry up in about 1970. Top-notch talent has come to direct some of its effort toward mass transportation.

University researchers also got into the act with Section 6—the

RD&D part of the Urban Mass Transportation Act—research during the early years of the federal effort, primarily as participants in demonstration programs. In recent years UMTA has apparently become disillusioned with university grant research under Section 6 and unhappy about the inability of universities to complete contract research on schedule. Most university work is now carried on under the University Research and Training Program of Section 11 of the act, which is, perhaps, better suited to the more casual and independent efforts that seem to typify university research effort.[9]

As noted earlier, the work under the sixth section is now geared primarily to begin with contract research and development and finish up, if necessary, with a demonstration contract. Some research, development, and demonstration work is being carried on at the Department of Transportation Rail Laboratory at Pueblo, Colo. There, in addition to laboratory work on the interaction of wheel, truck assembly, and rail, DOT and UMTA are researching the use of linear induction motors, air-cushion vehicles, and flywheel energy storage. As part of this program, the development and construction of the so-called State-of-the-Arts Cars (SOAC) for rapid transit service have been done under contract. Work is also being carried out on a modern streetcar and on modern bus designs, although there does not seem to be any intent of testing this equipment at Pueblo. Some of the hardware under development is to be tested by regular transit properties. The SOAC cars are to be operated on several of the rapid transit systems in the United States.[10]

Of all the more formal RD&D work to date, the efforts directed at Personal Rapid Transit (PRT) systems seem to be getting the biggest publicity play, and apparently the largest infusion of research dollars in a single activity. PRT systems were center-ring attractions at the Transpo '72 "trade fair" held at Dulles Airport. The PRT system at Morgantown, W. Va., has also been the subject of press reports and nationwide TV news coverage—good evidence of the ability of a demonstration to be broadly newsworthy.[11]

There is no denying that newsworthiness of some projects has had much to do with the growth of general interest in transit from the man in the street and public officials as well. Since 1961 a new attitude on the part of municipalities toward mass transit is noticeable; the demonstrations share the credit. In the 1950's it would have been unthinkable for most city officials, or the general public, to give serious thought to the problems and potential of mass transportation, much less take any public action to help solve the problems and exploit the possibilities. Other federal programs—particularly the capital grants—have played a vital role in the awakening process in given localities, but the publicity and attention derived from the demonstrations—one might call it a gospel of achievement—have been a critical factor in generating a broader national interest in the potential of mass transportation on the part of the general public, public officials, and transit management.

Demonstration programs have helped to make up for the many years in which there was little or no experimentation of any sort in the urban transport field. Over the past fifty years, as the mass transit industry languished, it grew less able to afford experimentation. A general policy in the industry has always been to keep fares low, in large part because of pressures from local public officials. This meant there was precious little money for research and development even in the relatively prosperous days of the industry.[12] In any event, only the largest properties would have been likely to possess the expertise to carry on large-scale research and development efforts independently. Research and innovation were common at rather modest-sized properties in Great Britain, and the U.S. transit industry was highly successful in its united effort to design the President's Conference Committee (PCC) streetcar in the early and middle 1930's.

Management within the industry also grew more and more conservative in its outlook, and therefore increasingly unable and unwilling to act aggressively and imaginatively toward solutions to its problems. The transit industry ceased to attract young men with the vigor and ideas necessary to a vital and healthy industry. Moreover, transit failed to develop within management that important echelon of middle-level staff professionals who are able to deal easily with professionals on the same level in government and other industries. The kind of professional interplay that develops innovative ideas and that makes smooth the way in dealings between industries and between an industry and government was missing. This latter point is probably a major reason that it took so long for government aid for mass transportation to develop; within the transit industry no one knew the correct buttons to push.

All these minus factors conspired to squelch creativity on the part of transit management. As the situation grew more bleak, the costs and risks of experimentation were too high, if borne entirely from the resources of suppliers, local government, and/or public transport firms.

It is fair to say that what little innovation did occur in the twenty years before the advent of the federal programs was primarily the result of the action of the transit supply industry. However, once the postwar switch from streetcars to buses was over, the market and profit potential for transit equipment was apparently too small to provide much incentive for manufacturers to do other than produce the same old stuff. New systems development was unthinkable.[13] At the same time, it should be noted that the practice of choosing equipment offered by the low bidder, common in the acquisition and purchase practices of government bodies—and the bulk of the work done by the U.S. transit industry is conducted by publicly owned properties—seems to be a sure way of doing little to get the best equipment or stimulate the supply industry to produce equipment with a high initial cost. The incentive for innovation is lacking in the process.[14]

By providing needed seed money, the federal demonstration grants have helped to change the picture somewhat; a new and innovative breath of life is stirring within the industry.[15] Moreover, new types of equipment and completely new modes of transport are under development for the first time in many years. For its part, the supply industry has begun to react with vigor to the stimulus given by the demonstrations—and high-dollar R&D work—and the expectation of profit in meeting the burgeoning needs of a revived transit industry.

Valuable and interesting information has been provided as a result of the demonstrations. Apart from the purely technical findings, some demonstrations have borne out the notion that mass transport service of good quality—especially in terms of easy access to the service and reduced travel time—can attract new patrons and retain old ones. This finding provides some firm backing to the hope that mass transport can play an important part in improving urban mobility, relieving congestion, and improving the quality of urban life.

Also, there is an opportunity in the demonstration program to experiment with marketing mass transport. Aside from the very largest cities, where the need to move huge numbers of people is primarily a technical problem, as noted in earlier pages, the crux of transit's failure and potential success in serving the public seems to lie in the field of marketing. Finding out what the traveling public desires and needs, and then providing it in the way it is wanted, is old hat for most business firms producing consumer goods or services. But marketing is strange territory indeed to operations-oriented transit managers. When they are unwilling or unable to try innovations on their own, the demonstrations provide the opportunity. Of course, old habits are hard to break, and much of the marketing effort has been modest. Worse yet, hard-won ideas generated by the demonstrations have often been left to gather dust in unread reports.

The demonstrations have provided useful mass transport services for the traveling public. Even if certain services have not continued for more than the one- or two-year period typical of the operating demonstrations, during that time the public has enjoyed better transportation. This is a benefit not to be counted lightly in an industry where erosion of service quality has been the common fact of life since the end of the Second World War. In some low-income ghetto areas—such as Watts—transit demonstrations have also made it possible, apparently for the first time, to gear bus service more realistically to the travel needs of the population of a particular area.

The demonstrations have permitted necessary service to continue to operate on a short-run basis while longer-range solutions were sought. Because of financial problems and an unwillingness or inability to plan ahead, it is no surprise that state and local officials often find it difficult to act quickly to save necessary but unremunerative services. In some cases the demonstrations have provided a cushion of federal funds to permit service to be maintained while probing for the most practical long-run means of insuring service retention—and eventual improvement. As a major case in point, the New York area commuter services operated by the New Haven Railroad (INT-MTD-11 [IT-06-0014]) fall into this category. That financially embarrassed carrier, now part of the even more embarrassed Penn Central system, was kept alive for several years while the *sturm und drang* of New York and Connecticut politics developed a means of assuring continued commuter service. Some local bus operations that have been on shaky ground have also been able to keep running and improve services to some degree.

To summarize, the benefits of the demonstrations, even if precisely unquantifiable, are most certainly noticeable. In conjunction with the other mass transportation programs, especially the capital grants, the demonstrations were effective in stirring interest in transit. This was particularly important in the early years of the federal programs before major amounts of capital were available and before major transit construction programs could get under way. The practical demonstrations provided interesting "events" to help draw interest to transit in a way that more precise but esoteric research projects could not.

Despite the relatively small amount of money spent on the demonstrations, they are in large part responsible for the new spirit of interest in mass transportation at large in the United States today, a spirit that has probably not been felt since the development of the electric street car in the 1880's. This reinvigorated spirit is perhaps the most critical element of all in a resurgence of mass transportation to serve the citizens of America's urban places. The prime evidence of growing support is the heavily favorable vote of Congress in the mass transportation legislation passed in 1970 and in the compromise that made possible the Highway Act of 1973. This "era of good feeling" toward transit is probably more important than any specific finding or result of any particular demonstration.

Some Gaps in the Demonstration Program

If there is a glow of hope discernible as a major result of the mass transportation demonstration program, it is only fair to remark on some of the warts that are also evident in the picture. The faults as carried out so far are mainly those of omission rather than commission:

The demonstrations, as a group, do not fit into any over-all plan of research and development. From the viewpoint of knowledge gained, what has been produced, particularly by the projects up to 1970, is a mosaic of bits and pieces of information that do not make a complete picture. For example, despite the relatively large number of demonstrations undertaken, nowhere can an interested party find out how to run a modern transportation system.[16] This failing is understandable; the earlier projects were principally products of local initiative rather than federal sponsorship of segments of an over-all plan of demonstration to be carried out locally. Some inhibitions can be attributed to the short supply of talent and money on the local level; others to the conservative nature of transit management and the fear that they may be "stuck" with a demonstration operation that is highly unremunerative after the demonstration period is over. This is not an atmosphere that generates highly imaginative, all-embracing—and perhaps costly—demonstrations. Thus, the earlier projects, either as a whole or in any individual case, have not covered the complete spectrum of urban transport in any systematic fashion, primarily because they were really not supposed to.

Most of the more recent demonstrations are part of a more complete and systematic search for knowledge, as part of a research, development, and demonstration program carried on by UMTA with more specific goals. Few results are available from the newer projects because they have not been long under way. Even when they are completed, however, there is no evidence that anyone will be any wiser about actually doing a better total job of operating a modern transit system, since much of the research work is hardware oriented.

A number of projects are clearly needed which cover all elements of mass transportation—not only operations or new technology, but employee selection, management and supervision, maintenance, routing and scheduling, marketing, and advertising and public relations. No one of these facets of mass transport exists in a vacuum. To continue to treat only one aspect in a given project is shortsighted and likely to produce relatively meaningless results as far as general application of findings is concerned.

The new policy, evidenced by the September 1970 request for applications of project managers, promises some changes.

The grievous shortcoming of the new direction in demonstrations is its strong bias toward technology. To harp on a point raised earlier, the essence of the failure of mass transportation in the United States, and the hope for its future success in meeting the urban travel needs, is not primarily a technical problem. It is a problem of management, particularly marketing management. The lack of attention to various aspects of managing the manipulation of transit resources that is evidenced in the new demonstration philosophy is a serious shortcoming.

There have been few citywide demonstrations. If mass transportation is viewed as a system, as it should be, it is clear that insufficient attention has been paid to meaningful system-wide experiments involving the whole of public transit in a given city. Thus it has been virtually impossible to experiment meaningfully with an integrated system of transport combining private automobile and public transportation. A lack of federal funds has contributed to this gap; a really complete demonstration in a large city would be very costly. Those citywide transit demonstrations that have been undertaken so far were carried out in small cities (Rome, N.Y., NY-MTD-6 [NY-06-0010] and New Castle, Pa., PA-MTD-6 [PA-06-0012]) where the financial commitment was relatively small.

Few demonstrations have been carried out in smaller urban places. Smaller urban places are just as much in need of improved mass transit as big cities. So far, however, relatively little has been done on either the federal or local level to understand their plight or take steps to relieve it. Exceptions may be found in the New Castle and Rome demonstrations cited above, and in IND-MTD-1 (IN-06-0002); the latter involving a handbook for the management of small-scale mass transportation enterprises, aimed primarily at small-city situations. Most projects are concentrated in larger cities in the Washington-Boston corridor and in the San Francisco area; the rest are scattered about, principally north of the Ohio River and east of the Mississippi River. The financial problems of smaller cities often make it difficult for them to participate in a demonstration where they must provide funds on a matching basis. Moreover, smaller cities often lack the staff people—either in local government or in the transit enterprise—who can handle the formulation, data gathering, and analysis that is a necessary adjunct of a demonstration.

One of the reasons that RD&D effort since 1970 has been of the contract type, involving professional research firms, is that such organizations are easier to deal with than a scattering of persons who are not professional researchers and who tend to be pragmatic rather than scientific in their approach.

Much of the information provided as a result of the demonstrations

*has not been in a form useful to the transit industry or public ad-
ministrators with mass transport responsibilities.* Demonstration participants are required to provide reports of the findings of their
demonstrations. Frequently, the reports are of little use to those who
are in greatest need of information. In other words, the findings
are not interpreted or presented in a meaningful form relative to
different mass transport circumstances. Admittedly, it is often difficult to generalize about the demonstration findings in a meaningful
way or, on the other hand, write a demonstration—or research—
report with specialized sections aimed at a host of special circumstances. This limits the payoff possible from these projects. For
example, a certain technique of big-city express bus operations
may be applicable in a city of medium size, but the lack of interpretation or comment on methods of implementation over a broad set
of circumstances makes it unlikely that the technique will be
adopted. This need not be a problem with research and demonstration projects contracted out to professional research firms. Such
contractors generally enjoy the services of a staff of professional
writers who can gear output to the needs of a variety of audiences
if requested to do so.

The demonstration projects have lacked boldness. The demonstration program provides a rare opportunity for a bold approach to
the problems of urban congestion and the breakdown of urban
mobility. For the most part, this opportunity has not been grasped.
Few of the projects, with the exception of those involving new kinds
of hardware, and the service innovations in Peoria and Skokie, Ill.;
Flint, Mich.; Haddonfield, N.J.; and the Shirley Highway in northern Virginia, have made any radical departure from conventional
mass transportation experience.[17] This is not to say that demonstrations have to be radical or exotic to be worthwhile, but past
techniques have failed to retain transit customers, and it is important to recognize the problem as far too serious for limited thinking
or a timid approach.

Conservatism was understandable in the earlier demonstrations
because of the reliance on local initiative and the necessity, until
recently, for one-third funding on the local level. Local participation is obviously desirable on as large a basis as possible, because
of the hope for possible future uptake of ideas, but the limited
funds and talent usually available in most places are not likely to

generate advanced thinking or vastly new approaches to problems. More money and the application of professional research may stimulate greater innovation and a more vigorous approach. Of course, professionals may lack any basic knowledge of mass transit and in ignorance may develop bold solutions for which there are no problems. Research firms with a background in space or military technology and a firm foundation in the systems approach may have no knowledge relevant to means of delivering a consumer service. Solving space and military problems may not be the best background for a contractor probing the field of urban mass transportation.

The early reluctance of the federal government to exercise initiative is unfortuate, but also understandable. Back in the early 1960's, projects originated in Washington for exercise on the local level could easily be construed as "more federal interference." Again, until 1970 Congress had not been generous in terms of appropriations. Beyond that, before the programs were switched over to DOT, HUD was in the process of getting organized. Not only was HUD trying to digest the mass transport programs in as smooth a manner as possible, it was also pulling itself together after its creation as a separate, cabinet-level agency in December 1965. Lack of staff, lack of funds, the problems of establishing a pecking order, and few guidelines to go by, are not the sort of stuff that bold and exciting programs are made of. Much the same thing happened when the mass transportation programs were placed in DOT.

Probably the boldest, most effective step that UMTA could take would be to develop a systematic approach to a better understanding of mass transportation. Broad programs of research would be laid out aimed at reaching given information objectives. The major goal would be to plug the gaps—"gulfs" might be a better word—in knowledge concerning mass transport. Locally initiated projects that fit would become integral parts of broader projects. Where local initiative did not produce a suitable demonstration "segment" proposal, UMTA could conduct one on its own. Of course, worthwhile but strictly independent demonstration ideas from the local level that did not fit into any particular research pattern should be encouraged as strongly as possible.

To a very large extent the thrust at UMTA has been as outlined above, yet the program of research, development, and demonstration is still incomplete. It focuses on hardware and technology to the exclusion of needed work on the management and marketing side of transit.[18]

By no means should local-initiative demonstrations be put aside completely in favor of a more structured approach. Dealing with locally conceived ideas is probably the best way for the RD&D personnel to stay abreast of what its most important constituency and strongest supporter, the cities themselves, feel is important. Failure to keep in touch—to communicate—through the demonstration program would be unwise in the extreme. These projects are also, to some extent, an index of the attitudes and initiative of the mass transit industry. Furthermore, there is no better way to help build a spirit of innovation than to have persons working in transit management help to educate themselves by being closely involved in an innovative demonstration project.

Demonstration Findings

So much for a broad and general view of what the demonstrations have or have not accomplished. What of the findings of some of the individual demonstrations? Unfortunately, there are so many projects that it is impossible to provide a detailed discussion of them by any means short of a book exclusively on that subject. Even so, one can pull together the experience and information gathered in many of the projects and get a fair handle on what has been learned. As might be suspected, the findings in many cases are not particularly new or surprising, but merely serve to confirm long-held notions or hypotheses.

It is evident that the United States is not yet prepared to solve traffic congestion by prohibiting the use of automobiles in certain places at certain times—at least on a large-scale, nationwide basis, the energy shortage notwithstanding. Hence the major goal of many demonstrations is to find a way to make mass transportation more attractive to those who might use transit as a matter of choice. Many of the most interesting experiments concentrated on attracting customers—of their own free choice—into using mass transportation, through a variety of service innovations. Another group of experiments concentrated on technical demonstrations of equipment or techniques which did not directly involve the stimulation of consumer acceptance of mass transit. Other projects sought to improve the efficiency as a means of helping increase access to employment or to community services for those in poverty.

Going Where People Want to Go

The most basic question that might be posed is what attracts people to transit. Based on the demonstrations so far completed, three major elements seem to stand out. The first is perhaps most obvious. Mass transport operations must link places between which people wish to travel in fairly large numbers; essentially, this means services which correspond to people's so-called "desire lines" of travel. Demonstrations dealing with radial transit service focusing on downtown areas have shown that increasing the frequency or speed of service will attract increased ridership. Improved commuter train services in Philadelphia (PA-MTD-1 [PA-06-0002]) and Boston (MASS-MTD-1 [MA-06-0007]) bear out this conclusion. New radial express bus service has also proved attractive to consumers in St. Louis (INT-MTD-8 [IT-06-0011]) and Baltimore (MD-MTD-1 [MD-06-0004]). Much the same is true of the express bus service offered on a reserved lane of the Shirley Highway connecting northern Virginia suburbs with Washington, D.C. (INT-MTD-23 [IT-06-0024]), and of the reserved reversed lanes for buses on the New Jersey approaches to the Lincoln Tunnel (Urban Corridor Demonstration Program USDOT Contract FH-11-7646). Some findings in the St. Louis area (INT-MTD-8 [IT-06-0011]) tend to contradict this point; however, in the St. Louis case the "cross-suburban" line linked together a number of well-used radial local and express lines. The key factor appears to be the degree of integration with other parts of the system.

There are important considerations, besides the obvious one of providing service where there is need, in operating services that draw large ridership. Few informed persons today believe that mass transit service of reasonably good quality can be offered on a profitable or even a break-even basis; the difficulty in improving productivity of operating staff and the peaked nature of demand for transit conspire against operations that cover cost. Still, mass transportation service that serves few persons and rings up a smashing deficit cannot be supported for long. Minimizing the subsidy while hauling large numbers of passengers who are rather pleased with the service appears to be a reasonable goal, especially if the economic and social cost of having to provide alternatives to transit is much more expensive. The most potent factors in achieving this admittedly limited goal appear to be such items as schedules, reliability of service, equipment characteristics, fare structure, convenience and comfort, cleanliness, availability of parking (especially for longer distance services linking suburbs with the center city), and advertising and public relations.[19] These are the factors management can do something about.

Despite the obvious importance of service quality, providing good service cast in the usual transit mold is no guarantee of success in terms of substantial ridership or minimized financial loss. It must be recognized that the distribution of population and jobs, and alterations in shopping habits and needs, have changed a great deal since the days of the streetcar and the highly transit-oriented city of a half-century ago. Many travel needs cannot be met by public mass transit competing with the private automobile—transit is simply not a reasonable alternative. Blue-collar workers living on the outskirts of a city and employed in factories that provide ample free parking are likely to be very poor prospects for mass transportation. So are suburban shoppers who need an easy way to lug the groceries home; the auto is obviously the easiest way to accomplish such a journey.

In short, what are principally "crosstown" or "cross-suburb" operations have usually not panned out well as demonstrations, nor have services oriented to suburban factories or other places with abundant free parking. This was made evident in the projects carried out in Memphis (TENN-MTD-1 [TN-06-0001]) and Nashville (TENN-MTD-2 [not given]). The subscription bus service demonstration in Flint, Michigan (MICH-MTD-2 [MI-06-0007]), had dismal results because it was aimed at workers in automobile factories who owned cars, were relatively affluent, were provided with free parking, and needed the flexibility provided by the private car in order to take advantage of overtime work possibilities.

The difficulty of effectively serving thinly populated areas, economically, with regular fixed route service has prompted experimentation with demand-achieved service—typically called dial-a-bus —that can respond to given demands and provide door-to-door service. The Haddonfield, N.J., dial-a-bus is the only federally sponsored demonstration exclusively involving that concept, but there has been some private experimentation. Demand-activated service was a part of the Hempstead, Long Island, feeder service project (NY-MTD-11 [NY-06-0014]).[20]

Access

As a second major demonstration finding, the critical importance of access to transit has been revealed in the findings and in the relative success or failure of attracting patrons in a number of the demonstrations. Access, as the term is used here, has both a time and a physical dimension. In its time dimension, this involves both scheduling, and all the knotty problems connected with it, as well as operating services with a fair degree of frequency. Schedules and frequency are, of course, interrelated factors. The more frequent the service, the less troublesome is the matter of scheduling times that optimize patron's convenience rather than the convenience and economic constraints of an entire transit operation. Commuter railway demonstrations in Philadelphia (PA-MTD-5 [PA-06-0011]) and Boston (MASS-MTD-1 [MA-06-0007]) and the Skokie Swift in the Chicago area (ILL-MTD-1 [IL-06-0007]) bear out the importance of frequent service in attracting new patrons to transit, as opposed to optimum times of departure. On the other hand, the less frequent Baltimore express bus operation (MD-MTD-1 [MD-06-0004]) illustrates the problem of selecting schedules convenient to patrons. The total demand involved and the particular departure and arrival needs of the consumers in a given market segment are the critical factors.

Physical access is a somewhat different problem. It has two aspects. Direct physical access involves the relatively old-fashioned notion of getting transit service near the people using a fixed route structure. By skillfully plotting a route it is possible to situate a service so that a maximum number of patrons live within the one-eighth mile—roughly two-block walking distance—critical patronage area of transit routes. It should be noted that standard transit thinking considers the patronage area to be one-quarter of a mile, with routes spaced one-half mile apart. Some demonstrations indicate that patronage drops very sharply for those who live more than about an eighth of a mile from a bus line. The distance people are willing to walk is probably somewhat greater for rapid transit and commuter rail service.[21]

Another, highly successful approach—one of the really original innovations of the whole demonstration program to date—involved utilizing the full potential of the bus to its maximum extent by going after the customers with a flexible routing program. This approach —tested in Peoria and Decatur, Ill. (ILL-MTD-3 and ILL-MTD-4 [not given])—requires a contractual, or subscription, fare agreement in which customers pay in advance through purchase of a special monthly pass. A considerable amount of effort is required to plot routes that link patrons' homes with destination points in the central business district or some other major employment concentration within relevant constraints of operating time, cost, and revenue. In actuality, one might call it a kind of personal selling or personalized service approach to marketing transit.

By having the bus go after the passengers, rather than the other way around, the usual inherent defect of patrons having to walk some distance to transit is eliminated. The willingness of patrons to contract in advance for service opens the possibility of fine-tuning bus service to meet travel needs more exactly than regular fixed route service. While less flexible than a demand-actuated system such as a dial-a-bus, the subscription bus may be less costly to operate and the supply of service may be more closely related to demand by means of more accurate prediction. There is the possibility that subscription service may be applicable to trips other than the journey to work, particularly if the bundle of service and price—particularly price—were more attractive to potential off-peak patrons than alternate means of transit. Substantial increases in mobility at reasonable cost to all concerned might be feasible with subscription bus service aimed at the elderly and handicapped and oriented to origin and destination points outside the Central Business District. This is especially so if such patrons must make some relatively regular trip, such as to a doctor, hospital, or site of therapy, or for regular shopping excursions. The possibly high unit cost per patron in a dial-a-bus operation may discourage the not-so-well-off from using it if they have to pay the charges that might go with such a level of flexibility. Welfare agencies, if they pick up the tab for transportation, may also be reluctant to pay the higher costs. In any event subscription service may provide a happy medium between fixed route service and completely flexible service in terms of time, origin, and destination.

Access may also be of an indirect nature. In other words, instead of attempting to take transit as close as possible to a maximum number of people, good interchange facilities may be provided so that as many people as possible may easily put themselves in a position to use certain transit facilities. In such situations, a maximum amount of properly located parking space seems to be a key ingredient. The same thing may be accomplished with buses feeding into a rail line or an express bus facility. Another method is to use the same fixed route bus for both the pickup and delivery as well as line-haul operations, with the line-haul operated as an express to minimize travel time. The attractiveness of the feeder line seems closely related to the frequency of service and the amount of time needed for this segment of a trip. Unless it is feasible to operate service frequently and the elapsed travel time is short, it seems best to let this element of "pick-up" service remain in the hands of the individual patron by providing adequate parking space and a fast transit ride to destination.[22] Whatever the means used, people will obviously not use transit if they can't get to it, or if it can't get to them.

Time

The third major element affecting transit attractiveness is the elapsed time necessary to make a trip. Clearly, this should compare favorably with the amount of time required to travel by means of the private automobile if mass transit is to be at all competitive. The survey research findings in the Seattle Monorail demonstration (WASH-MTD-1 [WA-06-0003]) give a clear indication of the emphasis given to this factor in public thinking. Over-all travel time is, obviously, a function of access as well as running speed on the line-haul part of the journey. Just running trains or buses faster is not enough. In order to utilize mass transport a patron may have to use his automobile for a portion of the journey, transfer to a line-haul link provided by means of mass transit, and perhaps utilize walking or some means of mass transport for the final stage of a journey into the central city. For mass transportation to be attractive these connections have to be coordinated, fast, and the transfer between them relatively painless.

Several of the demonstrations were particularly enlightening as to proper linkage, access, and transit time. The express bus operations in St. Louis (INT-MTD-8 [IT-06-0011]), wherein the buses operated as locals in the pickup stage within various outlying communities and then ran express downtown where they again ran as locals for delivery, indicated the efficacy of this sort of operation. The Premium Special Service in Peoria (ILL-MTD-3 [not given]) is another example of combining access on both ends with relatively high speed line-haul and convenience; likewise the Shirley Highway Express Bus (INT-MTD-23 [IT-06-0024]) and the Seattle Blue Streak Express Bus operation (WASH-MTD-2 [WA-06-0004]).

More surprising, perhaps, was the so-called Skokie Swift experiment conducted in Skokie, Ill., utilizing the abandoned right-of-way of an electric interurban railway (ILL-MTD-1 [IL-06-0007]). The high-speed, rapid transit shuttle train linking Skokie with the northern terminus of the major north-south elevated line of the Chicago Transit Authority proved to be enormously successful; indeed, the Swift has continued in operation to the present day. This particular demonstration flew directly in the face of a transit operating tradition which holds that people should never be made to transfer if it can be avoided. The shuttle train ran non-stop between its terminals; all passengers making journeys to or from Chicago's Loop (which amounted to well over 90 per cent of the patronage during the demonstration period) had to transfer at least once. Many of them drove their cars to the Skokie terminal, transferred to the Skokie Swift, transferred again to the main Chicago-North-South Elevated, and then transferred once more to another transit vehicle in the Loop. It seems clear that the high-speed link simply provided a better alternative, in terms of travel time and relative difficulty to people traveling from the northwestern suburbs of Chicago into the Loop than did driving their car all the way, or using some other mode or combination of modes of mass transportation. The "Swift" was the vital link that opened up the speed potential of the Chicago Rapid Transit System to many erstwhile motorists who otherwise would not have had access to it.

If more or less conventional mass transport can be made attractive when it matches traveler's desire lines, is accessible and competitive on a time basis, can new forms of transport technology offer added attraction to customers? In other words, is newness a virtue in itself; does a "freak" approach provide certain benefits in customer appeal, reduction in operating cost, or some other dimension that makes for a genuine improvement in mass transit? The answer is a guarded "yes." The reason for the caveat is the circumstances under which some of the new technological wrinkles were tested. The very positive reaction of the public noted in the Seattle Monorail Study (WASH-MTD-1 [WA-06-0003]) was doubtlessly much affected by the use of the monorail in connection with the festive occasion of the Seattle World's Fair. The same is true of the Westinghouse Transit Expressway (PA-MTD-2 [PA-06-0009]) which was tested in conjunction with the Allegheny County Fair. Its continued operation for several years in a park near Pittsburgh was more like a ride at an amusement park than transit. How long the enthusiasm of the public would last under more normal conditions is another question. Furthermore, neither demonstration was on a large enough scale to prove whether either form of transit system is really feasible as a key part of a dependable, comprehensive mass transport system. In both cases, it was obvious that a major plus factor was novelty.

On the negative side, both of the new modes mentioned above are burdened by a guidance system, i.e., "what keeps it on the track," that is the acme of cumbersomeness. Both rely on a complex system of rubber-tired wheels on horizontal and vertical axes to replace the conventional flanged steel wheel on a steel rail. Operating and maintenance costs would appear to be suspiciously high for economical use as a part of a mass transportation system. Added to this is the difficult, slow, and apparently costly problem of switching between "tracks" on such offbeat modes. Considerable work will be needed to provide foolproof operations under the demanding conditions of mass transit service. Nevertheless, the demonstration in Pittsburgh gave additional proof of the practicality of automatic train control. Undeniably, new modes may provide means of avoiding the shortcomings of more conventional systems, but they are practical only if they do not create more problems than they solve. It is unlikely they will become a part of existing rapid transit systems unless the new systems are somehow made compatible with existing investments in rapid transit.[23] However, such means of transport may function admirably in special service installations, as in providing a link between parking lots and the main terminal of an airport.

Since 1970, UMTA has become particularly interested in research and demonstration work involving so-called Personal Rapid Transit (PRT) systems. PRT systems operate upon a fixed guideway, utilizing vehicles of about automobile size that operate individually by means of automatic control systems. All stations are served by sidings, so that vehicles on the main line need not stop between the origin and destination stations. "Horizontal automatic elevators" is a phrase often used to explain the PRT concept. Morgantown, W.V., is the principal demonstration site for PRT's. The installation there joins together several parts of the West Virginia University campus and the downtown part of Morgantown.

The PRT systems were literally the centerpiece of the Transpo '72 exhibition, strong evidence of the importance UMTA attaches to PRT. In addition to the Morgantown project (WV-06-0005, WV-06-0006), UMTA is financing the construction of a PRT system in Denver. Planning work has been carried out for application of PRT to Minneapolis, and a "revenue" version of the Westinghouse system is planned for Pittsburgh.[24]

The hovercraft linking San Francisco Bay area airports and air terminals (CAL-MTD-3 [CA-06-0022]) was less successful than some of the other innovations in modal technology. The public obviously did not clasp this service to its bosom as it did the monorail and transit expressway. Perhaps this was because it was used in a regular service not enjoying the aura of excitement connected with a fair. Moreover, there were some significant operating problems. For example, the hovercraft could not be used safely at certain times, particularly during the hours of darkness and when the water was rough in the bay. It was also quite noisy. In brief, although such vehicles have enjoyed considerable use abroad—mainly in Great Britain—the general result in this country was less than encouraging as regards passenger appeal or practical operations. The important thing is, of course, that the hovercraft was tried out.

Although the final report is not yet completed, the demonstration of a gas-turbine propelled commuter car—tested on the Long Island Rail Road (INT-MTD-12 [IT-06-0015])—indicated that this form of propulsion is not yet reliable enough for commuter railroad operations. The potential is enormous, however, and if perfected could be utilized in providing high-speed commuter services where demand did not justify the heavy cost of electrification. The demonstration has been extended and expanded to develop a car that can operate directly from an electric power source or by means of gas turbine driving a generator supplying power to the car's traction motors. If perfected, Long Island trains could operate from Manhattan as electric trains using the third rail pickup—as at present—and when the end of third rail territory is reached, continue on by means of the gas turbine driving the electric traction motors. No more changing at Jamaica!

In San Francisco, the decision to build a high-speed, automated rapid transit system gives rise to many problems not faced by older and more conventional systems. The test track setup provided under demonstration grants (CAL-MTD-2 and 7 [CA-06-0021, CA-06-0026]) permitted automatic control devices to be tested under laboratory conditions,[25] along with such items as power collection, truck design, braking, acoustics, etc. This rapid transit laboratory —which is now part of BART's Walnut Creek line—has been so successful and useful that, as mentioned earlier, the UMTA is cooperating in constructing a permanent rapid transit laboratory as part of the DOT railway technology test track near Pueblo, Colo.

One case of a modal technology winning cheers from patrons while operating under normal conditions was the Washington Minibus (DC-MTD-2 [DC-06-0006]). The service was a downtown shuttle in the main shopping area of the District of Columbia. The service was frequent, the fare was a low five cents, and the small, highly maneuverable buses used were considered attractive. Indeed, in questionnaire and interview responses, the public was overwhelming in its classification of the minibuses as "cute." Cuteness must count, for this demonstration was considered to be quite successful, and the operation has been continued—at a higher fare—since the conclusion of the demonstration period. Several other cities—Los Angeles, Sacramento, and Detroit, among others—have felt the downtown minibus idea to be fetching enough to operate similar services.

Pricing, at first glance, seems to play a rather ambiguous role in the matter of attractiveness or unattractiveness of mass transportation. From the results of several demonstrations, it is rather obvious that, in general, customers don't mind paying for good service.[26] In a few of the demonstrations the improved service was not offered at a reduced rate; indeed, the rates were often higher for use of express service, as in the St. Louis Express Bus experiment (INT-MTD-8 [IT-06-0011]). Even so, the service was well received. This obviously does not mean that people don't value money in our affluent society, but, rather, that they run through a rough mental evaluation of the quality of service they receive for their expenditure. While people may not precisely calculate what it costs them to drive, they have a notion of the general range of cost and can compare the relative comfort of mass transport and private transportation. So, while prices may not be the major determining factor in transit use, they cannot be too far out of line with what the general public feels it costs them to use alternatives, or what the mass transportation service is worth.

Perhaps the importance of the quality of service relative to price was most clearly revealed in the SEPACT II and SEPACT III studies in Philadelphia (PA-MTD-4 [PA-06-0010]; PA-MTD-5 [PA-06-0011]).[27] In the survey research interviews most patrons saw nothing wrong with raising fares if it meant improvements in the quality of transport service provided. In the SEPACT III, Operation Reading project, fares were raised and service was improved with an increase in ridership and revenue; this had the happy effect of cutting the deficit. In the same demonstration, reducing service levels and cutting fares did not attract sufficient patronage or produce enough revenue to materially affect the deficit. Of course, in general, increases in fares have had much to do with chasing patrons away from mass transportation. The key point in this apparent contradiction is that for transit in general fares were raised without improvement in service; in fact, service cutbacks often accompanied the fare hike. Under such circumstances rider defection should be expected.

Even so, a price change can dramatize some alteration or improvement in mass transit services and be counted as an important factor in the success of an operation. In other words, the critical, long-run element in attracting and holding patronage to mass transit appears most likely to be the quality of the service in terms of speed, convenience, access, and so on. A lowered price is merely another attraction; in this case one that is easily measured in terms of the differential between the previous charge and a new "package" of service offered to the public. Once the public has tested and approved the wares, the price may be adjusted upward without loss of patronage, as was the case in Philadelphia and Boston (PA-MTD-1 and MASS-MTD-1 [PA-06-0008 and MA-06-0007]).

How important is advertising and promotion in attracting patronage? Without doubt, good promotion is important to the success of either a demonstration or the regular operations of mass transit service. Almost all of the demonstrations attempting to woo passengers to mass transit have relied on some promotional work; all of the mass media have been utilized. In a demonstration study of the effectiveness of the different mass media carried out in Pittsburgh (PA-MTD-7 [PA-06-0013]), it is clear that radio and television have an impact—perhaps a subtle one—on the potential transit patron. This project also revealed that improved maps and schedules also play an important part in making transit service more attractive.

One project (INT-MTD-10 [IT-06-0013]), carried out in Washington, D.C., was aimed at finding "what could be done through better information aids to encourage wider and more frequent use of mass transit."[28] While the general purpose of the demonstration seemed reasonable enough, the demonstration was unable to prove any of its hypotheses very definitely. Indeed, many of them could not be tested at all for a variety of reasons, including civil disorders that badly disrupted Washington, D.C., during the course of the demonstration. Practically everything one could imagine went wrong in the project; the special informational signs even mildewed so badly that it was difficult to read them. In any case, it was apparent that people will use information if it is made available to them; whether or not better maps, timetables, and information signs can actually boost transit use remains to be seen.

Very unsubtle, but seemingly highly important forms of promotion are visibility of the transit vehicles in operation and word of mouth. Seeing an actual operation is a constant reminder of availability and perhaps a good indication of potential access. The best form of promotion seems to be the word-of-mouth opinion of a friend or acquaintance who has been satisfied by the service offered —at least, results in the demonstrations in Skokie, Peoria, New Castle, and Watts points in this direction.

Do the mass transport demonstrations indicate whether or not improved transit can pay its own way? It should be noted that self-supporting operation was not always a factor to be tested in the demonstrations. In some instances, such as the commuter rail experiments in Philadelphia (PA-MTD-1 [PA-06-0008]), a major aspect of the desired payoff was in reduced automobile traffic congestion.

In other related projects (PA-MTD-3 [not given] and PA-MTD-4 [PA-06-0010]) reducing but not necessarily eliminating the deficit was a factor sought. In any case, most of the demonstrations did not pay their way through the farebox during the period of project operation. Again, in most of the demonstrations the period of testing was too short to effect a change in the habits of potential patrons to a sufficient degree to render an operation profitable.[29] A good upward trend in ridership may point to profitability in time, if the service is continued.

There were some exceptions to the rule of unprofitability. Both the Skokie Swift in the Chicago area (ILL-MTD-1 [IL-06-0007]) and the Premium Special Service operation in Peoria (ILL-MTD-3 and 4 [not given]) were profitable to a degree. The Skokie Swift returns about $10,000 per month over and above operating costs; the Chicago Transit Authority maintains that the Swift is a profitable venture at the present time. After about a year's operation in Peoria, the Premium Special Service went over the break-even point and showed a strong trend toward handsome profitability. In this case, however, the buses used were those which proved to be redundant at rush hours. No new equipment was purchased for this experiment; excess capacity was merely utilized. The costs would be higher and the profit potential lower in a situation where new buses were purchased in order to operate the service.

Are there untapped markets for mass transportation? Apparently so. The demonstrations have indicated that it is possible to attract more riders to certain types of services, even if these riders have alternative transport available. Many experiments revealed this—especially those in Peoria, St. Louis, Philadelphia, and Boston.

Perhaps it comes as no surprise that transit was doing a very poor job of serving even those persons who did not have a reasonable alternative to the use of mass transportation. This was clear in the Watts area; the existing transit system in this part of Los Angeles seemed uniquely geared toward *not* meeting the mobility needs of a low-income, low-skill community. The relevant job opportunities for its residents lie east and west of Watts; the transit system was oriented north and south. In other words, the transit system was molded to fit the needs of those wishing to go to the downtown Los Angeles area; this radial pattern of operations is typical of most mass transit service in the United States. Some of the very largest cities, such as Chicago, New York, San Francisco, and Philadelphia, have a considerable amount of crosstown service, although it is not always as high in service level and quality as the major radial lines. Somewhat smaller cities, such as Indianapolis, still have the major route focus on the CBD, and through riders or crosstown riders must transfer physically at some central point.

How many transit routes and transit systems operate in a fashion completely inappropriate to today's needs is at present not a matter of definite knowledge. As noted earlier, it is probably not too bad a guess to estimate that a significant portion of today's service religiously follows the pattern and routes established from fifty to a hundred years ago by the streetcar. Such routing may provide a serious time, money, and energy burden to those persons whose access to mobility is limited to public transportation. At the same time, the awkwardness of travel to non-CBD points actively discourages non-captive riders from choosing mass transportation.

Several studies have been undertaken on the subject of mobility and job opportunity, and in all probability, a considerable amount of work should be done on the pattern of transit operations in light of today's patterns of distribution of population and economic activity.[30] Many of the plans supported in part by federal money (under Section 9 of the Urban Mass Transportation Act, as amended in 1966) have sought to devise routing meeting present-day needs.

Of all these, the Watts demonstration is the best known. It involved, among other things, the inauguration of a new east-west bus line on Century Boulevard, which has been criticized as costing too much per patron and is not significantly reducing unemployment in Watts. Employment and employability involve much more than the spatial mobility afforded by transit. Low-income ghetto residents have problems of health, education, skill level, etc., that cannot be met by transportation alone, even though transport and the mobility it provides are a vital part of the package of supporting services needed in getting and keeping a job. Moreover, the scatteration of economic activity in the Los Angeles area makes the automobile the only practical means of travel in many cases.[31]

Few of the demonstration projects—or any of the other types of project, for that matter—have dwelt on the subject of transit management, despite the importance of management sensitive to consumer needs in improving the attractiveness, acceptance, and utilization of mass transportation by the public. One project, IND-MTD-1 [IN-06-0002]), put together a handbook for the management of small-scale mass transportation undertakings. Another demonstration (VA-MTD-2 [VA-06-0002]) devised a management game aimed primarily at maintenance and equipment utilization. Another management-oriented demonstration project was carried out for the purpose of developing a modern information system for mass transportation companies, including a new approach to accounting (OHIO-MTD-1 [not given]). This project included data-gathering devices mounted on buses that could be periodically probed to extract the stored information and make it available for use in a computer.[32]

This discussion only touches upon the demonstration projects. Nevertheless, the goal here has been to give some flavor of what has been discovered, not to present an exhaustive coverage. Since many of the nondemonstration research projects, conducted mainly on a contract basis, have either not yet been completed or implemented at the time of this writing, it is difficult to say just what their contribution to over-all knowledge of mass transit will be.[33]

The technical study and capital projects carried out with federal aid, while not designed to provide the same kind of information as the demonstrations and other research projects, nevertheless give some interesting insights into the transit situation at the present time. The technical studies have provided an opportunity for an evaluation of the transit situation in many cities. In many places these studies are often the first such probe in many years; in other cases, they are the first such study ever undertaken. Many of these are of interest in the light they shed on the adequacy of transit service compared to the distribution and needs of the population. Depending upon the quality of the research, some of these studies are an important contribution to general knowledge about urban transportation and transportation planning as well as providing specific information about given places.

Some of the technical studies are excellent pieces of work. The one in Denver (COLO-T9-7 [CO-09-0007]), for example, is probably one of the most thorough planning studies ever carried out and will probably stand as a model of its type for many years. On the other hand, some of the studies, particularly those done for small cities, are real production-line quickies done at a low price.

(For most small cities UMTA limits its contribution to about $20,000; this means, with the local one-third match, that only $30,000 is available to carry out the work.) One federal official admitted that some of the studies are cranked out using exactly the same format, approach, and advice, regardless of the place in question, changing only the city name and some of the numbers to suit the local situation. Such work is really poor value for the money even though they are relatively inexpensive.

The capital grant applications are revealing in their own way. By reading through them, one can grasp the depths to which the transit industry has fallen in terms of ancient equipment and rickety, substandard facilities. In some cities, transit operators are trying to carry on with maintenance facilities originally built as horsecar barns and that threaten, literally, to cave in from age and deterioration.

Conclusion

The mass transportation demonstrations revealed the major importance of linking together places travelers wish to go, the need for easy access to transit, and an elapsed travel time comparable to that of the automobile if transit is to gain greater acceptance by the public. Among other findings, the role of fares as a promotional device and the apparent willingness of patrons to pay higher fares for quality service was perhaps the most interesting. Most of the findings of importance could have been expected even before an actual given demonstration project was carried out. Indeed, one could almost have written the report of the importance of these factors before the demonstration. How to achieve these ends by actually mounting a transportation service is another matter. Probably surprising to some persons was the unexpected failure of higher fares to reduce patronage once a high quality level of service was reached. Also unexpected may be seen the success in attracting patrons by merely using conventional transit technology in a new and more attractive fashion. It is fair to observe that a brand new technology weighted down with space-age gadgets would have to be enormously attractive to do a better job of attracting masses of riders than some of the express bus services or improved commuter rail and rapid transit services that have been demonstrated and that continue to operate.

Urban travel is a serious business; people rarely do it for fun. Essentially, the urban traveler is buying performance in making his choice of travel modes. He is, apparently, willing to pay a fairly high price—witness the use of the automobile—for that performance. The gloss of new technology won't attract patronage unless there is performance under the cosmetic appeal. Perhaps this is the basic lesson of the demonstrations. Those that successfully appealed to the public delivered performance; research and demonstration efforts now and in the future will also have to deliver.

In brief, then, the mass transportation demonstrations have been successful in adding to our knowledge about the role that transit can play in our cities. With more money for experimentation and a vigorous and well-designed program of research projects that help fill informational gaps, the demonstration program can be even more useful a part of the federal package of aid to urban mass transportation. Whether it will, indeed, be so depends primarily on the boldness, imagination, and initiative of those guiding the federal programs in the future.

CHAPTER FIVE

The Federal Mass
Transportation Programs:
What Went Right
and What Went Wrong

Introduction

The previous chapter discussed in some detail the demonstration projects financed under the federal policy toward mass transportation. In this chapter a broad review of the more general accomplishments of the mass transportation programs is given, along with some of the principal shortfallings of federal policy and its execution. More discussion is devoted to shortcomings than to successes, not to minimize that success, but to spell out problem areas that need action.

There is little doubt that the federal mass transportation programs have had solid accomplishments. The renaissance of urban mass transportation can be traced to the federal policy and programs. Even so, in looking at any one point in time, progress may appear to be slow or nonexistent. Without doubt, many of the future bright spots in transit progress will rest on a foundation now being patiently put down, but it is obviously difficult to know which of the present actions will enjoy a substantial payoff. What follows, then, is based on what is now known, or what now seems to be a candid view of the situation.

What the Programs Have Accomplished

There is much that can be counted in a strictly numerical sense in reviewing the twelve years of a federal role in mass transit. The decisive action starts, of course, after the passage of the Urban Mass Transportation Act of 1964, because, as the reader will recall, the Housing Act of 1961 made provisions only for demonstration grants and low-interest loans. The capital grants authorized in the 1964 Act began to be parcelled out in the early part of 1965. To look at one five-year period, between February 1965, and January 1, 1971, the federal government made 154 capital improvement grants totalling $729,534,678, along with three capital improvement loans amounting to $63,100,000. In this period, the transit properties of thirty-eight cities had their bus systems rescued through federally aided purchases of financially distressed, privately owned carriers. In addition, much new equipment was purchased. In those first five years of the capital grant program, 4,566 new buses, 950 rail rapid transit cars, and 630 commuter railroad cars were bought as a result of federal aid. Seventy miles of rail rapid transit track extensions were financed, in part, with federal money. Five cities received money to assist in modernizing outmoded rail rapid transit station facilities. Aid was also provided for the improvement or construction of forty-two bus garage and service facilities. Financial aid was given as well for the modernization or upgrading of 181 miles of commuter railroad right-of-way.[1]

The emphasis on the purchase of equipment in the early years of the capital grant program is worthy of some discussion. New rolling stock was badly needed in most U.S. cities in order to replace worn equipment. Furthermore, while a new bus or rapid transit car is not what most people would consider cheap, it it far less costly to supply equipment than to finance major extensions of rapid transit subway lines, or to fund new rapid transit systems. Moreover, it is not hard to argue in favor of replacing a bus over fifteen years of age or a forty-year-old subway car. Essentially, then, most of the early grants of capital went to provide replacements on a one for one basis. This is a fairly uncomplicated procedure and could be handled quite well by the limited staff of the UMTA and its predecessor agencies in this time period. In addition, if visible evidence of a program was wanted, the relatively short lead time needed to get new buses on the street brought a fast show of something happening. Finally, even though the money was limited, in this general stage of mainly replacing overage rolling stock, the need was so widespread that the money was distributed about rather well on a geographic basis so that the benefits were not confined to any one section of the country.

The Urban Mass Transportation Administration points with considerable pride to calendar 1971, the first year in which the amount of money available for mass transportation can, in charity, be said to have advanced beyond the relatively microscopic stage. In that year there were 269 grants totalling $558,554,289 in federal funds, to which were added local matching funds of $298,136,413, for a total of $856,690,702 spent nationally on mass transportation. There were ninety-nine capital grants for a total of $485,683,830; these funds were used toward the purchase of 4,121 new buses and 493 commuter rail and rapid transit cars. Funds were provided to fifty-five cities for aid in upgrading maintenance and other facilities. Sixty-two new technical studies (planning) grants were funded, at a federal cost of $15,066,505. Thirteen new and eighteen amended demonstration grants and contracts were awarded totalling $15,-275,761. Eighteen research and development grants and twenty-four additions to previous grants were awarded, amounting to $38,218,-403. Sixty managerial training grants amounting to a sum of $334,356 were awarded. Research and training grants at thirty-three universities were approved. Funding of $1,046,191 was provided in seven new service development grants.[2] To anyone at all familiar with the early cheese-paring days of the federal programs, the scope and magnitude of the effort in 1971 are truly astounding.

These countable things are important and obviously cited with justifiable swagger by those responsible for the federal programs. The importance of these actions lies not so much in the impact they have had in terms of generating ridership (which, as will be noted later, appears to be negligible) or in making over a generally lacklustre and shabby industry, but because *something* was done, and that something was definitely a positive step. By the early sixties, the transit industry as a whole had not gone through a major re-equipment undertaking since immediately after World War II; some rapid transit facilities had not enjoyed a major renovation since the time of their original construction in the first two or three decades of the twentieth century. By the end of the first half-dozen years under the Urban Mass Transportation Act, a large amount of badly needed equipment was made available to a severely distressed industry.

The most important factor in all the federal activity is not so much the details of what was done, but the fact that federal money is available at all for mass transportation. For better or worse, the trend since the Depression has been for state and local government to forfeit the mantle of leadership in solving problems to the federal government. Federal interest in an area, backed by federal money, is a surefire means of bringing attention and perhaps action by state and local government in an area of need. Regardless of what may appear to be quibbling in the pages that follow, the continuation and growth of federal aid to transit has changed the outlook of U.S. cities in regard to mass transportation. It has also helped to start a trend toward more involvement by state government. By the first half of 1974 there were twenty-one state departments of transportation. Most of these played a role in urban mass transportation and some provided financial aid for transit, usually as a portion of the local matching funds required for federal grant aid.[3]

Before the federal urban mass transportation program was instituted, those urban residents and officials who wished seriously to make improvements in mass transit were stymied by severe financial malnutrition in the local coffers and a lack of outside funding. It is strange that almost a whole nation can tune out a given problem or go blithely along a given path—no matter how misguided the direction may have been in the clarity of hindsight. Despite the warning signals of the early 1950's, aid for mass transit, or an important role for urban mass transportation, was not an issue in most localities. In the absence of federal interest, no person or institution was able to pull off the blinders.

For example, most so-called transportation planning that was performed through the mid-60's was only highway planning carried on under the aegis of the highway-oriented state highway departments. Even the generally excellent Chicago Area Transportation Study —one of the real landmarks in transportation planning—almost ignored mass transportation. Indeed, highways, education, housing, and the various problems associated with population dispersion were probably viewed by public officials as the principal urban problems in the fifteen years immediately following the Second World War. Not until transportation planning was required by federal law, under the Highway Act of 1962 and the capital grant provision of the Urban Mass Transportation Act of 1964, did planners really address themselves fully to the over-all problems of urban transportation. The money for transit planning has finally started many cities on the way to taking a good look at their mobility problems and the alternative solutions that are possible. Work is being done in an area that has long been neglected in the United States.

The development of a fairly well-organized lobbying effort in behalf of mass transportation has been both cause and effect in developing the federal role in urban mass transport. As noted earlier, the main organizational force and focus of the lobby has been a combination of the U.S. Conference of Mayors and the National League of Cities. To this has been added the transit and commuter rail operators, equipment manufacturers and suppliers, construction firms, and engineering and consulting firms. This group provides a good blend of grass-roots interests along with powerful firms that enjoy national reputations and political clout to match.

Too often the word "lobby" is thought of only in a pejorative sense. There is nothing wrong with an organized approach to the Congress—and the administration in power—in order to bring a problem to the fore and suggest remedies. In so doing, especially in a broad national issue such as transit, the lobbying process is educational for the lobbyists as well as those lobbied. This learning process has begun to pay dividends on the state and local level as more public officials address themselves to constructive mass transportation activity close to home.

On the fringes of the interest group involved with mass transport, one might add the academic community, although its members are divided on the issue. Academicians have discovered mass transportation rather late in the game as a subject for serious academic consideration. Many have questioned the usefulness of mass transportation in the typically decentralized American city, as well as the wisdom of the federal effort, in a welter of often destructive criticism. Others, sensing an opportunity to sell their expertise as consultants, have found a wave of the future on which to hitch a ride. Whether or not academic interest has been useful is debatable, but at least some of the many and varied talents harbored in the universities are beginning to investigate numerous aspects of mass transit. The consequences may be fruitful.

Another benefit of the transit programs is that at long last a firm place has been established within the governmental framework for consideration and support of mass transportation. The Federal Highway Administration and its predecessors always provided a strong voice within the federal establishment on matters involving highways. UMTA can now do the same for urban mass transportation. This new member of the federal government has not always carried out its admittedly fuzzy mission with the alacrity or in the direction many outsiders would wish. Its new internal organizational structure may help UMTA to work much more effectively in the future. The staff is small, as federal agencies go, but apparently the dedication of many of the staff matches that of the early days when only a handful of men and women manned the transit battlements and succeeded in getting the federal program started.

Having an agency charged with responsibility for transit programs is not an unmixed benefit. For one thing, it tends to dry up support for transit-related projects from other sources of funding: this means that UMTA's whims and fancies can push or hold back much of what it wants. The crotchets of just a few bureaucrats can effectively roadblock necessary and important matters. Moreover, the stronger the bureaucracy, the greater the likelihood that it will come to represent its own interests rather than those of the constituents it is supposed to serve. A party line develops within all bureaucracies; those inside or outside the bureaucracy who deviate have the corrective bastinado applied until groupthink is achieved. Clearly, the agency operating in such a fashion is doing something less than its best.

In many federal programs, objectives beyond the usual scope of an agency's affairs sometimes become evident. For example, in recent years in dispensing its grants to colleges and universities under Section 11 of the Urban Mass Transportation Act, special favor was given to places of higher education with a high proportion of minority group students. Mass transportation programs are thus educational support programs as well.

At the same time, the programs have been touted by DOT and UMTA in a highly political fashion in mimeographed press releases that speak of "President Nixon's aim to make transit the success story of the 1970's." Clearly, the administration assumes that there must be political Brownie points associated with transit, as noted earlier in this work, and it is a refreshing change from the relatively low level of presidential interest evidenced in the Kennedy and

Johnson administrations. Nevertheless, one cannot help but wonder why, if the Nixon administration is so anxious to make transit the success story of the 1970's, the office of Management and Budget slashed the amount of money available for transit in 1971.[4]

If one had to choose just one positive facet of the federal mass transit program that had clearly been beneficial, the capital provided to assure the continuation of transit service is the winner. From the end of the Second World War until the passage of the Urban Mass Transportation Act of 1964 over two hundred transit firms had gone out of business; many communities were left without transit service. Since passage of that act, with capital available to help cities or public agencies buy out private companies about to go bankrupt, fewer than a dozen transit operations have completely ceased operations. If great improvements have not been forthcoming in urban mass transportation, at least the complete loss of transit service is now a rare occurrence.[5]

Furthermore, all over the United States, the statistics cited at the beginning of this chapter are available to the people, not as mere figures on a sheet of paper, but as equipment and facilities that are providing needed service to members of the public.

The Shortcomings of the Federal Programs

The failures of the mass transportation programs—or, put another way, the problems that loom very large despite federal transit programs—are many. These shortfalls are also quite understandable, especially considering the dismal situation that existed in mass transportation when the federal programs finally got under way in 1961. A later chapter will deal at length with the reasons behind these failures, many of which are related to lack of clear-cut direction for the programs. What follows is put forth as constructive criticism.

The Continuing Decline in Ridership and Other Disasters

Perhaps the most serious failure of the federal mass transportation program is that it has not stemmed the rapid erosion of patronage that has plagued urban mass transportation in the postwar era.[6]

Despite well over a billion dollars spent on urban mass transportation by the federal government since 1961, transit patronage has dropped from 8.8 billion in 1961 to 6.5 billion in 1972, a loss of over two billion annual riders.[7] Most certainly the federal programs have had positive impacts, but an aggregate increase in transit ridership is not one of them. Regardless of the rosy glow presented in UMTA news releases on the progress made by the mass transit programs, on a national basis they have been a dismal failure in maintaining or building patronage.

The ramifications of patronage losses nationally go beyond just the lamentable dip in the number of riders. Since transit is a labor-intensive business, falling patronage can only mean rising costs per passenger; moreover as long as patronage plummets, productivity of labor can only fall. So far has transit patronage fallen that in many cities it is difficult to conceive of the enterprise as *mass* transportation any longer; perhaps this is one of the reasons that many —including federal officials—have come to refer to it as *public* transit. In short, whatever else it has done, the federal effort by itself has not changed the transit trend away from an increasingly more expensive way of handling fewer and fewer people.

The agonizing part of the whole business of thrashing around with the figures on the loss of passengers is that the definitive reasons lying behind the decline are quite unknown. For example, it is reasonable to assume that the patronage declines of the fifties reflect the suburbanization of a large proportion of the population. Even if these new suburbanites were former users of transit, in their new suburban homes they were either not served, or served poorly and inconveniently. In other words, there is a question as to whether some people stopped using transit because it did not serve their needs at all, or they had a reasonable choice in the means of transportation available and that choice was exercised against mass transportation. Increasing affluence put many people in their own cars for the first time, without doubt, accounting for some of the patronage loss, but how much and when? The drop-offs of the late 1950's, 1960, 1961, and 1969 to 1971, may reflect the depressed economic conditions of those years, but there is no definitive answer to the questions in terms of who rode, who did not ride, and why.

Perhaps, the conventional type of transit service being offered is simply increasingly irrelevant to today's needs. For example, commenting on transit and the changes in the distribution of population in the United States, one writer notes:

For the most part, urban mass transit systems have not developed in response to . . . changing needs and conditions. Routes have remained constant despite population shifts and land use changes. Central city systems often stop for no other valid reason than having reached the city's boundaries. When transit routes were first established, few people lived outside of the city so there was no need to extend service beyond the city limits. As suburbs grew, transit charters and legal restraints limited transit expansion that could have responded to the new growth. What in essence has happened is that traditional urban mass transit systems established to serve the downtown oriented city of the 1900's have not changed despite the growth and decentralization of people and jobs in the modern metropolitan area.[8]

Did the defection from mass transportation occur because the concept of mass transportation is increasingly unacceptable to the American public, relative to the automobile, or was the delivery of mass transportation so poor that only captive riders would use it? There is an important difference here, and there is no way to give a sure answer. In effect, automobile users may be captive riders, too, if where they live, or the mass transportation provided for them, gives them no choice as rational persons but to use the car. If the mass transportation concept itself is unacceptable to the American public as a free choice—and some of the demonstrations appear to give contrary evidence—then the whole of the federal mass transportation policy is useless.

The gentler decline in transit use in the mid-1960's may stem from better economic conditions, meaning more people taking the bread-and-butter trip to work, which would explain the sharp drop-offs in economically troubled 1970 and 1971. Contradicting this would be the patronage decline during the prosperous mid-fifties. The federal programs have sometimes been cited as a possible reason for the modest decline between 1961 and 1969. This is somewhat unlikely, however, since the major impact of the expenditures under the capital programs would not have been felt until the latter 1960's, which is when the most serious declines occurred. Moreover, there were not enough demonstrations involving enough people to have had any great impact on the over-all patronage trends before 1969. The patronage figures of the 1960's may reveal only a slowly eroding base of elderly and/or lower-income captive riders. This may or may not explain the sharp drop-off in patronage in 1970 and 1971. On account of rapidly escalating operating costs, fares rose sharply in those years, which may have discouraged some patrons, although if the captive patrons were truly captive, more modest defections in patronage would probably have been more likely. Or could it be that the captive transit rider is in the group most likely to be laid off in hard times? At the moment there is no way of telling.

The exact fare system (often dubbed "ready-fare") now used in many of the larger cities is a practice which may have discouraged patronage. This system, whereby bus operators will no longer make change, has been implemented since 1968 as a reaction to a sharp increase in the robbery and murder of bus drivers. This reflects yet another factor undoubtedly affecting patronage—the fear of crime and violence in the city, particularly on big-city transit systems. A less convenient method of paying fares and fear of the city itself can have only negative impact on transit ridership.[9]

Lacking other information, to understand better why transit patronage has fallen despite federal aid, one can examine the trend in commuter rail ridership, since commuter railway service has also received substantial injections of capital for new equipment as well as funds for other improvements of property.[10] Total patronage on commuter railways has stayed about the same since the federal programs got started; losses in some cities or on some lines have been balanced by growth in ridership on other lines or in other cities. Since such service is generally of high quality in terms of elapsed trip-time—as compared with regular mass transit service or even the private automobile—quality of service, it seems clear, has much to do with retaining or building patronage. One suspects that the federal expenditures have not really raised the over-all quality of transit to the point that it could hold its own against the fierce competition of the automobile.

Glum as the over-all picture on transit ridership is, there are, nevertheless, some dramatic success stories. Atlanta, Ga.; Iowa City, Iowa; Denver, Colo.; Madison, Wisc.; and the operations of the Golden Gate Bridge, Highway, and Transportation District, all enjoyed gains in ridership in 1971. The Shirley Highway Demonstration project, in the northern Virginia portion of the Washington, D.C. metropolitan area, also enjoyed considerable increases in patronage as the result of a demonstration program. A sharp reduction in fares and some service improvements greatly boosted patronage in San Diego. However, these properties enjoyed imaginative and aggressive management—something rare in the industry—along with an improvement in the quality of the transit services offered.

There is no magic in the relative success of the above named cities. Local governmental institutions in each of these places provided substantial support for the operations of the transit service —that is, operating subsidies to assure a high level of service. None of the cities was content to stop with the not inconsiderable advantage of federal capital aid for equipment and facilities, as well as federal transit planning aid. All of the cities enjoyed a vigorous marketing and promotional effort, new transit routes, express bus and other quality improvements, along with fare cuts or a policy of fare maintenance. The cities or properties in question were willing to invest local money in transit operations along with the federal money. As might be expected, the shortage of fuel experienced in the winter of 1973–1974 helped to increase the number of patrons using mass transportation in these and many other cities.[11]

There is, of course, a question as to how many localities can afford such subsidies at the present time, although federal revenue sharing may give some help. In any case, it is an argument in favor of at least short-term federal operating subsidies. Without the addition of some federal operating aid, it may not be possible to gain the full advantage of existing federal programs. The examples of success, limited though they may be, are evidence that, properly handled, mass transportation can increase its patronage.

There is no way of escaping from the fact that the transit industry, despite all that the federal government has done, is in worse shape today as a whole than it was in 1961. It is anything but President Nixon's "success story of the 1970's." One public transit manager, reflecting on the dismal situation, was quoted as saying: "I won't say our position is hopeless, but if we were a ship, people would be on our deck singing 'Nearer My God to Thee.' "[12]

There are good reasons why it is difficult to attract more patrons to mass transportation, and it is clear that the continued decline in ridership did not occur because of the federal programs but largely in spite of them. But by any measure that now exists, considered from the viewpoint of patronage, the federal transit programs have been ineffective.

Despite the rather glum patronage history of public transportation, given the proper policy direction and financial nourishment from all levels of government, future patronage may present a somewhat happier picture. Indeed, the U.S. Department of Transportation predicts a two per cent annual increase in local transit patronage from the middle 1970's through 1990. This increase is largely predicated on a policy aimed at producing more rational land use, reducing pollution and congestion, and increasing the level of mobility available to various segments of society, especially low-income persons, the elderly, and the handicapped.[13]

Looking at patronage alone may be an inadequate means of judging performance, but it is an obvious and relatively clear-cut measure. That very clarity is cause for some concern. Under the worst circumstances, a continued sharp decline in transit patronage may cause Congress to re-evaluate its current positive attitude toward mass transportation. Moreover, the congressional evaluation of federal programs in transit and other areas of need may be negative if over-all federal deficits continue to mount at the alarming rate of the early '70's. The continued patronage drops, especially the steep falling off of 1970 and 1971, may be seen as a sign that mass transit is a hopeless loser and that little can be done to help it. An upturn in patronage—soon—seems necessary if Congress is not to feel that it has been throwing money down the proverbial rat hole.

On the more positive side, perhaps the Congress will interpret the ridership figures as evidence of a need for even greater federal expenditures. Apparently this happened in the case of the passage of the Highway Act of 1973. There is no doubt that transit proponents have developed some firm supporters in the Congress, who understand the magnitude of the job that lies ahead. Adding to reasons for additional support of mass transportation by all levels of government is concern over the environment, particularly the air pollution attributable to automobiles. Providing alternative means of transportation is one possible means of reducing pollution. Another factor is the energy crisis and gasoline shortage that began in 1973. While there was some doubt that the crisis was real—some persons thought it was a ploy of the petroleum industry to raise prices—if it is, mass transportation could provide an alternative to continued heavy use of automobiles in urban areas. Indeed, so serious had shortages become in some places that there were dramatic increases in transit patronage during the first few months of 1974. For example, transit ridership was up 24 million, or about 5 per cent, in January 1974 over the same month in 1973. Whether or not this patronage trend is indicative of the beginning a long-range increase in transit ridership is difficult to say. In short, there may be forces at work that will demand that significant improvements be made in mass transportation as at least a part of an over-all policy aimed at solving problems in addition to mobility.[14]

The Information Gap

If attempts to interpret the patronage and other figures in the previous section seemed to be mainly fiddling in the dark, it is hardly a matter for wonder. In sad fact, no reliable information is generally available on mass transportation.[15] The aggregate data compiled and made public by the American Transit Association are really about all there is to go on. The transit industry does not have the funds to do a more complete job of information gathering. It is a serious deficiency in the federal effort that, despite more than a dozen years of federal programs and expenditures reaching the one-billion-dollar-a-year level, there is still no reliable, nationwide information base for mass transportation. Standards of performance are also lacking. No measure of quality is available, so the question of whether or not transit is better today than it was at some time in the past cannot really be answered. Measures of the quality of anything involve a host of difficult conceptual problems, yet there is no evidence that UMTA is taking vigorous steps to develop a standard.[16] If one assumes that the federal programs were initiated to make things in transit somehow "better," then there has to be some measure of that "better." Otherwise, the only readily available information that can be used is the patronage figures, and these seem to have damaging implications insofar as the mass transit programs are concerned. A certain reluctance to provide definitive means of evaluating federal programs is not unusual in Washington. Nevertheless, it can be potentially damaging to a program when almost the only news available is bad.

Perhaps the riders of transit in 1972 were deliriously happy in comparison with the two billion more riders who utilized transit in 1961; there is no way to tell. The federal government, somewhere along the line, should have gathered some benchmark data so that comparisons could be made. Failure to do so means working in the dark, or working with the aggregate information from given transit operations around the United States. This does not seem to be a satisfactory means of carrying out a large-scale federal program.

The gaps in information are appalling. No definitive information is available on what it costs to carry a passenger on either a time series or cross-section basis, on the productivity of labor in transit, or on effective utilization of equipment or facilities. There is no broad cross-section and time series information on who rides and who does not ride transit and why.

The federal government has not required that uniform reports or accounting systems be utilized by the transit properties receiving aid. The transit industry itself collects little management information for decision-making purposes as a matter of course in regular operations. Few transit operations can give day-by-day, trip-by-trip information on patronage or on origins and destinations of patrons, or can provide a data profile of its patrons. Few can, as a matter of course, detail the cost of given routes or trips, or the revenue contributions such routes or trips make or the benefits conferred to the public by such trips. Much of the federal program is based on the assumption that there are overspill benefits from transit sufficient to warrant the subsidy of transit operations, yet there is no definitive, standardized method of calculating the benefits. The lack of information is probably a major cause for the evident lack of success in boosting patronage. Even if the federal government does not provide operating aid for mass transportation—and the policy of the Nixon administration and UMTA is that such assistance not be given, despite the wishes of the Congress to do so—it would seem most prudent to provide federal funds to mass transportation operators to gather necessary information. This would, of course, involve mainly the salaries of persons skilled in data collection and analysis, a type of person in notably short supply in the mass transportation industry.[17]

Worse yet, perhaps, as regards knowing and understanding exactly what is happening in mass transportation, there is no systematic follow-up by UMTA on how the suggestions made in the technical studies grants have worked out when the planning is carried out in the form of a capital program. Most capital grant applications assert as justification that the new equipment or facilities will have a beneficial effect, yet there is no regular effort to check up on this assertion.[18] In terms of definitive and useful information for management or program evaluation, the federal transit programs can only be judged as being largely built upon a foundation of ignorance.

The need for good information—useful to operators, planners, and policy makers—is so obvious that the failure of UMTA to take steps in this direction is certainly grounds for suspicion that UMTA management is not doing its job properly, or has a peculiar set of priorities. Lack of good information, except on the number of grants and the amount of dollars that have been handed out, leaves UMTA wide open for unfriendly questioning. Such questions are likely to be asked as the sums spent for transit mount and as diversion of Highway Trust Fund money to transit is carried out. True, implementation of a complete compilation of all needed information would probably not be cheap, but it would seem to be less costly than continuing to work in the dark.[19]

This is not to say that UMTA has not collected some important information or that it is insensitive to informational needs. The funds to do the job have evidently not been available, either because Congress was close-fisted or because UMTA did not do a convincing sales job or chose to move other items to higher priority in the expenditure of its limited funds. The UMTA Appropriations hearings for fiscal 1973 disclosed a number of instances of congressional chiding for more information and proposals by UMTA to collect and disseminate more information.[20] In 1973, it was apparent that UMTA was seeking better information about program impact and other facets of its own performance as well as that of its clientele.

Little Uptake of New Ideas

Despite the fact that well over a hundred demonstration projects have been carried out under federal auspices—virtually all purporting to have engendered practical innovations for adoption by the transit industry—there has been almost zero uptake of the ideas generated in such projects.[21] Part of this reluctance to use new ideas is the need for outside funding to help pay the inevitably high start-up costs of innovative services. New ventures in mass transportation, even if tested out empirically in one location, are by their very nature likely to show a dollar figure in the initial stages that is higher than the revenue or benefits that will flow from them once they are fully integrated into the operations of a going concern.

For example, if a city transit agency wishes to use a fairly long-distance express bus service from a suburban area into downtown in order to attract relatively high-income riders (similar to the demonstration carried out in Baltimore as MD-MTD-1 [MD-06-0004]) there might be a need for the purchase of several suburban-type buses with high seatbacks, greater room between seats—thus fewer seats—and only one door at the front of the coach. There would also be planning expense and the cost of advertising to attract attention to the new service. On top of this there might be a need to pave some parking areas in order to encourage potential patrons to drive to the suburban express stops. All of this would cost money; since building ridership is generally a relatively slow business, it might take several years before the operation was viable on a dollars and cents basis in the category of operating expense. Federal support—or some other outside funding—would seem a necessity to help cover at least some of the operating costs. Unfortunately, federal funding is generally not available to try out a demonstration idea for the second time in another location, which is what this hypothetical example would amount to. Under the present interpretation of the law, only if the subject of the innovation is strictly a capital measure can federal money be applied. Thus in the example above the new equipment could be purchased, land acquired, and paving done, but the operating cost, which is likely to be the largest single cost element, and the promotional expense will fall on the shoulders of the local transit property.

Another problem associated with the reluctance to attempt transit innovation is the likelihood of mistake or error that will be picked up and smeared about the media in a tantrum of muckraking. Such a risk is not one to be taken lightly by the typical breed of transit managers. As products of an inbred industry that has been ailing for a half-century, transit managers as a group are not very likely to be any great shakes at risky innovations, especially if the *Wall Street Journal* lies in anticipation of a gaffe that will be reported nationwide.

Just such an awful experience befell one of the few instances where an idea that worked out quite well in one demonstration was funded in a different city with, unfortunately, exactly the opposite results. The subscription bus service that had panned out rather nicely in Peoria (ILL-MTD-3, 4 [not given]) was a total disaster when tried out with minor modifications in Flint (MICH-MTD-2 [MI-06-0007]). The subscription bus service in Peoria, focused principally on the employee concentration at the gigantic Caterpillar Tractor Company works, was built up one route at a time, reflecting gradual increases in demand. After a year, there were seventeen routes in operation, most of them focused on Caterpillar. In Flint, two dozen routes were started at once; the howling emptiness of the buses was a matter of immediate newsworthiness. At Caterpillar, which does not make a consumer product, the possibility of working overtime is a matter typically known in advance by the employee. In Flint, dependent upon a large number of General Motors automobile plants scattered about the town, the chance for overtime work is generally not known to employees until after a shift begins; such a fact of life is not uncommon in consumer goods industries attempting to be as sensitive as possible to the demand shifts of a constantly changing market. In other words, the Flint factory employee has to have his car at work in order to provide transportation flexibility on the chance he might pick up a few overtime hours. Subscription bus service is geared to definite time of arrival and departure and could not readily be adjusted on a day-to-day basis. The debacle at Flint, with losses of over $900,000 in one year, was well publicized. Understandably, transit operators are reluctant to preside over such disasters.

Another reason for the lack of innovation is that the reports of the various demonstrations, depending upon the talents of those writing them, quite reasonably center upon the given situation and circumstances of the demonstration. Little or no effort is made to generalize findings or to develop the application of the basic ideas to different settings. It would be most helpful if synopses of the projects and their likelihood of application in different settings were provided. Moreover, since there is really no general management journal in urban transportation (as opposed to a news journal such as *Passenger Transport*), generalized treatments of research and demonstration findings are not likely to be available anywhere for transit managers. Reporting what has happened is good, but a more analytical approach is also needed. Meetings and seminars can be a great help in spreading the gospel of innovation, but not all transit managers can get to meetings, nor can many lower-level staff persons attend because of the cost involved.

Another factor hampering wide adoption of the ideas generated in the demonstrations is the temporal and geographic scatterization of these projects. A really interested transit manager or public official would need the time and money resources to do a fair amount of traveling over a period of time to see what was going on and attempt to judge the applicability of an idea to his own home setting.

There has also been apparently little uptake of the notions fermenting in the various research projects funded by UMTA. Much of this work has been hardware and technology oriented. To the usually conservative transit manager or public official some of this technology seems outlandish from the very start. It is unlikely that any innovation that is not fully compatible with existing facilities or equipment will be seriously considered, unless it obviously will do a better job of serving the public at a lower cost than existing methods. The political implications of scrapping an existing system for something exotic and unfamiliar are another factor to conjure with.[22]

The various people-mover or personal rapid transit (PRT) systems are a case in point of utilizing a system costly both to install and to operate. Such new-fangled devices will probably be installed only with continued operating support as well as with initial capital support from the federal government or other source of funding from outside. On the other hand, relatively nonexotic and compatible ventures, such as dial-a-bus, are not particularly expensive or difficult to inaugurate. If such an innovation lays an egg, the equipment can always be used in other services with little difficulty.[23]

In short, the means so far utilized to instigate innovation have not been those most likely to succeed in an industry that appears to need it desperately. Financially risky operating innovations will not be adopted in the absence of external support nor will exotic and costly technology that involves hardware not easily used for alternative purposes. Drastic innovation without continuing operating and maintenance support would be like saddling a transit undertaking with a boat in its basement. Getting conventional transit systems to work more effectively would seem to have a higher priority.

Transit as a Shaper of Urban Development

Except in a few cases of new or expanded rapid transit systems, as in San Francisco, transit does not seem to be playing a significant role in shaping urban growth. In any case, there is no publicly available information on the subject. One of the reasons for this lack of perceptible impact is the apparent unwillingness on the part of many planners to acknowledge the role that mass transit might play in shaping a city's growth. This seems to stem either from ignorance on the part of planners or from a shyness about integrating into their plans forms other than fixed-facility transit. Many urban planners know what highways will do in the development of a city; mass transit is often dismissed or assumed to carry an ever diminishing number of patrons. This cavalier treatment is a source of concern to transit observers.

Vigorous interest in transit is, of course, a relatively recent phenomenon, and work involving mass transport has been added to the curriculum a planner is likely to face in his schooling. Moreover, there is a natural lag in implementing what has been learned. Meanwhile, mass transit will probably be excluded from plans as to how a city should grow.

One serious problem is the lack of communication between planners and transit management. Planners often possess information of potential interest and importance to transit managers; managers often have information, or the possibility of gathering information, that could be of great use to planners. The twain rarely meet.

Plans also never seem to get carried out as intended by those who put them on paper, partly because of the extensive time involved in conducting a really good transportation planning study, and the lack of relevance that most plans seem to have to real-life situations when decisions—often reactions not well considered but necessary at the moment—have to be carried out with dispatch.

Clouding the whole planning issue, of course, are the unresolved questions of how big or how dense a city should be, or how it should be shaped. Moreover, many forces pull and tug at planners and the political decision makers responsible for seeing that plans are carried out.[24] For example, downtown business interests are becoming more friendly to transit because it appears to have a concentrating effect beneficial to downtown property values and sales of merchandise. Indeed, in some larger cities, downtown property owners have even agreed to an extra property tax assessment to help pay for downtown transit improvements. On the other hand, in small cities downtown merchants will often oppose the surrender of even one parking space for a bus stop. Good outlying highways are essential for industrial plants wishing to enjoy the economies of spread-out, single-level factories. Manufacturers usually push for more and better highways. Environmental groups are generally opposed to highways and may also oppose transit plans, especially those that involve increasing population concentrations. The various shapes of a city—satellite form, multi-nodules, starlike-corridors—are related to transport patterns, but determining which may be best for a given place is still a matter that is very much up in the air, and thus a subject for debate and disagreement.

A good deal has been written in recent years about techniques of determining the split between use of public transit and the private automobile in assigning trips between points in a city for planning purposes. No one seems particularly happy about the various modal split techniques. A major shortcoming of these models is that no provision is made in the analysis for improvements in transit quality —admittedly a difficult matter to come to grips with.[25] In any case, transit seems to be shortchanged in these techniques.

Much transportation planning has been fostered by the UMTA Technical Study Grants. Some of the work done under these grants has been, to say the least, rather shabby. Rarely does one come across a really top-notch job of planning. Often left out of such plans is any comment on the necessary reorganization of the management of the transit property in question. This is a serious shortcoming, since what to do with a carefully planned system is equally as important as where service should be offered and how many vehicles of what type may be needed.

For many years to come, the motor bus is likely to be the major means of providing mass transit service in U.S. cities. However, the impact of bus service on city shaping and development is also an unknown factor. Since a bus is dependent upon the provision of streets, and streets have apparently well-understood developmental impact for auto-related transportation, whatever separate impact the motor bus might have has been muffled. It would make sense to conduct studies on the impact of the bus on urban development.

Such studies might involve not only buses using regular city streets, but also buses providing different levels of service and with various degrees of control over the operating environment, short of completely separate busways. The impact of trolleybus and streetcar could also be studied to ascertain the potential of such modal tools in development. (The visible evidence—track and wires—of the streetcar and trolleybus may make them seem to be more permanent, and thus more likely to have a developmental impact. A permanent busway facility may have the same impact.)

The planning requirements of the federal laws and the monies available for planning have been a boon to planning. Probably there has never been a period when so much effort labeled as planning was being conducted in the United States, a good deal of it devoted to mass transportation. Probably little of this effort rises above mediocrity. The fault is not so much with the planners as with the lack of a genuine basic urban policy and the ability of public officials and the public to articulate what they want their cities to be like. On the matter of the public input, the people in general may not be able to state precisely what they wish their cities to be like; more and more, however, they are making perfectly clear what they do not want. The days seem to be over when the "planners" and the plans were synonymous with a highway crashing through a city. The climate for creative planning, properly emphasizing mass transportation, abundantly sensitive to human needs, and put forth in terms meaningful to the general public has rarely been better.

The Marketing Gap and the Hardware Panacea

Looking back over twelve years of federal mass transportation programs, there seems to have been remarkably little effect in the area of marketing mass transportation to the consumers. Given the clear need to attract more riders to mass transportation, more research and development aimed at understanding the needs of consumers would seem to be the obvious direction to take. Many of the early demonstration projects seemed to be particularly directed toward improved marketing or increasing the attractiveness of mass transport. Unfortunately, since there is no coherent body of marketing thought or relevant internal institutional structure in the mass transportation industry, those projects are difficult to assess. The new

UMTA research project in marketing may be the remedy, but the results will not be known for several years.[26]

As the matter now stands, any marketing improvement will probably have to be imposed—or cajoled—from the outside, since the transit industry has no real marketing tradition. Indeed, as the reader will recall, the great majority of transit firms do not possess an organizational structure that lends itself to consumer-oriented marketing. Whatever the thinking at UMTA may have been in the past several years, its actions indicate the clear assumption that hardware is the key to making transit more attractive. The strongest evidence of this bias is given in the time, effort, and money devoted to the personal rapid transit (PRT) systems.

All of these systems are an engineer's delight, overflowing with electronic doo-dads; they are to be totally automated, working on the principle of the public's push-button selection of destination. The systems displayed or under consideration are aimed at handling relatively small passenger loads; they are not intended for mass movement of patrons in the 10,000–60,000 passengers per hour range of conventional "heavy" rapid transit. The PRT's have price tags that would choke the proverbial horse.[27] The most costly PRT of all is being installed at Morgantown, W. Va. When completed that system will be two and one-fourth miles long and is now expected to cost about $125 million. Supposedly it will have sufficient capacity to move 1,100 passengers in a peak 20-minute period.[28] Even with its high price tag, one UMTA official admitted the Morgantown experiment would have only limited payoff.

> While we may learn from the Morgantown experiment regarding the costs of building, maintaining and operating an isolated, "closed system" PRT, it won't tell us how to operate and market PRT in the open and dynamic atmosphere of an American city. Therefore, we should not lean very heavily on the Morgantown experience, except for data on the command and control system itself. The operation of PRT in a real, congested city, with its attendant "unknown problems of vandalism and passenger security," requires a comprehensive approach to the city itself and to indicators of the external impacts of PRT. For that reason PRT ought to be fit into a larger city plan to market the city itself as an attractive place to be.[29]

What is particularly bothersome about the PRT schemes is that they are generally ballyhooed as new systems when, in truth, they are not new systems at all, but merely new technology applied to the old system of the railway. Like the railway, the PRT's use a fixed guideway with fixed station stops and the concomitant burden of fixed costs of such facilities that become a problem when they are not shared by many users, as is the case with highways. Some of the "systems" have been designed to be used by a limited number of dual-mode vehicles that can circulate on regular roads and streets as well as upon the specialized guideway. One strong virtue of the PRT is the lack of need for human crew members or even single operators; cutting down on manpower is a matter to ponder seriously in light of the sharp and consistent increase in the wages of transit operating personnel.

Unfortunately, the PRT designs advanced so far don't enjoy one of the principal virtues of a more conventional railway: capacity. All of the proposed PRT systems use cars or modules of relatively low capacity. Handling peaked loads will be difficult without a large number of the vehicles, which, of course, would sharply increase the capital cost of the venture. Coupling modules together, or using modules of very large capacity, would apparently defeat the objective of developing a truly personalized rapid transit mode. So far, at least, the PRT's seem far too expensive for modest demands of patronage and too limited in capacity to meet heavy or highly peaked demand. PRT technology may be practical, but probably only under certain limited conditions. Enthusiasm waxes strong for PRT's, however, and Denver proposes making PRT's the backbone of its recently planned transit system.

The expression of faith in hardware and relative lack of interest in finding what the consumer wants is typical of undertakings dominated by engineers and other assorted technocrats. It is also typical of U. S. society; its apparent reluctance to try to come to grips with people problems in realistic terms forces it toward hardware, regardless of whether or not hardware makes sense. In short, the PRT technology, despite the funds and attention directed toward it, may only provide solutions for which there is no great and pressing problem.

The real need, of course, is not to cease exploration in new or improved types of hardware, but to direct effort as well toward understanding the transit market and the problems and needs in transit as consumers see them.[30] The key to making mass transportation attractive and useful to increasing numbers of people is quite likely not to have much to do with hardware. Indeed, UMTA itself admits that key factors in developing more transit ridership are really a coupling of factors that are nothing more or less than what one would expect of a well-managed, systematic, marketing-oriented, businesslike transit organization. The factors are:

1. Fast, frequent service.
2. Convenience of routes and schedules.
3. Adequate route and service information.
4. Ease of transfer intra- or inter-modal.
5. Clean vehicles and stations.
6. Courteous personnel dealing with the public.

Unfortunately, UMTA has done little to promote or research activities related to these factors in recent years.[31]

The Matter of Image

Another matter of concern is the image of transit to the American public at large. Although there are no definitive studies on the topic, it is probably safe to assume that mass transportation presents generally negative connotations to the public mind. Riding the bus to work is definitely not part of the American dream. The trouble in discussing image is that it is so intangible a concept that it defies neat and precise handling. Even so, a product or service that is viewed in a favorable light is usually much easier to sell or promote.

It is probably fair to say that transit is viewed by the great American middle class as a service for the disadvantaged. It has been mentioned in previous pages that, repeatedly, at conferences and meetings, representatives of the transit industry, industry suppliers, and government officials speak almost exclusively of transit as a service to the poor and the halt, rather than as one that the whole public might find useful. Apparently, none of these parties, even when speaking of the future, can really conceive of transit having a very broad attraction, despite the evidence that where service quality is high a broad public can be attracted. Of course, the quality of present-day service in most cities is such that the clientele is made up almost exclusively of captive riders—those outside the mainstream of upwardly mobile, relatively prosperous middle-class citizens. If transit is a service for losers—and this is a real detriment in a society that takes winning so seriously—the job of attracting the mainstream of the public into the transit market is a very difficult job indeed, especially in attempting to combat not only the potent symbolism of the car but also the automobile's conveniences and virtues. The task of selling transit down on the operating level in given cities is incredibly difficult if transit is not even viewed as a reasonable travel alternative to the car by a hefty segment of what otherwise might be a large part of the market. The task is doubly difficult if those responsible for managing transit properties or administering government programs appear to have so little faith in the potential broad appeal of the product.

Part of the image and, unfortunately, part of the fact, is the danger of crime associated with transit, particularly in the subway systems of the great cities. In New York, Chicago, and Philadelphia, only unwary or captive patrons use the rapid transit systems at night. Real violence and criminality are common and usually well reported. Vandalism, especially graffiti, make the use of transit not only aesthetically unpleasant, but frightening and unsettling to the average person. Indeed, the graffiti problem in Philadelphia is so bad that using almost any part of the transit system is akin to traveling in a lavatory patronized by mental defectives. Transit is not the only victim of criminals and vandals, of course; the whole problem of "crime-in-the-streets" in urban areas is a part of a reputed general social decay in the United States. This part of transit's image problem can only be solved by general solutions to urban and social problems; such solutions have so far eluded the nation.[32]

The federal programs have had little direct impact on the image problem, again reflecting an interest in hardware and engineering rather than marketing and consumer orientation. Here, however, hardware can play a role, because most transit service is quite visible to the public. Certainly, any transit property running bedraggled buses or weary rail cars has a very large and material image problem. The federal programs will help buy new hardware and thus improve at least the visual image.

The quality of transit service is made up of a more complex mix of factors than just the age and shininess of the equipment or facilities. A poorly managed, non-consumer-oriented service will remain much the same even if the equipment is new. Image can be aided by the tone of the graphics, by the advertising and other information made available to the public, and by the attitude of employees. How the public views transit is more than mere puffery or pleasant pastel interiors; image must be backed up by reliable, fast, direct, on-time service at convenient times, bearing a price consistent with the quality of the service. In short, truly satisfied users are the real heart of building an image that, in turn, will attract still more users.

All of which raises an interesting matter to consider. How many transit managers or UMTA personnel make regular use of mass transportation? How many know, on the basis of regular, personal experience, just how good or how bad transit service really is? One possible way of improving transit service, marketing, and image, might be to require all transit managers aided with federal mass transportation money and all federal personnel involved in the mass transit programs to ride mass transit on a regular basis. (This suggestion is made with tongue in cheek, but not totally in jest!)

Lack of Coordination and Integration of Transit

It is obvious to any traveler that the United States as a nation does not enjoy a true transportation system. Rather, it has a structure of different modes that manage, somehow, to touch each other fitfully at times. Consequently, it is often very difficult to make a through journey from city to city via public means of transport and enjoy convenient transfer between modes. On the local scene the same holds true. Except in Cleveland, Ohio, the trip from the airport to the downtown area is rarely one that can be accomplished expeditiously by use of mass transportation, if it is possible at all. Likewise, even transfer between different lines of the same system can be a trial and a tribulation, particularly to the person strange to a system.

Much of this has to do with the history of the development of the various pieces of the transport structure; as the independent parts grew, there was no intention of coordinated service and the structure still shows it. As a case in point, despite the rather careful planning of the Bay Area Rapid Transit District's service in San Francisco, extension of the rapid transit line to the San Francisco and Oakland airports is being studied only as an afterthought. Again, BART is only one more part of a mass transport structure in the Bay Area and is being overlaid upon the existing AC Transit System (Alameda—Contra Costa Transit District) on the Oakland side of the Bay and the Municipal Railways on the San Francisco side. A more recent entrant is the Golden Gate Bridge, Highway and Transportation District, which covers the territory in Marin County, across the Golden Gate Bridge from San Francisco itself. Although all four systems have received federal aid, including support for a study on coordination, each participant is apparently viewing the other warily and up until recently the degree of coordination hoped for is apparently just that—a hope.[33] The Metropolitan Transportation Commission, established in 1970, was formed by the California legislature to quench local animosities and to plan and help direct a coordinated transportation system for the Bay area.

Even though sincerely committed to improving coordination of mass transportation service on the local level, UMTA has moved at a glacial pace to provide incentives for real coordination or integration of the services. For the most part, this reflects the reluctance or the inability of UMTA's clients, the cities, to seek better metropolitan coordination. The reluctance is understandable because of fierce local infighting that is likely to develop.[34] A great deal of effort and cajoling, which may be possible only by some nonlocal party, such as the federal government, seems needed to iron out the gaps in the structure. Depending on their interpretation and enforcement, UMTA's capital grant criteria that went into effect on July 1, 1972, may go a long way toward achieving better intergovernmental coordination on the local level.[35]

Even where there is but one local transit operation, it appears that insufficient pressure has been brought to make it easier for the public to have access to the transit system. Too often service is not close to patrons or potential patrons. As discussed earlier in more detail, one of the glaring problems for transit in the United States today is that with the increasing suburbanization of the population, many citizens live outside the reach of viable conventional mass transit service. The pickup and delivery service in thinly populated areas almost has to be handled either by automobile, a dial-a-bus type of service, or perhaps a combination of each, coupled with park-and-ride terminals and parking lots. Such services are still the exception rather than the rule. The success of the Skokie Swift, which is nothing more than an access device; the parking facilities and integrated bus service offered in Cleveland; and the New Brunswick, N.J., parking lot built in conjunction with the Penn Central commuter service all show the efficacy of such undertakings. The Northwest Passage in Chicago, linking the Lake Street Elevated with the Northwestern Station, is another example.[36]

Granted, some of the coordination and integration will not be easily won. Where different transit organizations operate in the same jurisdiction, especially when some are privately and some publicly owned, there is the stuff that wars are made of. Much more federal effort—meaning more incentives—is needed to aid in ironing out the coordination problem.

Management Upgrading

There are other shortcomings to the federal mass transportation programs. One of these is their failure to raise the quality of transit management. The other is the continued fragmentation of government in United States metropolitan areas. This latter failing is a symptom of the larger problem of the lack of a true and effective national urban policy. While both of these matters are pointed out here as factors where federal policy—mass transportation or otherwise—has been relatively ineffective, at the same time it must be understood that these are some of the very basic reasons behind the failure of the federal effort to markedly improve transit. As some of the basic problem areas, they will be treated more extensively in the next chapter. For now, a few observations are in order on just where the federal programs have fallen down.

One of the reasons that the federal programs have not been more effective in improving transit service, and in attracting more patronage as evidence of that improvement, is that the present management of transit operating properties lacks the skill required to discover what services the public wants and needs and how to promote them effectively. In short, management is not geared to meet the challenge and the opportunities afforded by the federal mass transportation programs. It is no secret that management is one of the weakest links in the chain of improvement and this weakness was the reason that the 1966 amendments to the Urban Mass Transportation Act contained provisions for managerial training.

Unfortunately, the federal managerial training and upgrading program is not large in either scope or dollar input. For example, only 100 fellowships per year are currently available in the program, paying a maximum of $12,000 or 75 per cent of the regular annual wage of the fellow. These are to be used mainly for the purpose of sending present management-level personnel to graduate school for advanced degrees in economics, business administration, or public administration. Money is also available for short courses and seminars and other brief means of upgrading talent. There is a clear place for these approaches in improving management, but the effort seems puny in comparison with the need. Small injections of federal money—at the present time, money for management training is spent at the rate of about $500,000 per year, about equal to the cost of a dozen new, air-conditioned buses—will hardly faze an industry as tightly set in its ways as is the transit industry. The present limited program will do little to break the chain of performing the same old job in the same old way, guaranteeing the same old dismal results.[37]

Incentives are badly needed to upgrade management and the organization structure of mass transportation firms so that managerial effort can be brought to bear more efficiently. Beyond that, training programs should not be confined to retreading or upgrading present management. Much effort is needed over the coming years to recruit and educate a whole new managerial team for the mass transportation industry. Moreover, personnel improvement should not be limited to the upper echelons of management, but should be available for supervisory personnel on all levels. There seems, as well, to be a need for job training for lower-level employees. Like so much of the transportation industry, the public's contact with transit is in the hands of low-level, rank-and-file employees. Whatever human impression of an operating property the transit-using public has is probably that provided by the bus driver. Most of the transit employees have not been trained to deal with the public in a felicitous manner or to handle problems with ease, skill, and sympathy. This is a serious deficiency, particularly if the public is to be attracted rather than coerced into using mass transportation. No element of the service can be laid aside as if it existed in a vacuum. This is apparently what has happened in the area of personnel.

Managerial improvement may be the key to effective transit improvement. Unfortunately, it is hardly a glamorous undertaking. On the local level, the receipt of a substantial grant for new hardware may appear to public officials to be far better evidence to the public that improvement is on its way. The same holds true on the federal level; ticking off the items of hardware purchased with UMTA money has a satisfying ring. Counting the number of transit firms having their management structures reorganized, or persons sent for schooling, is not the sort of stuff that makes headlines. Neither is it likely to be very impressive to congressional watchdogs of federal money. The renaissance in management that is needed to really improve mass transportation is apt to be bypassed in the effort to do things that appear to be more noteworthy.

Local Fragmentation

The essence of the disease that has wrought such damage to the quality of American life is the inability of local governments to meet the needs and challenges of the twentieth century. The popular media are full of the problems of the city in the United States and one of the most serious is the impending bankruptcy that seems to haunt urban places of all sizes. As Daniel Moynihan pointed out:

> At least part of the relative ineffectiveness of the efforts of urban government to respond to urban problems derives from the fragmented and obsolescent structure of urban government itself. The federal government should constantly encourage and provide incentives for the reorganization of local government in response to the reality of metropolitan conditions.[38]

Cities in all parts of the country are hemmed in and strapped down by laws of the nineteenth century that may have made sense for a largely rural and agricultural society, but are witless and ineffective when applied to a highly urbanized industrial society. Direct federal aid to cities is clear evidence of the past unwillingness or inability of the states to do much of anything to ameliorate urban problems.

The situation has not changed much over the decade of federal mass transportation programs. Indeed, much of the hue and cry associated with urban problems focuses on the problem of urban fragmentation, yet in correcting this problem almost nothing has been achieved.[39]

The Need for a Showcase

There is an obvious efficacy in showing off one's wares and abilities; hence the attraction of fairs and expositions to show the public —or specialized groups—what can be done. The New York World's

Fair of 1939 and 1940 showed the masses the wonders of freeways and express highways. The Interstate Highway System, for better or worse, is part of the legacy of the fair. Hundreds of monumental courthouses and public buildings still attest to the impact on the public and on public officials of the classical architecture of the World's Columbian Exposition in Chicago in 1893.

It is most surprising that there is still no national showcase for transit ideas. This would seem to be particularly appropriate to an industry that needs the invigoration of new ideas and the warm support of the local public officials. Yet there is no place one can go to see a complete, modern transit system in action, and make the comparisons—invidious or otherwise—with one's own local scene. Transit should lend itself well to such an effort and could be effective if shown in regular operation, not as part of a huckstering carnival, à la Transpo '72.[40]

Taken individually, none of the factors discussed in this chapter would be totally debilitating in a national effort to upgrade mass transportation in order to make it a critical and catalytic part of a resurgence of the good life in U.S. cities. Taken altogether, however, these factors act as a damper that assure the lack of meaningful success in improved quality and increased patronage. It is unfair merely to harp on shortcomings; rather support is needed to overcome them. Before that, however, it is prudent to review some of the basic factors that act to hinder the efficacy of the federal role in mass transportation.

CHAPTER SIX

Why Do Problems Persist?

Introduction

It is very difficult to carry through a program of improvements to urban mass transportation that will be reflected in rising patronage and increased usefulness of mass transportation service to more U.S. citizens. Since the time of the First World War, over a half-century ago, billions of dollars have been spent for the improvement of highways, and highways tend to benefit the private motorist. Additional billions have been spent to promote the purchase and use of the automobile. There is no doubt that the auto provides a high standard of service, a standard that is very difficult for mass transportation to compete with under most circumstances. Moreover, a rising standard of living and dispersed pattern of population distribution—a pattern difficult to service with conventional mass transportation—have made the private car not only obtainable by a majority of U.S. citizens but also necessary for mobility.

At the outset, then, it must be understood that the job of making mass transportation a relevant service to an increasing number of travelers is extremely hard to achieve in the present situation. Given the best of all possible worlds in the foreseeable future, it is fair to say that mass transportation may increase the proportion of urban trips it handles relative to the automobile, but it will not replace the automobile. Given sufficient time, mass transportation may play a positive role in shaping cities once more. Perhaps many of those persons who are now unable to participate fully in American society, because of lack of regular access to the automobile, will, through improved mass transport, gain mobility advantages now closed to them. In time, automotive congestion may be relieved to a degree. Nevertheless, given the conditions of wealth and population distribution, and the advantages the automobile undoubtedly possesses as a means of transportation, mass transportation probably will not come close to playing its dominant, pre-1920 role in society. If it does so, it will take many years, unless there is a very sudden shift in U.S. values, or a substantial increase in the cost of using automobiles. Even so, the rise in interest in protecting the environment may work to effect a shift in American values. The shortage of gasoline that arose in early and mid-1973 increased the price of driving a car and there were threats of fuel prices rising to a dollar a gallon or more. At the same time, the pollution control devices installed on cars as a requirement of the Environmental Protection Act, and the trend to heavier automobiles, cut the mileage that could be obtained with each gallon of gasoline. A sharp rise in automobile operating costs is now a fact of life thanks to escalating fuel prices.

The future of mass transportation in the United States needs much more than adequate funds, talented transit management, and a vigorous, well-staffed bureaucracy parcelling out the federal money. The problems discussed subsequently involve the clarity of the mission of the federal programs and the tools necessary to do the job. In the absence of clear goals and the necessary resources, meaningful attempts at enlarging the role of mass transportation, difficult under ideal circumstances, are virtually impossible.

The Need for a Clear-cut Mission

If one traces the history of U.S. transportation policy in general, he will find that it consists of a series of reactions to given problems at given times.[1] It is not the story of the pursuit of a carefully defined objective along a clearly marked path. The legislation that has been passed was aimed mainly at solving a given problem at a given time. The phasing of regulatory legislation and promotional efforts in transportation, moreover, are largely the result of compromise in Congress as well as cooperation between Congress and the administration in power. Much the same is true, as the initial chapter pointed out, in the development of the federal mass transportation program.

The trouble with this piecemeal approach, while it is not lacking in achievement, is that the needs of the moment are likely to obscure the proper path to follow over the long haul. That is pretty much what has happened in both general transportation policy and in the policies, as expressed in laws and action, in urban mass transportation. Stated objectives, as seen in earlier pages, tend to be general and incapable of measurement in any precise fashion. If clear objectives are put forth in the efforts mounted to pass given legislation, they tend to be extremely short-run in nature, with little or no concern over the long-run impact. The effort of transit interests to secure federal operating subsidies in 1972 and 1973 is a case in point.

Given a firm, rational, and workable set of long-range goals that are either quantifiable or observable and have a target date set for completion, those involved can begin to plan effectively how to achieve the objectives within the time period allowed. They can make rational calculations on the resources that will be needed, evaluate alternative approaches to the objectives, and establish guidelines; they may develop strategy and set up programs. The effort can be programmed with care, and progress toward the workable objective can be measured.

At the present time there is no clear-cut, workable objective for the federal mass transportation program. What is needed is something akin to the goal President Kennedy set for the space program back in 1961. He called for the United States to put men on the moon and bring them back by 1970; Congress agreed with him. From that point it was possible to set in motion the effort and gather the resources needed to do the job.

In order to function with maximum effectiveness, the federal urban transportation program needs to have its mission set forth clearly in terms of workable objectives. These objectives must, of course, be consistent with concurrent objectives for over-all transportation policy and general urban policy.

There are major difficulties in writing such a prescription. Legislators and administrators are naturally reluctant to make firm declarations of aims; such goals form yardsticks against which performance may be measured, and neither politicians nor government agencies are anxious to have such measurement carried out. Further-more, various vested interests, content with the status quo, may mount a strenuous opposition if they feel threatened. Another prob-lem with setting goals is that if they do not appear to be dramatic or interesting to the general public they may not claim much public support. The fact remains, in the absence of workable objectives, it is impossible to chart a course or to determine when the destination has been reached.

The Urban Mass Transportation Administration does not have a firm set of workable objectives by which to gear its efforts, so its failure to achieve more should not be unexpected. It has tried to make do as best it can under the laws passed by the Congress. For example, the UMTA administrator, in appropriations hearings be-fore a subcommittee of the House of Representatives, noted that:

> Several broad objectives are derived from the UMTA Act which gener-ally direct UMTA to promote the "welfare and vitality of urban areas" through the improvement of mass transportation facilities, equipment, techniques, and methods of regional planning. These objectives are to:
> Promote mobility to urban residents; improve urban transportation systems; and encourage areawide urban transportation planning.[2]

There is nothing wrong with these objectives, but they are hardly specific enough to be of much help. Other rather loose objectives for specific functions within the UMTA structure were noted earlier in the chapter on institutions.

Unfortunately, this is evidence of the fact that the Department of Transportation has taken no decisive steps to carry out the mandate expressed in the act giving it life, that of setting goals for national transportation policy.[3] Likewise, no discernible action has been taken to establish workable, rational goals for urban transportation. To say the least, it is a serious omission. As far as urban mass trans-portation is concerned, one of the best opportunities for goal-setting arose in the work leading up to the publication of *Tomorrow's Transportation: New Systems for the Urban Future* in May 1968. However, the opportunity was allowed to slip by; there was no call for decisiveness in the report and no suggestions for definite legisla-tive action. The report merely listed some possible directions that might be taken and discussed some interesting hardware that might be applicable to urban mass transportation.[4] The failure to grasp this opportunity is perhaps best explained by the fact that by the time the report was being written it was already clear that the urban mass transportation programs were to be shifted from HUD into DOT. *Tomorrow's Transportation* was the last hurrah for HUD in the area of direct concern with urban transportation.

Without a good map to steer by, UMTA must do the best it can to take action reasonably expected of it within its bailiwick. It must work, therefore, to keep the goodwill of the Congress and it must do things that are relevant in real and political terms on the local level. Capital grants for facilities construction are understandably popular with UMTA's urban constituents, if for no other reason than that they are visible, tend to create jobs locally, and are a sign of success in local dealings with the federal government. This support is obviously important to public officials of local government, who are constantly faced with the need to answer the question "What have you done for us lately?" that is raised by their constituents. Insofar as grants for equipment are concerned, bus projects are rather popular with both local government and UMTA because they are generally noncontroversial, provide visible evidence of action, and, because of the relatively short lead-time involved in acquiring such equipment, can achieve visibility in a brief span of time.

Within the framework of the limitation with which it is forced to work, UMTA has attempted to improve the effectiveness of its work. For example, the "new" criteria established for the evaluation and awarding of capital grants are an effort to provide a means for choosing capital grant projects so that funds are provided for those with the greatest payoff.[5] No longer is it enough for a city just to show a need for capital funds; almost any city's transit operation has a desperate need. With only $3.1 billion authorized under the 1970 Act plus an additional $3 billion under the Highway Act of 1973, and an estimated $5 billion in applications already in hand, something has to be done to help select the most worthy recipients or at least provide UMTA with a cushion against charges that political influence determines who gets the money. As the UMTA administrator summed up the revised capital grant guidelines:

> The new guidelines, as a matter of public policy, indicate that resources will be allocated among grantees on the basis of the transportation-related purposes of the program, not just the need for financial assistance. . . .
> In general, the guidelines categorize applications by size groups to ensure

fair distribution of program assistance. Applications in each size group will be considered with reference to one another rather than to the entire caseload of applications. The size groups are:

urban areas with SMSA populations under 250,000
urban areas between 250,000 and 1,000,000 population
urban areas with 1,000,000 population or over

The existing priority to projects intended to prevent cessation of service will continue. In addition, for cities in the medium and large categories, priority will also be given projects designed to affect traffic congestion in conjunction with the Federal Highway Administration's TOPICS program which finances projects to provide such things as: exclusive or preferential transit streets, bus lanes, or expressway ramps; control of traffic lights by buses, bus turnouts; fringe parking spaces in suburban areas in conjunction with terminals for express or improved bus services; and similar improvements.

In the medium and large categories a priority will also be given to projects which are part of programs demonstrating current or proposed use of non-capital means by which to affect congestion and modal choices —such means as regulating the supply and pricing of off-street parking, staggering of work hours, auto-free zones, and pricing adjustments to vehicular facilities (such as bridges and tunnels) in order to encourage transit riding. . . . The intent of the guidelines is not to exact service improvements *per se* as a condition for project approval. The intent is to assign a priority to projects specifically associated with service improvements.[6]

The transit industry and the coalition that supports it did not greet the revised criteria with warm feelings. Apparently, from the tone of the criteria, acquiring federal capital funds would become more difficult and time consuming. Discussion among the Department of Transportation, UMTA, American Transit Association, Institute for Rapid Transit, Rail Progress Institute, and National League of Cities/U.S. Conference of Mayors occupied about a year; the new guidelines went into effect, nevertheless, with the transit coalition expressing the following concerns:

Most of the data needed to comply with the criteria was not presently available, particularly in medium and small transit systems where no data existed at all. [This is a sad reflection on the status of planning in the United States, the attitude or lack of knowledge of planners, and the need for help from the state level in seeing that planning is done.]

No resources were available at the local level to collect the data and develop the analysis that would be necessary to comply with the criteria. *It is the combined industry position that before criteria are employed, the*

*federal government must make the funds available to the local applicant
so that they are capable of complying with the criteria.*
    As initially drafted, some of the criteria lacked relevance to ongoing
transit operations.[7]

Both sides of the situation are understandable. UMTA would like
to have firmer grounds on which to base its judgments in allocating
capital grant funds. Since the transit industry traditionally has carried out its activities with only the most modest information base, it
was disturbed over having to provide information that was just not
readily or cheaply available. The most logical complaint of the transit interests revolves around the fact that technical studies grants
have been funded and carried out for a number of years with no
requirement from UMTA that much of the information demanded in
the new capital grant criteria be unearthed in the process of carrying out the planning study, although that would have been the most
logical occasion on which to do the needed work.

The new guidelines seem to be a step in the right direction, a
move away from simple injections of money for capital purposes.
If UMTA carries through on the criteria, it means more emphasis
will be put on marketing effort by transit management and cooperative efforts on the part of urban areas. Pricing schemes affecting
downtown parking, more control of the operating environment by
mass transit agencies, and means of attempting to assess the full
costs of automobile travel against the motorist are necessary steps in
the right direction. Just how these new criteria are to be evaluated,
especially the difficult task of comparing project applications from
different places with widely varying conditions, remains to be seen.
UMTA may have to page King Solomon to handle the job.

At the same time, some of the flaws in the execution of mass transit policy—the lack of basic information on mass transit; the lack of
work in the area of marketing, management organization, the development of effective management teams, and a body of useful modern
transit management concepts; the lack of a real showcase transit
system; and the lack of a national effort to upgrade the tarnished
and threadbare image of mass transit—all come home to roost. All
the goodwill and criteria in the world will not make up for the lost
opportunities of the past.

In any case, the attempt to set new criteria for a program is very
difficult without workable objectives. No one really knows what the

federal transit programs are supposed to achieve. As a result, the capital grant program, and all the other UMTA programs, tend to exist for themselves and for the immediate, perceived needs of the potential recipients. The threat to the status quo wrung an understandably unfavorable reaction from mass transit's vested interests, since changing grant criteria would appear to make an already difficult job even more burdensome. It is also clear that the transit interests felt that the revised criteria were unfair.

The above instance is a good example of how the lack of meaningful goals can frustrate the efforts of groups normally in accord with one another. All in all, the lack of specific direction for the federal mass transportation program is probably the most serious factor inhibiting improvement in urban mass transportation. Until this situation is changed, there is small likelihood that the status of mass transportation and its role in U. S. life will be markedly improved.

The Money Shortage

The lack of adequate goals may be the principal flaw in the achievement of major transit improvements and gains in patronage; however, a more obvious reason to most persons concerned is the lack of money that has been made available over the years since the federal programs got under way. As discussed earlier, the initial and rather understandable reluctance of Congress to provide much in the way of money has given way to relatively generous authorizations for funding, at least in comparison with past efforts. Before 1971 there was never more than $175 million per annum available; a billion dollars was to be available in fiscal 1973 and again in fiscal 1974. The $3 billion in UMTA funds and the money potentially available from the Highway Trust Fund under the Highway Act of 1973 are assuredly moves in the right fiscal direction. The rise in funding is commendable, but still falls far short of what is deemed necessary by some observers.

The Federal Highway Administration—of all people!—has estimated that somewhere between $30 and $35 billion should be spent on mass transportation in the decade of the 1970's. The Institute for Public Administration estimated that about $50 billion needed to be spent within the next two decades. Other studies give ranges as high as $60 billion to be spent in the decade from 1972.[8] This money is needed just to bring mass transit up to reasonably good standards and to prevent the highway system from breaking down in critical spots in urban places. Yet the Department of Transportation has not really advocated transit spending on anything approaching that scale. The Nixon administration has proposed, and Congress had adopted in the 1970 Act, a $12 billion program for mass transportation in this decade. It seems barely enough when one estimate puts a price tag of over a half billion dollars just on cleaning and refurbishing New York City's subway stations. Secretary Volpe's brave attempt to use some of the Highway Trust Fund money to gain some assured financing for transit, while well intended, is still on too small a scale in light of the needs defined within DOT itself.[9] The same is true of Secretary Brinegar's efforts.

Of course, it is not just the amount of money available for transit purposes that is important, but the certainty that funds will continue to be available. Such certainty is not possible when a program must live with the vagaries of annual appropriations. The contract authority provisions of the Act of 1970 were designed to help assure cities that funds would be available when needed. Still, in times of vast federal deficits, there is always the danger of the axe falling on some programs. Federal transit funds, unlike federal highway money, are spooned out of the general fund and are thus not insulated from other fiscal demands on the federal government. One consultant's report put the situation very well:

> [Transit] . . . grants are discretionary; the Secretary [of Transportation] is authorized, not obliged, to make them. Consequently, receipt of federal funds for mass transportation improvement projects is dependent upon the availability of funds and demonstrated need when compared to other applications. Federal assistance is not assured, and is subject to delays even when granted. Further, the availability of discretionary funds from the federal government is subject to administrative whims, economy waves, and the needs of other branches of the government.[10]

The whacking away by the Office of Management and Budget of $300 million of the $900 million appropriated by Congress for transit in fiscal 1972 shows the difficulty of getting a bird in the hand when the administration has its mind set on economy. The new criteria, discussed a few pages earlier, are another example of hurdles to be jumped in getting what funds are available. The Highway Trust Fund was an obvious sitting duck as a potential source of financing for mass transportation programs, simply because the fuel pump turns out to be about the most effective and painless tax collector ever invented.

It may be questioned whether the whole trust fund idea is a good one to begin with. This is especially pertinent if an effort is made to create a transit trust fund. Once started, such devices seem to take on a life of their own. They help interpose rigidities in the use of funds and make the job of the federal government in trying to effect some control over the economy more difficult than it would be otherwise. Congress, ever jealous over its control of the purse strings—about the last real power that Congress has, according to Neil MacNeil of *Time*—is beginning to take a dim view of such devices, since it amounts to an erosion of congressional power, with review possible only at infrequent intervals.

Even given a strong willingness on the part of the Congress and the administration in office at a given time to devote more federal resources to mass transportation, without some rational urban policy and rational general transportation policy—meaning that there would have to be workable objectives, priorities, and policies established in both areas—there is no way of logically or rationally determining the extent of funding needed to do the job. More important than just the amount of money, of course, is the wisdom with which it is spent, so that maximum benefits will be yielded by whatever expenditure is made.

Assuming more money becomes available from the federal level, there remains the problem of finding local matching funds. Many local areas are unwilling or unable to bite the bullet and commit the needed local share to do a decent job on a transit undertaking. Much of the reluctance stems from the overwhelming use of the property tax to fund local government. The public is crying for property tax relief, and tax revolts are feared by local government. This, of course, touches on the whole business of the dire need for the restructuring of local government so that full local fiscal resources may be brought to bear on local problems. The point of all this is that the money problem in transit is far more complicated than just raising the federal ante. It is plain that there are no easy answers on sources of funds on either the national, state, or local level. Perhaps the studies on financing transit mandated by the Highway Act of 1973 will prove valuable on this score.

The Nixon administration proposed several plans of federal revenue sharing specifically aimed at transit; nothing came of these efforts.[11] Local and state governments reacted in a generally favorable way to these proposals, in which money from Uncle Sam would be apportioned according to a formula, with some stipulations on the use. Some observers, including the Congress, were not happy about the idea of revenue sharing. A cry arose that it would loosen congressional and federal control and turn billions of dollars over to levels of government that are often felt to be, at best, inept and, at worst, corrupt. Some saw it as a gigantic pork barrel with little control over who gets the pork or control of the barrel, a definite sore point in Congress.

Nevertheless, the fact remained: Something had to be done about the fiscal crunch that bogs down local government. With some misgivings, Congress passed a general revenue sharing bill shortly before the 1972 election. The funds may be used for a variety of purposes, at the discretion of state and local government. Public transportation is a high priority category for the use of the funds.[12] It is still too early to see how this program will work out. With no real information at the time of this writing on the effectiveness of the revenue sharing policy, one is obliged to listen to comments from sincere observers ranging from, "Revenue sharing is the most fiscally irresponsible action ever taken by the federal government," to "Revenue sharing is the most helpful action for local government ever taken by Congress." Basking in the ignorance of what is really going on, one can merely shrug and wait for definitive information. At the same time, it should be noted that many local officials see the start of a withering away of the federal categorical grant programs. There is reason for this concern in the avowed goal of the Nixon administration to dismantle and discontinue many of the Great Society programs of the Johnson administration. If much of the categorical aid is done away with, revenue sharing may leave the local governments of the United States worse off than before.

Management: Ridership and Transit Performance as a Marketing Problem

If UMTA is to be seriously faulted—recognizing, of course, the lamentable difficulty of operating with an indefinite mission—it lies in its tendency to interpret the mass transit problem as primarily a technological difficulty. As chronicled in these pages, much of the recent thrust of the federal effort has been on technical innovation. Certainly, technical innovation is needed; nevertheless, those responsible for managing the federal transit program have to deal with the problem of boosting transit ridership. Whether right or wong, that is likely to be the ultimate short-run test of the effectiveness of federal mass transportation policy and managerial effectiveness on the local level. Increasing the utilization of mass transportation is essentially a marketing problem. In other words, it depends largely upon the skill and the insight of management personnel. Technology, whether simple or sophisticated, is useful only as a set of tools management can utilize to meet the needs of consumers in the various segments of the transit market. Unfortunately, improving management's skill at marketing transit is not very dramatic stuff; the delivery of fifty new buses rates a headline and a ribbon cutting; a well-planned cost control system, internal organization, route structure, or carefully designed schedules are not newsworthy. A law can be passed providing money for various types of hardware; just passing a law will not provide good management.[13]

Old style, nonmarketing, nonconsumer-oriented managers still rule the roost in most transit organizations. The dead hand and obsolete concepts of managerial styles fifty years out of date are a cross that transit—and transit's present dwindling parcel of riders—must put up with. Even so, the time is ripe for some significant changes. To begin with, many of the top echelon of today's transit managers are not far from retirement. Regardless of any federal action, within a decade it will be necessary to find new people to run the nation's transit systems. This provides an excellent opportunity to introduce new managers with new ideas and put them in key positions.

Secondly, public ownership and public support—including the various federal-aid-for-transit programs—provide a pivot by which management standards can be established and required. Of course, the obvious danger is that publicly owned systems could become a haven for political hacks. Federally imposed standards of education and/or performance could help to remove this threat. Such standards would be nothing new, but would echo the requirements imposed by the federal government when the federal-aid highway program began; state highway departments had to have a certain level of professional personnel in order to qualify for federal funds. Incentives to managerial performance could be effected through a sliding scale of capital and other grant contributions favoring managerial quality, innovation, and performance.

Beyond the skills of the individual manager, transit firms are generally not organized to do a job of selling anything. As mentioned before, the organization chart of most transit organizations is totally devoid of any box labeled marketing.[14] Even if there is such a box, because of the lack of relevant information, the transit industry may be said to be in relative ignorance of those it serves, those it doesn't serve, and those whom it might serve.[15]

Included in a set of standards could be one on organizational form and informational requirement. The new capital grant criteria, discussed earlier in this chapter, could be a vehicle for imposing such standards.

Another related factor that makes decent mass transportation the exception rather than the rule in the United States is the ability of those responsible for urban planning and the public officials responsible for overseeing urban transport. Many planners, particularly those with extensive background and experience in highway planning or highway-oriented planning, are either totally innocent of any understanding or feel for mass transportation or may be hostile to it. As a result, what passes for transportation planning is often nothing more than highway planning with a crust thrown to mass transportation to make it "comprehensive."[16]

The public official responsible for mass transportation in any given city is likely to be mainly highway-oriented, or to have a background in sanitation or operation of a city-owned public utility, or other training that does not apply to transit. Probably the biggest problem here, as with transit management, is the lack of understanding of the marketing job needed for successful transit use. An official whose experience is based principally on managing a city-owned sanitation or water service has probably never been faced with the necessity to sell the service he is responsible for. A former street commissioner, on the other hand, is not likely to be sympathetic to transit, particularly if the operations he has seen have been churning along poorly for years; all he can see is a losing operation, with supposed benefits that no one can state clearly or consistently. The hostile public official is most likely to view the nebulous concept of "balanced transportation" as meaning fifty per cent asphalt and fifty per cent concrete. This is a problem that may fade as provision of transit as a city service becomes a regularly accepted part of urban administration, but it will take some time.

In summary, the management problem is critical; without good management of the day-to-day operations of transit there is little hope for success, regardless of the quality of federal objectives or the quantity of money provided. Unfortunately, the federal government has not stressed management, and the transit industry shows little interest in changing the status quo. Shifts to public ownership may not offer much in the way of progress. It remains to be seen if the new UMTA Office of Management will alter this situation.

Some Gordian Knots: Pricing and Population Distribution

Two of the best reasons that the federal programs have not had more glowing success are the way in which automobile use is priced (especially in relationship to transit pricing) and the distribution of population in U.S. metropolitan areas.

Pricing is an especially thorny matter. In attempting to do its job of improving mass transportation, which implies increasing transit patronage, UMTA has one hand tied behind its back because it has no control whatsoever over the pricing of the use of urban highways. (On the other hand, while it has no fare-setting powers now, if the federal government provided operating subsidies, it is possible that UMTA could have a voice in the setting of transit fares.) Present automobile user charges do not reflect congestion cost or the cost of environmental damage caused by automobiles. The federal user charges collected reflect an average cost per vehicle of using the highways, at least in the sense of putting money into the till to cover the federal expenditures for highways made through the Highway Trust Fund. In the aggregate, it is usually assumed that the user charges collected through fuel, license, and other levies is about equal to what is spent on highways; obviously, what is spent on highways does not reflect all the costs associated with highway travel, either in cities or in rural areas. To some extent, automobile users are beginning to pay some of the pollution costs through the prices charged for antipollution devices on new cars and the cost of operating automobiles equipped with such devices. Automobile insurance rates reflect, probably to a large degree, the pecuniary costs of accidents, although the social costs involved cannot very well be covered in the usual auto insurance premium. How does one calculate the cost of fatal accidents that wipe out enough people each year to populate Bloomington, Indiana, or Great Falls, Montana?

One of the great weaknesses of user charges as now collected is that there is no charge levied for congestion. In a very indirect way fuel burned up in congested driving conditions is a way of paying for such costs, but no one seriously considers that it is a very effective way of pricing such breakdowns of mobility, so as to reflect the burden such congestion foists on society. Various "economic" pricing ideas have been tinkered with in books and articles, but no city in the United States has been bold enough to institute a scheme for charging cars for congestion costs, or has tried to levy tolls at certain times to discourage the use of cars on certain roads or streets, or to otherwise match the price of automobile travel with cost. In a sense, then, driving an automobile in the city is always a bargain because the motorist is never asked to cough up the full cost of his journey.[17]

Adding to the advantage of automobile use for those who are not concerned with cost matching price is the separation of the pecuniary cost of car use from the individual trip, over and above the almost total disassociation of the social costs of automobile travel. Commonly, no overt payment must be made each and every time the motorist uses his car. The highway user charge is neatly buried in the price of fuel and is often completely obscured by the use of gasoline credit cards. Few motorists calculate the cost of an urban journey relative to the cost of the same trip via public transportation. Even if they did, in all likelihood only the direct cost of fuel and perhaps oil and tires would be included. The full monetary costs— including depreciation, insurance, and maintenance—are rarely considered. Social costs, at least at the present state of the art and available information, are not considered at all.

In comparison to the private automobile, mass transportation— even very good mass transportation—is at a decided disadvantage. A fare must be paid each time a trip is taken. Even if commuter tickets, tokens, passes, or automatic fare collection schemes (such as are used by BART in San Francisco, the Illinois Central commuter service in Chicago, or the Lindenwold Line in the Philadelphia area) are utilized, a substantial sum of coin-of-the-realm must be parted with at some point. An overt act is still required to pay for the ride each time mass transportation is used. Perhaps even more annoying, and tending to make the transit fare more burdensome still, is the growth in the use of exact-fare plans in most of the larger and many of the smaller cities in the United States. There is no doubt about it: having to present the exact change for anything from a vending machine to a parking meter to a bus farebox is a bother —yet another deterrent to the use of mass transportation.

It is worse yet, in many eyes, that the amount of that fare is likely to be substantial for even a single trip. Even with the growth of subsidized, publicly owned transit firms, the sharp rise in cost—particularly for labor—has been accompanied by steep fare hikes. The customer who must pay 40 or 50 cents for a service that is likely to strike him as being dear at half that price is hard-pressed to see transit as a bargain.

For mass transportation to be reasonably competitive with the private automobile for urban travelers with the luxury of choice, either the service must be markedly improved, the price lowered to a level deemed reasonable, or the price of automotive travel raised to a level representing its total cost. None of these alternatives is easy to carry out. On the surface, fare cuts may appear to be the easiest to accomplish, but this is a difficult step to take in a deficit-ridden industry that has trouble finding funds to cover costs even when fares are high. The risk of cutting fares to boost patronage, unless there is some assured source of countervailing income, is probably too much to face for either the managers of a privately owned company or public officials shepherding a publicly owned transit firm. Since, at the present time, funds are not generally available to provide for substantial cuts in transit fares, the price of automobile use is below total cost, and major quality improvements in transit are slow in coming, transit continues to appear expensive and automobile use cheap in comparison.[18]

If the federal programs in mass transportation have trouble finding a victory because of pricing handicaps, add to that the difficulty of servicing a population that has spent the last half-century busily scattering itself in a dispersed pattern around metropolitan areas, and the full difficulty of the task of providing for meaningful transit improvement and customer appeal is painfully obvious. Improved planning and greater control of development on the local level is a partial solution to sprawled development, but it takes time. Transit, of course, can play a part in helping to control sprawl and concentrate development in line with judicious planning, depending on the type of development desired in a given metropolitan area.

On the matter of population distribution, the trouble is there are no definitive answers to how much or how little dispersion is desirable. As noted elsewhere, nineteenth-century levels of concentration are no doubt intolerable in the modern United States, but the present scatterization may be economically and socially undesirable, too. The trouble is nobody seems to know what is best. Sociologists, economists, and other social scientists have not yet provided clues as to where the good life might lie in terms of development patterns.

Assuming the urban sprawl has at least some undesirable factors, restructuring cities to higher density forms just to make federal transit policy more successful doesn't qualify as a red-hot idea. Equally silly, considering the complex forces that have shaped our metropolitan population distribution patterns over the past half-century, would be bland acceptance of sprawl as the ultimate desire of the people.

The trouble with the sprawled metropolis is that by its very size and multiplicity of governmental jurisdictions, the sprawl can only get worse; there is no body with the power to pull it all together. Unless some form of unified metropolitan government is adopted, there is no way that the total resources of the metropolitan area can be gathered to come to grips with metropolitan problems, such as sprawl and uneconomic land use—and mass transportation, of course.

The urban aimlessness is the product of a lack of a rational urban policy for the nation. There are no long-range, rational, workable objectives for urban policy. For longer than a decade, the federal government—and some state governments, too—have fumbled with various urban problems and symptoms of problems on a piecemeal, patchwork basis. As in so many of our difficulties, even though a flurry of laws are passed, the nation is adrift with no star to steer by. In short, solutions to urban mass transportation problems require solutions to urban problems in general.

In this chapter some factors were discussed that cause urban mass transportation problems to persist in the face of federal efforts to improve matters. Considering the difficulties, it is, indeed, amazing that the federal mass transportation programs have seen even the modest success so far enjoyed.

CHAPTER SEVEN

What Can Be Done About the Problems?

Introduction

All books about problems inevitably and invariably end up with a list of solutions to the problems, as if the author really knew. Sometimes it might be more realistic simply to say that there are no solutions—or at least none that are generally acceptable to the public and the politicians—that will provide a genuine service in really settling what ails us.

In time-honored fashion, therefore, suggestions for long-term and short-term solutions are provided in the pages that follow. However, a caveat should be observed: the long-run solutions put forth will probably not be adopted. One might observe, somewhat cynically, that in the never-never land of politics an acceptable solution that won't work is often preferred to a workable solution that may be unpalatable. The short-run recommendations mentioned here are more likely to see the field of action, but even these depend on men of goodwill ready to act in ways unfamiliar to them.

The chances for quick and effective action seem dim when one reflects upon the glacial pace of U.S. developments in mass transportation. Especially if government action is required, accomplishing almost anything seems to take forever, and this seems particularly true in the years since the end of the Second World War. Certainly, in the area of urban mass transportation, most other advanced nations of the world seem to be making substantial strides in the improvement of transit. Comparisons can be made with progress in Montreal and Toronto, Canada. For example:

> . . . Metropolitan Toronto, so far as public transportation and urban planning is concerned, is doing an excellent job of living up to its name. A refreshing willingness by the provincial government on the one hand and the city and its 12 suburbs on the other to meet and work together to avoid urban strangulation has earned this thriving area the reputation of being a public transportation showcase. While others plan and talk, Toronto plans and digs; while others plan and consult, Toronto plans and lets contracts; while others plan and haggle, Toronto plans and grows.[1]

The United States has planned, consulted, and haggled and has relatively little to show for it. Sisyphus and his rock come to mind as an apt simile.

Long-Run Solutions

No effective program of government actually depends on the actions of just one element. The legislative, executive, and judicial must work together. Still, the onus is on the Congress to take the definitive steps; the urging and support of the executive branch is also a necessity.

In order to provide for lasting relief of urban transportation problems, Congress must take two actions that are closely interrelated. First, it must set workable goals for urban mass transportation in the United States and then provide the financial capability and authority needed by the Department of Transportation so that the task may be accomplished within some specified time period. Second, Congress must help cities solve their financial and jurisdictional problems, particularly by providing strong incentive for coordination or integration of government on the local level. This means that the states, too, must be pressed to act so that local government will have the resources necessary to solve problems either independently or in conjunction with state government. At the very least, states must not impede local efforts. In short, what this means is that the Congress must establish practical, workable objectives for urban transportation policy in particular, and for urban policy in general.

It is easy enough to say that workable objectives should be set, but another thing to set them. As with a business firm's goal of a given return on investment, an objective which can be quantitatively defined is needed. The end goal must be specific and measurable, and a target date is necessary.

The purpose of transportation is to provide mobility; therefore, the workable objectives should focus logically on mobility. Possibly the best way to do this is to develop an index of urban physical mobility—based on research studies—for some base year, and then require a reasonable level of improvement by a given target date. For example, Congress could order that a mobility index measurement be taken in 1975; the findings would serve as a benchmark, using the base year as a starting place. Congress could then mandate that there be a 15 per cent (or some percentage) improvement in mobility by 1985 and a 25 per cent improvement by 1990. The mobility index studies would be taken on a regular basis, perhaps as part of the biennial DOT-sponsored "Transport Need Studies," in order to determine how successfully the goal was being met. Once the measure had been taken and the degree of improvement and target period established, DOT and UMTA could back up from the goal to the base-year measure and investigate alternative approaches to reaching the goal and determine the methods and levels of expenditure needed. Obviously various combinations of capital expenditures, operating aids, and policies for various modes of transport—including highways—would be necessary.

The mobility index itself would aim at measuring the stock of assets available for mobility purposes and the difficulty imposed on persons utilizing those assets in moving about a given metropolitan area as a whole. Furthermore, the specific level of mobility enjoyed by given portions of the urban population on the basis of age, income, location, and other demographic and geographic factors would have to be measured. On calculating the index, several dimensions of mobility should be included. For the individual the index would measure the time, effort, and money costs as these affect him personally. At the same time, the index would have to measure the social, environmental, and monetary costs as they affect a given metropolitan area as an economic and social entity. Perhaps several indices would be needed to assure the sensitivity of the testing method so that key factors would not get lost in the shuffle. Factors relating to environmental quality would also have to be included. The stock of mobility assets would include highways, automobiles, and mass transportation, and the degree of availability of the automobile and mass transport assets to the public.

A three-dimensional personal mobility index, considering time, effort, and money costs, would provide a clearer picture of mobility as it affects citizens than is afforded by any existing measure. In the past, various studies have attempted to clock the time involved in journeys and some have measured the money cost. However, the effort factor involved in mobility has rarely been measured, and, to the best of this writer's knowledge, has never been combined with time and money cost in an attempt to calculate fully the relative ease or difficulty of enjoying mobility. Yet effort cost of mobility must be included if the full cost of personal mobility, and the aggregate cost of mobility as it affects all segments of urban society, are to be realistically evaluated.[2]

The relative weighting of the personal cost factor would be expected to vary considerably depending on the age, income, and location of persons within a given urban area. For instance, elderly persons may enjoy sufficient time and money to make certain journeys, but the effort involved may be beyond their limited energies; for practical purposes, such persons are immobilized unless travel is relatively easy. A program to enhance the mobility of senior citizens should probably give priority to reducing the effort involved rather than diminishing time cost, or perhaps even the money cost. Conversely, it is possible that the mobility of young people may be affected more by their lack of financial resources rather than lack of time or the effort costs involved.

In addition to reflecting the mobility of given segments of the urban population, any reasonably good measure must also reflect the social, environmental, and economic costs as these factors affect the community as a whole. This is necessary as a primary measure of the costs of mobility as they affect all—or very large chunks—of society in the process of providing enhanced mobility for given segments. As an example, a new urban expressway may cut the personal time, effort, and money costs of a majority of citizens; nevertheless, the side effects of concentrated automotive air pollution, neighborhood fracturing by impingement of the roadway, and loss of land from the tax rolls may have a deleterious effect on the city as a whole and create a substantial burden on some segments of the population. As an instance of such a burden, the hypothetical highway improvement may divert so many car owners from using mass transportation in a given corridor that transit service may be cut back substantially; noncar owners have their mobility diminished by the reduction in transit quality, yet at the time are obliged, through their property taxes, to pay part of the cost of a highway facility that confers few benefits on them. On the other hand, the new highway may divert cars from the regular streets so that transit buses can move more quickly and dependably, thus improving the mobility of transit riders.

The mobility index should provide a useful tool for policy makers and for those whose job it is to implement policy. It will provide hitherto unavailable insight on the mobility for the nation—or a given city—at a given time. It will also provide a means of discovering, over time, whether or not progress is being made in the task of improving mobility. For example, establishing a base-year benchmark in a community will allow comparisons in future years in order to see if changes—such as capital investment in transit and highways—have really improved mobility. Likewise, if Congress should set workable objectives for urban transportation programs—a certain standard of mobility to be achieved nationally by a given date as noted earlier—the mobility index would permit evaluation and monitoring of efforts aimed at meeting congressional objectives. The findings from a repeated series of regularly performed indexes would be an aid in planning future policy and programs on the national, state, and local levels.

Perhaps the most valuable and important use of the mobility index will be in the evaluation of public investment decisions, where, despite the understandable political considerations, the key indicator for government decision has often been efficiency. Of course, as painful experience has shown in regard to highways, efficiency may be so narrowly defined—pecuniary costs only—that the results are nothing short of disastrous.

The workable objectives for urban transportation and the policies and guidelines necessary to implement such objectives must tie in with workable objectives for transportation as a whole throughout the nation and with the establishment of a rational urban policy. While it is beyond the scope of this work to get into the complex business of national transportation policy, it would be absurd for urban transportation policy to exist in a vacuum relative to the intercity transport structure. Ideally, wise policy would smooth off the rough edges that now exist in most places between strictly intra-urban transport and interurban transportation. (Indeed, in some places—such as the Northeast corridor between Washington and Boston—it is hard to draw the line between intraurban and inter-urban transport.)

In addition to assuring a fit between workable objectives and national transportation policy and urban transportation, it is nec-essary that the second major step mentioned earlier be taken by the Congress. Nothing less than a national urban policy with work-able objectives is needed, otherwise urban transportation policy will hang in limbo in relation to the cities it is to serve, as well as in its association with intercity transport. Some rational objectives must be set to help give direction to city growth, population density, structure, and location, and to provide cities with the financial base and authority to solve more of their own problems. This is essential if U.S. cities are ever to be masters of their own household. Some of their difficulties have been discussed in Chapter 1 and the point made that the reason behind a federal policy in urban mass trans-portation is the lack of financial ability of cities to solve their own problems. Indeed, the relationship of cities to the state and federal governments is probably the stickiest internal political problem now facing the nation and will not be easily or quickly resolved.

What direction should workable objectives for a national urban policy take? That, too, is beyond the scope of this book. In a broad sense, whatever the objectives, they must be consistent with the efforts in urban transportation and intercity transportation, and vice versa. As Wilfred Owen has noted, we must not continue to let urban transportation policy—such as it is and such as it might be —take the place of a meaningful urban policy.[3] Moreover, what-ever the particulars, it would seem most logical for the Congress to create an environment that would help cities solve as many of their problems as possible from local resources. At the same time, local inadequacies in administrative talent, imagination, and the often unwholesome political scene should not be allowed to act as a bur-den on national development, or the over-all quality of national life.

Just about as evident as is the need for rational workable objec-tives for U.S. urban places and for urban transportation is the need for a rational national pricing policy on highways. Indeed, pricing, properly applied, is a critical part of any useful effort to improve transport. The user charges levied on highways should reflect the costs of particular sections of the road system. In addition, rational pricing should also reflect the cost at certain times of day, week, or year; in other words, charges should be imposed on highways to reflect congestion costs. Environmental costs should also be reflected in pricing. More rational pricing of mass transport is needed, too, but such a policy cannot be implemented in the absence of a realistic highway pricing scheme.

The likelihood of any of these three actions being taken by the Congress is exceedingly slim, at least in the near future. It is a sad fact, but the population of the United States does not think in systematic terms about much of anything. In short, there will probably be no general pressure from the electorate for a rational approach to transportation policy. Moreover, government objects to workable objectives—such as the suggested mobility index—because they permit performance to be measured. The federal agencies responsible for carrying out policy would be reluctant, in all probability, to be measured. For example, at the present time, because no one is quite sure what UMTA is really supposed to be doing, it is difficult to criticize; but with workable objectives as a help in measurement, the fat would be in the fire if UMTA's performance were not up to par. Internal pressures within the federal establishment would undoubtedly serve to hinder setting of workable objectives. Congress, too, would be measured in a sense, since it would be responsible for supplying the resources needed to carry out the objectives it set. Congressional shortchanging on the amount of money or authority required by a federal agency to do a proper job would be quite apparent.

As a consequence, however desirable the establishment of logical objectives of a workable nature might be, it will probably be many years before Congress takes such steps. Yet, in the meantime, it is possible for Congress, the Department of Transportation, and the Urban Mass Transportation Administration to help provide some short-run solutions that would improve the quality of mobility in the nation's cities, increase patronage of mass transport, and to at least some extent improve the quality of urban life in the United States.

The main objective of the short-run efforts would aim at the consumer level by improving management of mass transit resources and improving the channels of communication with present and potential users of mass transit.

Short-Run Solutions

More Money

As starters for short-run solutions, Congress can provide more money for transit. The funds, however, should not be simply thrown at transit in the vague hope that more is better, but should be carefully directed for maximum results for the dollar spent. How much more Congress will be willing to part with is probably dependent upon the degree of improvement shown in transit's performance and the chance of tapping some source of reliable financial input—such as the possibility of a bite of the Highway Trust Fund through the Highway Act of 1973. To avoid a pitched battle with the highway interests over the Highway Trust Fund revenues, Congress might impose an extra penny or two on the federal fuel tax, with the receipts earmarked for urban mass transportation purposes. There is somewhat of a chicken and egg relationship here, but money for noncapital improvements that promised major increases in patronage, in addition to the continued financing of capital improvements, would probably be attractive to Congress.

There are excellent arguments in favor of increased funding, not the least of which is the obvious demand for funds that already far exceeds the amounts authorized under the Act of 1970 or the Highway Act of 1973. Just how much is needed? As discussed in an earlier chapter, estimates range from $30 to $60 billion for the decade of the 1970's.[4] How much can reasonably be expected from Congress is hard to assay. A continuation of capital spending on a somewhat higher level than at present along with some of the programs outlined below might be achieved without too much strain. Programs and projects that actually increased patronage would probably prove to be increasingly easy to fund as time went on.

The need to provide some visible evidence of success in mass transportation especially in the form of steadily mounting ridership cannot be overstressed. Some clear, here-and-now type of benefit must manifest itself to the public. This lack of apparent benefit from U.S. moon landing programs led to severe budget cuts in the space effort; the mass transportation budget can face the same fate unless it shows tangible results—and a rise in patronage is most certainly tangible—in the very near future.

Leadership by UMTA

As the agency charged with administering the mass transportation programs, UMTA has an opportunity and a responsibility to do more than merely see that administrative matters are handled smoothly. UMTA should provide vigorous leadership with the goal of accomplishing nothing less than remolding the transit industry to insure a more effective delivery of mass transportation service to the public. The eventual result desired would, of course, be increased patronage reflecting the rise in the usefulness of mass transportation to a larger proportion of the public. This does not mean that UMTA must involve itself directly in the day-to-day operations of local transit firms. However, by setting certain standards of performance, it can alter the whole approach of the mass transportation industry toward the public.

In the first of the subsequent sections, a detailed discussion of what is needed is given. Folowing that is a section on the means UMTA might use in accomplishing the changes.

Precipitating a Transit Revolution: The Goal

The present management philosophy and organizational structure of the typical transit firm are not only obsolete, but irrelevant, since they follow a pattern appropriate only to a firm operating under near monopoly conditions. There are lessons for the revision of this managerial philosophy to be found in the modern business firm and its concepts. Such a firm focuses on sharply defined goals and organizes all of its component parts in a fashion to maximize the chances of reaching those goals. Understanding the market is essential for designing and delivering the product or service in a way that meets the needs and desires of the consumer. The consumer is the central focus and, because the marketing arm of the modern firm is charged with the responsibility of understanding and dealing with the consumer, the marketing function takes on critical importance within the organization. In a nutshell, the aim of the modern, consumer-oriented business firm is to produce and sell goods and services that consumers want, not necessarily what the firm wants to make or what it can produce most cheaply.

In order to function effectively, transit management and public officials charged with jurisdiction over a city's transit operations have to be specific about what the enterprise is supposed to do. This means that workable objectives—that is, clear, attainable, measurable, and with a given target date for accomplishment—must be established. Simply to use "transit must be better" as a goal is useless. A more useful goal would be "to provide transit service on at least a 20-minute headway, within two blocks of every resident within four miles of the Courthouse Square by July 1, 1982." Goals might also take the form of setting patronage targets, or sighting in on hauling a given proportion of the person-trips in a city each day.

Of course, any enterprise may have a number of major and minor goals; there is no problem as long as the objectives are not in conflict. In transit, increasing the frequency of service and increasing the numbers of patrons would be compatible goals. However, a goal of increasing the reliability of service and another of cutting maintenance expenditures 85 per cent would most likely conflict with one another.

Generally, because of the shift of mass transportation from private to public enterprise, goal setting should concentrate mainly on service quality and patronage rather than on profit or least-cost operations. From past history and the evidence of many of the federally sponsored demonstrations, it is apparent that in marketing transit service the quality of the service is paramount if there is to be, over time, even a remote hope of minimum loss, break-even, or profitable operations. This is not to suggest that there is anything wrong with a publicly owned enterprise operating at a surplus if it can. It does mean that public enterprise transit is ill-advised to try to operate out of the farebox or engage in drastic cost-cutting to the exclusion of marketing a quality service to the public. The general goal should be service and the principal public policy should be to provide sufficient financial support to encourage consumer-oriented management practices.

It is unlikely that any city would wish to force its citizens to

Figure 7–1
Model of Human Behavior

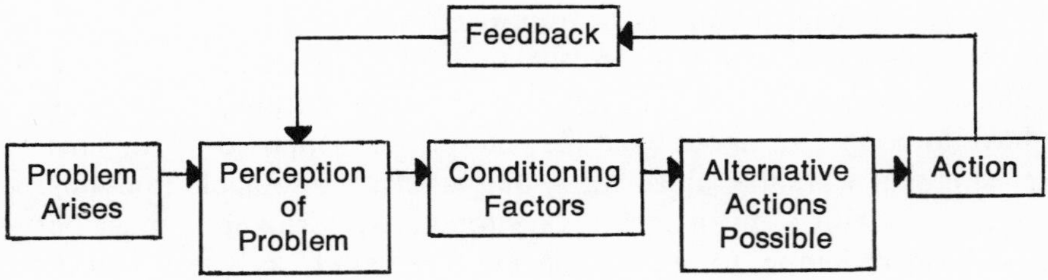

utilize mass transit service; it is also unrealistic to expect the public to patronize transit as an act of civic virtue. Public utilization of transit depends on providing a service that customers want; therefore, successful operation of mass transportation depends on vigorous marketing, which in turn must be built upon an understanding of consumer behavior. There is logic and motivation behind any act of the consumer. The simple model of human behavior shown in Figure 7–1 will help to illustrate this point. In a marketing context its elements are as follows:

A problem arises. The consumer will act to solve his problems through the purchase of goods and services.
Perception. The senses communicate the problem to the brain.
Conditioning. This is a filter that affects the consumer's attitudes and his approaches to solving his problems. While some conditioning is biological, the most important conditioning to the marketer is that imposed by society. A long-time resident of the United States would be affected and conditioned by Western civilization in general; the nation as a whole and the regional society in which he lives; his general group or class within the region; the immediate group in which he finds himself; and the group he looks up to and attempts to copy. For the last three conditioning factors, symbols and images are highly important.
Alternatives. The consumer will select among alternatives that are open, acceptable in light of his conditioning, and known to him. An unknown option is a choice that does not exist to the consumer in any meaningful or useful form. In evaluating alternatives, a consumer mentally performs a rough calculus of the time, energy, and money costs of each alternative and compares this with his resources of time, energy, and money.
Action. The consumer now behaves in accordance with the alternative he has chosen.

Feedback. This element reflects whether or not the particular problem has been solved by the action taken. If the consumer is satisfied with his action—choice of product or service—he is likely to behave in a similar fashion again.

The elements in the model that seem to offer the best opportunities for managerial action in the transit field are the conditioning factors and the alternatives perceived by the consumer. Transit management can, for example, make a vigorous effort toward affecting conditioning so that mass transportation is acceptable to many sectors of society. Goals and policy should be shaped with improvement of transit's image and acceptability by the public kept carefully in mind. By means of advertising, community relations efforts, and exemplary performance, the conditioning factors may be affected positively. This process would take time; no overnight miracles are probable.

A particularly fertile ground for marketing effort lies in promoting mass transportation as a reasonable alternative to the private automobile for many types of journeys. Obviously, transit is not always perceived as a reasonable alternative by most persons in the United States. In addition to some social stigma, the use of mass transportation may be perceived as more costly in terms of time, energy, and money expended than is the private automobile. Even if that is not really the case, as long as the consumer with a choice perceives transit to be more costly than the automobile, he will choose the automobile.

To effect the necessary consumer cost reductions, careful rethinking and perhaps restructuring of transit routes and schedules as well as other service improvements are needed to make mass transportation a reasonable travel choice for an increasing number of citizens. Assuming that transit is less expensive in pecuniary terms than the full cost of auto travel (a factor that should be the subject of diligent advertising and promotion work) the time and energy costs associated with transit use must be cut. Clearly, long walks to transit stops, lengthy running time, infrequent service, inconvenient transfers, unpleasant and uncomfortable equipment, a lack of waiting shelters, and surly employees, are all factors that increase the energy and time cost of transit patrons. To cut these costs is not easy, especially since it requires management to rethink many elements of the service, and rethinking is hard work.

Moreover, the task is made more difficult because most transit managers have little or no control over the right-of-way—or environment—in which they must operate. If substantial improvements are to be made in the quality of service, transit management must work closely with city officials, planners, and others involved in the handling of traffic. Results will probably not be achieved with ease, but the effort is necessary if reserved lanes, no-parking at bus stop zones, bus-only streets, or other means to help management exercise better control over transit's operating environment are to be found. The burden is on city officials to cooperate in such measures. Most certainly, it is foolish for public officials to set goals for greatly improved transit service and then give no help in providing the means to do the job.

Image improvement is probably as difficult as it is important. Advertising, new equipment, and other attractive viable facilities are critical factors. Most essential, however, is the quality of the service package; if service is undependable, slow, and uncomfortable, the image of mass transportation is not likely to improve even if the externals are superficially attractive.

In reaching toward the goal of better service geared to meet the wishes and desires of consumers and potential consumers of transit service, there are many internal elements over which the transit manager has control. Traditionally, of course, transit managers have acted as if they could control only the fare charged (and that usually only with the approval of a regulatory body) and the quantity—hence the quality—of the service. Also, it is normal to attempt to minimize the cost of each of the subfunctions under their control, since each function is typically thought to exist independent of other elements. For example, cutting maintenance costs to the bone may appear to be a sign of an efficient maintenance supervisor; however, excessive equipment breakdowns because of poor maintenance may make schedules highly unreliable and alienate customers, resulting in severe losses in patronage and revenue. All of the subfunctions must also be geared to achieve the goals of the transit service. This fits very directly into the marketing orientation, which demands recognition of all factors under management's control and concurrently molding them to fit the requirements of consumer satisfaction. The factors of subfunctions under managerial control include:

The goals of the firm and the organization of the firm to meet those goals.
The information collected by the firm and how it is used for management
purposes (including accounting information and other facts necessary
for effective managerial control and decision making).
The personnel selected by the firm, how they are recruited and
trained, and the methods utilized in dealing with them.
The equipment and its maintenance.
The routes and schedules.
Communication for efficient and dependable operation, particularly
between operators and supervisory personnel.
The advertising program.
Public information, such as maps, timetables, and informational signs.
Relations of the firm with the community as a whole, public officials,
and the mass media.

Organization is critical. Typically, transit enterprises have operations as the central function, with maintenance and the office and
other administrative functions as adjuncts. In an organization that
is geared to the consumer, as transit must be, marketing must be
the core function around which the organization is built. This is
illustrated graphically in Figure 7–2. In this functional organization
chart (the boxes represent functions and their relationship with one

Figure 7–2
Functional Organization of Consumer-Oriented Transit Operation

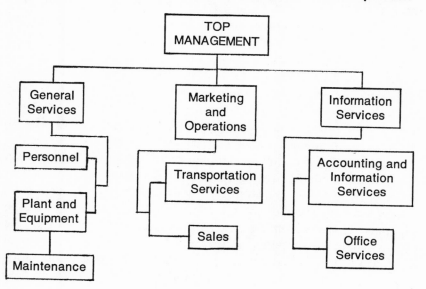

another, not persons), "Operations" carries out the marketing tasks that serve the goals of the enterprise. "Marketing," charged with being sensitive to consumer needs and wishes, must call the tune; the operating subfunction operates the service as designed by marketing. "Information Services" includes not only the usual accounting and office functions, but is also involved in gathering information for managerial decision making and marketing. "General Services" includes the hardware and personnel functions, maintenance of equipment and facilities, and the purchase and control of supplies.

The precise details of the organization would depend in large measure on the size and complexity of the operation. Enterprises of modest size may combine some of the necessary tasks and assign them to one individual. The larger the property in question, the greater the degree of specialization.

The essential business of vigorously marketing mass transportation service will not come easily to the transit industry. Traditionally, the market has been considered, if at all, as homogeneous. One service was made available to all and whatever selling effort was made was the same to all. Given relatively slender resources, a wiser approach would be to consider the market as consisting of a series of possibly nonhomogeneous segments. Different combinations of service, promotion, and pricing should be considered in reaching each segment. For example, selling mass transportation service to middle-income auto-commuters for the journey to work might require special express bus services in the morning and afternoon peak hours. Promotional effort might concentrate on special advertising spotted in the sports pages of newspapers, and radio commercials specially aimed at the motorist fretting in a traffic jam. The major thrust of the promotional campaign might be toward saving driving effort, parking frustration, and money, and would be aimed at a segment composed mainly of men between 30 and 60 years of age.

On the other hand, appealing to a market segment composed of housewives in single-car families, where the car was not available at home during the day, would require a different approach. The trip purpose for which the mass transportation service would be geared would be shopping or personal business. The promotional effort would focus on the mobility available to women in the home without an automobile. Operations and fares would be geared to the off-peak hours. The main point here is that two different segments of the market would require different packages of service, promotion, and—perhaps—pricing to be reached successfully. One service and one sales pitch will not suffice.

Probably the best marketing strategy for a transit enterprise using the market segment technique would be to appeal initially to the most accessible segment or segments of the local market. At first, they would probably consist mainly of those patrons already being served and, of course, those who may not be regular patrons but who do not possess alternate means of transportation. Much of the early effort would center on improving the quality and status of mass transportation. Also involved would be the promotion of destinations—the zoo, museums, sports events—and the use of transit to reach them. By concentration on reliability, convenience, and other quality factors, the initially served segment or segments of the market should be held onto and the usual pattern of eroding patronage halted. With a service worth pointing to with pride, quality improvements and high standards of service should be promoted through the relevant media. After the potential of the first segment is tapped, then the next best segment should be pursued, and so on.

Finding the segments of the market is not easy and probably should not be based on simple demographic information. Possibly the best way to discover the segments of the transit market is by first offering a service to those most likely to use it, emphasizing reduced time, energy, and money costs of travel. Emphasis should also be placed on new equipment, on-time performance, and reasonable prices. It is important that there be an actual offering of service of known quality so that users will have a known factor to relate to. Once patrons have become accustomed to the service, research should be conducted to see who—that is, what segments—are using the service and why. What patrons think about an actual service is likely to provide far better information than asking potential patrons what they would do if so-and-so were offered. This suggests that accurate prediction of patronage resulting from improved service is very difficult. People can only evaluate a product or service that they have sampled.

The next logical step is to conduct research to discover who is not using transit and why. Some additional segments or potential segments may be revealed by this work. Particularly important is the discovery of some market segment that might provide more users of mass transportation if some slight change in the basic service offering were made. For example, speeding up service from a suburban area to the central business district by means of express buses might attract a number of persons using automobiles. It is only natural, of course, that some segments of the market would remain completely inaccessible to the blandishments of transit, however excellent its quality. Salesmen who must carry bulky samples with them are one example; housewives who must bring home a week's groceries are another. Only those segments that are accessible and large enough to warrant separate cultivation should be followed up.

The marketing mix is a useful concept in the process of reaching and developing various segments of the transit market. The mix consists of all the service, price, and promotion factors under the control of management that may be varied or manipulated to meet the needs of the different segments.

For transit, the product portion of the mix involves the types of service offered, the quality of the service, and the access to it that is afforded consumers. The types of transit service include regular route, special services, and charters. For regular route operations, the configuration of the routes and the schedules operated are the principal variables. Special services are those operating under special conditions and not following the regular route pattern; such services may be offered on special occasions or to sports events or points of special interest. Special subscription bus services offering door-to-door transportation on a monthly contract basis would fit into this category, as would dial-a-bus. Charters involve private service under contract to a special group.

The quality of the service is a vital part of the product factor. It includes such items as air-conditioned equipment, seating comfort, decor, reliability, waiting shelters, courtesy of personnel, physical transfer requirements, travel time, and access. Access to transit is usually determined by route spacing or by direct service to given traffic generators. The typical route spacing used at the present time —about a half-mile apart outside the central business district—is out of touch with reality today when many potential patrons have their own private means of transport; to maximize the ease of access, routes should be closely spaced, probably no more than three or four blocks apart. The provision of outlying parking lots for cars, with quality service to major destination points, is another way of providing access. Still other means of access are given by dial-a-bus and subscription bus services where the transit vehicle goes after the people rather than the other way around.

Pricing is the second ingredient in the marketing mix and one that cannot be considered in isolation from the other ingredients. Whether the price of transit is deemed high or low is probably a matter more closely connected with the quality of the service as perceived by the consumer than with any absolute sum of money. High-quality service—frequent, dependable, and clean, with air-conditioned vehicles operating on a fast schedule—is likely to be perceived as good value for money and therefore relatively inexpensive. On the other hand, undependable, infrequent service, utilizing old, dirty vehicles manned by rude personnel may be judged as high in cost even though the price charged may be the same in both cases. Whatever the charge, it should be carefully fitted into the mix.

Free transit service should not be offered as a means of compensating for low-quality service. If free service for some or all of the segments of the market is carried out for some social goal, that may be a different matter, but as noted elsewhere in this book, consumers are usually willing to pay for value received.

The final part of the marketing mix is promotion. This includes advertising in various media, ranging from radio and newspapers to circulars, television, and local magazines. Promotion is not confined to advertising; it includes public information devices such as maps and timetables (designed to be understood readily by members of the general public) and information signs. Community relations are also part of the promotional package. This latter factor is really a two-way street of communication dealing directly with the members of the community and public officials and media. It includes finding out what is on the public's mind as well as passing out information.

What all this lengthy discussion boils down to is a way of approaching the management of a transit enterprise in the most constructive fashion. It focuses on the consumer logically enough because transit is a consumer service. It is nothing more than an outline of a means by which the resources of transit can be most effectively brought to bear to meet consumer needs. All of this is essential if transit is to fulfill the role of providing improved mobility in urban areas.[5]

The Role of UMTA in the Revolution in Transit Management

What role can UMTA play in leading transit properties to the trough of improved management and encouraging them to drink? Since better management cannot be achieved instantly by either wishful thinking or proclamation, financial incentives are necessary to encourage transit firms to adopt at least certain minimum management improvements.

Assuming that local matching funds continue to be required in order to receive federal capital and other transit grants, incentives for managerial reform could be given by means of a sliding scale for the federal portion, provided various management and marketing practices were carried out. For example, if a given transit operation had key positions filled by persons with marketing or other stipulated management skills, the federal proportion of a capital or planning grant might be increased from the present 80 per cent of net project cost to 85 per cent. If the firm collected certain data as a matter of course and regularly conducted marketing surveys, the federal share might rise to 90 per cent.

Since much of the success of effective transit service depends upon the operating environment outside the direct control of management and under the control of the city itself, incentives could be provided to elicit more cooperation from the city. For example, a certain basic minimum of cooperative effort might be expected from the city before it would be eligible for any federal mass transit grants. A suggested list of minimum standards would include:

> Police enforcement of no-parking at bus stop zones.
> Right-of-way for all transit vehicles in traffic, with strict enforcement by the police.
> Preferential treatment for transit vehicles at traffic signals, in congested places, and in making turns.
> No parking along crowded transit streets during rush hours.

Once the minimums were met, other improvements in the operating environment, as with the management efforts mentioned previously, would be encouraged by a sliding scale of capital and planning grants. For instance, assuming the management had carried out all the efforts mentioned above, the proportion of federal aid might increase to 92 per cent if the city provided reserved lanes for transit vehicles during the rush hour; 95 per cent aid might be granted if there were transit-only streets during high traffic times. A maximum of 95 or even 100 per cent federal capital aid for a given time period might encourage cities to permit the transit enterprises to have an active role in planning and development, such as veto power over the streets platted in new subdivisions or on new street developments in older parts of the city or metropolitan areas; as yet another option, private rights-of-way might be provided by city government for mass transportation vehicles in newly developed portions of a metropolitan area, in order to qualify for an increased proportion of federal aid. Similar incentives might be used to encourage cities to establish areawide mass transportation (or total transportation) authorities or districts.

Likewise, the federal portion of grants might slide upward where localities provided a certain proportion of local financial support for transit operating costs in order to improve service quality. The greater the proportion of the local contribution the greater the federal support for capital and planning grants—and perhaps management training and demonstration grants as well.

If the federal government ever provides operating subsidies for mass transit, then incentives to better management, better marketing, and greater cooperation from the city might be achieved by means of a sliding scale of support. Assuming that there were some basic level of operating support, say three cents per passenger per year for five years, the transit firm experiencing a five-per-cent increase in annual patronage might receive six cents per passenger. If patronage increased by ten per cent per year, it might receive twelve cents per passenger, and so on. In short, increasing the number of patrons would mean more federal money for the local coffers to help offset any local deficits.[6]

To carry out such an incentive program would mean that UMTA would need to have some persons well versed in management on its own staff to establish management and organizational standards and evaluate local efforts. UMTA leadership through a program of incentives should insure that the maximum efforts will be made on the part of transit enterprises and cities to deliver high-quality mass transportation service to the public. The program suggested would offer a means for beginning a turnaround in transit patronage and insuring some major victories in transit patronage performance.

Manpower

Providing properly trained manpower for transit management is of vital importance in moving out of the 1920's and into the 1970's. Those responsible for the marketing, operation, and information-gathering functions of the transit firm should be trained in modern business management skills. This should include a basic knowledge of transportation economics, management and organization behavior, cost and management accounting, electronic data processing, marketing, and production management. Graduates of the better business schools have such an education; however, it would probably be best to assure that there was, in addition to "regular" academic work, a strong input of institutional work relating to transit in the college program.[7]

The transit academy idea has potential merit. Transit academies located at several points in the United States might perform a valuable service. They should probably be housed in a small number of major state universities. In addition to the regular business-oriented programs for students aiming at degrees, work could also be provided through short courses, institutes, and other brief programs to upgrade present managerial and supervisory personnel in the transit field. Some academies could specialize in certain fields, since some academic eggs should be kept in one basket. Beyond that, transit academies could help train and educate all levels of employees on a vocational school basis. Good diesel mechanics or scheduling men are rare. None of this need be terribly expensive. The present very modest federal transit management training program could be expanded somewhat and certain selected institutions could receive aid to set up programs. Probably the best way to administer an expanded program would be to give grants through the transit firms to selected employees, who could choose which academy they would attend. This would keep each of the participating schools on its toes. At the same time UMTA would have to watchdog the programs to make certain they did not merely embalm past transit practices in ivy-covered halls.

Another area in which UMTA could provide aid and incentives

is through encouragement of better utilization of present hardware. Better use of the technology we already have is, of course, another way of saying more effective management. However, the present UMTA approach of stressing new technology puts too much emphasis on "things" and the future and not enough on delivering good service to the public now. New technology, no matter how worthwhile it proves to be, always bears the risk that accompanies any innovation; worse yet, it often takes considerable time to implement. Things being what they are in mass transit, it would certainly seem best to make improvements in the quality and quantity of service as soon as possible. If patronage continues to fall, all the customers may be long gone by the time sensible but radical technological changes are finally made.

Utilizing present technology better is no big deal.[8] For example, by improved routing and scheduling, or the use of subscription-bus or demand-activated service (dial-a-bus), conventional buses can be used to provide better, more consumer-oriented transit service. As has been noted, present policy precludes grants to replicate ideas already tested in demonstrations previously. Such a policy almost guarantees that ideas will not be adopted once tested. "Initiative" grants could be provided—say a federal operating subsidy of 30 per cent of net operating costs of new, innovative services for a period of three years—to encourage transit operators to get the ball rolling as soon as possible. Whatever the proportion of federal aid, it would have the purpose of fostering here-and-now service improvements over and above covering a portion of capital expenses. Without some incentive the transit industry may be led to the water of innovation but no reason is provided to imbibe. Relatively high payoff would probably also be gained by UMTA-sponsored research aimed at improvement in vehicle maintenance and other efforts to increase the reliability of operation and the efficiency of transit service. UMTA could, in addition, sponsor research at modest cost to provide helpful, easily adapted methodology for quick uptake.

Other UMTA-sponsored research with fairly quick return could be directed toward means of cutting the cost of facility construction or vehicle fabrication. Reducing the cost and increasing the reliability of air conditioning and heating and ventilating devices would also provide major savings in maintenance cost.[9] At the moment construction and equipment costs are skyrocketing, but apparently little has been done by UMTA to foster economy. Such steps are needed, particularly in the short run, to encourage expansion of quality mass transit services. That UMTA is not merely interested in providing capital or pushing for radical new technological change was pointed up at the 1973 appropriations hearings in a statement by the UMTA official supervising the capital grant program:

> I think that Federal capital grants alone are not going to reverse the ridership trend. They are going to permit us to retain service and to extend service to new growth areas. But I think that all of us are convinced that factors other than merely new equipment will be more influential in increasing, or on the opposite side of the coin, losing ridership. These factors include convenience of service; they include speed of operation, reliability—the things which the passenger is looking for when he seeks to use transit.[10]

Nevertheless, performance leaves much to be desired, and the appropriation subcommittee directed some very pointed questions to UMTA administrators, bespeaking a real interest for nonhardware-oriented managerial action.[11]

Nor would it hurt, in seeking avenues for quick improvement, to browse through the (probably dusty) pages of *Potential Near Term Improvements in Urban Transportation*, prepared by Day and Zimmerman under a HUD contract in March 1968 as part of the studies in new systems in urban transportation.[12]

Information and Communication

A great deal could be done by UMTA on the information front; the same, of course, holds true for DOT in general. This fact has been recognized by the Department of Transportation in a report to the Committee on Appropriations of the U.S. House of Representatives.[13] On some important informational problems in the area of urban transportation the report stated:

> *Urban Transportation Demand:* Transportation problems of crisis proportions exist in many cities. Although valuable pioneering work has been accomplished over the past 15 years in the fields of urban transportation and demand (including "simulation" of flows in transportation networks, and quantification of land use-travel interrelationships), substantial additional work remains to be done to provide a sound basis for effective urban transportation analysis, planning and policy-making at local, state, and national levels.

For the necessary studies compatible data are required from a cross-section of metropolitan areas on a time-series basis for: (i) origins and destinations of trips and shipments by all modes of transportation with door-to-door times and costs, and descriptions of the land uses at origins and destinations; (ii) land use locations, distributions and densities; and (iii) the networks of transportation facilities on a basis that will facilitate multimodal and intermodal "simulations" of network flows.[14]

Despite the obvious importance of having such basic information available, Congress did not provide DOT with the needed funds for fiscal 1970. Nevertheless, the Department of Transportation has been attempting to construct a small-scale information base with limited funds beginning in fiscal 1971. DOT hopes to build on this base in the future.[15]

The fact remains that even though DOT has been in business since 1967, reliable or useful information is hard to find, even for highway impact.[16] Especially important would be information of value to transit managers and administrators. The proposed DOT information system does not seem to be oriented in that direction. In addition, systematic management information should be collected. Included in the bundle of data would be demographic information and facts on the distribution of urban population kept up on a more timely basis than is currently available in the decennial census. Management information on operations and performance, including cost and patronage data and material relevant to marketing efforts, should also be gathered. The collection and dissemination of some of this information on the local level by mass transportation agencies might be required as a part of an UMTA grant. The process could be considerably eased within the mass transportation industry by a uniform system of accounts and reporting of information. Some of what was gathered would, of course, be useful to UMTA itself for the management of projects under its jurisdiction.

The dissemination of the information is as important as the gathering. Understandable, useful information has to be provided on a regular basis. It might be published or made available through computer interconnections or other electronic links. Of value to management and administrative personnel would not only be cost and performance comparisons, but publications—perhaps government-sponsored or published with UMTA cooperation—that would give thoughtful writeups on new ideas or practices that might be beneficially shared with others. Reports on given research and demonstration projects could be written up in a transit management journal in a fashion that would make sense and be of use to operators facing somewhat different circumstances and scales of operations. Translations of relevant material appearing in foreign language journals would also be of value. The main objective would be to get useful information to transit managers.

UMTA's record on promoting better information is spotty; however, there are some indications that the situation may be improving. Promised soon is an information dissemination system based on a keyword index and a retrieval system.[17] Perhaps the most lamentable shortcoming is the footdragging concerning the development of Transman.

> Transman is an acronym for transportation management information system. This is a system for collecting, processing, and providing to the various levels of management that maintain and operate mass transit systems the information necessary to actions and decisions. Such data as miles operated, fuel and oil consumed, cost of labor and parts required for maintenance, and parts inventory levels are involved. The objective is to apply to transit modern and in many cases automated management information methods so as to reduce costs, increase service levels and reliability, and enable more effective reaction to changes in vehicle performance, fleet performance, or total system performance.[18]

The development project was initiated at Kent State University as Ohio-MTD-1, but an imbroglio apparently developed between UMTA and the project director. As a result, Transman was pulled back into the hands of UMTA—where little has been heard from it since.[19]

One of the sad facts of transit, noted earlier, is that there is no place in the United States where a public official, transit manager, or member of the public can go to observe the operation of a complete and truly modern transit system. A showcase is needed for mass transportation ideas and practices, as a kind of continuing demonstration. Many good ideas have been tested over the years as a result of the demonstration projects. Real-life use is an excellent means not only of testing but also revealing ideas. Indeed, the notion behind the highly touted Transpo '72 Exposition was that an exhibition of hardware can help to stimulate interest and generate still more ideas. What is badly needed is a regular showcase of mass transit operated in one or more locations around the United States to show the relevant ideas and hardware for different scales of operation. The appetites of city fathers, transportation administrators, and transit managers could be whetted by a model transit city, which could also function as a laboratory, much like the DOT rail test site near Pueblo, Colo. In a model transit city, however, the hardware could be tested under actual operating conditions. To create such sites, UMTA could subsidize the capital and operating costs involved. To keep costs relatively low, the most valid sites for such demonstrations might be small and medium-sized cities, where the level of knowledge and degree of inspiration also seem to be most lacking. An essential ingredient of such a setup would be the implementation of an organization structure and the services of a management team following modern business procedures.

National information campaigns are also needed to stimulate more public support for and greater use of transit service. Again, there is nothing particularly new about promotional efforts for activation in the public sector; witness the various safety campaigns, anticigarette commercials, and ads to encourage the armed services as a career.

The campaign should consist of two parts. The first should be aimed basically at providing information on the benefits that accrue to the public from the presence of a well-managed, useful, consumer-oriented mass transportation service. The value of this program would be to make it much easier for local transit managers and administrators to get public support, through referenda or other means, for transit improvements. At the present time, each city has to mount its own campaign with limited resources and without the advantages of the most talented media people available. A continuing national campaign could break the ice and make major, universal points. Local efforts could then stress particular local issues, and the city-level campaign would have the advantage of the momentum generated nationally.

The other aspect of the national media campaign would be aimed at improving the image of mass transportation. Clearly, the very names Rolls-Royce and Volkswagen both summon up images in the mind of the public; after Ralph Nader, so did Corvair. Again, an image-building campaign on the national level would make the job of local transit marketing people much easier. It would help to provide a base upon which to build a local marketing effort. In any case, the objective would be to show that using mass transit is not a threat to the nation's manhood or something used only by the lame, the halt, and girls who can't get dates. A major goal of this effort would be to help make transit appear as a reasonable travel alternative in the public mind.

That all of the above suggestions, regardless of their simplicity, would be carried out assumes that UMTA would want to do these things, all of which bear the burden of being, individually at least, not very spectacular. On the other hand, if the Congress really wanted obvious results for its money, it might insist that such actions be taken, thus forcing UMTA to proceed with a program that lacks the aura of exotic hardware or the distance from the problem that appears to be so common to many federal programs.

Of course the steps mentioned above could be taken in such a manner that the whole process would be awash with red tape. That would be self-defeating. Early in the game, UMTA in its various guises and locations was refreshingly free of this encumbrance; there is evidence that the dead hand of increasing bureaucracy may be affecting UMTA's performance now. Surely, improving mobility in urban areas is the major thrust that must lie behind the federal mass transit program. To thwart this aim would be a pity, because over the long haul UMTA's value—and the worth of federal mass transportation policy—will not be gauged by having forms filled out correctly, but by the enhancement of mobility.

The short-run approaches suggested here will not produce the milennium, but they should help garner a few more satisfied patrons to the bosom of mass transportation by putting more of the action and resources down on the level where the job will be done—with the operating companies and their managers. Also, the suggested approach would help provide the resources so that local areas could be better armed to fight their own battles.

All this means that stronger local efforts are needed to capitalize on the potential benefits that could flow from adopting the simple programs oulined above. Already UMTA's planning requirements and those necessary to obtain federal highway money are long steps in the right direction. More pressure could be applied by placing more incentive on regional transit undertakings. "Regionalize or no federal help" may sound drastic, but local government pushed into a tight corner might feel the urge to do the job properly. Intermodal planning groups, fostered by DOT beginning in 1970, and the institutionalization of the Unified Work Programs—combining airport, highway, and transit planning—in March 1973 may be a step in the direction of regionalism; according to a proposed DOT rubric, all planning and, eventually, implementation money will be funnelled through a single local or regional agency. Much local and state action will depend upon the efforts made by transit interest groups working at the grass-roots level and just slightly above. A better flow of relevant information can help gird these forces for battle.

Since its beginnings in 1961, the federal role in urban mass transportation has come a long way. Obviously, those first paces along the thousand-mile journey have been taken, but there is still a very long way to go.

A Practical View of the Future

What is a reasonable assessment of the future of mass transportation in the United States? All things considered, great changes will probably not come about. Not that more money won't be forthcoming for transit improvement, nor that major improvements such as service quality and, perhaps over time, some increases in patronage will not occur. Rather, the track record of success of federal urban aid programs, with the fuzzy goals typical of such ventures, makes an objective judgment difficult. All in all, it is hard to think of a major success.

Probably UMTA will go on to do what most federal agencies do—respond to pressure groups, especially those within its particular constituency. Whether the constituents will press not only UMTA but the Congress and the resident administration to take vigorous and useful steps is strictly a matter of conjecture. The U.S. Conference of Mayors/National League of Cities is probably the best oriented and best situated of the lobby groups to pull it off. However, the notion of directing effort toward enhancing mobility may seem a bit esoteric. A patchwork of short-run victories may be the best that can be expected.

For its part, Congress will probably be unable or unwilling to do much. This reflects the increasing weakness of the legislative arm of the government relative to the executive branch. This fact of life does not seem likely to change in a big hurry.[20] Even if it did, Congress is probably less likely than the administration to instigate substantial change in the absence of strong pressure from a broad constituency.

In short, for the time being, the only way a city will get decent mass transportation is to accomplish the feat pretty much on its own. The city must really want to make its mass transportation operation first class in every way. The will to do the job and the necessary commitment to the task are the crucial factors.

Next, a city must organize itself for transit. Ideally it would set clear goals for what it hopes to achieve through mass transportation improvements, and then draw up a good plan for the achievement of those goals. This would include the development of strategies to gain the necessary local powers needed for jurisdiction and finance of transit improvements. Even if the federal government provides more monetary aid in the future, it will probably always have the requirement of local matching funds. A regular infusion of local supporting funds will also have to be guaranteed if the deficits from operations are to be covered. Another important factor is local action to insure that the management retained to run the transit operation is properly organized and skillful in the tricky business of marketing the service. In the best of all possible worlds this would mean that the transit agency would not be allowed to deteriorate into a political football. Managerial talent rather than political influence would be the critical factor for line management. Of course, politics is important, and one transit official, probably the chairman of the board of a public transit agency, would have the job of keeping the political fences in repair, freeing the line managers to manage.

An interested city would probably be well advised to build a strong rapport and community of interest with other cities in the same state wishing to make transit improvements. Together a coalition could be developed to press the state legislature and the state administration for needed legal powers, or even financial aid from the state coffers if that is possible.

Finally, the city will have to do a good job of politicking at UMTA in order to get the necessary federal aid with a minimum of ruffles and flourishes. If the city is big enough to afford it and serious enough to try hard, it will probably have at least one man charged with the full-time responsibility of acting as a liaison with UMTA.

For its part, UMTA will probably serve as a valve to control emissions of money. On the basis of past performance it is hard to see it playing a highly vigorous or constructive role of leadership, unless it is fortunate enough to have men of talent and dedication at the top. The UMTA reorganization of 1973 may provide such leadership. In addition, the agency would have to recruit and retain skilled and dedicated staff. Unhappily, like many federal agencies, it may simply occupy much time in setting standards that are attempts at compromise of the uncompromisable, and in shuffling paper and causing its constituents to shuffle paper as well. That means that what is gotten out of UMTA will be whatever can be pried out by effective liaison and political work on the local level. It need not be that way, of course, because the task assigned to UMTA is one of the most interesting and exciting challenges now facing any federal agency. UMTA should be able to attract a fine staff, and given strong support by the Congress and the administration it could play an important role in the future of life in U.S. cities.

CHAPTER EIGHT

Conclusion

It is not difficult to find fault with U.S. cities. The daily newspapers and broadcast media regale the public with items on the decay of the cities. A journey through most urban areas is hardly cheering; evidence of decay, blight, fear, violence, bad taste, and waste, lies on every side, making the few oases of life and vigor seem almost out of place in comparison. It is very easy to view this segment of the national situation with dismay, if not despair. Perhaps even more dismaying is the fact that considerable attention has been focused on urban problems for well over a decade through a variety of federal programs. In sad fact the various efforts and the billions of dollars sunk into them have apparently not worked very well. Perhaps the worst thing is the disappointment resulting from the lack of fulfillment of high expectations. Mass transportation, as covered in this book, is merely one case in point.

Despite the gloom, the situation is not hopeless. The important thing is to take the proper action in pursuit of a worthwhile, clearly articulated objective. The time may be ripe for taking steps down new paths, for fresh thinking and new approaches, simply because so much effort has failed. In truth, although it is not an original thought, Americans have just about run out of places to go to escape from urban problems. The bright promise of the move to the suburbs, which has been the dominant fact of life in the United

States since the end of the Second World War, has dimmed considerably. The lack of felicity that was responsible for the urban exodus is catching up with the suburbs and the rural fringe. The time to do battle is at hand, and sheer necessity may force government to react in an organized, well-directed fashion that may prove to be more beneficial than the piecemeal actions of the past.

In most cities, regardless of their size, transit improvement that is likely to attract patronage is a matter of getting down to business and deciding, at long last, to put the house in order, grasp the nettle, and move ahead. Reflecting on what has happened over the past decade, it seems clear that for transit improvement to work, an effort must be initiated locally, where the problems are most obvious and the route to improvement most visible. This does not mean that there is no role for the state or federal levels of government, but vision grows clouded the further one stands from a problem. On the local level this means nothing less than community leaders making up their minds that mass transit deserves better than the usual second- or third-class treatment. Such decisions led to the development of the BART system and the progress being made in Atlanta, to cite just two examples. Community leaders and public officials of real vision may take action on their own, particularly if they are far-sighted and work seriously to lead and better their community. Happily, more public officials are willing to provide leadership on this issue today than just a few years ago. Less often now do citizens have to bring strong pressure before public officials will act. Still, even far-sighted leaders can't move far or fast if the general public sits on its hands. For decisive and vigorous action, the public and its leadership must move together with a common will for better mass transit. Among other things, this means a massive information and community relations program. There are enough success stories —Atlanta, San Francisco, Washington, D.C.—so that no one can say the situation is really hopeless, even though the job may be difficult.[1]

For all cities, but particularly the large ones, it means sufficient will, generated by the public and its leaders, to design an approach to the delivery of mass transportation that will provide maximum choice and opportunity to the public. No one should be expected to use transit simply because it may be in the public interest to do so. In a democracy it is clearly far better to attract than to coerce the public into using a service because it is worthy of their use. Management sensitive to public needs and desires is a vital ingredient. Cooperation in use of the streets—such as reserved bus lanes—is a minimum effort that can be made early in the game by public officials. Providing needed funds—from local sources if other funds aren't available—for improvement and operation on a first-rate basis is essential in order to make service continually attractive. This may not be easy, but it must be done.

Because of the long lead-time involved in making new systems operational as well as economical, large cities and small ones must learn how to use familiar transit modes and technology more effectively in the present and near future than has been true in the past. Those who expect the transit millenium to arrive on the wings of a shiny new technology will be collecting Social Security long before such means of transport are economically, technically, and politically feasible. Improvement is needed now and cities must act now to make sure that transit assets are managed with the maximum degree of effectiveness by demanding high performance of transit managers and providing them with the needed resources to do the job.

For all cities, but particularly for the smaller ones, it means that they must form a strong coalition with other urban areas within their state in order to build support for legislative action at the state level. In other words, the cities must help each other to get the state government to help them so they can get the rules, regulations, jurisdiction, and finances necessary to help themselves as much as possible locally as well as to qualify for, obtain, and match federal grants. A state department of transportation, perhaps supplying funds for both capital and operating needs, may be the ideal to work toward. The course of greatest wisdom appears to be with city and state action that will provide the powers and money to give quality service without the need to depend heavily on federal action and support. In transit, Washington can help most in supplying money and information; the federal government cannot deliver the service needed locally and should not be expected to do so, but federal funds can act as a most helpful windfall.

What good will it do to improve mass transportation? Improved mass transportation won't solve the problem of poverty, but it may help. Better circulation and improved mobility for all citizens of urban areas is possible with widespread, high-quality mass transportation available so that all citizens may have better access to job opportunities. This will be an advantage for employers as well as employees, since the job market will be considerably broader; workers and employers will have wider opportunities to get what they both want and need. In addition, large-scale construction of facilities should create useful jobs in the building trades, especially those requiring low to medium skills. Much unemployment or underemployment may be reduced or eliminated in the very process of supplying transit improvements. Furthermore, increased mobility will open up access to health, educational, recreational, and other services to citizens without the necessity of car ownership.

Improved mass transit won't solve the problem of crime, but it may help get at its roots by providing wider job and recreation opportunities and by so doing raise the economic level of the poor above the point of desperation that apparently leads to crime in many places. By improving access and opportunity, transit will have played a part in tackling the complex and difficult problem of U.S. criminality associated with poverty.

Improved mass transportation won't solve the air pollution problem, but it will help. There is no doubt that the automobile in its present form is too useful a means of mobility to be completely phased out. Motive power more salutary to the environment may be devised soon, but the automobile is likely to be with us for a long time. Mass transportation, however, if it is fostered to act as a reasonable alternative, can cut down the number of automobile trips and over time can help cut present air pollution levels. Reduction in the number of vehicles is apt to cut noise levels as well, a factor that could be a major blessing to U.S. cities.[2]

Improved mass transportation won't solve the problems of the elderly, but it will help. With high-quality mass transportation available, older American need not fill the ranks of those outside the pale of normal society for want of mobility. Better access to recreation, social activities, employment, and health care can do much to alleviate the bleakness of life now so common among the old.

Improved mass transportation won't solve the congestion problem, but it will help. As noted earlier, much congestion is a result of institutionalized work hours, but such work patterns are not easy to change. As long as such rigid work hours are maintained, mass transportation may be the most effective means of cutting congestion by making more efficient use of limited urban space. Indeed, if work hours stay as they are now, shifting more support to mass transportation is probably a much more effective use of our urban public resources than continuing to build more roads and parking space.

Improved mass transportation won't make U.S. cities more beautiful, but it will help. The disfigurement of American cities has more complex roots than blemishes such as expressways that are caused by transportation alone. However, mass transportation improvements may cut down on the need for such cataclysmic projects as pushing multiple lane highways through built-up parts of the city. In cities where rapid transit facilities will be constructed there is an opportunity for considerable renewal in the high-accessibility areas around station facilities.

Improved mass transportation won't make us better or happier people, but it may help. It may help to make the urban environment somewhat more pleasant. More integration of the population may help. Idealists are usually guilty of claiming that there is great benefit in mixing a large and varied population together, whether that population likes it or not. Mass transportation is one way of facilitating such togetherness if it is, indeed, desirable. Nevertheless, getting to know one another better, by whatever means, may have its advantages in healing the national hostility and overcoming the spirit of despair that hangs over many urban places.

In short, quality mass transportation, not just new hardware, is likely to act as a great catalyst and a major rallying factor in the push to convert American cities to a level beyond mere livability to a high standard of pleasant, exciting, felicitous, civilized life. Perhaps a great deal can be accomplished by using a large-scale mass transit project as a direction for a city's energy. San Francisco in the construction of the BART system and the beneficial effects in Toronto from rapid transit construction give strong evidence of the exciting possibilities in this direction. Certainly, improved transit and all the other activities that go into rebuilding the cities can combine American energy and idealism and provide a worthy use for our vast resources and power.

In the ideal sense, the modern city should be the monstrance of all that is best in our civilization, rather than grubby, desperate, disaster areas. This has been the case in all great and long-lasting civilizations. Programs to help cities improve mass transportation will not by themselves provide another Eden, demi-paradise, or new Jerusalem. But mass transportation clearly has a role to play in the over-all improvement of the urban life. It is the task—and a challenging one—of public officials and the general public working in harmony to see that role fulfilled.

Appendices

The following listings were derived from information supplied by the United States Department of Transportation and its predecessor agencies. Additional information for these listings was gathered through correspondence with the grant recipients.

The projects are listed by state, with the states arranged in alphabetical order. Within each state listing, the projects are given in project number order. The Urban Mass Transportation Administration changed its project numbering system several years ago. Each project is shown with the number assigned at the time the initial proposal was received. Projects that cover a multi-state jurisdiction are listed under Interstate; the prefix is INT under the old numbering system and IT under the new one.

Federal Mass Transportation
Capital Grant Projects

The initial project numbering system for capital grants used a three- or four-letter state identification, the letters UTG to indicate that it was a capital grant, and then a number for the particular project. For example, CAL-UTG-1 would be the first capital grant for the state of California. Under the new numbering system, a two-letter code is used for the state, a two-digit code for the type of project, and a four-digit code for the project number. Under this system, the first California capital grant project would be listed as CA-03-0001. A gap in a project number indicates the project is not funded.

CAPITAL GRANTS

PROJECT	YEAR	LOCATION	DESCRIPTION	TOTAL COST	FEDERAL
AL-03-0002	1973	BIRMINGHAM	ACQUIRE SYSTEM, 10 BUSES	2,250,000	1,500,000
ARK--UTG--1	1965	LITTLE ROCK	42 BUSES	574,744	287,372
ARK--UTG--3	1972	LITTLE ROCK	ACQUIRE SYSTEM, 44 BUSES	3,652,941	2,435,294
AZ-03-0001-1	1973	TUSCON	9 BUSES		235,116
CAL--UTG--1	1965	VALLEJO	7 BUSES	115,500	77,000
CAL--UTG--2	1965	OAKLAND	300 TWO-WAY RADIOS	269,000	134,500
CAL--UTG--3	1966	ALAMEDA COUNTY	30 BUSES	820,000	410,000
CAL--UTG--4	1966	SAN FRANCISCO	NEW FACILITIES AND TUNNELS	39,683,261	23,500,000
CAL--UTG--5	1966	SAN BERNARDINO	15 BUSES	421,767	281,178
CAL--UTG--6	1966	SAN FRANCISCO	BUILD 12 MILES RAIL LINE	34,098,000	13,100,000
CAL--UTG--7	1965	POMONA	12 BUSES, GARAGE, OFFICE	277,700	185,133
CAL--UTG--8	1966	OXNARD	9 BUSES, GARAGE, OFFICE	318,195	212,130
CAL--UTG--9	1966	BERKELEY	BUILD SUBWAY	20,811,060	4,733,000
CAL--UTG--10	1966	STOCKTON	20 BUSES, EQUIPMENT	580,980	387,320
CAL--UTG--11	1966	SAN FRANCISCO	BUILD TUNNEL,ROADBED	45,204,850	13,200,000
CAL--UTG--11	1967	SAN DIEGO	ACQUIRE SYSTEM, 100 BUSES	7,902,000	3,951,000
CAL--UTG--13	1967	MODESTO	4 BUSES	82,100	41,050
CAL--UTG--14	1968	SANTA BARBARA	12 BUSES	620,770	310,385
CAL--UTG--15	1968	SAN FRANCISCO	BUILD SUBWAY	54,995,550	26,000,000
CAL--UTG--16	1968	SAN FRANCISCO	192 TWO-WAY RADIOS	190,705	95,352
CAL--UTG--17	1968	MONTEBELLO	10 BUSES	1,100,018	550,000
CAL--UTG--19	1968	SACRAMENTO	15 BUSES, GARAGE	970,270	435,135
CAL--UTG--19	1968	SAN FRANCISCO	125 TRANSIT CARS	60,210,000	28,000,000
CAL--UTG--20	1968	CULVER CITY	8 BUSES	274,374	137,187
CAL--UTG--21	1968	ALAMEDA COUNTY	30 BUSES,160 TWO-WAY RADIOS	1,178,050	589,075

CAPITAL GRANTS

PROJECT	YEAR	LOCATION	DESCRIPTION	TOTAL COST	FEDERAL
CAL--UTG--22	1969	SAN FRANCISCO	50 BUSES	2,073,750	1,036,875
CAL--UTG--23	1969	FRESNO	19 BUSES, 12 SHELTERS	715,186	357,593
CAL--UTG--24	1969	LOS ANGELES	1500 FAREBOXES	896,750	448,375
CAL--UTG--25	1972	SAN DIEGO	GARAGE, OFFICE	478,550	319,032
CA-03-0036	1972	SAN FRANCISCO	132 BUSES	9,464,000	6,209,332
CA-03-0038	1972	SAN FRANCISCO	54 BUSES	2,657,544	1,771,696
CA-03-0036	1972	SAN FRANCISCO	3 FERRIES, 3 TERMINALS	24,717,405	16,478,270
CAL--UTG--42	1972	OAKLAND	215 BUSES,GARAGE	11,505,042	7,676,028
CAL--UTG--43	1971	SAN FRANCISCO	CAPITAL IMPROVEMENTS	48,168,000	28,778,666
CAL--UTG--44	1972	LONG BEACH	9 BUSES, GARAGE, EQUIPMENT	3,171,263	2,114,175
CAL--UTG--47	1972	SAN FRANCISCO	PEDESTRIAN WALKWAY	16,143,700	1,000,000
CA-03-0049	1972	LOS ANGELES	220 BUSES,EQUIPMENT		10,762,466
CA-03-0050	1972	MODESTO	1 BUS	33,000	22,400
CA-03-0052	1972	SAN FRANCISCO	EQUIPMENT	52,205,000	38,136,666
CA-03-0053	1973	OXNARD	4 BUSES	157,800	105,200
CA-03-0056	1973	SAN FRANCISCO	REBUILD ELECTRIC SYSTEM	26,650,000	19,756,666
CA-03-0057	1972	SANTA MONICA	30 BUSES	1,467,216	978,143
CA-03-0058	1973	SAN FRANCISCO	TRANS-BAY TUBE	2,550,000	1,700,000
CA-03-0059	1972	SAN FRANCISCO	100 TRANSIT CARS	40,798,000	27,198,656
CA-03-059-01	1973	SAN FRANCISCO	100 TRANSIT CARS		34,646,400
CA-03-0061	1973	SANTA CLARA CO	ACQUIRE SYSTEM,140 BUSES	7,385,301	4,923,534
CA-03-0062	1973	OCEANSIDE	GARAGE		451,200
CA-03-0064	1973	ORANGE COUNTY	162 BUSES	16,351,521	10,901,000
CA-03-0067	1973	SAN BERNARDINO	16 BUSES,EQUIPMENT		699,108
CA-03-0068	1973	SIMI VALLEY	3 BUSES, EQUIPMENT		134,896

CAPITAL GRANTS

PROJECT	YEAR	LOCATION	DESCRIPTION	TOTAL COST	FEDERAL
CA-03-0069	1973	SAN FRANCISCO	BART	32,522,000	21,661,333
CA-03-0071	1973	SAN DIEGO	58 BUSES	3,047,130	2,031,420
COLO-UTG--1	1965	PUEBLO	ACQUIRE SYSTEM,5 BUSES,GARAGE	269,051	179,366
COLO-UTG--4	1971	DENVER	ACQUIRE SYSTEM,37 BUSES	8,527,698	4,263,850
CC-03-0006	1973	DENVER	32 BUSES	1,716,000	1,144,446
CT-C3-0004	1972	NEW HAVEN	RAIL LINE	27,100,000	11,400,000
DEL--UTG--1	1970	WILMINGTON	55 BUSES	2,562,000	1,281,000
FLA--UTG--1	1965	CORAL GABLES	20 BUSES	647,325	431,550
FLA--UTG--2	1965	ST PETERSBURG	5 BUSES	145,000	72,500
FLA--UTG--3	1966	ST PETERSBURG	5 BUSES,EQUIPMENT	182,569	91,284
FLA--UTG--4	1968	ST PETERSBURG	5 BUSES	148,000	74,200
FLA--UTG--5	1969	ST PETERSBURG	5 BUSES,EQUIPMENT	156,000	77,500
FL-03-0010	1973	ST PETERSBURG	10 BUSES,EQUIPMENT	468,815	313,210
FLA--UTC--14	1972	FT LAUDERDALE	ACQUIRE SYSTEM,81 BUSES	3,831,000	2,554,533
FLA-C3-0015	1972	CLEARWATER	ACQUIRE SYSTEM,17 BUSES	795,150	523,433
FLA--UTG--16	1972	JACKSONVILLE	ACQUIRE SYSTEM,45 BUSES	5,319,250	3,539,566
FLA--UTG--17	1972	MIAMI	74 BUSES	2,730,000	2,184,000
FL-03-0018	1973	MIAMI	10 BUSES	425,050	283,366
GA--UTG--1	1967	ROME	10 BUSES	154,200	77,100
GA--UTG--2	1968	COLUMBUS	20 BUSES,GARAGE	1,000,120	495,660
GA-C3-0006	1973	SAVANNAH	33 BUSES	1,028,888	685,925
GA-C3-0008	1973	ATLANTA	RAIL BUS RAPID TRANSIT	104,300,000	69,533,333
ILL--UTG--1	1966	CHICAGO	EXTEND ELEVATED	6,632,125	4,526,066
ILL--UTG--2	1967	CHICAGO	BUILD 5.2 MILES RAIL LINE	38,767,900	25,936,333
ILL--UTC--3	1967	CHICAGO	MODERNIZE STATION	333,000	222,000

CAPITAL GRANTS

PROJECT	YEAR	LOCATION	DESCRIPTION	TOTAL COST	FEDERAL
ILL--UTG--4	1967	CHICAGO	BUILD 9.5 MILES RAIL LINE	29,941,000	20,006,666
ILL--UTG--5	1968	CHICAGO	150 TRANSIT CARS	19,500,000	13,000,000
ILL--UTG--6	1968	SPRINGFIELD	20 BUSES	656,250	328,125
ILL--UTG--7	1968	CHICAGO	130 COMMUTER CARS	37,829,050	18,914,525
ILL--UTG--8	1970	CHICAGO	3135 FARE BOXES	2,373,500	1,186,750
IL-03-0020	1973	JOLIET	20 BUSES,EQUIPMENT	303,010	907,900
ILL--UTG--21	1972	AURORA	11 BUSES,GARAGE,OFFICE	3,015,723	606,006
IL-03-0011	1973	CHICAGO	52 BUSES	11,180,640	2,010,486
IL-03-0022	1973	CHICAGO	15 COMMUTER CARS	60,690,750	7,453,760
IL-03-0024	1973	CHICAGO	1000 BUSES,100 TRANSIT CARS		40,460,500
IL-03-0028	1973	CHAMPAIGN	GARAGE,OFFICE	629,600	419,086
IL-03-0029	1973	ROCK ISLAND	ACQUIRE SYSTEM,27 BUSES	1,750,049	1,173,366
IL-03-0030	1973	PEORIA	GARAGE,OFFICE	612,750	421,833
IND--UTG--1	1965	TERRE HAUTE	18 BUSES	271,530	181,020
IND--UTG--2	1969	FT WAYNE	40 BUSES	1,753,700	876,850
IND--UTG--3	1970	EVANSVILLE	24 BUSES	827,163	137,965
IND--UTG--4	1970	SOUTH BEND	30 BUSES,EQUIPMENT	1,433,722	716,861
IN-03-0004	1973	SOUTH BEND	ADDITIONAL FUNDING		238,953
IN-03-0011	1973	LAFAYETTE	ACQUIRE SYSTEM,26 BUSES	1,445,400	963,600
IN-03-0013	1972	TERRE HAUTE	12 BUSES	399,970	259,980
IN-03-0016	1973	WASHINGTON	3 BUSES	553,600	63,928
IA--UTG--1	1966	WATERLOO	30 BUSES	702,898	276,800
IA--UTG--2	1967	CEDAR RAPIDS	ACQUIRE SYSTEM	493,000	351,449
IA--UTG--3	1968	SIOUX CITY	ACQUIRE SYSTEM,2 BUSES		241,500
IA-03-0011	1973	CEDAR RAPIDS	C-TYPE FUEL INJECTORS		3,692

CAPITAL GRANTS

PROJECT	YEAR	LOCATION	DESCRIPTION	TOTAL COST	FEDERAL
IA-03-0012	1973	DES MOINES	ACQUIRE SYSTEM		2,271,480
KANS--UTG--1	1966	TOPEKA	GARAGE	401,400	200,700
KANS--UTG--2	1967	WICHITA	32 BUSES,GARAGE	1,402,000	701,000
KANS--UTG--3	1971	WICHITA	14 BUSES,EQUIPMENT	553,909	369,272
KY-03-0002	1973	LEXINGTON	ACQUIRE SYSTEM,42 BUSES,GARAGE	2,538,125	1,692,083
LA--UTG--1	1965	KENNER	2 BUSES,GARAGE	73,590	49,060
LA--UTG--2	1966	LAFAYETTE	15 BUSES,TERMINAL	575,024	383,848
LA-03-0008-1	1973	ALEXANDRIA	GARAGE		82,976
LA--UTG--10	1972	SHREVEPORT	ACQUIRE SYSTEM,32 BUSES		1,753,706
LA-03-0011	1973	NEW ORLEANS	108 BUSES	5,083,987	3,339,322
ME-03-0001	1973	PORTLAND	ACQUIRE SYSTEM,15 BUSES	874,095	582,730
MD--UTG--1	1970	BALTIMORE	ACQUIRE SYSTEM,370 BUSES	19,700,000	14,854,450
MD-03-0004	1972	BALTIMORE	BUILD 8.5 MILES RAIL LINE	33,750,000	22,500,000
MD-03-0025	1973	BALTIMORE	ACQUIRE SYSTEM,10 BUSES	7,434,000	4,956,000
MASS--UTG--1	1965	BOSTON	REPAIR 4 SUBWAY STATIONS	9,115,920	6,077,280
MASS--UTG--2	1965	BOSTON	150 BUSES	4,800,000	3,200,000
MASS--UTG--3	1966	BOSTON	1 MILE RAIL TUNNEL	18,000,000	12,000,000
MA-03-0003-1	1966	BOSTON	AMENDMENT		13,956,153
MASS--UTG--4	1968	BOSTON	76 TRANSIT CARS,RAIL LINE	51,921,000	35,164,133
MASS--UTG--5	1969	BOSTON	44 TRANSIT CARS,RAIL LINE	75,293,000	50,862,000
MA-03-0005-1	1973	BOSTON	READING RIGHT OF WAY	19,689,615	13,126,410
MA-03-0029	1973	BOSTON	ORANGE LINE		4,456,872
MASS--UTG--1	1972	BOSTON	GREEN LINE	33,000,000	25,413,333
MA-03-0022	1972	BOSTON	150 STREETCARS	49,200,000	32,800,000
MA-03-0019	1973	BOSTON	PENN CENTRAL RIGHT OF WAY		19,500,000

CAPITAL GRANTS

PROJECT	YEAR	LOCATION	DESCRIPTION	TOTAL COST	FEDERAL
MA-03-0024	1973	BOSTON	80 TRANSIT CARS	27,615,900	18,410,600
MA-03-0025	1973	BOSTON	SUBWAY IMPROVEMENTS	15,902,460	10,601,640
MA-03-0026	1973	BOSTON	SUBWAY IMPROVEMENTS	11,899,638	7,933,092
MA-03-0028	1973	BOSTON	50 STREETCARS	2,672,250	1,781,500
MICH--UTG--1	1965	SAGINAW	14 BUSES	209,308	139,539
MICH--UTG--2	1965	DETROIT	471 SHELTERS	526,000	263,000
MICH--UTG--3	1966	LANSING	19 BUSES	567,900	283,950
MICH--UTG--4	1966	DETROIT	100 BUSES,GARAGE	15,048,400	7,656,900
MICH--UTG--5	1967	KALAMAZOO	34 BUSES	1,484,922	742,401
MICH--UTG--6	1967	DETROIT	51 BUSES,EQUIPMENT	1,640,000	820,000
MICH--UTG--7	1968	FLINT	27 BUSES	711,585	355,792
MICH--UTG--3	1969	BATTLE CREEK	17 BUSES	207,750	103,875
MT-03-0021	1973	DETROIT	CAPITAL STOCK	1,500,000	1,000,000
MN-03-0008	1973	MINNEAPOLIS	60 BUSES		2,166,096
MINN--UTG--1	1965	MINNEAPOLIS	BUILD MALL	769,000	513,266
MINN--UTG--2	1970	MINNEAPOLIS	19 BUSES	277,755	256,483
MINN--UTG--3	1970	MINNEAPOLIS	ACQUIRE SYSTEM,93 BUSES	14,585,700	9,723,800
MINN--UTG--5	1972	MINNEAPOLIS	408 BUSES	27,000,000	18,000,000
MS-03-0004	1973	JACKSON	12 BUSES	437,292	291,528
MO--UTG--1	1966	COLUMBIA	10 BUSES,GARAGE	307,215	153,607
MONT--UTG--1	1972	BILLINGS	ACQUIRE SYSTEM,5 BUSES	172,800	115,200
MT-03-0002	1973	BILLINGS	5 BUSES,GARAGE		228,112
NEB--UTG--1	1971	LINCOLN	ACQUIRE SYSTEM,40 BUSES	1,900,000	1,286,666
NJ--UTG--1	1965	NEW JERSEY	ALDENE PLAN	7,234,648	4,826,298
NJ--UTG--2	1966	NEW JERSEY	35 COMPUTER CARS	9,991,874	6,661,259

CAPITAL GRANTS

PROJECT	YEAR	LOCATION	DESCRIPTION	TOTAL COST	FEDERAL
NJ--UTG--5	1969	TRENTON	20 BUSES	2,360,584	1,573,722
NM--UTG--1	1966	ALBUQUERQUE	ACQUIRE SYSTEM,18 BUSES	1,226,590	817,726
NY--UTG--1	1965	NEW YORK CITY	400 TRANSIT CARS	45,840,000	23,420,000
NY--UTG--1	1967	UTICA	ACQUIRE SYSTEM	793,000	396,500
NY--UTG--3	1967	NEW YORK CITY	EXTEND ELECTRIC RAIL 16 MILES	45,394,300	30,292,866
NY--03-0003-1	1973	NEW YORK CITY	AMENDMENT	15,750,000	10,500,000
NY--UTG--4	1967	JAMESTOWN	9 BUSES,GARAGE	314,000	157,000
NY--UTG--5	1968	ROME	8 BUSES	73,520	36,750
NY--UTG--6	1968	BROOME COUNTY	35 BUSES,GARAGE	1,451,782	725,891
NY--UTG--7	1968	NEW YORK CITY	TWO-WAY RADIO SYSTEM	2,046,000	1,023,000
NY--UTG--8	1969	NIAGARA FALLS	15 BUSES	434,744	217,372
NY--UTG--9	1969	ROCHESTER	ACQUIRE SYSTEM,27 BUSES	6,100,000	3,050,000
NY--UTG--10	1969	UTICA	27 BUSES	784,462	392,231
NY--UTG--11	1969	NEW YORK CITY	3 FERRY BOATS	20,130,000	13,382,000
NY--UTG--24	1971	NEW YORK CITY	RAIL LINE IMPROVEMENTS	11,600,000	7,709,887
NY--UTG--37	1971	ROCHESTER	GARAGE	7,923,348	5,500,232
NY--03-0039	1972	POUGHKEEPSIE	6 BUSES,GARAGE,EQUIPMENT	300,000	200,000
NY--UTG--42	1972	SYRACUSE	ACQUIRE SYSTEM,97 BUSES	8,474,000	5,650,000
NY--UTG--44	1972	NEW YORK CITY	BUILD SUBWAY	37,500,000	25,000,000
NY--03-0045	1973	NEW YORK CITY	BUILD SUBWAY	94,100,000	62,733,333
NY--UTG--46	1972	NEW YORK CITY	320 TRANSIT CARS	95,133,760	63,422,502
NY--03-0050	1973	NASSAU COUNTY	ACQUIRE SYSTEMS,50 BUSES	9,318,492	6,212,328
NC--UTG--1	1968	ASHEVILLE	34 BUSES,GARAGE	1,315,600	658,300
NC-03-0002	1972	WINSTON-SALEM	ACQUIRE SYSTEM,35 BUSES,GARAGE	2,412,770	1,608,513
OHIO--UTG--1	1965	ZANESVILLE	8 BUSES,GARAGE	165,690	110,460

CAPITAL GRANTS

PROJECT	YEAR	LOCATION	DESCRIPTION	TOTAL COST	FEDERAL
OH-03-0002	1973	COLUMBUS	ACQUIRE SYSTEM,31 BUSES	18,644,210	5,356,000
OHIO--UTG--2	1966	CLEVELAND	BUILD RAIL LINE TO AIRPORT		12,326,840
OHIO--UTG--3	1966	SPRINGFIELD	12 BUSES	185,220	123,480
OHIO--UTG--4	1968	HAMILTON	15 BUSES	255,428	127,714
OHIO--UTG--5	1968	WARREN	ACQUIRE SYSTEM,24 BUSES	704,264	352,132
OHIO--UTG--6	1968	EUCLID	12 BUSES,GARAGE	1,591,000	795,500
OHIO--UTG--7	1969	CLEVELAND	105 BUSES,10 TRANSIT CARS	13,260,100	6,630,050
OH-03-0021	1973	DAYTON	ACQUIRE SYSTEM	2,977,250	1,984,833
OKLA--UTG--1	1968	OKLAHOMA CITY	61 BUSES	908,960	454,480
OKLA--UTG--3	1971	TULSA	45 BUSES,EQUIPMENT	2,036,133	1,018,075
ORE--UTG--1	1966	SALEM	ACQUIRE SYSTEM	443,070	295,513
OR-03-0006-1	1973	PORTLAND	80 BUSES	4,451,500	2,697,666
PA--UTG--1	1965	PITTSBURGH	180 BUSES,GARAGE	8,863,114	5,908,742
PA--UTG--2	1965	PHILADELPHIA	MODERNIZE SUBWAY STATION	4,385,000	2,923,333
PA--UTG--3	1966	PITTSBURGH	200 BUSES,4 GARAGES	16,935,502	11,290,334
PA--UTG--4	1967	PHILADELPHIA	REPAIR RAIL VIADUCT	1,800,000	900,000
PA--UTG--5	1967	ERIE	50 BUSES	2,328,633	1,164,317
PA--UTG--6	1968	ALTOONA	17 BUSES	454,760	227,380
PA--UTG--8	1969	WILLIAMSPORT	ACQUIRE SYSTEM,4 BUSES	375,330	187,665
PA--UTG--9	1970	PHILADELPHIA	EXTEND ELECTRIC RAIL LINE	1,725,220	862,610
PA--UTG--10	1967	PHILADELPHIA	144 COMMUTER CARS	42,000	21,000
PA--UTG--25	1971	PITTSBURGH	158 BUSES	6,801,873	3,400,936
PA-03-0025-1	1971	PITTSBURGH	AMENDMENT	10,449,150	1,823,638
PA--UTG--32	1972	PHILADELPHIA	300 BUSES,EQUIPMENT	12,400,000	8,262,000
PA-03-0032	1972	PHILADELPHIA	300 BUSES,EQUIPMENT	12,258,500	8,172,333

CAPITAL GRANTS

PROJECT	YEAR	LOCATION	DESCRIPTION	TOTAL COST	FEDERAL
PA-03-0032-3	1973	PHILADELPHIA	140 BUSES,110 STREETCARS	11,831,085	7,887,390
PA-03-0034	1973	ERIE	6 BUSES,EQUIPMENT	248,300	165,533
PA-03-0036	1972	PHILADELPHIA	BUILD 1.3 MILES RAIL LINE	14,530,000	9,686,666
PA-03-0037	1973	PHILADELPHIA	STATIONS,SHELTERS	2,036,480	1,357,653
PA-03-0038	1973	ALLENTOWN	50 BUSES,EQUIPMENT	3,004,090	2,002,726
PA-03-0039	1973	WILKES-BARRE	43 BUSES,EQUIPMENT	2,139,102	1,426,068
RI--UTG--1	1965	PROVIDENCE	102 BUSES	2,457,000	1,638,000
RI--UTG--2	1970	PROVIDENCE	45 BUSES	1,012,133	759,000
TENN--UTG--1	1965	MEMPHIS	75 BUSES	2,120,355	1,413,570
TENN--UTG--2	1966	JACKSON	12 BUSES,GARAGE	345,528	172,764
TENN--UTG--3	1967	MEMPHIS	67 BUSES	2,561,090	1,280,545
TENN--UTG--5	1971	KNOXVILLE	40 BUSES,GARAGE	1,902,516	1,268,344
TN-03-000E	1973	NASHVILLE	ACQUIRE SYSTEM,101 BUSES	6,688,950	4,459,300
TEX--UTG--1	1966	DALLAS	310 BUSES	12,045,000	8,045,000
TEX--UTG--2	1966	ABILENE	6 BUSES,GARAGE	140,605	70,303
TEX--UTG--3	1966	CORPUS CHRISTI	ACQUIRE SYSTEM,19 BUSES	1,056,000	704,000
TEX--UTG--4	1969	SAN ANGELO	9 BUSES	227,884	113,942
TEX--UTG--E	1972	SAN ANTONIO	EQUIPMENT	55,094	36,725
TX-03-0008	1972	FORT WORTH	ACQUIRE SYSTEM,100 BUSES	8,119,122	5,412,748
TEX--UTG--9	1972	WACO	ACQUIRE SYSTEM,12 BUSES	601,000	401,000
TX-03-0010	1972	DALLAS-FT WORTH	AIRPORT TRANSPORTATION	21,700,000	7,635,540
VA--UTG--1	1967	MARTINSVILLE	7 BUSES	111,084	55,542
VA-03-0003	1973	NORFOLK	ACQUIRE SYSTEM,47 BUSES	5,261,717	4,177,811
VA-03-0005	1973	RICHMOND	ACQUIRE SYSTEM,76 BUSES		5,068,280
WASH--UTG--1	1965	TACOMA	34 BUSES	917,000	611,333

CAPITAL GRANTS

PROJECT	YEAR	LOCATION	DESCRIPTION	TOTAL COST	FEDERAL
WASH--UTG--2	1965	SEATTLE	4 FERRIES	22,824,600	15,216,400
WASH--UTG--4	1968	SEATTLE	70 BUSES	4,770,431	3,180,280
WASH--UTG--5	1968	TACOMA	10 BUSES	305,987	203,990
WASH--UTG--9	1972	SPOKANE	CAPITAL IMPROVEMENTS	3,914,100	2,609,400
WA-03-0010	1972	EVERETT	18 BUSES	568,610	379,073
WA-03-0012	1972	TACOMA	32 BUSES	1,475,904	983,936
WA-03-0014	1973	SEATTLE	ACQUIRE SYSTEM,91 BUSES,GARAGE	1,537,900	1,025,266
WI-03-0008	1973	FOND DU LAC	4 BUSES,GARAGE		84,484
WI-03-0009	1973	MADISON	ACQUIRE SYSTEM,22 BUSES	1,204,899	803,266
WI-03-0010	1973	GREEN BAY	ACQUIRE SYSTEM,6 EUSES		975,548
WV-03-0001	1973	HUNTINGTON	ACQUIRE SYSTEM,23 BUSES,GARAGE	1,655,900	1,103,933
INT--UTG--1	1965	NEW YORK CITY	44 COMMUTER CARS	15,020,000	5,100,000
INT--UTG--2	1967	BRISTOL	ACQUIRE SYSTEM	458,672	229,336
INT--UTG--3	1967	NEW YORK CITY	144 COMMUTER CARS	56,300,000	28,400,000
INT--UTG--4	1968	NEW JERSEY	BUILD TERMINAL	34,099,000	23,232,656
INT--UTG--5	1968	ST LOUIS	40 BUSES	1,983,542	991,771
INT--UTG--6	1968	KANSAS CITY	ACQUIRE SYSTEMS,30 BUSES	6,407,000	3,203,500
INT--UTG--7	1969	ST LOUIS	EQUIPMENT	340,000	170,000
IT-03-0010	1973	CAMDEN	45 TRANSIT CARS	34,904,100	23,269,400
IT-03-0019	1973	WASHINGTON D C	ACQUIRE SYSTEM,620 BUSES	105,517,000	70,344,666
IT-03-0020	1973	KANSAS CITY	BUILD TERMINAL	3,850,000	7,829,832
IT-03-0023	1972	NEW YORK CITY	BUS-RAIL IMPROVEMENTS	760,000	2,566,666
PR--UTG--1	1965	SAN JUAN	30 BUSES	407,899	506,666
PR--UTG--2	1966	SAN JUAN	FERRY TERMINAL	753,666	271,932
PR--UTG--3	1966	SAN JUAN	29 BUSES		502,444

CAPITAL GRANTS

PROJECT	YEAR	LOCATION	DESCRIPTION	TOTAL COST	FEDERAL
PR--UTG--4	1968	SAN JUAN	151 BUSES	5,865,040	3,910,020
PR-03-0007	1972	SAN JUAN	3 FERRIES,TERMINAL	2,550,700	1,700,466
PR-03-0010	1972	SAN JUAN	EQUIPMENT	493,229	329,819

Federal Mass Transportation
Demonstration Grant Projects

The initial project numbering system used a three- or four-letter state identification code, the letters MTD to indicate that it was a demonstration grant, and a number for the particular project. For example, CAL-MTD-1 would be the first demonstration grant for the state of California. Under the new numbering system, the first California capital grant project would be listed as CA-06-0001. A gap in the project number indicates the project is not funded, and the project number originally assigned will not be used for another project.

DEMONSTRATION GRANTS

PROJECT	YEAR	LOCATION	DESCRIPTION	TOTAL COST	FEDERAL
ALAS--MTD--1	1964	ANCHORAGE	TWO NEW ROUTES DOWNTOWN	311,884	207,923
ALAS-MTD-2	1972	ANCHORAGE	DIAL A BUS	442,695	295,130
AL-CE-CC42	1973	TUSKEGEE	CITY-COUNTY TRANSIT STUDY	30,000	20,000
CAL--MTD--2	1963	SAN FRANCISCO	HIGH SPEED TEST TRACK	3,329,000	6,219,333
CAL--MTD--3	1965	OAKLAND	AIR CUSHION VEHICLE	1,159,221	772,814
CAL--MTD--4	1965	SAN FRANCISCO	AUTOMATED FARE SYSTEM	1,700,000	1,133,333
CAL--MTD--5	1965	ALAMEDA COUNTY	COORDINATE TRANSIT MODES	299,449	199,632
CAL--MTD--6	1965	SAN FRANCISCO	COORDINATE TRANSIT MODES	508,149	338,765
CAL--MTD--7	1966	SAN FRANCISCO	TEST TRACK	1,200,000	800,000
CAL--MTD--8	1966	LOS ANGELES	HELICOPTER SERVICE	735,175	490,112
CAL--MTD--9	1966	LOS ANGELES	TRANSIT IN POVERTY AREAS	2,700,000	2,700,000
CAL--MTD--10	1968	SACRAMENTO	STUDY CHANGES IN LOCAL SYSTEM	426,900	284,600
CAL--MTD--11	1968	OAKLAND	ELIMINATION OF CRIME	309,133	206,092
CAL--MTD--12	1969	SAN FRANCISCO	STEAM POWERED BUS	610,000	450,000
CAL--MTD--13	1972	SAN FRANCISCO	AMENDMENT		683,041
CAL--MTD--14	1969	SAN FRANCISCO	DEVELOP 10 CARS FOR BART	7,500,000	3,000,000
CAL--MTD--15	1969	ALAMEDA COUNTY	COMPUTER INFORMATION SYSTEM	270,364	180,242
CAL--MTD--16	1969	SAN FRANCISCO	CUT BUS NOISE AND EXHAUST	90,000	60,000
CA-CE-0014	1973	SAN FRANCISCO	KINETIC ENERGY WHEEL	450,000	300,000
CO-06-0002	1972	DENVER	TEST PRT SYSTEM		11,000,000
CONN--MTD--1	1969	HARTFORD	INNER CITY TRANSPORT NEEDS	23,721	25,849
DC--MTD--2	1963	WASHINGTON DC	CENTRAL CITY MINIBUS	240,103	160,069
DC--MTD--3	1968	WASHINGTON DC	TRANSIT FOR THE JOBLESS	25,000	25,000
DC--MTD--4	1969	WASHINGTON DC	ROUTE AND SCHEDULE MODEL	52,477	49,977
DC--MTD--5	1969	WASHINGTON DC	INSTITUTIONS AND TRANSIT	317,700	302,765

DEMONSTRATION GRANTS

PROJECT	YEAR	LOCATION	DESCRIPTION	TOTAL COST	FEDERAL
DC--MTD--5	1969	WASHINGTON DC	TEST OF CENTRAL CITY CONCEPT	285,000	270,000
FL-06-0007	1972	ST. PETERSBURG	MOBILITY FOR THE ELDERLY	50,000	33,333
FL-06-0008	1973	MIAMI	BUS RESERVED LANES		366,408
GA--MTD--1	1969	ATLANTA	CIVIC CENTER SHUTTLE	60,000	30,000
ILL--MTD--1	1964	CHICAGO	HIGH SPEED SHUTTLE TRAIN	523,825	349,217
ILL--MTD--2	1964	SKOKIE	TEST A SUBURBAN BUS SYSTEM	142,816	85,690
ILL--MTD--3	1964	PEORIA	HOME TO JOB BUS SERVICE	230,133	153,422
ILL--MTD--4	1965	DECATUR	SUBSCRIPTION BUS SERVICE	99,336	66,224
ILL--MTD--5	1967	CHICAGO	BUILD A COVERED WALKWAY	595,750	397,186
ILL--MTD--6	1968	CHICAGO	BUS MONITORING SYSTEM	2,000,000	1,549,000
ILL--MTD--8	1969	CHICAGO	BUS SERVICE TO AIRPORT	147,000	132,300
IND--MTD--1	1969	BLOOMINGTON	MANAGEMENT HANDBOOK	111,433	100,566
IND--MTD--2	1969	GARY	LOW INCOME BUS SERVICE	18,337	78,058
KANS--MTD--1	1963	KANSAS STATE	COMPUTER SCHEDULING OF BUSES	24,163	12,224
MD--MTD--1	1966	BALTIMORE	EXPRESS BUS SERVICE		16,116
MD--MTD--2	1968	COLUMBIA	BUS SYSTEM FOR NEW CITY	416,600	277,733
MD--MTD--3	1968	BALTIMORE	BUS ROUTES FOR UNEMPLOYED	170,000	100,000
MD--MTD--4	1969	ANNAPOLIS	RADIO COMMUNICATION		89,731
MASS--MTD--1	1962	BOSTON	FARE AND SERVICE ADJUSTMENTS	5,228,947	3,485,965
MASS--MTD--2	1966	BOSTON	SUBWAY CONSTRUCTION METHODS	240,900	100,600
MASS--MTD--3	1967	M.I.T.	JOB OPPORTUNITIES AND BUS SERV	160,635	151,975
MASS--MTD--4	1957	HARVARD	TRANSIT LEGAL PROBLEMS		22,624
MASS--MTD--5	1968	M.I.T.	COMPUTER AIDED ROUTING SYSTEM	129,750	128,250
MASS--MTD--6	1968	BOSTON	*DIAL A BUS* COMPUTER SYSTEM	855,350	812,200
MASS--MTD--7	1969	BOSTON	TRANSIT IN INDUSTRIAL CENTERS		45,554

DEMONSTRATION GRANTS

PROJECT	YEAR	LOCATION	DESCRIPTION	TOTAL COST	FEDERAL
MICH--MTD--1	1962	DETROIT	INCREASE LOCAL BUS SERVICE	295,454	196,969
MICH--MTD--2	1968	FLINT	PERSONALIZED BUS SERVICE	1,171,189	780,793
MICH--MTD--3	1966	DETROIT	COMMAND CONTROL COMMUNICATIONS	55,556	50,000
MO--MTD--3	1969	KANSAS CITY	MULTI SERVICE TRANSPORTATION	494,359	444,923
MO--MTD--1	1967	ST LOUIS	NEEDS OF LOW INCOME RESIDENTS	1,275,000	1,147,274
MO--MTD--2	1968	G WASHINGTON U	UNEMPLOYMENT AND MOBILITY	127,318	120,952
NFB--MTD--1	1969	OMAHA	TRANSIT FROM SLUMS TO INDUSTRY		105,778
NJ--MTD--1	1967	RUTGERS	LOW ALTITUDE AIR SHUTTLE	131,206	99,206
NY--MTD--5	1963	NEW YORK CITY	CONNECT BUS AND RAIL SERVICE	4,778,000	3,185,000
NY--MTD--6	1964	ROME	TEST SMALL CITY BUS SYSTEM	268,408	178,939
NY--MTD--8	1964	NEW YORK CITY	REPAIR SUBWAY STATION	750,805	500,537
NY--MTD--9	1966	NEW YORK CITY	EFFECTS OF TRANSIT STRIKE	75,740	56,493
NY--MTD--10	1967	BUFFALO	TEST A MODAL SPLIT MODEL	682,105	454,736
NY--MTD--11	1967	HEMPSTEAD	FEEDER BUS LINE	270,562	180,375
NY--MTD--12	1967	NEW YORK CITY	STUDY SUBWAY AIR CONDITIONING	255,000	170,000
NY--MTD-13	1968	NEW YORK CITY	STUDY RAILWAY FACILITY SHARING	63,160	60,002
NY--MTD-14	1968	BUFFALO	HOW TO AID LOW INCOME AREAS	547,074	492,367
NY--MTD-16	1968	NEW YORK CITY	DEMAND ACTIVATED TRANSIT	66,367	59,857
NY--MTD-17	1969	SYRACUSE	DEVELOP COMMUNICATIONS	158,109	146,000
NY--MTD-18	1969	TROY	DESIGN SMALL BUS	290,430	290,430
NY-05-0041	1973	SYRACUSE	DIAL A BUS FOR ELDERLY	500,000	333,333
OHIO--MTD--1	1968	KENT STATE UNIV	MANAGEMENT CONTROL SYSTEM	342,539	304,995
OHIO--MTD--2	1968	CLEVELAND	DOWNTOWN TRANSIT PROBLEMS	309,000	206,000
OHIO--MTD--3	1969	CLEVELAND	TRANSPORT TO SUBURBAN JOBS	390,000	260,000
OHIO--MTD--4	1969	KENT STATE UNIV	SCHEDULING PROBLEM SOLUTIONS		422,295

DEMONSTRATION GRANTS

PROJECT	YEAR	LOCATION	DESCRIPTION	TOTAL COST	FEDERAL
PA--MTD--1	1962	PHILADELPHIA	IMPROVE COMMUTER RAIL SERVICE	4,674,300	3,116,200
PA--MTD--2	1963	PITTSBURGH	TEST SKYBUS SYSTEM	7,400,000	4,472,000
PA--MTD--4	1963	PHILADELPHIA	RAIL COST BENEFIT ANALYSIS	437,500	291,667
PA--MTD--5	1965	PHILADELPHIA	RESTRUCTURE RAIL SERVICE	4,742,000	2,877,000
PA--MTD--6	1965	NEW CASTLE	SMALL BUS FOR SMALL TOWN	548,847	365,898
PA--MTD--7	1967	PITTSBURGH	ADVERTISING AND PROMOTION	300,000	200,000
PA--MTD--8	1967	PHILADELPHIA	CENTRAL CITY SMALL BUS SERVICE	1,023,151	999,029
PA-06-0007	1972	PITTSBURGH	STUDY HIGH CAPACITY BUSES		226,080
PA-06-0028	1972	WILKES-BARRE	DEVELOP MANUAL FOR EMERGENCIES	1,500,000	300,000
RI--MTD--1	1964	RHODE ISLAND	DESIGN A STATE WIDE AUTHORITY	30,753	20,000
RI--MTD--2	1967	PROVIDENCE	EXPRESS BUS SERVICE	54,887	36,591
TENN--MTD--1	1962	MEMPHIS	BUS SERVICE EXPERIMENTS	345,934	230,623
TENN--MTD--2	1963	NASHVILLE	NEW ROUTE EXPERIMENTS	600,000	400,000
TENN--MTD--3	1964	NASHVILLE	SUBURBAN EXPRESS BUS	128,667	85,778
TENN--MTD--4	1966	NASHVILLE	EXPRESS BUS FOR HOSPITALS	723,000	482,000
TEX--MTD--2	1969	DALLAS	NON-POLLUTING BUS	464,684	309,789
TEX--MTD--3	1969	DALLAS	COMPUTERIZED BUS MAINTENANCE	189,582	123,735
TEX--MTD--4	1969	HOUSTON	CIRCULATORY TRANSIT SYSTEM	252,000	168,000
TEX--MTD--5	1970	DALLAS	TRANSIT SYSTEM AT AIRPORT	1,855,315	1,021,315
VA--MTD--1	1965	CHESAPEAKE	EXPRESS BUS SERVICE	361,899	241,266
VA--MTD--2	1968	V.P.I.	DEVELOP A SIMULATION GAME	33,069	29,433
VA--MTD--3	1969	BLACKSBURG	DESIGN BUS SHELTERS	123,634	113,461
WASH--MTD--1	1962	SEATTLE	STUDY MONORAIL OPERATION	15,000	10,000
WASH--MTD--2	1967	SEATTLE	EXPRESS BUS ON FREEWAY	1,546,445	1,030,963
WASH--MTD--3	1965	SEATTLE	TRANSIT FOR YOUNG PEOPLE	27,370	11,770

DEMONSTRATION GRANTS

PROJECT	YEAR	LOCATION	DESCRIPTION	TOTAL COST	FEDERAL
WVA--MTD--1	1965	MORGANTOWN	COMPUTERIZED RUN CUTTING	25,377	16,727
WVA--MTD--2	1967	MORGANTOWN	DEVELOP TRANSIT SURVEYS	109,600	73,000
INT--MTD--1	1962	NEW YORK CITY	NEW STATION AND PARKING LOT	242,825	161,883
INT--MTD--2	1963	NEW YORK CITY	AUTOMATIC FARE COLLECTION	266,518	177,678
INT--MTD--5	1963	NEW YORK CITY	HARLEM DIVISION RAIL SERVICE	1,915,339	1,210,225
INT--MTD--7	1963	NEW YORK CITY	IMPROVED FEEDER BUS SERVICE	148,740	99,160
INT--MTD--8	1964	ST LOUIS	EXPRESS BUS SERVICE	536,631	357,754
INT--MTD--9	1964	ST LOUIS	MONTHLY PASS STUDY	14,432	9,621
INT--MTD--10	1964	WASHINGTON DC	USE OF SCRIP TO CUT CRIME	262,634	175,089
INT--MTD--11	1965	NEW YORK CITY	INFORMATION AIDS FOR RIDERS	4,500,000	3,000,000
INT--MTD--12	1966	NEW YORK CITY	CONTINUE COMMUTER SERVICE	2,477,635	1,651,750
INT--MTD--13	1967	NEW YORK CITY	TEST GAS TURBINE PROPULSION	2,222,222	2,000,000
INT--MTD--14	1967	WASHINGTON DC	PROVIDE JOB ACCESSIBILITY	106,500	71,000
INT--MTD--15	1968	WASHINGTON DC	ROLE OF COMPUTER IN TRANSIT	86,700	86,700
INT--MTD--16	1968	WASHINGTON DC	EMPLOYMENT INFORMATION CENTER	25,000	25,000
INT--MTD--17	1968	WASHINGTON DC	DEVELOP EXPRESS SERVICE	745,338	670,804
INT--MTD--18	1969	WASHINGTON DC	TRANSPORT FOR YOUTH PROJECTS	1,000,000	750,000
INT--MTD--20	1969	WASHINGTON DC	BUS POLLUTION CONTROL	172,936	164,936

Appendix 3

Federal Mass Transportation
Technical Study Grant Projects

The initial project numbering system used a three- or four-letter state identification code, the term T9 to indicate that it was a technical study grant, and a number for the particular project. For example, CAL-T9-1 would be the first technical study grant for the state of California. Under the new numbering system, the first California technical study grant project would be listed as CA-09-0001. If the project is not funded the project number originally assigned will not be used for another project.

Since all technical studies are for transit planning purposes, there is no column in the listing to describe each project.

TECHNICAL GRANTS

PROJECT	YEAR	LOCATION	TOTAL COST	FEDERAL
ALA--T9--1	1969	MOBILE	40,000	26,666
AL-09-0003	1972	TUSCALOOSA	50,000	33,333
ARIZ--T9--1	1968	PHOENIX	71,832	54,832
CAL--T9--1	1967	LOS ANGELES	3,380,000	2,253,333
CAL--T9--2	1968	LOS ANGELES	369,500	246,333
CAL--T9--3	1968	FRESNO	60,000	40,000
CAL--T9--4	1968	SAN BERNARDINO	25,000	16,666
CAL--T9--5	1968	OAKLAND	52,763	35,174
CAL--T9--6	1968	SAN JOSE	233,000	155,334
CAL--T9--7	1968	SANTA CLARA CO	234,100	156,066
CAL--T9--8	1969	SAN DIEGO	46,600	31,066
CAL--T9--19	1971	SACRAMENTO	50,000	33,000
CAL--T9--20	1971	SAN FRANCISCO	3,000,000	2,000,000
CA-09-0022	1972	LOS ANGELES	1,537,500	1,025,000
CA-09-0023	1972	SAN DIEGO	501,000	334,000
CA-09-0025	1972	BERKELEY	1,800,000	1,200,000
COLO--T9--1	1968	PUEBLO	20,760	13,840
COLO--T9--2	1968	DENVER	100,000	66,667
COLO--T9--3	1969	DENVER	185,000	135,000
COLO--T9--7	1971	DENVER	573,500	382,300
COLO--T9--7	1972	DENVER		424,850
FLA--T9--1	1967	MIAMI-DADE CTY	399,270	266,180
FLA--T9--2	1968	HOLLYWOOD	11,250	7,500
FLA--T9--3	1969	PENSACOLA	25,000	18,000
FLA--T9--4	1969	TAMPA	34,960	23,306
FL-09-0010	1972	ST PETERSBURG		160,000
GA--T9--1	1966	ATLANTA	692,900	461,933
GA-09-0011	1973	VALDOSTA	13,395	8,930
GA-09-0012	1972	ATLANTA	4,800,000	3,200,000
HAWA--T9--1	1968	HONOLULU	103,960	69,300
HAWA--T9--2	1969	HONOLULU	270,000	180,000
HI-09-0005	1970	HONOLULU	1,965,000	1,310,000
ILL--T9--1	1968	CHICAGO	98,687	63,596
ILL--T9--2	1968	SKOKIE	71,100	47,400
ILL--T9--3	1968	CHICAGO	265,980	177,320
IOWA--T9--2	1970	IOWA CITY	16,316	10,877
KY-09-0005	1973	COVINGTON	31,632	21,088
LA--T9--1	1968	NEW ORLEANS	57,000	38,000
LA--T9--2	1970	SHREVEPORT	25,320	25,320
LA--T9--3	1970	NEW ORLEANS	89,500	59,666

TECHNICAL GRANTS

PROJECT	YEAR	LOCATION	TOTAL COST	FEDERAL
MD--T9--1	1967	BALTIMORE	1,350,000	900,000
MD--T9--2	1968	BALTIMORE	450,000	300,000
MD--T9--3	1968	BALTIMORE	600,000	400,000
MD-09-0007	1972	BALTIMORE	1,477,200	984,400
MASS--T9--1	1967	BOSTON	746,726	497,817
MASS--T9--2	1961	LAWRENCE	15,415	10,276
MASS--T9--3	1968	BROCKTON	84,000	56,000
MASS--T9--4	1968	BOSTON	664,151	442,767
MASS--T9--5	1969	BOSTON	300,000	200,000
MASS--T9--6	1969	LOWELL	167,000	100,500
MASS--T9--10	1970	BOSTON	2,940,250	1,693,500
MASS--T9--11	1968	WORCHESTER	64,794	43,196
MICH--T9--1	1968	DETROIT	120,000	80,000
MICH--T9--2	1968	ANN ARBOR	15,000	10,000
MICH--T9--3	1969	DETROIT	181,500	121,000
MINN--T9--1	1968	ST. PAUL	594,400	396,266
MINN--T9--2	1969	DULUTH	33,000	22,000
MINN--T9--7	1971	ST. PAUL	108,000	72,000
MO-09-0002	1973	JEFFERSON CITY	127,500	85,000
MONT--T9--1	1967	GREAT FALLS	7,250	4,833
NEB--T9--1	1968	OMAHA	121,758	81,172
NEB--T9--2	1969	OMAHA	43,506	29,004
NEB--T9--3	1969	LINCOLN	15,000	10,000
NJ--T9--1	1968	NEWARK	45,000	3,000
NJ--T9--2	1969	MERCER COUNTY	17,500	11,666
NJ--T9--3	1969	ATLANTIC CITY	21,000	14,000
NY--T9--1	1968	BROOME COUNTY	58,596	39,064
NY--T9--2	1968	NASSAU COUNTY	37,522	25,014
NY--T9--3	1968	SYRACUSE	46,580	29,980
NY--T9--4	1970	BUFFALO	786,000	524,000
NY---T9--12	1971	BUFFALO	149,976	99,984
NY-09-0014	1972	BUFFALO	442,700	295,133
NY-09-0017	1972	BUFFALO	1,850,000	1,233,333
OHIO--T9--1	1967	AKRON	26,530	17,687
OHIO--T9--2	1968	TOLEDO	31,830	21,220
OHIO--T9--4	1969	STARK COUNTY	66,000	44,000
OH-09-0012	1973	CLEVELAND-AKRON		96,620
OKLA--T9--1	1969	TULSA	51,993	34,662
ORE--T9--1	1968	EUGENE	20,400	13,600
ORE--T9--2	1969	PORTLAND	64,753	43,168

TECHNICAL GRANTS

PROJECT	YEAR	LOCATION	TOTAL COST	FEDERAL
ORE--T9--4	1971	PORTLAND	99,000	66,000
PA--T9--1	1968	PITTSBURGH	450,000	300,000
PA--T9--2	1968	ERIE	24,000	16,000
PA--T9--3	1969	LANCASTER	33,850	22,566
PA-09-0010	1972	PHILADELPHIA	6,225,000	4,150,000
TENN--T9--1	1968	CHATTANOOGA	37,320	24,840
TENN--T9--2	1969	NASHVILLE	103,531	69,020
TEX--T9--1	1968	WICHITA FALLS	212,210	135,848
TEX--T9--2	1969	DALLAS	600,000	400,000
TEX--T9--5	1970	TEXAS COLLEGE	395,000	263,333
TEX--T9--6	1970	DALLAS	502,000	334,666
TEX--T9--12	1972	ARLINGTON	292,500	195,000
TEX--T9--14	1967	TEXAS A+M	98,176	98,176
JTAH--T9--1	1969	SALT LAKE CITY	73,136	48,756
VA--T9--1	1968	RICHMOND	90,000	60,000
VA--T9--2	1968	FAIRFAX COUNTY	45,000	30,000
VA-09-0005	1973	RICHMOND	110,322	73,548
VA-09-0006	1973	LYNCHBURG		26,898
WASH--T9--1	1967	SEATTLE	1,434,000	816,000
WASH--T9--2	1969	SPOKANE	108,000	72,000
WA-09-0007	1973	WASHINGTON		62,600
WIS--T9--1	1968	MILWAUKEE	550,000	220,000
WISC--T9-8	1972	MILWAUKEE		181,849
WI-09-0010	1973	LA CROSSE	36,000	24,000
INT--T9--1	1967	KANSAS CITY	15,000	10,000
INT--T9--2	1967	WILMINGTON	120,000	80,000
INT--T9--3	1967	KANSAS CITY	34,900	23,266
INT--T9--4	1968	ST LOUIS	400,000	266,666
INT--T9--5	1968	KANSAS CITY	182,200	121,466
INT--T9--6	1970	KANSAS CITY	100,000	75,800
INT--T9--7	1971	CINCINNATI	321,000	214,000
INT--T9--8	1970	PORTLAND	505,000	336,666
INT--T9--9	1972	CAMDEN	426,000	250,726
INT--T9--11	1970	ST LOUIS		146,666
INT--T9--20	1972	WASHINGTON DC	4,699,950	3,133,300
IT-09-0023-1	1973	NEW YORK CITY	5,250,000	3,500,000
IT-09-0025	1973	TRENTON	150,000	100,000
PR--T9--1	1969	SAN JUAN	1,069,500	713,000

Suggested Readings

As anyone can see from the heft of the bibliography, a great deal of material is available on the subject of urban mass transportation. For the person wishing to bolster his or her knowledge of the field without reading through all of the items in the bibliography, here are some suggested items that afford a good perspective on urban mass transportation and federal policy. See the bibliography for full citations.

For a comprehensive view of the whole urban transportation situation, *The Metropolitan Transportation Problem* by Wilfred Owen is probably the best single source. For somewhat more detail and an analytical approach to solutions, the reader should see *The Urban Transportation Problem* by John R. Meyer, John F. Kain, and Martin Wohl.

For more extensive discussion on policy matters relating to urban mass transportation policy, see *Urban Transportation and Public Policy* by Lyle Fitch and Associates; *Urban Transportation: The Federal Role* by George M. Smerk; *Metropolitan Transportation Politics and the New York Region* by Jameson Doig; and *Federal-Metropolitan Politics and the Commuter Crisis* by Michael Danielson. Coverage of the events leading up to the enactment of federal transit legislation through the amendments of 1966 may be found in *Readings in Urban Transportation,* edited by George Smerk.

The problems of implementing mass transit policy on the local level and the difficulty of breaking away from the conventional highway approach are illustrated very well in *Rites of Way: The Politics of Transportation in Boston and the U.S. City* by Alan Lupo, Frank Colcord, and Edmund P. Fowler, and *Highways to Nowhere: The Politics of City Transportation* by Richard Hebert.

Apart from the statistics published annually by the American Transit Association in its *Fact Books,* it is not easy to corral statistical information about urban mass transportation. The Department of Transportation's publication entitled *Economic Characteristics of the Urban Public Transportation Industry* is a great aid in supplying information about transit, commuter railroads, and taxicabs. Certain aspects of the transit industry are covered in *Principles of Urban Transportation,* edited by Frank H. Mossman; *Marketing Urban Mass Transit* by Lewis M. Schneider; and *Mass Transit Management: A Handbook for Small Cities* prepared by the Institute for Urban Transportation.

Keeping up on transit issues of all sorts can most easily be done through the pages of *Passenger Transport,* the weekly newspaper of the American Transit Association.

BIBLIOGRAPHY

Books

Abrams, Charles. *The City Is the Frontier*. New York: Harper & Row, 1965.

Anderson, J.E., J.L. Davis, W.L. Garrad, and A. L. Kornhauser (eds.). *Personal Rapid Transit*. Minneapolis: University of Minnesota, Institute of Technology, April 1972.

Bayer, Harold. *The Transportation Industries—1889–1946: A Study of Output, Employment and Productivity*. New York: National Bureau of Economic Research, 1951.

Beal, Denton (ed.) *Leland Hazard on Transportation*. Pittsburgh: Carnegie-Mellon University, 1969.

Bendtsen, P.H. *Town and Traffic in the Motor Age*. Copenhagen: Danish Technical Press, 1961.

Bernstein, Marver H. *Regulating Business by Independent Commission*. Princeton, N.J.: Princeton University Press, 1955.

Burby, John. *The Great American Motion Sickness*. Boston: Little, Brown, 1971.

Carman, Harry James. *The Street Surface Railway Franchises of New York City*, Vol. 88, No. 1. New York: Columbia University Press, 1919.

Danielson, Michael. *Federal-Metropolitan Politics and the Commuter Crisis*. New York: Columbia University Press, 1965.

Dearing, Charles L. *American Highway Policy*. Washington, D.C.: Brookings Institution, 1941.

Debout, John E. and Ronald J. Grele. *Where Cities Meet: The Urbanization of New Jersey*. Princeton, N.J.: Van Nostrand, 1964.

Doig, Jameson W. *Metropolitan Transportation Politics and the New York Region*. New York: Columbia University Press, 1966.

Dommel, Paul R. *The Politics of Revenue Sharing*. Bloomington: Indiana University Press, 1974.

Fellmeth, Robert. *The Interstate Commerce Omission: The Public Interest and the ICC*. New York: Grossman, 1970.

Fitch, Lyle C. and Associates. *Urban Transportation and Public Policy*. San Francisco: Chandler, 1964.

Foster, C.D. and M.E. Beesley. "The Victoria Line," in *Transport*, ed. Denys Munby. Hermondsworth: Penguin (Middlesex, England), 1968.

Gans, Herbert J. *People and Plans: Essays on Urban Problems and Solutions*. New York: Basic, 1968.

Ginger, Ray. *Altgeld's America*. New York: Funk & Wagnall's, 1958.

Gordon, Mitchell. *Sick Cities*. Baltimore: Penguin, 1966.

Gottman, Jean and Robert A. Harper. *Metropolis On the Move*. New York: John Wiley, 1967.

Grodinsky, Julius. *Jay Gould: His Business Career*. Philadelphia: University of Pennsylvania Press, 1957.

Gruen, Victor. *The Heart of Our Cities*. New York: Simon and Schuster, 1964.

Haworth, Lawrence. *The Good City*. Bloomington: Indiana University Press/Midland Books, 1966.

Hebert, Richard. *Highways to Nowhere: The Politics of City Transportation*. New York: Bobbs-Merrill, 1972.

Hilton, George. *The Transportation Act of 1958*. Bloomington: Indiana University Press, 1969.

Hirsch, Mark D. *William C. Whitney: Modern Warwick*. New York: Dodd, Mead, 1948.

Hoel, Lester A. et al. *Latent Demand for Urban Transportation*. (TRI Research Report No. 2) Pittsburgh, Pa.: Carnegie-Mellon University, Transportation Research Institute, 1968.

Hudson, William J. and James A. Constantin. *Motor Transportation*. New York: Ronald, 1953.

Hunnicutt, James Madison, Jr. "Parking Conceptions and Misconceptions," in *Downtown Action on Traffic—Parking—Transit*, ed. Laurence A. Alexander and James J. Bliss. New York: National Retail Merchants Association, 1965.

Johnson, Philip. "Why We Want Our Cities Ugly," in *The Future of Man's Environment*. Washington, D.C.: Smithsonian Institution Press, 1968.

Kent, T.J., Jr. *The Urban General Plan*. San Francisco: Chandler, 1964.

Kuhn, Tillo E. *Public Enterprise Economics and Transport Problems*. Berkeley and Los Angeles: University of California Press, 1962.

Leavitt, Helen. *Superhighway-Superhoax*. New York: Ballantine, 1970.

Levin, Melvin R. and Norman A. Abend. *Bureaucrats in Collision: Case Studies in Area Transportation Planning*. Cambridge, Mass.: M.I.T. Press, 1971.

Locklin, D. Philip. *Economics of Transportation*, 6th ed. Homewood, Ill.: Irwin, 1966.

Lupo, Alan, Frank Colcord, and Edmund P. Fowler. *Rites of Way: The Politics of Transportation in Boston and the U.S. City*. Boston: Little, Brown, 1971.

Mandelker, Daniel R. "Legal Strategy for Urban Development," in *Planning for a Nation of Cities*, ed. Sam Bass Warner, Jr. Cambridge: M.I.T. Press, 1966.

Manson, R. Joseph and Mark W. Cannon. *The Makers of Public Policy: American Power Groups and Their Ideologies*. New York: McGraw-Hill, 1965.

McKelvey, Blake. *The Urbanization of America 1860–1915*. New Brunswick, N.J.: Rutgers University Press, 1963.

Meyer, John R. "Knocking Down the Straw Men," in Benjamin Chinitz, *City and Suburb: The Economics of Metropolitan Growth*. Englewood Cliffs, N.J.: Prentice-Hall, 1964.

Meyer, John R., John F. Kain, and Martin Wohl. *The Urban Transportation Problem*. Cambridge: Harvard University Press, 1965.

Miller, John Anderson. *Fares, Please!* New York: Dover, 1960.

Modernizing Local Government. New York: Committee for Economic Development, July 1966.

Mossman, Frank H. (ed). *Principles of Urban Transportation*. Cleveland, Ohio: The Press of Western Reserve University, 1951.

Moynihan, Daniel P. "Toward a National Urban Policy," in *Toward a National Urban Policy*, ed. Moynihan. New York: Basic, 1970.

Mumford, Lewis. *The City in History*. New York: Harcourt, Brace and World, 1961.

Mundy, Ray A. *Marketing Urban Mass Transit—1973*. University Park: Pennsylvania State University, Transportation and Traffic Safety Center, January 1974.

Mundy, Ray A. and John C. Spychalski. *Managerial Resources and Personnel Practices in Urban Mass Transportation*. University Park: Pennsylvania State University, Transportation and Traffic Safety Center, November, 1973.

Murin, William J. *Mass Transit Policy Planning*. Lexington, Mass.: Heath Lexington, 1971.

Oi, Walter Y. and Paul W. Shuldiner. *An Analysis of Urban Travel Demands*. Evanston, Ill.: Northwestern University Press, 1962.

Owen, Wilfred. *The Metropolitan Transportation Problem*. Washington, D.C.: Brookings Institution, 1966.

———. *A Fable: How the Cities Solved Their Transportation Problems*. Washington, D.C.: Urban-America, Inc., 1967.

———. *The Accessible City*. Washington, D.C.: Brookings Institution, 1972.

Peters, G.H. *Cost-Benefit Analysis and Public Expenditure* [Eaton Paper 8]. London: The Institute of Economic Affairs, 1966.

Rasmussen, Steen Eiler. *London: The Unique City*. Cambridge: M.I.T. Press, 1967.

Regional Plan Association. *Urban Design Manhattan*. New York: Viking, 1969.

Schmidt, Emerson P. *Industrial Relations in Urban Transportation*. Minneapolis: University of Minnesota Press, 1937.

Schneider, Kenneth R. *Autokind vs. Mankind*. New York: Norton, 1971.

Schneider, Lewis M. *Marketing Urban Mass Transit*. Boston: Harvard University, Graduate School of Business Administration, Division of Research, 1965.

———. "Urban Mass Transportation: A Survey of the Decision-Making Process," in *The Study of Policy Formation*, ed. R. A. Bauer and Kenneth J. Green. New York: Free Press, 1968.

'71–'72 Transit Fact Book. Washington, D.C.: American Transit Association, 1972.

'72–'73 Transit Fact Book. Washington, D.C.: American Transit Association, 1973.

Smerk, George M. *Urban Transportation: The Federal Role*. Bloomington: Indiana University Press, 1968.

Smerk, George M. (ed). *Readings in Urban Transportation*. Bloomington: Indiana University Press, 1965.

Smith, Wilbur and Associates. *The Potential for Bus Rapid Transit*. Detroit: Automobile Manufacturers Association, February 1970.

Taff, Charles A. *Commercial Motor Transportation*. Homewood, Ill.: Irwin, 1955.

Technical Description of the Stockholm Underground Railway: 1964. Stockholm, Sweden: Stockholm Passenger Transport Company, 1965.

Tomazinis, Anthony R. *The Role of the States in Urban Mass Transit*. Philadelphia: University of Pennsylvania, Transportation Studies Center for Urban Research and Experiment, July 1971.

Traffic in Towns [The Buchanan Report]. London: Her Majesty's Stationery Office, 1963.

Transportation and Parking for Tomorrow's Cities. New Haven, Conn.: Wilbur Smith and Associates, 1966.

Urban Rapid Transit: Concepts and Evolution. Pittsburgh: Carnegie-Mellon University, Transportation Research Institute, 1968.

Warner, Sam Bass, Jr. *The Private City: Philadelphia in Three Periods of Its Growth*. Philadelphia: University of Pennsylvania Press, 1968.

Wood, Robert. "Intergovernmental Relationships in an Urbanizing America," in *Toward a National Urban Policy*, ed. Daniel P. Moynihan. New York: Basic, 1970.

Periodicals and Journals

"Administration Fails to Back Operating Aid," *Passenger Transport*, June 16, 1972, p.1.

"Administration Plan Would Allow Operating Aid," *Passenger Transport*, January 25, 1974, p.1.

"Anderson Re-Introduces Trust Fund Bill," *Passenger Transport*, January 12, 1973, pp.1, 5.

Asher, Joe. "Highway Money for Transit? That's What the Man Said," *Railway Age*, April 10, 1972, pp.22–25.

———. "How Are Things in Glocca Washington?" *Railway Age*, August 9, 1971, pp.24–25.

———. "What Does Lindenwold Prove?" *Railway Age*, December 11, 1972, pp.24–25.

Ashford, Norman. "The Developing Role of State Government in Transportation," *Traffic Quarterly* 22, 4 (October 1968), 455–468.

"ATA Asks Senate to Raise Transit's '72 Funding Level," *Passenger Transport,* July 16, 1971, pp.1, 3.

"At Last: Congress Approves Transit Aid," *Railway Age,* July 6, 1964, pp.28–29.

"Atlanta Fares Down, Riders Up," *Passenger Transport,* March 27, 1972, pp.1, 6.

Avery, George A. and James C. Echols. "The Shirley Highway Project: Achieving Effective Intergovernmental Cooperation," *Traffic Quarterly* 26, 3 (July 1972), 373–390.

Barbera, Kevin G. "Introduction to the City of Boston Taxicab Industry," *Traffic Quarterly* 26, 2 (April 1972), 279.

Barkley, Bruce T. "Problem Solving in Urban Transportation," *Traffic Quarterly* 27, 4 (October 1973), 491–502.

————. "Some Public Policy Strategy Considerations," *New Concepts in Urban Transportation,* March 15, 1973, p.320.

Bartley, Robert. "Why an Orderly Transport Growth Makes Toronto's System a Showcase," *Railway Age,* June 11, 1973, p.30.

Bennett, James W., Jr. and William J. DeWitt, III. "The Development of State Departments of Transportation—A Recent Organizational Phenomenon," *Transportation Journal* 12, 1 (Fall 1972), 5–14.

"Better Urban Transportation," *Proceedings of the American Municipal Congress 1959.* Washington, D.C.: American Municipal Association.

"Bill Passes!" *Passenger Transport,* October 2, 1970, pp.1–7, 10–12.

"Boston—San Francisco Trolley," *Rollsign* 9, 10 (October 1972), 2–10.

Brdlik, Hal. "A Legislative Miracle," *Metropolitan Management, Transportation, and Planning* 60, 5 (September 1964), 26, 50.

Brune, Barry A. "Developing State DOT Organizations," *Proceedings—13th Annual Meeting, Transportation Research Forum* 13, 1 (1972), 243–256. (Richard B. Cross Co., Oxford, Ind.)

Burke, Vincent J. "The Tangled Path of a Transit Bill," *The Reporter,* July 16, 1964.

"Can You Top This: San Diego Story 53 Miles for 25¢," *Passenger Transport,* November 24, 1972, p.4.

"Center City Transportation," *Nation's Cities* 8, 2 (February 1970), 9–32.

"Chicago: Institute for Rapid Transit," *IRT News Letter* 6, 7 (December 1966), 11.

"The Cleveland Rapid," *IRT News Letter,* November 15, 1961, p.1.

"Cochran Leads Industry Support for Senate Bill 870," *Passenger Transport,* April 9, 1971, pp.1, 7.

"A Commentary: Capital Grant Criteria," *Passenger Transport,* June 2, 1972, p.1.

"Conferees Agree to Expand Use of Highway Trust Fund to Transit," *Passenger Transport,* July 27, 1973, pp.1, 5.

"Congress Okays $900 Million for Transit," *Passenger Transport,* August 6, 1971.

332   Bibliography

Conway, Thomas, J. "1950–1960 Population Shift Poses Transportation Problem," *Traffic Quarterly* 15, 1 (January 1961), 62.

————. "Rapid Transit Must Be Improved to Alleviate Traffic Congestion," *Traffic Quarterly* 16, 1 (January 1962), 103.

"CTS Is Ten Years Old," *Going Places,* Third Quarter 1965, p.4.

"DOT Picks Denver for PRT Test," *Passenger Transport,* October 27, 1972, p.5.

" 'Damnedest Coalition' Fights for Transit Aid Bill Passage," *Passenger Transport,* July 3, 1970, pp.4–5.

"Down But Not Out," *Pittsburgh Press,* July 26, 1972, p.26.

"Editorial," *Metropolitan* 69, 3 (May/June 1972), 36.

Entwistle, Clivè. "Roads to Ruin," *The New York Times Book Review,* September 4, 1966, pp.3, 22–23.

"The Escalating Cost of a People Mover," *Business Week,* March 16, 1974, pp.50–52.

"An Evaluation of a Report Entitled 'Technology and Urban Transportation,' " *IRT News Letter,* August 15, 1963.

Farmer, Richard N. "Whatever Happened to the Jitney?" *Traffic Quarterly* 19, 2 (April 1965), 263–279.

"Federal Action: S. 502 Becomes A Law," *IRT Digest,* September/October 1973, pp.1–10.

"Federal Environmental Legislation and Regulation as Affecting Highways," *Research Results Digest* No. 25, January 1971.

"Governor Gives Green Light to Transit in Massachusetts," *Passenger Transport,* December 8, 1972, pp.1, 4, 5.

"The Governor's Transportation Program," *Rollsign* 9, 11 (November 1972), 1–3.

Gruen, Victor. "Needed: A Prompt End to the Old Luxury of Limited Thinking," *Architectural Forum,* October 1963, p.94.

Gutman, Robert. "Urban Transports as Human Environment," *The Journal of the Franklin Institute* 286, 5 (November 1968, Special Issue on New Concepts in Urban Transportation Systems), 533–539.

Haar, Charles M. "Transit and the Ghetto," *Nation's Cities* 5, 1 (January 1967), 7–9.

" '. . . A Harder Look at Transit'—Blatnik," *Passenger Transport,* August 6, 1971, pp.1, 4–5.

Havemann, Joel. "Revenue Sharing Report/Problems Snag Nixon Plan as Complaints from Local Areas Mount," *National Journal,* March 17, 1973, pp.389–390.

Hendrick, Burton J. "Great American Fortunes and Their Making," *McClure's Magazine* 30 (1907–1908), 33–48, 236–250, 323–338.

Herbert, Evan. "Transporting People," *International Sciences and Technology,* October 1965, pp.30–42.

"Herringer Announces UMTA Reorganization," *Passenger Transport,* September 14, 1973, p.4.

"Highway Act of 1973: What's in It for Mass Transit," *Passenger Transport,* August 10, 1973, pp.4, 5.

Hilton, George W. "Rail Transit and the Pattern of Modern Cities: The California Case," *Traffic Quarterly* 21, 3 (July 1967), 379–393.

Hooper, William L. "Transportation Demonstrations: Link Between Analysis and Decision," *Proceedings—7th Annual Meeting, Transportation Research Forum* 7, 1 (1966). (Richard B. Cross Co., Oxford, Ind.)

"House Adds a Transit Panel," *Passenger Transport,* March 16, 1973, pp.1, 6.

"House Says 'No' to Anderson, 'Yes' to Three Other Proposals," *Passenger Transport,* April 20, 1973, p.3.

IRT Digest, Special Issue, Annual Conference 1972, pp.4–10, 15–19.

IRT News Letter, March 30, 1962; *IRT News Letter,* August 15, 1963; *IRT News Letter* 7, 7 (December 1966).

"Industry Calls for Operating Aid at Senate Hearings," *Passenger Transport,* February 4, 1972, pp.1, 4–5.

Karr, Albert R. "Mass-Transit Groups Say Upsurge Is More Than Token Victory," *Wall Street Journal,* March 21, 1974.

"Kelm Points Out PRT Shortcomings," *IRT Digest,* Special Issue, Annual Conference 1973, pp.36–39.

Kessler, Felix. "London Cab Drivers Are Polite, and They Are Safe and Honest," *Wall Street Journal,* September 8, 1972.

Kohl, John C. "The Federal Urban Transportation Demonstration Program," *Traffic Quarterly* 18, 3 (July 1964), 303.

"Lack of Quorum Kills Transit Aid," *Passenger Transport,* October 27, 1972, pp.1, 5.

Lago, Armando M. "United States Subway Requirements 1968–1990: Projections and Benefits," *Traffic Quarterly* 23, 1 (January 1969), 79–88.

Larson, Thomas D. "Toward a More Effective State Role in Transportation," *Proceedings—13th Annual Meeting, Transportation Research Forum* 13, 1 (1972), 257–269. (Richard B. Cross Co., Oxford, Ind.)

Lilley, William III. "Urban Report: Urban Interests Win Transit Bill with 'Letter-Perfect' Lobbying," *National Journal,* September 19, 1970, pp. 2021–2029.

————. "Urban Report: Mayors and White House Prepare for Battle Over $40 Billion Subway Program for 1970's," *National Journal,* March 18, 1972, pp.484–492.

"Mapping Transit's Future: All Eyes Focus on Pittsburgh," *Railway Age,* January 24, 1966, pp.18–19.

"MARTA: Setting Atlanta in Motion by Bus and Rail," *Passenger Transport,* January 19, 1973, pp.4, 5.

"Mass Transport: A $10 Billion Market," *Railway Age,* February 18, 1963, p.25.

McConnell, R.M. "Watching Washington: Mass Transit and the Handicapped," *Railway Age,* October 8, 1973, p.16.

Miller, David R. "New Challenges, New Institutions," *Public Administration Review* 33, 3 (May/June 1973), 236–242.

"More Transit Funding Sought: Volpe Urges Additional $3 Billion," *Passenger Transport,* September 8, 1972, pp.1, 4.

Motor Coach Age 24, 8 (August 1972), 12–19.

"Muskie Bill Would Open Trust Fund," *Passenger Transport,* January 26, 1973, p.4.

"New York's MTA: Light at the End of the Tunnel," *Railway Age,* April 9, 1973, pp.16–31.

"92nd Congress Kills Federal Aid Bill," *IRT Digest* No. 14 (November/December 1972), pp.2–6.

"Nixon Proposes 'Revenue Sharing,' " *IRT Digest* No. 3 (March/April 1971), p.2.

"Nixon Proposes Separate Transit Revenue Sharing," *IRT Digest* No. 4 (May/June 1971), pp.1–4.

"Nixon, Rep. Mills Agree on Revenue Sharing Proposal," *Passenger Transport,* December 10, 1971, pp.1, 7.

"Nixon: Transit Is High Priority," *Passenger Transport,* February 23, 1973, p.1.

"Nixon Urges Rail Use of Trust Fund," *Passenger Transport,* March 16, 1973, p.6.

"Notes and Comments," *Motor Coach Age* 24, 5 (May 1972) 32.

"On the Right Track," *Monsanto Magazine* 47, 1 (March 1967), 16–20.

"On the Washington Scene," *Metropolitan* 24, 6 (November/December 1968), 28, 30; *Metropolitan* 65, 5 (September/October 1969), 36–38; *Metropolitan* 65, 6 (November/December 1969), 44; *Metropolitan* 66, 1 (January/February 1970), 29; *Metropolitan* 67, 4 (July/August, 1971), 12–13.

Papp, Albert L. "Why a Commuter Crisis in New Jersey," *The Journal of Business* (Seton Hall University) 4, 1 (December 1965), 24–29.

―――. "Alleviating the Commuter Crisis," *The Journal of Business* (Seton Hall University) 4, 2 (May 1966), 23–29.

Passenger Transport, February 21, 1969; March 21, 1969; August 15, 1969; January 7, 1972 through February 25, 1972.

"People First Plan: Transit—The New Way to Go in Ontario," *Passenger Transport,* December 8, 1972, pp.1, 4, 5.

"People Mover Dedicated in Morgantown," *Passenger Transport,* October 27, 1972, p.1, 4.

Peters, C. Lovett. "Transportation in the Free Market," *Transportation Journal* 6, 2 (Winter 1967), 41–47.

"President Nixon Signs Transit Aid Bill," *Passenger Transport,* October 16, 1970, p.1.

"Private Investments Nearly as Much as Subway Costs," *IRT News Letter* 10, 2 (April 1969), 27–28.

"Pueblo: Test Tube for Tomorrow's Railroads," *Railway Age,* September 13, 1971, p.38.

Rapid Transit (San Francisco Bay Area Rapid Transit District) 6, 2 (September/October 1963).

"Revenue Sharing Checks to Be Mailed Soon," *Passenger Transport,* November 24, 1972, p.1.

Reynolds, D.J. "Review of *Urban Mass Transit Planning,*" *Journal of Transport Economics and Policy* (London School of Economics) 2, 2 (May 1968), 250–251.

Roe, B. John. "The Evolution of the Motor Bus as a Transport Mode," *High Speed Ground Transportation Journal* 5 (Summer 1971), 221–235.

Rosenbloom, Sandi. "Taxis, Jitneys and Poverty," *Trans-Action* (February 1970), pp.47–54.

"St. Germain Offers Transit Aid Bill," *Passenger Transport,* January 26, 1973, p.4.

"San Franciscans Fight for that Cable Car Charm," *Business Week,* September 4, 1971, p.64.

Schenker, Eric and John Wilson. "The Use of Public Mass Transportation in the Major Metropolitan Areas of the United States," *Land Economics* 43, 3 (August 1967), 361–367.

Schneider, Lewis. "A Marketing Strategy for Transit Managers," *Traffic Quarterly* 22, 2 (April 1968), 283–294.

"Senate Holds Hearings on S. 386: DOT Head Fails to Back Operating Aid," *Passenger Transport,* February 9, 1973, pp.1, 4, 6.

"Senate OKs Operating Aid," *Passenger Transport,* March 3, 1972, pp.1, 7.

"Senate Passes Landmark Transit Aid Legislation," *Passenger Transport,* March 16, 1973, pp.1, 8.

"Senate Passes Transit Aid Bill," *Passenger Transport,* February 6, 1970, pp.1, 6.

Shannon, William V. "The Highwaymen," a syndicated column of the *New York Times,* appearing in the Bloomington, Ind. *Herald-Telephone,* September 18, 1972, p.8.

"Skybus Land Buying Banned," *Pittsburgh Press,* August 20, 1972, p.1.

Smerk, George M. "An Evaluation of Ten Years of Federal Policy in Urban Mass Transportation," *Transportation Journal* 11, 2 (Winter 1971), 51.

————. "Federal Urban Transport Policy: Here . . . and Where Do We Go From Here?" *Traffic Quarterly* 21, 1 (January 1967), 47–50.

————. "The 'Hardware' Gap in Urban Transport," *Business Horizons* 9, 1 (Spring 1966), 5–16.

————. "Mass Transit Management," *Business Horizons* 14, 6 (December 1971), 5–16.

————. "The Streetcar: Shaper of American Cities," *Traffic Quarterly* 21, 4 (October 1967), 569–584.

————. "The Urban Mass Transportation Act of 1964: New Hope for American Cities," *Transportation Journal* 5, 2 (Winter 1965), 37–38.

Staher, B.R. "How San Francisco Is Solving the Transportation and Traffic Problem," *Going Places* (Fourth Quarter 1970), pp.10–11.

"State Department of Transportation Directory," *IRT Digest* (March/April 1974), 12–21.

"Taxis Clock Up Woes for the Urban Planner," *Business Week,* December 23, 1967, p.51.

Taylor, George Rogers. "The Beginnings of Mass Transportation in Urban America," *The Smithsonian Journal of History* (Part I) 1, 2 (Summer 1966), 35–50; (Part II) 1, 3 (Autumn 1966), 31–54.

Thelen, Gilbert C. "Mass Transit: Up Against the Concrete Wall," *The Nation,* February 21, 1972, p.238.

Thorp, Bruce E. "Transportation Report: House Resists Plan to Use Road Funds for Urban Transit," *National Journal,* September 9, 1972, pp.1437–1443.

"Transit and the Trust Fund: Senate Panel Reports Bill," *Passenger Transport,* July 28, 1972, pp.1, 4.

"Transit Guide to Transpo '72," *Passenger Transport,* May 19, 1972, pp.1, 10.

"Transit Riders Coming Back," *Passenger Transport,* September 7, 1973, pp.1, 2.

"Transit Riders Coming Back Coast to Coast," *Passenger Transport,* February 15, 1974, p.1.

"Transit Ridership Continues Dramatic Rise," *Passenger Transport,* March 1, 1974, pp.1, 5.

"269 Grants Went to Improve Transit in '71," *Passenger Transport,* April 14, 1972, pp.1, 5.

"UMTA Administrator Herringer Talks of Reorganization," *IRT Digest,* Special Issue, Annual Conference 1973, pp.29–32.

"UMTA's New Thrusts: Marketing and Management," *Railway Age,* July 9, 1973, pp.46–49.

"The U.S.' Lopsided Transportation Budget," *Forbes Magazine,* October 1, 1968.

"Utah Transit Ridership Up," *Passenger Transport,* June 8, 1973, p.5.

"UTAP: Administration Plan Set," *Passenger Transport,* February 8, 1974, pp.1, 3.

"UTAP: 'One Hand Giveth, and One Hand Taketh Away,'" *Railway Age,* March 11, 1974, p.24.

Vigrass, William J. "The Lindenwold Hi-Speed Transit Line," *Railway Management Review* 72, 2 (Summer 1972), 28–52.

"Villarreal Answers Questions About Nixon's Public Transportation Bill," *Passenger Transport,* September 12, 1969, p.1.

Villarreal, Carlos C. "Guidelines: Capital Grant Project Selection," *Passenger Transport,* July 21, 1972, pp.1, 3.

"Volpe Urges Transit Aid from Highway Trust Fund," *Passenger Transport,* March 17, 1972, p.1.

Walker, P.J. "America's New Standard Tramcar," *Modern Tramways* 36, 425 (May 1973), 150–155.

"The War Over Urban Expressways," *Business Week,* March 11, 1967, pp.94–103.

Weaver, Robert C. "The Federal Interest in Urban Mass Transportation," *Traffic Quarterly* 17, 1 (January 1963), 25, 29.

Weiner, Edward. "Modal Split Revisited," *Traffic Quarterly* 23, 1 (January 1969), 5–28.

Whalen, Richard J. "The American Highway: Do We Know Where We're Going?" *Saturday Evening Post,* December 14, 1968.

"What the Highway Act Will Do for Mass Transport," *Railway Age,* October 8, 1973, p.34.

"Where Does Transit Stand?" *Passenger Transport,* April 6, 1973, pp.1, 2.

"Williams Introduces Transit Bill," *Passenger Transport,* January 19, 1973, p.3.

"Williams Named Man of the Year," *Passenger Transport,* October 10, 1969, pp.1–2.

Wohl, Martin. "Public Transport Pricing, Financing, and Subsidy Principles," *Traffic Quarterly* 27, 4 (October 1973), 619–634.

"A Word to the Thrifty," *Passenger Transport,* August 11, 1972, p.1.

Government and Special Publications

"Agreement Between the Secretary of the Department of Housing and Urban Development and the Secretary of the Department of Transportation." Mimeographed document signed by HUD Secretary Robert Weaver on September 9, 1968, and Transportation Secretary Alan Boyd on September 10, 1968. For commentary on the agreement, see "On the Washington Scene," *Metropolitan* 24, 6 (November/December 1968), 28–30.

Allegheny County Rapid Transit. Pittsburgh, Pa.: Port Authority of Allegheny County, 1969.

Allott, Gordon. "Urban Transit: Paper or Progress." Paper delivered at the Third International Conference on Urban Transportation. Pittsburgh, Pa.: WABCO Mass Transit Center, Westinghouse Air Brake Co.

Altshuler, Alan. "The Politics of Urban Mass Transportation." Paper delivered at the annual meeting of the American Political Science Association, September 4–7, 1963 (Mimeo).

Ames, ArDee. "An End to Highway Aid," pp.1–4 in *A Look at Urban Transportation.* Washington, D.C.: National League of Cities, 1966.

"Analysis of the New Federal Urban Transportation Act." Chicago: Institute for Rapid Transit (Mimeo).

Avoidable Cost of Passenger Train Service. Cambridge, Mass.: Aeronautical Research Foundation, September 1957.

Banks, R.L. & Associates. *Study and Evaluation of Local Transit Regulation and Regulatory Bodies* (Part I, No. PB 211077 and Part II, No. PB 211078). Springfield, Va.: National Technical Information Service, 1972.

Bond, Langhorne and Richard Solomon. *The Promise and Problems of High Capacity Buses in the United States.* Pittsburgh, Pa.: National Transportation Center, 1971.

Burco, Robert A. "International Activity in Personal Rapid Transit Development and Assessment," in *Advanced Transportation Systems and Technology* (Highway Research Record No. 427). Washington, D.C.: Highway Research Board, 1973.

Bureau of Population and Economic Research. *The Socio/Economic Impact of the Capital Beltway on Northern Virginia* prepared in cooperation with the Virginia Department of Highways and the U.S. Department of Transportation, Bureau of Public Roads. Charlottesville: University of Virginia, 1968.

Cherniak, Nathan. "A Statement of the Urban Passenger Transportation Problem," *Urban Transportation Planning: Concepts and Application* (Bulletin 293). Washington, D.C.: Highway Research Board, 1961.

City-by-City Directory of Urban Rail Systems. Schenectady, N.Y.: General Electric Co.

The Collapse of Commuter Service. Washington, D.C.: American Municipal Association, 1959.

The Composite Report, Bay Area Rapid Transit. San Francisco: Bay Area Rapid Transit District, May 1962.

Coordinated Transit for the San Francsico Bay Area—Now to 1975. Final Report of the Northern California Transit Demonstration Project, prepared by Simpson and Curtin, Transportation Engineers, Philadelphia and San Francisco, October 1967.

Crosstown Line 9—An Evaluation of a New Route. FASTRIP. Sacramento Transit Authority: Interim Technical Report No. 8, January 1971.

Dashaveyor People Mover. Ann Arbor, Mich.: Transportation Systems Marketing, Bendix Corp., 1972.

Demand-Responsive Transportation Systems (Special Report 136). Washington, D.C.: Highway Research Board, 1973.

A Demographic Procedure for Bus Route Design. Federally assisted Sacramento Transit Research and Improvement Project (FASTRIP), Interim Technical Report No. 5 (CAL-MTD-10 [CA-06-0028]), October 1970.

Downtown Loop Bus Program. Cleveland Transportation Action Program, Report No. 2, October 1970.

Dueker, Kenneth J. and James Stone. *Final Report: Mass Transit Technical Study.* Iowa City: University of Iowa, Institute of Urban and Regional Research, September 1971.

————. *Iowa City Transit Revival* (Technical Report No. 3). Iowa City: University of Iowa, Institute of Urban and Regional Research, January 1972.

Eastern Railroad Problems: The Serious Situation and Its Causes. Jersey City, N.J.: Eastern Railroad Presidents Conference, October 1961.

An Evaluation of Free Transit Service. (N.T.I.S. No. PB 179845). Cambridge, Mass.: Charles River Associates, August 1968.

Federal Register, September 24, 1973, pp.26624–26625.

Final Report, FASTRIP. Sacramento Transit Authority. (Undated).

Final Report, Test and Demonstration of Automatic Train Control for San Francisco Bay Area Rapid Transit District. San Francisco: Westinghouse Electric Corp. (part of CAL-MTD-2 [CA-06-0021]), June 1966.

Forecast of Urban 40-Foot Coach Demand, 1972–1990, Summary Report, prepared by Simpson and Curtin Co. for Transbus Program, Booz Allen Applied Research, under UMTA Contract No. DOT-UT-10008, December 1972.

Go: Toronto's Transportation Triumph. Madison, N.J.: Board of Public Transportation of Morris County, 1968.

Government Expenditures for Construction, Operation, and Maintenance of Transport Facilities by Air, Highway, and Waterway and Private Expenditures for Construction, Maintenance of Way, and Taxes of Railroad Facilities. Washington, D.C.: Association of American Railroads, Bureau of Railway Economics, March 1965.

Hammond, D.G. "The BART Demonstration Programs." Paper for presentation at the Transportation Demonstration Projects Conference, Washington, D.C., November 19–20, 1969, Capital Section of the American Society of Civil Engineers and the U.S. Department of Transportation.

Heenan, G. Warren. "The Influence of Rapid Transit on Real Estate Values in Metropolitan Toronto." Address delivered before a joint meeting of the Cleveland Real Estate Board and the Cleveland Chamber of Commerce, November 25, 1966; mimeographed and distributed by the Institute for Rapid Transit, November 29, 1966.

Highway Research Board. *Demand-Actuated Transportation Systems* (Special Report 124). Washington, D.C.: National Research Council, 1971.

Highway Research Board, *New Transportation Systems and Technology* (Highway Research Record No. 397), Washington, D.C.: National Research Council, 1972.

Highways, Safety and Transit: An Analysis of the Federal-Aid Highway Act of 1973. Washington, D.C.: Highway Users Federation for Safety and Mobility, 1973.

Hoover, Edgar M. *Motor Metropolis: Some Observations on Urban Transportation* (Reprint No. 2). Pittsburgh, Pa.: University of Pittsburgh, Center for Regional Economic Studies, 1966.

Immediate Action Program (Interim Report No. 1). Prepared by Simpson and Curtin Co. for Broward County (Florida) Transportation Authority, November 1971.

Implementation of Transit Improvements (Interim Report No. 7). Prepared by Simpson and Curtin Co. for the Twin Cities Area Metropolitan Transit Commission, St. Paul, Minn. 1971.

The J. & L. Story: A Manpower/Transportation Demonstration Project (CTAP Report No. 1). Cleveland Transportation Action Program, September 1970.

Job Accessibility for the Unemployed: An Analysis of Public Transportation in Chicago. Chicago Committee for Economics and Cultural Development, March 1972.

Lawrence, David G. *The Politics of Innovation in Urban Mass Transportation Policymaking: The New Systems Failure.* Washington, D.C.: Urban Transportation Center, Consortium of Universities, Spring 1970.

Manchester Rapid Transit Study, commissioned jointly by the Corporation of Manchester, Ministry of Transport, in association with British Railways, Vol. 1, September 1967; Vol. 2, August 1967; Vol. 3, November 1968.

Mass Transit Management: A Handbook for Small Cities (IND-MTD-1 [IN-06-0002]). (N.T.I.S. No. PB 222386). Bloomington: Indiana University, Institute for Urban Transportation, February 1971.

A Master Plan for Transportation. Trenton, N.J.: State Department of Transportation, 1972.

Metro Hospital Bus Demonstration Project (CTAP Report No. 3), Cleveland Transportation Action Program, November 1970.

Metro Memo, Issue No. 40 (July/August 1972), Washington, D.C.: Washington Metropolitan Area Transportation Authority.

Morgantown PRT Control System. Ann Arbor, Mich.: Transportation Systems Marketing, Bendix Corp., 1972.

Operating Guidelines and Standards for the Mass Transportation Assistance Program. Harrisburg: Bureau of Mass Transit Systems, Pennsylvania Department of Transportation, January 1973.

Optimisation of Bus Operations in Urban Areas. Paris: Organisation for Economic Co-Operation and Development, May 1972.

Paine, Frank, Alan Nash, Stanley Hille, and Alan Brunner. *Consumer Conceived Attributes of Transportation.* College Park: University of Maryland, Department of Business Administration, June 1967.

Plan and Program 1955. Urban Traffic and Transportation Board, City of Philadelphia, April 1956. (Conclusions and Recommendations of the Board —Report of Staff to the Board).

The Preliminary Report (October 1967) and *Final Report* (May 1968), Los Angeles: Southern California Rapid Transit District.

Proposed Regional Transportation Plan. Berkeley, Cal.: Metropolitan Transportation Commission, June 1, 1973.

Public Transportation Research Needs (Special Report 137). Washington, D.C.: Highway Research Board, 1973.

Questions and Answers from PAT. Pittsburgh, Pa.: Port Authority of Allegheny County, August 20, 1969.

"Rapid Transit Service to Cleveland Hopkins International Airport," Speech by Gaspare A. Cossco, Member of the Board, Cleveland Transit System, to Annual Meeting of American Transit Association, September 15–18, 1968. Cleveland Transit System, 1968.

San Francisco Bay Area Rapid Transit District Linear Parkway. San Francisco: B.A.R.T.D., May 1968.

SEPACT I: Commuter Rail Service Improvements for a Metropolitan Area (June 1971); *SEPACT II: Final Report: A Study of the 1975 Commuter Railroad System in the Southeastern Pennsylvania Metropolitan Region* (January 1971); *SEPACT III: Final Report: Operation Reading* (June 1971), Philadelphia: Southeastern Pennsylvania Transportation Authority.

Sloan, Anthony R. and John W. Baltteau. *Reestablishing the Link: A Study of the Commuter Rail Station.* Philadelphia: Southeastern Pennsylvania Transportation Authority, January 1970.

Solomon, Richard J. and Arthur Saltzman. *History of Transit and Innovative Systems.* Cambridge, Mass.: M.I.T. Urban Systems Laboratory, USL TR-70-20, March 1971.

Solomon, Richard J. and Joseph S. Silien. *Modes of Transportation.* New York: Urban Transportation Research Council, American Society of Civil Engineers, Sources of Information on Urban Transportation, Report No. 2, August 1968.

Southward Transit Area Coordination Study. Chicago: Southward Transit Area Coordinating Committee, 1971.

"Speech and Discussion by Dr. William Ronan," Chairman of the Board of the Metropolitan Transit Authority of New York at the Annual Meeting of the Ohio Public Transit Association. Cincinnati, August 28, 1972.

Statistics of Railroad Passenger Service. Washington, D.C.: Association of American Railroads, Bureau of Railway Economics, October 1966.

Studying Transportation from a Consumer Viewpoint. College Park: University of Maryland, Department of Business Administration, September 1967.

Subsidies and Reimbursements for 1971. Washington, D.C.: American Transit Association, March 1972.

Tomlinson, Graham. *Rides, Trips and Moves on a Bus* (Interim Technical Report No. 6, CAL-MTD-6). Sacramento, Calif.: Transit Authority, December 1970.

Transit Information Aids, Final Report. Washington, D.C.: Washington Metropolitan Area Transit Commission INT-MTD-10 (IT-06-0013), 1971.

Transit Option for the Twin Cities Metropolitan Region. Minneapolis: Twin Cities Area Metropolitan Transit Commission, January 1971.

Transport Technical Trends. Washington, D.C.: Transportation Association of America, October 1970.

Transportation and Aging: Selected Issues. Based on proceedings of the Interdisciplinary Workshop on Transportation and Aging, May 24–26, 1970. Washington, D.C.: U.S. Government Printing Office.

Transportation Needs of the Handicapped: Travel Barriers. Prepared for the Department of Transportation, Office of Economics and Systems Analysis, by Abt Associates, Inc. Cambridge, Mass.: Clearinghouse for Federal Scientific and Technical Information (PB 187327), August 1969.

Urffer, Richard T. *The First 22 Minutes.* Philadelphia: Port Authority Transit Corporation, Delaware River Port Authority, 1969.

U.S., Bureau of Public Roads. *Modal Split Documentation of Nine Methods for Estimating Transit Usage,* by M.J. Fertal, E. Weiner, A.J. Balek, and A.F. Sevin. Washington, D.C., 1967.

U.S., Congress. Law 88-365 (88th Congress, 2d session).

————. Public Law 91-190, 83 Stat. 852, 42. U.S.C. 4321-47.

————. *Housing Act of 1949,* Section 103(b) amended by Section 303 of the Housing Act of 1961.

U.S., *Congressional Record.* 89th Congress, 2d session, Vol. 112, August 15, 1966, pp.18576–18577, and August 16, 1966, pp.18712–18740; 91st Congress, 2d session, September 29, 1970, pp.H 9349, H 9350–9351, H 9359.

U.S., Department of Commerce. *Federal Transportation Policy and Program.* Washington, D.C.: U.S. Government Printing Office, March 14, 1960.

————. *A Five Year Market Forecast for Commuter Railroad Cars.* Washington, D.C.: Business and Defense Services Administration, 1966.

————. *Statistical Abstract of the United States.* 92nd Annual Edition, Washington, D.C.: Bureau of the Census, 1971.

————. *Rationale of Federal Transportation Policy,* by E. W. Williams and David Bluestone. Washington, D.C.: U.S. Government Printing Office, 1960.

U.S., Department of Housing and Urban Development. *Tomorrow's Transportation: New Systems for the Urban Future.* Washington, D.C.: Office of Metropolitan Development, Urban Mass Transportation Administration, May 1968.

U.S., Department of Transportation. *Capital Grants for Urban Mass Transportation: Information for Applicants.* Washington, D.C.: Urban Mass Transportation Administration, June 1972.

————. "Control of Highway Related Noise," pp.42–44 in *Highway and Urban Mass Transportation.* Issued jointly by the Federal Highway Administration and Urban Mass Transportation Administration, Washington, D.C., Summer 1972.

————. *Directory of Research, Development and Demonstration Projects* (through June 30, 1970), Washington, D.C.: Urban Mass Transportation Administration, 1970.

————. Institute for Defense Analysis, *Economic Characteristics of the Urban Public Transportation Industry.* Prepared for U.S. Department of Transportation, Assistant Secretary for Policy and International Affairs, Office of Systems Analysis and Information. Washington, D.C.: U.S. Government Printing Office, February 1972.

————. *Low Cost Urban Transportation Alternatives: A Study of Ways to Increase the Effectiveness of Existing Transportation Facilities; Executive Summary;* Vol. I, *Results of a Survey and Analysis of Twenty-One Low Cost Techniques;* Vol. II, *Results of Case Studies and Analysis of Busway Applications in the United States,* all prepared by P. R. Pratt Associates for Office of Urban Transportation Systems, Assistant Secretary for Policy, Plans and International Affairs, Washington, D.C., January 1973.

————. "Major Mass Transportation Related Provisions of the Federal Aid Highway Act of 1973," Department of Transportation News Release, UMTA 73-90.

————. *1972 National Transportation Report: Present Status—Future Alternatives,* Washington, D.C., July 1972.

————. *Research, Development and Demonstration Projects.* Washington, D.C.: Urban Mass Transportation Administration, June 30, 1972.

————. *Study and Evaluation of Local Transit Regulation and Regulatory Bodies* (Part I, No. PB 211077, Part II, No. PB 211078). Prepared by R.L. Banks & Associates. Springfield, Va.: National Technical Information Service, 1972.

U.S., Executive Office of the President, Bureau of the Budget. *Standard Metropolitan Statistical Areas.* Washington, D.C.: U.S. Government Printing Office, 1961.

U.S., Federal Electric Railway Commission. *Proceedings of the Federal Electric Railway Commission,* Vol. 3. Washington, D.C.: U.S. Government Printing Office, 1920.

U.S., House. H.R. 18185. 91st Congress, 2nd session.

————. *Department of Transportation and Related Agencies Appropriations for 1973.* Hearings before a Subcommittee of the Committee on Appropriations, (92d Congress, 2d session, Part 2), Washington, D.C.: U.S. Government Printing Office, 1972.

————. *EPA Pollution Regulations and Fuel Shortage: The Impact on Mass Transit.* Hearings before the Subcommittee on Urban Mass Transportation of the Committee on Banking and Currency, 93rd Congress, 1st session, July 26, 30, 31, 1973.

————. Committee on Banking and Currency. House Report No. 1487 Accompanying H.R. 14810, 89th Congress, 2d session, May 9, 1966.

————. *Reorganization Plan No. 2, 1968, for Transportation,* 90th Congress, 2d session, House Document No. 262. Washington, D.C.: U.S. Government Printing Office, February 26, 1968.

————. *Report to the President on Urban Transportation Organization by the Department of Housing and Urban Development and the Department of Transportation,* 90th Congress, 2d session, House Document No. 251, Washington, D.C.: U.S. Government Printing Office, March 13, 1968.

————. *Transportation Information, A Report to the Committee on Appropriations,* U.S. House of Representatives from the Secretary of Transportation, May, 1969.

————. *The Transportation System of Our Nation.* Message from the President of the United States, 87th Congress, 2d session, House Document No. 384.

————. *Urban Mass Transportation.* Hearing before the Subcommittee on Housing of the Committee on Banking and Currency, 92d Congress, 2d session, on Providing Financial Assistance for the Operating Expenses of Urban Mass Transportation, February 23, 1972. Washington, D.C.: U.S. Government Printing Office, 1972.

————. *Urban Mass Transportation Act of 1962.* Hearings before a Subcommittee on Banking and Currency, 87th Congress, 2d session on H.R. 11158, Washington, D.C.: U.S. Government Printing Office, 1962.

U.S., Interstate Commerce Commission. *75th Annual Report of the Interstate Commerce Commission* (fiscal year ended June 30, 1961). Washington, D.C.: U.S. Government Printing Office, 1961.

U.S., Senate. Hearings Before the Committee on Commerce, 87th Congress, 2d session on S. 3615, September 17, 18, 19, 20, 1962.

————. *National Transportation Policy,* Preliminary Draft of a Report Prepared by the Social Study Group on Transportation Policy for the United States, Senate Committee on Interstate and Foreign Commerce, 87th Congress, 1st session, January 3, 1961.

————. *Report on Regulatory Agencies to the President-Elect,* by James M. Landis, submitted by the Chairman of the Subcommittee on Administrative Practice and Procedure to the Committee on the Judiciary, 86th Congress, 2d session, Washington, D.C.: U.S. Government Printing Office, 1960.

————. *Older Americans and Transportation: A Crisis in Mobility,* a report by the Special Committee on Aging, 91st Congress, 2d session, Report No. 91-1520, Washington, D.C.: U.S. Government Printing Office, December 1970.

————. S. 2599, Bill to Amend the Urban Mass Transportation Act of 1964, 89th Congress, 1st session, October 5, 1965.

————. Senate Report No. 1436, Committee on Banking and Currency, 89th Congress, 2d session, August 8, 1966.

————. *American Ground Transport: A Proposal for Restructuring the Automobile, Truck, Bus, and Rail Industries,* by Bradford Snell, presented to the Subcommittee on Antitrust and Monopoly of the Committee on the Judiciary, 93d Congress, 2d session, February 26, 1974, Washington, D.C.: U.S. Government Printing Office, 1974.

————. *Urban Mass Transportation—1962.* Hearings before a Subcommittee of the Committee on Banking and Currency, 87th Congress, 2d session, on Bills to Authorize the Housing and Home Finance Agency to Provide Additional Assistance for the Development of Mass Transportation Systems, and for Other Purposes, April 24, 25, 26, 27, 1962.

User Determined Attributes of Ideal Transportation Systems. College Park: University of Maryland, Department of Business Administration, December 1965.

Vuchic, Vukan R. *Light Rail Transit Systems: A Definition and Evaluation.* (No. PB 213447), Springfield, Va.: National Technical Information Service, October 1972.

Notes

Introduction

1. Wilfred Owen, *The Metropolitan Transportation Problem* (Washington, D.C.: Brookings Institution, 1966), p.4.

Chapter One: The Urban Transportation Crisis and the Growing Role of Federal Government

1. Executive Office of the President, Bureau of the Budget, *Standard Metropolitan Statistical Areas* (Washington, D.C.: U.S. Government Printing Office, 1961), pp.1, 2. The criteria used for establishing SMSA's are detailed on pp.3–5. See also *Statistical Abstract of the United States,* 92d ed. (Washington, D.C.: U.S. Department of Commerce, Bureau of the Census, 1971), pp.2, 16, 17, 829.

2. Wilfred Owen, *The Metropolitan Transportation Problem* (Washington, D.C.: Brookings Institution, 1966), pp.5, 6.

3. Some interesting thoughts on urban population shifts and the need for improved mass transportation to meet the needs of rapidly growing suburban areas may be found in two articles by Thomas Conway, Jr., "1950–1960 Population Shift Poses Transportation Problem," *Traffic Quarterly* 15, 1 (January 1961), 62; and "Rapid Transit Must Be Improved to Alleviate Traffic Congestion," *Traffic Quarterly* 16, 1 (January 1962), 103. A convenient and valuable compilation of statistics and other information on urban transportation may be found in *1972 National Transportation Report: Present Status—Future Alternatives* (Washington, D.C.: U.S., Department of Transportation, 1972), 42–59, 185–254.

4. See Lewis M. Schneider, *Marketing Urban Mass Transit* (Boston: Harvard University Graduate School of Business Administration, Division of Research, 1965), esp. pp.33–34; and George M. Smerk, "Federal Urban Transport Policy: Here—and Where Do We Go From Here?" *Traffic Quarterly* 21, 1 (January 1967), 47–50.

5. For a more complete coverage of this decline see Lyle C. Fitch and Associates, *Urban Transportation and Public Policy* (San Francisco: Chandler, 1964), pp.37–54; Wilfred Owen, *The Metropolitan Transportation Problem,* rev. ed. (Washington, D.C.: Brookings Institution, 1956), ch. 3; and George M. Smerk, *Urban Transportation: The Federal Role* (Bloomington: Indiana University Press, 1965), pp.43–54.

6. For more detailed information on federal highway policy see William J. Hudson and James A. Constantin, *Motor Transportation* (New York:

Ronald Press, 1958), ch. 4; Charles A. Taff, *Commercial Motor Transportation* (Homewood, Ill.: Irwin, 1955), ch. 2; Charles L. Dearing, *American Highway Policy* (Washington, D.C.: Brookings Institution, 1941); and Smerk, ch. 6.

7. See *Modernizing Local Government* (New York: Committee for Economic Development, 1966) for a most interesting analysis of the problem. This study suggests a strengthening of county government as a means of better serving metropolitan area needs. See also Bruce T. Barkley, "Problem Solving in Urban Transportation," *Traffic Quarterly* 27, 4 (October 1973), 491–502.

8. See, for example, Jameson W. Doig, *Metropolitan Transportation Politics and the New York Region* (New York: Columbia University Press, 1966), pp.42–43, 96, 146–148.

9. For a more complete discussion of fragmentation see Michael N. Danielson, "Suburbia: Remedialism and Localism," ch. 4 in *Federal-Metropolitan Politics and the Commuter Crisis* (New York: Columbia University Press, 1965); Lyle Fitch and Associates, *Urban Transportation and Public Policy* (San Francisco: Chandler, 1964), pp.15–18; and ch. 5, "The Role of Government in Urban Affairs," in Smerk, pp.82–118, esp. pp.99–100.

10. A most interesting and enlightening book on this subject is R. Joseph Manson and Mark W. Cannon, *The Makers of Public Policy: American Power Groups and Their Ideologies* (New York: McGraw-Hill, 1965), esp. pp.1–23.

11. The most valuable and complete source of information on the events leading up to the beginning of federal participation in urban mass transportation programs is to be found in Michael Danielson's excellent study *Federal-Metropolitan Politics and the Commuter Crisis* (New York: Columbia University Press, 1965). Much of what follows is indebted to Danielson's work for its thought and spirit.

12. As a patron of the mass transport system in Philadelphia from the late 1930's to the early 1950's, the author can testify that some of the subway and commuter railroad equipment appeared to match Independence Hall in antiquity if not in charm. Facetiousness aside, Philadelphia probably did enjoy better public transport services that most other American cities. Even so, it was an uphill battle against the automobile as the move to the suburbs began in earnest after World War II.

13. City of Philadelphia, Urban Traffic and Transportation Board, *Plan and Program 1955* (Conclusions and Recommendations of the Board—Report of Staff to the Board), April 1956; and Danielson, pp.95–96.

14. See *The Composite Report, Bay Area Rapid Transit, May, 1962* (San Francisco: Bay Area Rapid Transit District, 1962).

15. For a few examples, see Fitch, pp.52–54.

16. The exact losses from passenger operations are a debatable issue. The $723.7 million figure represents the result of the ICC's method of fully apportioned costs. On the basis of solely related costs the deficit for 1957 was in the neighborhood of $114 million. In either case the losses involved

were hardly a matter to delight the railroads. See 306 ICC 419–425, 486 (ICC Docket No. 31954, May 18, 1959, *Railroad Passenger Train Deficit*); Association of American Railroads, Bureau of Railway Economics, *Statistics of Railroad Passenger Service* (Washington, D.C., October 1966), p.9; and *Avoidable Costs of Passenger Train Service* (Cambridge, Mass.: Aeronautical Research Foundation, September 1957).

17. Public Law 85-625, 85th Congress. For a brief recapitulation of the contents of this act, see D. Philip Locklin, *Economics of Transportation*, 6th ed. (Homewood, Ill.: Irwin, 1966), pp.254–258. For a more complete discussion, see George Hilton, *The Transportation Act of 1958* (Bloomington: Indiana University Press, 1969).

18. *75th Annual Report of the Interstate Commerce Commission for Fiscal Year Ended June 30, 1961* (Washington, D.C.: U.S. Government Printing Office), p. 72.

19. See, for example, Finance Docket No. 20443, Lehigh Valley Railroad Company Discontinuance of Service, All Passenger Operations, 307 ICC 239, 307 ICC 257, 312 ICC 399; Finance Docket No. 20606, Pennsylvania Railroad Company Discontinuance of Passenger Service between Trenton and Red Bank, N.J., 317 ICC 5; Finance Docket No. 20671, New Jersey & New York Railroad Company (Horace Banta Trustee) Discontinuance of Service from Hoboken, N.J., to Spring Valley, N.Y., 307 ICC 532; Finance Docket No. 20524, New York Central Railroad Company Discontinuance of Service, St. Lawrence Division, 312 ICC 4; and Finance Docket No. 20731, Pennsylvania Railroad Co. Discontinuance of Service between Camden and Trenton, N.J., 312 ICC 167.

20. Danielson, pp.47–52. See also Doig, esp. ch. 9; and Alan Altshuler, "The Politics of Urban Mass Transportation," mimeographed paper delivered at the annual meeting of the American Political Science Association, Sept. 4–7, 1963, pp. 16–21.

21. For more information on the Passenger Service Improvement Corporation of Philadelphia see *IRT News Letter*, 3, 2 (March 30, 1962), published by the Institute for Rapid Transit. Concerning activities in the New Jersey and New York area see Doig, chs. 8 and 9, and John E. Debout and Ronald J. Grele, *Where Cities Meet: The Urbanization of New Jersey* (Princeton, N.J.: Van Nostrand, 1964), pp.73–74.

22. U.S., Department of Commerce, *Federal Transportation Policy and Program* (Washington, D.C.: U.S. Government Printing Office, March 14, 1960).

23. The text of Williams' letter of transmittal, dated April 14, 1960, addressed to the Secretary of Commerce, is of interest:

"Transmitted herewith is a report, 'Rationale of Federal Transportation Policy,' which is supplemental to the report you recently released on 'Federal Transportation Policy and Program.'

"The attached report reflects the considered views of your Study Staff, arrived at after careful attention to the underlying reports of consultants and contractors as well as such other information as was available. Of course, it should be clearly understood that this report is the sole responsibility of the authors, and should in no way be construed as being attributable to you or the Department of Commerce.

"However, I feel that it may be helpful to have publicly available a somewhat simplified statement of the staff thinking on such conclusions as your report, necessarily very brief, has adopted."

From Ernest W. Williams, Jr., and David W. Bluestone, *Rationale of Federal Transportation Policy* (Washington, D.C.: U.S. Department of Commerce, U.S. Government Printing Office, 1969), p.iii.

24. Ibid., pp.52–54.

25. Danielson, pp.25–27.

26. See Smerk, pp.99–113.

27. For a more detailed treatment of this analysis, see Danielson, ch. 10, esp. pp.183–189.

28. Ibid., pp.101–103.

29. *The Collapse of Commuter Service* (Washington, D.C.: American Municipal Association, 1959), p.2.

30. Ibid., p.3.

31. Danielson, pp.104–105.

32. For example, the panel discussion on transport problems in large cities moderated by Dilworth, despite his efforts, constantly strayed from the rail issue. See "Better Urban Transportation," *Proceedings of the American Municipal Congress 1959* (Washington, D.C.: American Municipal Association).

33. See Altshuler, pp.27–28.

34. Danielson, pp.111–113.

35. Ibid., p.116.

36. Ibid., pp.129–133.

37. *Proceedings of the American Municipal Congress 1959*, p.24.

38. For an excellent summary of the work behind the various highway measures prior to 1970, especially the 1956 Act, see Vera Hirschberg, "CPR Report/Forces Gather for Stormy Debate over Highways with Trust Fund as Lightning Rod," *National Journal*, June 6, 1970, pp.1193–1207, esp. pp. 1194–1199.

39. For an interesting appraisal and analysis of the initial entrance of the federal government onto the urban scene, see Charles Abrams, *The City Is the Frontier* (New York: Harper & Row, 1965), pp.238–249.

40. Indeed, the criticism has been leveled that federal programs have often been far more beneficial to private business than to the general public.

41. *The Transportation System of Our Nation*, Message from the President of the United States, 87th Congress, 2d session, House of Representatives Document No. 384, 1962, pp.9 and 10.

42. James M. Landis, *Report on Regulatory Agencies to the President-Elect*, submitted by the Chairman of the Subcommittee on Administrative Practice and Procedure to the Committee on the Judiciary of the United

States Senate, 86th Congress, 2d session (Washington, D.C.: U.S. Government Printing Office, 1960).

43. U.S., Senate Committee on Interstate and Foreign Commerce, *National Transportation Policy, Preliminary Draft of a Report Prepared by the Special Study Group on Transportation Policy for the United States,* 87th Congress, 1st session, January 3, 1961, pp.552–635.

44. For a highly interesting account of the fortunes of the mass transportation program in the early days of the New Frontier, see Danielson, pp. 155–174.

45. Robert C. Weaver, "The Federal Interest in Urban Mass Transportation," *Traffic Quarterly* 17, 1 (January 1963), pp.25, 29.

46. For example, see *Urban Mass Transportation Act of 1962: Hearings before Subcommittee No. 3 of the Committee on Banking and Currency,* House of Representatives, 87th Congress, 2d session on H.R. 11158 (Washington, D.C.: U.S. Government Printing Office, 1962), pp.517–522.

47. See Smerk, pp.170–171, and ArDee Ames, "An End to Highway Aid," in *A Look at Urban Transportation* (Washington, D.C.: National League of Cities, 1966), pp.1–4.

48. The author is acquainted with a graduate city-planner who was unable to find a good job in his profession just before the Highway Act of 1962 was enacted. Shortly thereafter he had a half-dozen excellent offers, including one from the Bureau of Public Roads.

49. T. J. Kent, Jr., *The Urban General Plan* (San Francisco: Chandler, 1964), p.33.

50. Ibid., pp.40–43.

51. Abrams, pp.215–218.

52. See Section 103 (b) of the Housing Act of 1949 as amended by Section 303 of the Housing Act of 1961.

53. John C. Kohl, "The Federal Urban Transportation Demonstration Program," *Traffic Quarterly* 18, 3 (July 1964), p.303.

54. Danielson, p.176.

55. *The Transportation System of Our Nation,* p.10. The president's recommendations were based on a program of action advocated by Secretary of Commerce Hodges and HHFA Administrator Weaver as a result of a study prepared for them by the Institute of Public Administration. See Fitch, chs. 6, 7; and Danielson, pp.174–175.

56. See Altshuler, pp.38–39.

57. See *Urban Mass Transportation—1962, Hearings before a Subcommittee of the Committee on Banking and Currency,* U.S., Senate, 87th Congress, 2d session, *on Bills to Authorize the Housing and Home Finance Agency to Provide Additional Assistance for the Development of Mass Transportation Systems, and for Other Purposes,* April 24, 25, 26, and 27, 1962, esp. pp.397–403, 314–319, 273–281, 308–314. See also *Urban Mass Transportation Act of 1962;* Altshuler, pp.39–40; and Danielson, p.177.

58. See *Hearings Before the Committee on Commerce,* U.S., Senate, 87th Congress, 2d session on S. 3615, September 17–20, 1962. The senator

seemed particularly intrigued by the testimony of Dr. Leon Moses of Northwestern University (see pp.37–51). Also see Altshuler, p.41.

59. Altshuler, p.41.

60. Altshuler, pp.43–51.

61. Victor Gruen, "Needed: A Prompt End to the Old Luxury of Limited Thinking," *Architectural Forum* (October 1963), p.94.

62. An interesting treatment of the events leading up to the 1964 act, including division in the ranks of the transit and commuter rail industries and the role of the Urban Passenger Transportation Association, may be found in Lewis M. Schneider, "Urban Mass Transportation: A Survey of the Decision-Making Process," in *The Study of Policy Formation,* ed. R.A. Bauer and Kenneth J. Green (New York: Free Press, 1968), pp.254–266.

63. Mel Brdlik, "A Legislative Miracle," *Metropolitan Management, Transportation, and Planning* 60, 5 (September 1964), pp.26 and 50; and Vincent J. Burke, "The Tangled Path of a Transit Bill," *The Reporter,* July 16, 1964.

64. "The Administrator, on the basis of engineering studies, studies of economic feasibility, and data showing the nature and extent of expected utilization of the facilities and equipment, shall estimate what portion of the cost of a project to be assisted under Section 3 cannot be reasonably financed from revenues—which portion shall hereinafter be called 'net project cost.'" From Section 4 (a) of the Urban Mass Transportation Act of 1964.

65. The Urban Mass Transportation Administration hoped to end the "emergency" program on June 30, 1972, and provide only the full two-thirds (now 80 per cent) federal money "long-range" grants. Time will tell if this can be done.

66. Public Law 88-365, 88th Congress, 2d session, especially Appendix D; also see "At Last: Congress Approves Transit Aid," *Railway Age,* July 6, 1964, pp.28–29; "Analysis of the New Federal Urban Transportation Act" (Chicago: Institute for Rapid Transit, July 1964, mimeo); and George M. Smerk, "The Urban Mass Transportation Act of 1964: New Hope for American Cities," *Transportation Journal* 5, 2 (Winter 1965), 37–38.

67. *Government Expenditures for Construction, Operation, and Maintenance of Transport Facilities by Air, Highway, and Waterway and Private Expenditures for Construction, Maintenance of Way, and Taxes of Railroad Facilities* (Washington, D.C.: Association of American Railroads, Bureau of Railway Economics, March 1965), p.4. It was estimated that total expenditures of all levels of government for transportation would be $28,285,000,000 in 1973. Since records have been kept, all levels of U.S. government have spent $425,951,599,486 on transportation: ibid., May 1973, p.2 and table 1.

68. Railway commuter service on a large-scale basis is offered in Boston, New York, Philadelphia, and Chicago. More modest commuter services are to be found in Washington, D.C., Baltimore, San Francisco, Pittsburgh, and a few others. More detailed coverage of commuter railroad service may be found in Chapter 3.

69. See George M. Smerk, "The 'Hardware' Gap in Urban Transport," *Business Horizons* 9, 1 (Spring 1966), 5–16. Also see the excellent monograph by Vukan R. Vuchic, *Light Rail Transit System: A Definition and Evaluation* (Springfield, Va.: National Technical Information Service, October 1972), PB 213 447.

70. For some estimates of the amount of money needed in the time period under discussion, see Fitch, pp.55–57; "Mass Transport: A $10 Billion Market," *Railway Age*, February 18, 1963, p.25; *IRT News Letter* 7, 7 (December 1966) contains a most interesting review of transit developments in the preceding year; for some prognostication of the cities where rapid transit is a distinct possibility, see "Mapping Transit's Future: All Eyes Focus on Pittsburgh," *Railway Age*, January 24, 1966, pp.18–19.

71. Syracuse, N.Y., for example, was unable to match an approved federal grant of demonstration funds. On June 30, 1964, $185,353 was approved for use by that city, provided a matching sum of $92,657 was forthcoming. Syracuse could not find the money and the demonstration was cancelled in January 1965.

72. See Evan Herbert, "Transporting People," *International Science and Technology*, October 1965, pp.30–42.

73. *S. #2599, a Bill to Amend the Urban Mass Transportation Act of 1964 to Provide for Additional Technological Research*, 89th Congress, 1st session, October 5, 1965. This bill was introduced again in the next session of Congress.

74. Senate Report No. 1436 (Committee on Banking and Currency), 89th Congress, 2d session, August 8, 1966.

75. See House Report No. 1487 accompanying H.R. 14810 (Committee on Banking and Currency), 89th Congress, 2d session, May 9, 1966.

76. Ibid., p.10.

77. Ibid., p.5.

78. Ibid., pp.15–16.

79. *Congressional Record* 112, 89th Congress, 2d session, August 15, 1966, pp.18576–18577.

80. Ibid., p.18582.

81. Ibid., p.18585.

82. Ibid., August 16, 1966, pp.18712–18740.

83. Ibid.

84. David G. Lawrence, *The Politics of Innovation in Urban Mass Transportation Policymaking: The New Systems Example* (Washington, D.C.: Urban Transportation Center, Consortium of Universities, Spring 1970), pp.3–4.

85. Ibid., pp.7–8, 10–11.

86. Ibid., p.12, 14–16.

87. Ibid., p.21.

88. Ibid., pp.22–25.

89. Ibid., pp.25–34.

90. The findings from the studies were summarized in *Tomorrow's Transportation: New Systems for the Urban Future* (Washington, D.C.: U.S., Department of Housing and Urban Development, Office of Metropolitan Development, 1968).

91. A good example of the adverse criticism may be found in the paper by Senator Gordon Allott, "Urban Transit: Paper or Progress," delivered at the Third International Conference on Urban Transportation, Pittsburgh, 1968 (reprinted by the WABCO Mass Transit Center, Westinghouse Air Brake Co., Pittsburgh).

92. Lawrence, pp.42–44.

93. *Reorganization Plan No. 2, 1968, for Transportation,* 90th Congress, 2d session, House Document No. 262 (Washington, D.C.: U.S. Government Printing Office, February 26, 1968).

94. *Report to the President on Urban Transportation Organization by the Department of Housing and Urban Development and the Department of Transportation,* 90th Congress, 2d session, House Document No. 281 (Washington, D.C.: U.S. Government Printing Office, March 13, 1968), p.4.

95. *Hearing Before a Subcommittee of the Committee on Government Operations: Reorganization Plan No. 2 of 1968 (Urban Mass Transportation),* 90th Congress, 2d session (Washington, D.C.: U.S. Government Printing Office, April 22, 1968), esp. pp.14–17.

96. "Agreement between the Secretary of the Department of Housing and Urban Development and the Secretary of the Department of Transportation" (mimeographed document signed by the Secretary of Housing and Urban Development, Robert Weaver, on September 9, 1968, and by Transportation Secretary Alan Boyd on September 10, 1968). For commentary on the agreement, see "On the Washington Scene," *Metropolitan* 24, 6 (November/December 1968), 28, 30.

97. Senator Williams' bill was S. 1032, which in an amended version eventually became the Mass Transportation Act of 1970. See *Passenger Transport,* February 21, 1969 and March 21, 1969, for comment on the introduction of the legislation.

98. See *Passenger Transport,* August 15, 1969, p.1; and, for almost unalloyed gloom, *Metropolitan 65, 5* (September/October, 1969), 36.

99. See "On the Washington Scene," *Metropolitan* 65, 5 (September/October, 1969), 36.

100. See "Villarreal Answers Questions about Nixon's Public Transportation Bill," *Passenger Transport,* September 12, 1969, p.1.

101. See "Williams Named Man of the Year," *Passenger Transport,* October 10, 1969, pp.1–2.

102. "On the Washington Scene," *Metropolitan* 66, 1 (January/February, 1970), 29. This was changed in the final bill (H.R. 18185, 91st Congress, 2d session) in Section 4c, to read as follows: ". . . not to exceed $80,000,000 prior to July 1, 1971, which amount may be increased to not exceed an aggregate of $310,000,000 prior to July 1, 1972, not to exceed an aggregate of $710,000,000 prior to July 1, 1973, not to exceed an aggregate of $1,260,-

000,000 prior to July 1, 1974, not to exceed an aggregate of $1,860,000,000 prior to July 1, 1975, and not to exceed an aggregate of $3,100,000,000, thereafter."

103. See "On the Washington Scene," *Metropolitan* 65, 6 (November/December, 1969), 44.

104. "House Adds a Transit Panel," *Passenger Transport,* March 16, 1973, pp.1, 6.

105. See John Burby, *The Great American Motion Sickness* (Boston: Little, Brown, 1971), pp.234–235. Also, see William Lilley III, "Urban Report: Urban Interests Win Transist Bill with 'Letter-Perfect' Lobbying," *National Journal,* September 19, 1970, pp.2021–2029, for a penetrating analysis of what it takes to get legislation through the Congress.

106. See " 'Damnedest Coalition' Fights for Transit Aid Bill Passage," *Passenger Transport,* July 3, 1970, pp.4–5.

107. See "Senate Passes Transit Aid Bill," *Passenger Transport,* February 6, 1970, pp.1, 6; "Bill Passes!" *Passenger Transport,* October 2, 1970, pp.1–7, 10–12; and "President Nixon Signs Transit Aid Bill," *Passenger Transport,* October 16, 1970, p.1.

108. *Congressional Record,* 91st Congress, 2d session, September 29, 1970, p. H 9349.

109. Ibid., pp.H 9350–9351.

110. Ibid., p.H 9359.

111. For accounts of the activity, see: "Cochran Leads Industry Support for Senate Bill 870," *Passenger Transport,* April 9, 1971, pp.1, 7; "ATA Asks Senate to Raise Transit's '72 Funding Level," *Passenger Transport,* July 16, 1971, pp.1, 3; " '. . . A Harder Look at Transit'—Blatnik," and "Congress Okays $900 Million for Transit," *Passenger Transport,* August 6, 1971, pp.1, 4, 5; "Industry Calls for Operating Aid at Senate Hearings," *Passenger Transport,* February 4, 1972, pp.1, 4, 5; "Senate OKs Operating Aid," *Passenger Transport,* March 3, 1972, pp.1, 7; "Volpe Urges Transit Aid from Highway Trust Fund," *Passenger Transport,* March 17, 1972, p.1; "Administration Fails to Back Operating Aid," *Passenger Transport,* June 16, 1971, p.1; "Transit and the Trust Fund: Senate Panel Reports Bill," *Passenger Transport,* July 28, 1972, pp.1, 4; "Lack of Quorum Kills Transit Aid," *Passenger Transport,* October 27, 1972, pp.1, 5. Also, see *IRT Digest,* Special Issue, Annual Conference 1972, pp.4–10, 15–19; and "92d Congress Kills Federal Aid Bill," *IRT Digest,* No. 14, November/December 1972, pp. 2–6; "Nixon: Transit Is High Priority," *Passenger Transport,* February 23, 1973, p.1, and "Nixon Urges Rail Use of Trust Fund," *Passenger Transport,* March 16, 1973, p.6.

112. See "Anderson Re-Introduces Trust Fund Bill," *Passenger Transport,* January 12, 1973, pp.1, 5; "Williams Introduces Transit Bill," *Passenger Transport,* January 19, 1973, p.3; "St. Germain Offers Transit Aid Bill," and "Muskie Bill Would Open Trust Fund," *Passenger Transport,* January 26, 1973, pp.1, 4; "Senate Holds Hearings on S.386: DOT Head Fails to Back Operating Aid; Industry Says Williams Bill Is Essential," *Passenger Transport,*

February 9, 1973, pp.1, 4, 6; and the following bills introduced in the Senate and House in the first session of the 93rd Congress: S.386, S.502, S.885, H.R.576, H.R.991, H.R.2734. The Senate hearings on the Highway Act of 1973 (which is essentially S.502, as amended) are most informative. The dedicated reader might be particularly interested in the following portions: Testimony and discussion by Secretary of Transportation Claude Brinegar, pp.95–123; testimony and discussion by William D. Ruckelshaus, director, Environmental Protection Agency, pp.565–620; testimony of pro-highway advocates, pp.135–181, 351–371, and 520–535; and testimony of U.S. Conference of Mayors/National League of Cities, pp.671–701.

113. See "Senate Passes Landmark Transit Aid Legislation," *Passenger Transport,* March 16, 1973, pp.1, 8; "Where Does Transit Stand?" *Passenger Transport,* April 6, 1973, pp.1, 2; and "House Says 'No' to Anderson, 'Yes' to Three Other Proposals," *Passenger Transport,* April 20, 1973, p.3.

114. "Conferees Agree to Expand Use of Highway Trust Fund to Transit," *Passenger Transport,* July 27, 1973, pp.1, 5.

115. "What the Highway Act Will Do for Mass Transit," *Railway Age,* October 8, 1973, p.34.

116. The Highway Act of 1973 is a long and complex piece of legislation, so much so that definitive statements on it will not really be possible until it has been in effect for some time. The major portion of the final Highway Act, which is Public Law 93-87, is derived from S.502, 93rd Congress, 1st session, as amended. Important sections of the act are as follows: Urban System Flexibility, Section 121; Interstate Transfer, Section 137; Earmarking of Urban System Funds, Section 157; Urban Planning Funds, Section 112; UMTA Amendments, Section 301; Bicycle Transportation, Section 124; Provisions for the Elderly and Handicapped, Sections 165b, 140, and 301g. Also see *Highways, Safety and Transit: An Analysis of the Federal-Aid Highway Act of 1973* (Washington, D.C.: Highways Users Federation for Safety and Mobility, 1973); "Federal Action: S. 502 Becomes a Law," *IRT Digest,* No. 18 (September/October 1973), 1–10; "What the Highway Act Will Do for Mass Transit," pp.34, 35; R.M.M. McConnell, "Watching Washington: Mass Transit and the Handicapped," p.16; "Highway Act of 1973: What's in It for Mass Transit," *Passenger Transport,* August 10, 1973, pp.4, 5; "Major Mass Transportation Related Provisions of the Federal Aid Highway Act of 1973," Department of Transportation News Release, UMTA 73–90.

117. *IRT Digest,* No. 18, September/October 1973, p.8.

118. Ibid., p.9.

119. See "Administration Plan Would Allow Operating Aid," *Passenger Transport,* January 25, 1974, p.1; "UTAP: Administration Plan Set," *Passenger Transport,* February 8, 1974, pp.1, 3; and "UTAP: 'One Hand Giveth, and One Hand Taketh Away,' " *Railway Age,* March 11, 1974, p.24.

Chapter Two: Mass Transportation: Pro and Con

1. D.J. Reynolds in a review of *Urban Mass Transit Planning,* ed. Wolfgang Homburger (Berkeley and Los Angeles: University of California, Insti-

tute of Transportation and Traffic Engineering, 1968). The review appeared in the *Journal of Transport Economics and Policy* (London School of Economics) 2, 2 (May 1968), 250–251.

2. For example, see "More Transit Funding Sought: Volpe Urges Additional $3 Billion," *Passenger Transport,* September 8, 1972, pp.1, 4.

3. For an example of the classic opposition to mass transportation, see the position of the U.S. Chamber of Commerce in *Urban Mass Transportation Act of 1962,* Hearings before Subcommittee No. 3 of the Committee on Banking and Currency, U.S., House of Representatives, 87th Congress, 2d session on H.R. 11158 (Washington, D.C.: U.S. Government Printing Office, 1962), pp.581–608.

4. See "Governor Gives Green Light to Transit in Massachusetts," and "People First Plan: Transit—The New Way to Go in Ontario," *Passenger Transport,* December 8, 1972, pp.1, 4, 5. For the full text of Governor Sargent's speech see "The Governor's Transportation Program," *Rollsign* 9, 11 (November 1972), 1–3. Also see Alan Lupo, Frank Colcord, and Edmund P. Fowler, *Rites of Way: The Politics of Transportation in Boston and the U.S. City* (Boston: Little, Brown, 1971).

5. See, for example, John Burby, *The Great American Motion Sickness* (Boston: Little, Brown, 1971), pp.124–126.

6. One of the best reviews of rail versus highway positions can be found in Edgar M. Hoover, *Motor Metropolis: Some Observations on Urban Transportation in America* (Pittsburgh: University of Pittsburgh, Center for Regional Economic Studies, 1966), Reprint No. 2.

7. In this century the United States has experienced the tightly-knit, clustered city created by public transportation in the last half of the nineteenth century and the spread-out city created—in part—by the automobile. In all honesty, neither form seems to be much of a bargain, as both were executed as products of speculative enterprise aiming at the fast dollar rather than any sort of lasting value. Whether or not we can do better in the future is a matter to ponder. For an interesting treatment of the subject of urban sprawl, see Jean Gottmann and Robert A. Harper, *Metropolis on the Move* (New York: John Wiley, 1967).

8. For a penetrating investigation into some of the fruits of the spirit of privatism in the United States, see Sam Bass Warner, Jr., *The Private City: Philadelphia in Three Periods of Its Growth* (Philadelphia: University of Pennsylvania Press, 1968).

9. Wilfred Owen has written often and eloquently on this point. See, for example, *The Metropolitan Transportation Problem* (Washington, D.C.: Brookings Institution, 1966), chs. 7, 8; *A Fable: How the Cities Solved Their Transportation Problems* (Washington, D.C.: Urban-America, Inc., 1967); and *The Accessible City* (Washington, D.C.: Brookings Institution, 1972).

10. In *The City in History* (New York: Harcourt, Brace and World, 1961, pp.505–506), Lewis Mumford cogently sums up how dependence upon the automobile spawns still more dependence, until the automobile becomes a kind of snare.

11. *Department of Transportation and Related Agencies Appropriations for 1973, Hearings before a Subcommittee of the Committee on Appropriations,* House of Representatives, 92d Congress, 2d session, Part 2, (hereinafter referred to as *Appropriations Hearings—1973*) (Washington, D.C.: U.S. Government Printing Office, 1972, pp.591–592; see also pp.600, 671, 696, 883; *Older Americans and Transportation: A Crisis in Mobility, A Report by the Special Committee on Aging,* U.S., Senate, 91st Congress, 2d session, Rept. No. 91-1520 (Washington, D.C.: U.S. Government Printing Office, December 1970); *Transportation and Aging: Selected Issues,* based on proceedings of the Interdisciplinary Workshop on Transportation and Aging, Washington, D.C., May 24–26, 1970, sponsored by U.S. Department of Health, Education and Welfare, U.S. Department of Transportation, and U.S. Department of Housing and Urban Development (Washington, D.C.: U.S. Government Printing Office, DHEW Publication No. [SRS] 72-20232, 1971); *Transportation Needs of the Handicapped: Travel Barriers,* prepared for the Department of Transportation Office of Economics and Systems Analysis by Abt Associates, Inc., Cambridge, Mass., August 1969 (Clearinghouse for Federal Scientific and Technical Information, PB 187 327); and Lester A. Hoel et al., *Latent Demand for Urban Transportation* (Pittsburgh: Carnegie-Melon University, Transportation Research Institute, TRI Research Report No. 2, 1968).

12. See *Transportation and Parking for Tomorrow's Cities* (New Haven, Conn.: Wilbur Smith and Associates, 1966).

13. P.H. Bendtsen, *Town and Traffic in the Motor Age* (Copenhagen: Danish Technical Press, 1961), p.8.

14. *Transportation and Parking for Tomorrow's Cities,* p.69.

15. Ibid., p.59.

16. See, for example, the section on facilitating bus transit in Gordon Sessions, *Getting the Most from City Streets* (Washington, D.C.: Highway Research Board, 1967), pp.31–33.

17. See G. Warren Heenan, "The Influence of Rapid Transit on Real Estate Values in Metropolitan Toronto," address delivered before a joint meeting of the Cleveland Real Estate Board and the Cleveland Chamber of Commerce, November 25, 1966, mimeographed and distributed by the Institute for Rapid Transit, November 29, 1966. See also Mitchell Gordon, *Sick Cities* (Baltimore: Penguin Books, 1966), pp.48–49; "Private Investments Nearly as Much as Subway Costs," *IRT News Letter* (Institute for Rapid Transit, Washington, D.C.), 10, 2 (April 1969), pp.27–28; and B.R. Staher, "How San Francisco Is Solving the Transportation and Traffic Problem," *Going Places* (General Electric Transit Systems Department, Erie, Pa.) Fourth Quarter, 1970, pp.10–11.

18. One of the more vigorous indictments of wanton highway building may be found in Richard J. Whalen's "The American Highway: Do We Know Where We're Going?" *Saturday Evening Post,* December 14, 1968. See also "The War over Urban Expressways," *Business Week,* March 11, 1967, pp.94–103; and "San Franciscans Fight for That Cable Car Charm,"

Business Week, September 4, 1971, p.64; John Burby, *The Great American Motion Sickness* (Boston: Little, Brown, 1971), pp.94–96.

19. Public Law 91-190, 83 Stat. 852, 42 U.S.C. 4321–4327.

20. See Mitchell Gordon, *Sick Cities,* ch. 3; "Federal Environmental Legislation and Regulation as Affecting Highways," *Research Results Digest,* No. 25 (National Cooperative Highway Research Program), January 1971; "Control of Highway Related Noise," *Highway and Urban Mass Transportation* (Washington, D.C.: U.S. Department of Transportation, issued jointly by the Federal Highway Administration and the Urban Mass Transportation Administration, Summer 1972), pp.42–44; and William V. Shannon, "The Highwaymen," a syndicated column of the *New York Times,* appearing in the Bloomington, Ind. *Herald-Telephone,* September 18, 1972, p.8.

21. See, for example, Meyer, Kain, and Wohl, *The Urban Transportation Problem* (Cambridge: Harvard University Press, 1965), p.80; and *Transportation and Parking for Tomorrow's Cities,* pp.84–88.

22. Warner, pp.205–208.

23. Ibid. Warner points out that the transit improvements of the 1920's were only marginally beneficial to the city and the downtown, and that the money could probably have been better spent on education, public health, unemployment relief, etc. Of course, the long-range benefits of the past transit investment may be considerably higher.

24. See, for example, Wilfred Owen, *The Accessible City* (Washington, D.C.: Brookings Institution, 1972); and Regional Plan Association, *Urban Design Manhattan* (New York: Viking Press, 1969), esp. chs. 4, 5.

25. See Lawrence Haworth, *The Good City* (Bloomington: Indiana University Press, Midland Books, 1966), pp.19–38, 44–45, 54–57.

26. Some of the most literate and interesting arguments in favor of improved mass transportation may be found in Denton Beal (ed.), *Leland Hazard on Transportation* (Pittsburgh, Pa.: Carnegie-Mellon University, Transportation Research Institute, Research Report No. 4, 1969).

27. On this latter point see Herbert J. Gans, *People and Plans: Essays on Urban Problems and Solutions* (New York: Basic Books, 1968), chs. 11, 12.

28. "A Word to the Thrifty," *Passenger Transport,* August 11, 1972, p.1.

29. See "Exhibit" to *Eastern Railroad Problems: The Serious Situation and Its Causes,* Jersey City, N.J., Eastern Railroad Presidents Conference, Oct. 1961, p.89. This indicates that rail passenger crewmen in the New York suburban zone received 56.6 per cent of their time paid while actually off duty.

30. John M. Leavens, Jr., *The Cost of Commuter Transportation,* a thesis presented to the faculty of the Graduate School of Business Administration, New York University, in partial fulfillment of the requirements for the degree of Master of Business Administration, 1968.

31. The difficulty of putting values on nonpecuniary factors is one of the principal headaches of benefit-cost analysis. See, for example: G.H. Peters, *Cost-Benefit Analysis and Public Expenditure* [Eaton Paper 8] (London: Institute of Economic Affairs, 1966); C.D. Foster and M.E. Beesley, "The

Victoria Line," in *Transport,* ed. Denys Munby (Harmondsworth, Middlesex, England: Penguin Books, Penguin Modern Economics, 1968), pp.223–243; George M. Smerk, *Urban Transportation: The Federal Role* (Bloomington: Indiana University Press, 1965), pp.235–243; Tillo E. Kuhn, *Public Enterprise Economics and Transportation Problems* (Berkeley and Los Angeles: University of California Press, 1962).

32. See Mayer, Kain, and Wohl, *The Urban Transportation Problem,* esp. chs. 8, 9, 10, 11.

33. Ibid., pp.243–249. See also Wilbur Smith and Associates, *The Potential for Bus Rapid Transit* (Detroit, Mich.: Automobile Manufacturers Association, February 1970).

34. Ibid., pp.299–306.

35. *IRT Newsletter* (Institute for Rapid Transit, Chicago), 4, 3 (August 15, 1963), Appendix A, "An Evaluation of a Report Entitled Technology and Urban Transportation."

36. Clive Entwistle, "Roads to Ruin," *The New York Times Book Review,* September 4, 1966, pp.3, 22–23. Oddly enough, when the Association of American Railroads reproduced this review for distribution, in a format somewhat reduced in size from the original, the photo cut which was left in showed an empty rail line rather than a jammed highway; the original showed both.

37. Leavens, p.21. Leavens refers to Meyer, Kain, and Wohl, p.218.

38. Entwistle, p.22.

39. See Armando M. Lago, "United States Subway Requirements 1968–1990: Projections and Benefits," *Traffic Quartery* 23, 1 (January 1969), 79–88, esp. 79. Lago notes the problem of reaching firm conclusions on the basis of the Meyer, Kain, and Wohl analysis because of the understandable lack of information available on critical points. He also notes that cities may pursue plans for rapid transit systems, even where density is low, not just for the purposes of prestige, but also to revitalize downtown areas.

40. See, for example, Kenneth R. Schneider, *Autokind vs. Mankind* (New York: N. W. Norton, 1971), esp. chs. 1–4; and John Burby, *The Great American Motion Sickness,* ch. 3.

41. James Madison Hunnicutt, Jr., "Parking Conceptions and Misconceptions," in *Downtown Action on Traffic—Parking—Transit,* ed. Laurence A. Alexander and James J. Bliss (New York: National Retail Merchants Association, 1965), p.50.

42. For something of this flavor see John R. Meyer, "Knocking Down the Straw Men," in Benjamin Chinitz, *City and Suburb: The Economics of Metropolitan Growth* (Englewood Cliffs, N.J.: Prentice-Hall, 1964), pp. 85–93.

43. For an interesting treatment of not only amenities but also the sociology of the bus, see Graham Tomlinson, *Rides, Trips and Moves on a Bus,* Interim Technical Report No. 6 (CAL-MTD-6), Sacramento (California) Transit Authority, December 1970; also see Robert Gutman, "Urban Trans-

ports as Human Environment," *The Journal of the Franklin Institute* 286, 5 (November 1968, Special Issue on New Concepts in Urban Transportation Systems), pp.533–539, esp. pp.536–537.

44. On the problem of seating comfort in public passenger vehicles see *Urban Rapid Transit: Concepts and Evolution* (Pittsburgh: Carnegie-Mellon Institute, Transportation Research Institute, Research Report No. 1, 1968), pp.9–29. For more comment on vehicle comfort see George M. Smerk, "The 'Hardware' Gap in Urban Transport," *Business Horizons* 9, 1 (Spring 1966), pp.10–12.

45. On attempts to design more attractive transit vehicles see Burby, p.148.

46. A capsule view of the level of decreptitude achieved by some properties can be gained by a review of Exhibit C of the capital grant application of the Rochester-Genesee Regional Transportation Authority (NY-UTG-37). The wall of a sadly outdated garage was expected to collapse soon. For the problems of commuter railway stations, see Anthony R. Sloan and John W. Baltteau, *Reestablishing the Link: A Study of the Commuter Rail Station* (Philadelphia: Southeastern Pennsylvania Transportation Authority, January 1970).

47. Some examples of the quality of modern facilities design may be found in "On the Right Track," *Monsanto Magazine* 47, 1 (March 1967), pp.16–20; *San Francisco Bay Area Rapid Transit District Linear Parkway* (San Francisco: B.A.R.T.D., May 1968); and *Metro Memo* No. 40, July-August 1972, illustrates throughout the care taken in design in the Washington Metropolitan Area Transit Commission's rapid transit venture.

48. Almost every weekly issue of *Passenger Transport* (Washington, D.C., American Transit Association) from 1968 through 1970 reported one or more cities switching to the "Ready-fare Plan."

49. See, for example, "Center City Transportation," *Nation's Cities* 8, 2 (February 1970), pp.9–32, esp. p.27.

50. See *'71–'72 Transit Fact Book* (Washington, D.C.: American Transit Association, 1972), table 5, p.8.

51. Eric Schenker and John Wilson, "The Use of Public Mass Transportation in the Major Metropolitan Areas of the United States," *Land Economics* 43, 3 (August 1967), pp.361–367. See also *Transportation and Parking for Tomorrow's Cities,* ch. 5; and Walter Y. Oi and Paul W. Shuldiner, *An Analysis of Urban Travel Demands* (Evanston, Ill.: Northwestern University Press, 1962), esp. chs. 4, 5, 6.

52. See "The U.S.' Lopsided Transportation Budget," *Forbes Magazine,* October 1, 1968.

53. For information on the Cleveland system see "The Cleveland Rapid," *IRT News Letter* (Institute for Rapid Transit) 2, 5 (November 15, 1961), 1; "CTS is Ten Years Old," *Going Places* (Erie, Pa.: General Electric Co., Third Quarter 1965), p.4; "Rapid Transit Service to Cleveland Hopkins International Airport," (speech by Gaspare A. Cosse, Member of the Board, Cleveland Transit System, to Annual Meeting of American Transit Associa-

tion, September 15–18, 1968, Cleveland Transit System, 1968. Parking and mass transportation thinking are combined in Toronto, Canada; see *GO: Toronto's Transportation Triumph* (Madison, N.J.: Board of Public Transportation, Morris County, N.J., 1968).

54. See *Low Cost Urban Transportation Alternatives: A Study of Ways to Increase the Effectiveness of Existing Transportation Facilities; Executive Summary;* Vol. I, *Results of a Survey and Analysis of Twenty-One Low Cost Techniques;* Vol. II, *Results of Case Studies and Analysis of Busway Applications in the United States,* all prepared by R.H. Pratt Associates for Office of Urban Transportation Systems, Assistant Secretary for Policy, Plans and International Affairs, U.S. Department of Transportation, Washington, D.C., January 1973.

55. See Meyer, Kain, and Wohl, chs. 2, 3; John R. Meyer, "Urban Transportation Problems: Knocking Down the Straw Men." The interested reader might also examine pp.32–41 for Chinitz's own comments: *Transportation and Parking in Tomorrow's Cities,* pp.9–21, 347.

56. Proceedings of the Federal Electric Railway Commission, Washington, D.C., U.S. Government Printing Office, 1920, Vol. 3, pp.2156–2157, 2262.

57. For changes in apartment house starts see *Transportation and Parking for Tomorrow's Cities,* pp. 31–33. For an interesting discussion of the background to the prevailing desire for the single-family home on a fairly large plot of ground, see Steen Eiler Rasmussen, *London: The Unique City* (Cambridge: M.I.T. Press, 1967, first Danish Edition 1934, first English Edition 1937), ch. 4, esp. pp.70–71.

58. For a coverage of the Swedish method, see *Technical Description of the Stockholm Underground Railway: 1964* (Stockholm: Stockholm Passenger Transport Company, 1965), ch. 1. See also Victor Gruen, *The Heart of Our Cities* (New York: Simon and Schuster, 1964), pp.286–287; and the *Preliminary Report* (October 1967) and *Final Report* (May 1968) of the Southern California Rapid Transit District, calling for and justifying a rail rapid transit system for Los Angeles.

59. See Philip Johnson, "Why We Want Our Cities Ugly," in *The Futures of Man's Environment,* Smithsonian Annual II (Washington, D.C.: Smithsonian Institution Press, 1968).

60. See, for example, Nathan Cherniak, "A Statement of the Urban Passenger Transportation Problem," *Urban Transportation Planning: Concepts and Application* (Washington, D.C.: Highway Research Board, Bulletin 293, 1961), pp.21–29, and the discussion by J.W. McDonald on p.31.

61. See Bruce E. Thorp, "Transportation Report/House Resists Senate Plan to Use Road Funds for Urban Transit," *National Journal,* September 9, 1972, pp.1437–1443, esp. 1442, 1443; and William Lilley III, "Urban Report/Mayors and White House Prepare for Battle Over $40 Billion Subway Program for 1970's," *National Journal,* March 18, 1972, pp.484–492.

62. "The U.S.' Lopsided Transportation Budget."

Chapter Three: Urban Mass Transportation: The Institutions

1. By the Institute for Defense Analysis, prepared for the U.S., Department of Transportation, Assistant Secretary for Policy and International Affairs, Office of Systems Analysis and Information, February 1972 (Washington, D.C.: U.S. Government Printing Office). See pp.2-1 and 8-1 to 8-31.

2. For a general history of transit, see John Anderson Miller, *Fares, Please!* (New York: Dover, 1960). Also see Blake McKelvey, *The Urbanization of America 1860–1915* (New Brunswick, N.J.: Rutgers University Press, 1963), pp.75–85; and George Rogers Taylor, "The Beginnings of Mass Transportation in Urban America," *The Smithsonian Journal of History, Part I* 1, 2 (Summer 1966), 35–50, and *Part II* 1, 3 (Autumn 1966), 31–54; George M. Smerk, "The Streetcar: Shaper of American Cities," *Traffic Quarterly* 21, 4 (October 1967), 569–584; John B. Roe, "The Evolution of the Motor Bus as a Transport Mode," *High Speed Ground Transportation Journal* 5 (Summer 1971), 221–235; and George W. Hilton, "Rail Transit and the Pattern of Modern Cities: The California Case," *Traffic Quarterly* 21, 3 (July 1967), 379–393.

3. Frank H. Mossman, ed., *Principles of Urban Transportation* (Cleveland: The Press of Western Reserve University, 1951). See the article, "The Organization of the Transit Company," by Willits H. Sawyer, pp.77–90.

4. Sad to say, no comprehensive study has been written on this period of mass transportation history. Those interested in the subject must piece together information from a variety of sources. One of the most interesting is Burton J. Hendrick, "Great American Fortunes and Their Making," *McClure's Magazine* 30 (1907–1908), 33–48, 236–250, 323–338. The Chicago activities of Charles Tyson Yerkes—Theodore Dreiser's "Tycoon"—are touched upon throughout Ray Ginger's *Altgeld's America* (New York: Funk & Wagnalls, 1958). The finagling for operating rights in New York City is covered in Harry James Carman, *The Street Surface Railway Franchises of New York City* (New York: Columbia University Press, Studies in History, Economics and Public Law, Volume 88, No. 1, 1919). See also, Julius Grodinsky, *Jay Gould: His Business Career* (Philadelphia: University of Pennsylvania Press, 1957), ch. 15; Blake McKelvey, *The Urbanization of America*, ch. 5; Emerson P. Schmidt, *Industrial Relations in Urban Transportation* (Minneapolis: University of Minnesota Press, 1937), ch. 2; and Mark D. Hirsch, *William C. Whitney: Modern Warwick* (New York: Dodd, Mead, 1948), chs. 15, 17. The unhappy state of the industry is covered at great length in the three-volume *Report of the Federal Electric Railway Commission* (Washington, D.C.: U.S. Government Printing Office, 1920).

5. The twenties were, in terms of patronage, the golden age of mass transportation. According to available statistics, mass transit ridership reached its peak in 1926, when 17,243,000,000 passengers were hauled. The trend has been downward ever since with the exception of the wartime and immediate postwar period. In 1946 an all-time high total of 23,372,000,000 pas-

sengers were moved by transit. The decline of industry patronage in more recent years will be detailed subsequently. For patronage figures from 1922 to 1948, see Frank H. Mossman, p.8.

6. Much of the information in this section was derived from a highly valuable monograph by Richard J. Solomon and Arthur Saltzman, entitled *History of Transit and Innovative Systems* (Cambridge, Mass.: M.I.T. Urban Systems Laboratory, USL TR-70-20, March 1971). Also see United States v. National City Lines, Inc. et al., 186 F2d. 562, p.565; and Bradford C. Snell, *American Ground Transport: A Proposal for Restructuring the Automobile, Truck, Bus, and Rail Industries,* presented to the Subcommittee on Antitrust and Monopoly of the Committee on the Judiciary, United States Senate, 93rd Congress, 2d session, February 26, 1974 (Washington, D.C.: U.S. Government Printing Office, 1974).

7. A recent, though not complete, listing of publicly owned transit operations, revealed the following:

City Department	75
State Department	1
Regional Authority	43
Regional Taxing District	8
Total	127

The regional authority and regional taxing district have gained in popularity since 1960. See *Immediate Action Program, Broward County (Florida) Transportation Authority,* prepared by Simpson and Curtin, Interim Report No. 1, November 1971, Table 11.

8. See Ray A. Mundy and John C. Spychalski, *Managerial Resources and Personnel Practices in Urban Mass Transportation* (University Park: Pennsylvania State University, Transportation and Traffic Safety Center, November 1973).

9. All figures are from the *'72–'73 Transit Fact Book* (Washington, D.C.: American Transit Association, 1973), p.3.

10. Frank H. Mossman, p.10.

11. See *Subsidies and Reimbursements for 1971* (Washington, D.C.: American Transit Association, March 1972).

12. "Transit Riders Coming Back," *Passenger Transport,* September 7, 1973, pp.1, 2; and "Transit Ridership Continues Dramatic Rise," *Passenger Transport,* March 1, 1974, pp.1, 5.

13. Transit statistics are dominated by New York City. In the mid-sixties New York accounted for about 32 per cent of all transit ridership. See John B. Roe, p.227.

14. For an old but interesting comment on productivity in urban transportation see Harold Bayer, *The Transportation Industries—1889–1946: A Study of Output, Employment and Productivity* (New York: National Bureau of Economic Research, 1951), ch. 5.

15. *'72–'73 Transit Fact Book,* p.11.

16. See '71–'72 *Transit Fack Book,* p.1. All through 1972, *Passenger Transport,* the newspaper of the transit industry, stressed the fare stabilization theme. For example, see the eight-part special report on fare stabilization beginning in *Passenger Transport* January 7, 1972, through February 25, 1972.

17. See '71–'72 *Transit Fact Book,* p.20. Just how large the motor bus fleet may be is subject to some doubt. Some observers claim that the base fleet consists of about 20,000 vehicles. Extra coaches to meet peak demands may swell this to an operating pool totalling some 35,000 vehicles. The figures generally used by the American Transit Association—that is, about 50,000 buses—may reflect the old practice of the industry: rates of return based on the investment in rolling stock. A large bus fleet, even if only partially operational, kept the rate base up. See Langhorne Bond and Richard Solomon, *The Promise and Problems of High Capacity Buses in the United States* (Pittsburgh: National Transportation Center, 1971), note 9 to section 3. As part of the UMTA Transbus program, Simpson & Curtin did a survey of the present transit coach fleet and forecasted demand up to 1990. They estimated that there were 43,800 transit buses of all sizes in the United States as of June 1972. They predicted a net increase in the fleet of 40-ft. buses of 22,950 by 1990, bringing the number of large buses up to 52,850, but they made no estimate of the number of smaller coaches that would be needed by 1990. See especially Tables IV and X in *Forecast of Urban 40-Foot Coach Demand, 1972–1990, Summary Report* by Simpson & Curtin for Transbus Program, Booz Allen Applied Research. Prepared under UMTA Contract No. DOT-UT-10008, December 1972. There are few good statistics available in the transit field; the ATA figures depend entirely on the cooperation of individual properties and not all firms are ATA members. See also *Economic Characteristics of the Urban Public Transportation Industry* for its interesting investigation of the transit industry.

18. The streetcar and trolleybus waned in popularity in the days of private ownership in transit because of the fixed costs associated with the railway fixed structure and with power distribution systems, a burden the diesel-powered bus was happily free of. The rise of public ownership and public subsidy, along with mounting concern over air pollution, has increased the appeal of electrically propelled vehicles. As light rapid transit, the streetcar may return to provide a higher quality of service and greater capacity than is possible with the motor bus, without the great expense of construction of heavy rapid transit. See Vukan R. Vuchic, *Light Rail Transit Systems: A Definition and Evaluation* (Springfield, Va.: National Technical Information Service, October 1972), PB-213 447.

19. The Long Island Railroad is an exception, usually earning the lion's share of its revenues from its commuter services. Commuters also loom large in the total business of the Chicago, South Shore, & South Bend Railroad.

20. *Economic Characteristics of the Urban Public Transportation Industry,* p.7-5.

21. Ibid., p.7-3.

22. These tables are presented for information only. They are as accurate as possible, considering the difficulties in deriving information from the data available. The interested reader should consult the material on commuter railroads in *Economic Characteristics of the Urban Public Transportation Industry*. The authors of that work readily admit to the shortcomings of their information, but it is about the best available. To point up the sad state of affairs relative to commuter railroad statistics, there is not even a uniform definition of passenger traffic!

23. See *A Five Year Market Forecast for Commuter Railroad Cars* (Washington, D.C.: U.S. Department of Commerce, Business and Defense Services Administration, 1966). The tables on pp.15 and 17 reveal the antiquity of equipment. Guesstimates and prognostications on the need and the level of replacement are published about once a year by *Railway Age*. The *City-by-City Directory of Urban Rail Systems* distributed by the General Electric Company provides interesting information on commuter rail, rapid transit and light rapid transit facilities and equipment; possible equipment needs and line extensions are cited.

24. See *SEPACT I: Commuter Railroad Service Improvements for a Metropolitan Area*, April 1, 1969; *SEPACT II Final Report: A Study of the 1975 Commuter Railroad System in the Southeastern Pennsylvania Metropolitan Region*, January 1971; and *SEPACT III Final Report: Operation Reading*, June 1971, all published by the Southeastern Pennsylvania Transportation Authority, Philadelphia.

25. See, for example, Albert L. Papp, "Why a Commuter Crisis in New Jersey," *The Journal of Business* (Seton Hall University) 4, 1 (December 1965), 24–29; Albert L. Papp, "Alleviating the Commuter Crisis," *The Journal of Business* 4, 2 (May 1966), 23–29; *A Master Plan for Transportation* (Trenton, N.J.: State Department of Transportation, 1972), ch. 6; and *Southward Transit Area Coordination Study* (Chicago: Southward Transit Area Coordinating Committee, 1971), esp. ch. 9; "New York's MTA: Light at the End of the Tunnel," *Railway Age*, April 9, 1973, pp.16–31.

26. There is no extensive literature on the subject of taxicabs. The material contained in *Economic Characteristics of the Urban Public Transportation Industry* is probably the best available in the United States at present.

27. See *Economic Characteristics of the Urban Public Transportation Industry*, table 8.1, p.8-6. In the Boston area, as an example, it is estimated that the cab companies had about $18 million in revenue in 1966—about 40 per cent of the revenues of the Massachusetts Bay Transportation Authority. See Kevin G. Barbera, "Introduction to the City of Boston Taxicab Industry," *Traffic Quarterly* 26, 2 (April 1972), p.279.

28. Ibid., p.2-36.

29. Ibid., p.2-39.

30. See Ibid., p.8-17.

31. Ibid., pp.8-19 to 8-20.

32. "Taxis Clock up Woes for the Urban Planner," *Business Week,* December 23, 1967, p.51.

33. *Economic Characteristics of the Urban Public Transportation Industry,* p.8-24.

34. Ibid., pp.2-37 to 2-38 and 8-9 to 8-14.

35. See "Taxis Clock up Woes for the Urban Planner," p.51. For innovative use of cabs, see Sandi Rosenbloom, "Taxis, Jitneys and Poverty," *Trans-Action,* February 1970, pp.47–54; Richard N. Farmer, "Whatever Happened to the Jitney?" *Traffic Quarterly* 19, 2 (April 1965), pp.263–279; and Lovett C. Peters, "Transportation in the Free Market," *Transportation Journal* 6, 2 (Winter 1967), pp.41–47. For some interesting insights into cab service in London, see Felix Kessler, "London Cab Drivers Are Polite, and They Are Safe and Honest," *Wall Street Journal,* September 8, 1972.

36. In the study conducted by the author, despite prodding, only 38 of the 50 state commissions bothered to reply. The Urban Mass Transportation Administration commissioned a study on this subject which was carried out by R.L. Banks & Associates, Washington, D.C., entitled *Study and Evaluation of Local Transit Regulations and Regulatory Bodies* (Springfield, Va.: National Technical Information Service, 1972), Part I, No. PB 211077, and Part II, No. PB 211078.

37. For a detailed discussion of state activity in urban mass transportation and associated activities, see Anthony R. Tomazinis, *The Role of the States in Urban Mass Transit* (Philadelphia: University of Pennsylvania, Transportation Studies Center for Urban Research and Experiment, July 1971). Also published is an appendix volume which gives details of the research procedures used and more complete information on the findings in the various states and cities where investigation was carried out. Also, see Norman Ashford, "The Developing Role of State Governments in Transportation," *Traffic Quarterly* 22, 4 (October 1968), pp.455–468; and James W. Bennett, Jr., and William J. DeWitt, III, "The Development of State Departments of Transportation—A Recent Organizational Phenomenon," *Transportation Journal* 12, 1 (Fall 1972), pp.5-14; David R. Miller, "New Challenges, New Institutions," *Public Administration Review* 33, 3 (May/June 1973), pp.236–242; Barry A. Brune, "Developing State DOT Organizations," and Thomas D. Larson, "Toward a More Effective State Role in Transportation," both in *Proceedings—13th Annual Meeting, Transportation Research Forum* 13, 1 (1972), pp.243–256 and 257–269, published by Richard B. Cross Co., Oxford, Ind.; and "State Departments of Transportation Directory," *IRT Digest,* March/April 1974, pp.12–21.

38. For background information on the UMTA reorganization see: "UMTA's New Thrusts: Marketing and Management," *Railway Age,* July 9, 1973, pp.46–49; "UMTA Administrator Herringer Talks of Reorganization," *IRT Digest,* Annual Conference 1973, pp.29–32; "Herringer Announces UMTA Reorganization," *Passenger Transport,* September 14, 1973, p.4; and *Federal Register,* September 24, 1973, pp.26624–26625.

39. *Appropriations Hearings—1973,* p.583.

40. The UMTA style of numbering its "activities" is used in the *Appropriations Hearings—1973,* and will be followed here. It is, of course, impossible to cover all of the past, present, and proposed activities of UMTA in the limited space available in this book. The interested reader should peruse the vast amount of information provided by UMTA in *Appropriations Hearings—1973* and *Appropriations Hearings—1974,* as well as subsequent hearings in the years to come, in order to see the full scope of federal mass transit activities.

41. *Appropriations Hearings—1973,* pp.750–751.

42. UMTA is by no means alone in this apparent attitude. Transit industry meetings give an observer the strong feeling that only that portion of the U.S. public without access to automobiles is considered in the thinking of transit leaders.

43. Some direction might be found in Lewis Schneider, "A Marketing Strategy for Transit Managers," *Traffic Quarterly* 22, 2 (April 1968), pp. 283–294; and *Optimisation of Bus Operations in Urban Areas* (Paris: Organisation for Economic Co-Operation and Development, May, 1972).

44. See Wilfred Owen, *The Accessible City* (Washington, D.C.: Brookings Institution, 1972), esp. ch. 5.

45. *Appropriations Hearings—1973,* p.764.

46. Ibid., p.764.

47. Ibid., p.780.

48. Ibid., p.781.

49. Ibid.

50. Ibid., p.795.

51. See "Request for Proposal No. DOT-UT-30012 for an UMTA Transit Marketing Program," April 24, 1973.

52. *Appropriations Hearings—*1973, p.897.

53. Ibid., pp.899–922.

54. Ibid., pp.923–926 and 965–966.

Chapter Four: The Federal Demonstration Programs

1. A letter to the author, dated September 22, 1967, from Thomas R. Floyd, Jr., acting director, Division of Demonstration Programs and Studies, U.S. Department of Housing and Urban Development, contained the following comment on demonstration grant cost-sharing policy: "The Federal share has been increased for only two kinds of projects: (1) those dealing with transportation problems of the poor; and (2) those being conducted by public/or private institutions of higher learning which are strictly research projects. Grants for regular demonstrations which involve the actual operation of a service, are still being given for two-thirds of project [cost]."

2. Issue No. PSA-5149, September 11, 1970, p.2.

3. See *Department of Transportation and Related Agencies Appropriations for 1973 Part 2;* Hearings before a Subcommittee of the Committee on

Appropriations. House of Representatives, 92d Congress, 2d session (Washington, D.C.: U.S. Government Printing Office, 1972), pp.882–883, 950 (hereinafter called *Appropriations Hearings—1973*).

4. There is always a danger of sacrificing public appeal and observable usefulness for scientific respectability or administrative neatness. Academics often fall into this trap; esoteric scribblings, ping-ponging back and forth within a narrow group of specialists may have little real benefit other than academic promotion of the authors. Even those hostels of the pragmatic, the business schools, seem to have been so bent in recent years on impressing the local economists that they have, alas! alienated the business community by churning out what appears to the businessman to be nothing more than reams of printout and doubletalk.

5. See William L. Hooper, "Transportation Demonstrations: Link between Analysis and Decision," *Proceedings—Seventh Annual Meeting, Transportation Research Forum* 7, 1 (1966), esp. pp.23–24, published by Richard B. Cross Co., Oxford, Ind.

6. For some attitudes on how effective the more than $100 million spent on research, development, and demonstrations has been, see Joe Asher, "How Are Things in Glocca Washington?" *Railway Age,* August 9, 1971, pp. 24–25.

7. Using the state-by-state listing of the projects in serial number order is perhaps the least arbitrary means of presenting the demonstration projects in some logical order. Listing by type of project—that is, service improvement, new technology, pricing, etc.—is often difficult. For example, DC-MTD-2 (DC-06-0006), often called the Washington Minibus Project, is dubbed by DOT as "Downtown Shuttle Service with Small Buses and Low Fares." This could be listed as a service experiment (downtown shuttle service), as an equipment experiment (small buses), or a pricing experiment (low fares), depending upon how one might wish to classify it. The project listing used in Appendix 2 has been utilized to point out the salient aspect or aspects of each demonstration and should by no means be considered as an exhaustive description of a project.

Those interested in securing more information on a project should always use the project number. Also, because project names are often long and cumbersome, and may not be particularly definitive, the project number provides a handy shorthand reference to a particular undertaking; they are used throughout this book in that fashion. To add a note of confusion, UMTA has recently revised its project numbers; for convenience both the old and new numbers will be given whenever possible. A printout is available from UMTA giving both old and new project numbers.

UMTA publishes a directory of these projects at infrequent—too infrequent—intervals. See U. S. Department of Transportation, *Directory of Research, Development & Demonstration Projects* (through June 30, 1970), (Washington, D.C.: Urban Mass Transportation Administration, 1970); and *Research, Development and Demonstration Projects* (Washington, D.C.: Urban Mass Transportation Administration, June 30, 1972). The dedicated researcher should look through the latest UMTA project directory for projects that are of interest or seem of value. For ongoing projects, copies of reports may be requested from whoever is carrying out the work. For completed projects, the National Technical Information Service serial number for the report is given, along with the title of the report. Publications may be acquired from NTIS at a reasonable fee, usually $3 to $10.

Two valuable new publications on UMTA projects became available in early 1973. While they do not quite cover all projects that have been funded, the capsule summaries are excellent. The publications are: *Urban Mass Transportation Abstracts* (Washington, D.C.: Urban Mass Transportation Administration, October 1972), distributed by National Technical Information Service, Springfield, Va., (PB 213212); and *Transit Research Abstracts* (Washington, D.C.: Highway Research Board, January 1973). The latter publication deals with research projects only and does not contain information on capital grants.

8. See *Traffic in Towns* [The Buchanan Report] (London: Her Majesty's Stationery Office, 1963), pp.214–219; also, see G. H. Peters, *Cost-Benefit Analysis and Public Expenditures* [Eaton Paper No. 8] (London: Institute of Economic Affairs, 1966), esp. pp.33, 34.

9. Some of the most interesting early projects involved universities: ILL-MTD-3 and 4 [not given], the University of Illinois; PA-MTD-8 (PA-06-0014), the University of Pennsylvania; OHIO-MTD-1 (OH-06-0010), Kent State University; KANS-MTD-1 (KS-06-0001), Kansas State University; and MASS-MTD-5 and 6 (MA-06-0009), M.I.T. See *Appropriations Hearings—1973*, pp.846–847.

10. See *Appropriations Hearings—1973*, pp.863–882, for a lengthy discussion of some of the R&D work funded by UMTA. For a description of the testing laboratory at Pueblo, Colorado, see "Pueblo: Test Tube for Tomorrow's Railroads," *Railway Age, September* 13, 1971, p. 38.

11. See *Highway and Urban Mass Transportation* (Washington, D.C.: U.S. Department of Transportation, Summer 1972), esp. pp. 1–8; "Transit Guide to Transpo '72," *Passenger Transport,* May 19, 1972, pp.1, 10; *Personal Rapid Transit,* ed. J. E. Angerson, J. L. Davis, W. L. Garrard, and A. L. Kornhauser (Minneapolis: University of Minnesota, Institute of Technology, April 1972); "People Mover Dedicated in Morgantown," *Passenger Transport,* October 27, 1972, pp. 1, 4; and Robert A. Burco, "International Activity in Personal Rapid Transit Development and Assessment," in *Advanced Transportation Systems and Technology* (Washington, D.C.: Highway Research Board, Highway Research Record No. 427, 1973), pp.16–25, esp. pp.19–21.

12. Michael Cafferty, "Research and Reality," *Public Transportation Research Needs* (Washington, D.C.: Highway Research Board Special Report 137, 1973), p.27.

13. See Richard J. Solomon and Arthur Saltzman, *History of Transit and Innovative Systems* (Cambridge, Mass.: M.I.T. Urban Systems Lab [USL TR-70-20] March 1971); and Bradford C. Snell, *American Ground Transport: A Proposal for Restructuring the Automobile, Truck, Bus, and Rail*

Industries, presented to the Subcommittee on Antitrust and Monopoly of the Committee on the Judiciary, U.S., Senate, 93rd Congress, 2d session, February 26, 1974 (Washington, D.C.: U.S. Government Printing Office, 1974), pp.26–38.

14. For an interesting discussion of the problems associated with the low-bid process, see P. J. Walker, "America's New Standard Tramcar," *Modern Tramways,* 36, 425 (May 1973), 150–155. For specifications of the new U. S. streetcars, see "Boston-San Francisco Trolley," *Rollsign* 9, 10 (October 1972), 2–10.

15. It should be noted, however, that some transit managers are reluctant to undertake a demonstration project because they fear public pressure will force uneconomic operations to continue after the federally supported demonstration project has ended. This attitude is probably declining, however, because of the increase in the number of subsidized and publicly owned transit properties.

16. One exception to this was project IND-MTD-1 (IN-06-0002), which developed a handbook for the management of small-scale mass transit systems: *Mass Transit Management: A Handbook for Small Cities.* Unfortunately, after initial approval of publication and distribution, UMTA chose to suppress the *Handbook* for a time because of its suggestions, addressed to local public officials, that political action should be taken to expedite receipt of grants from the federal government.

17. For some very interesting hardware demonstrations see, for example, the Westinghouse Transit Expressway in Pittsburgh (PA-MTD-2 [PA-06-0009]), the hovercraft demonstration on San Francisco Bay (CAL-MTD-3 [CA-06-0022]), and the work with the Skylounge in Los Angeles (CAL-MTD-8 [CA-06-0027]). The experiments on propulsion and train control systems in conjunction with the Bay Area Rapid Transit District in San Francisco (CAL-MTD-2, CAL-MTD-7 [CA-06-0021, CA-06-0026]) would also qualify in this category, as would the experiments with a gas-turbine propelled commuter car on the Long Island Railroad (INT-MTD-12 [IT-06-0015]). The service innovations include the Premium Special Service (subscription bus service, one might say) in Peoria, Ill. (ILL-MTD-3 and 4 [not given]), the Skokie Swift highspeed shuttle train, also in Illinois (ILL-MTD-1 [IL-06-0007]), the combination express bus-premium special service in Flint, Mich. (MICH-MTD-2), the dial-a-bus project in Haddonfield, N.J. (NJ-DMG-2 [NJ-06-0002]), and the Shirley Highway Express Bus Service (INT-MTD-23 [IT-06-0024]).

Also, see George A. Avery and James C. Echols, "The Shirley Highway Project: Achieving Effective Intergovernmental Cooperation," *Traffic Quarterly* 26, 3 (July 1972), 373–390.

18. For example, see the list of RD&D projects for the near future in *Appropriations Hearings—1973,* p.597.

19. *SEPACT II Final Report: A study of the 1975 Commuter Railroad System in the Southeastern Pennsylvania Metropolitan Region* (Philadelphia: Southeastern Pennsylvania Transportation Authority [PA-MTD-4 (PA-06-

0010)], January 1971), p.44. The interested reader should ponder pp.44–48 and ch. 3.

20. See Highway Research Board, *Demand-Actuated Transportation Systems,* Special Report 124 (Washington, D.C.: National Research Council, 1971); Highway Research Board, *New Transportation Systems and Technology,* Highway Research Record Number 397 (Washington, D.C.: National Research Council, 1972); Solomon and Saltzman, *History of Transit and Innovative Systems,* pp.3–13 to 3–16; and *Demand-Responsive Transportation Systems* (Washington, D. C.: Highway Research Board Special Report 136, 1973).

21. See, for example, *A Demographic Procedure for Bus Route Design,* Federally Assisted Sacramento Transit Research and Improvement Project (FASTRIP), Interim Technical Report No. 5 (CAL-MTD-10 [CA-06-0028]), October 1970, p.30; *Final Report* FASTRIP (undated), p.7; *Crosstown Line 9—An Evaluation of a New Route,* FASTRIP, Interim Technical Report No. 8, January 1971, pp.59, 60; *Demand-Actuated Transportation Systems,* p.81; and John R. Meyer, John F. Kain, and Martin Wohl, *The Urban Transportation Problem* (Cambridge: Harvard University Press, 1965), pp.141–142.

22. Experiments involving the use of parking as an important factor include those conducted in Boston (MASS-MTD-1 [MA-06-0007]), Chicago's Skokie Swift (ILL-MTD-1 [IL-06-0007]), and New Brunswick, N.J., (INT-MTD-1 [IT-06-0007]). Express bus studies were included in demonstrations in Baltimore (MD-MTD-1 [MD-06-0004]), Nashville (TENN-MTD-2 and 3 [not given]), the Norfolk area of Virginia (VA-MTD-1 [VA-06-0004]), and the St. Louis area (INT-MTD-8 [IT-06-0014]). Also, see *SEPACT II* Final Report, pp.57–59.

23. Cafferty, p.29.

24. Because of considerable unhappiness, politically expressed, the Pittsburgh installation has been stalled. For details of what was proposed and what has happened, see *Allegheny County Rapid Transit; Questions and Answers from PAT* (Pittsburgh: Port Authority of Allegheny County, 1969); PAT News Release, August 20, 1969; *Appropriations Hearings—1973,* pp. 681, 715–772, 774–777, 869–873; "Skybus Land Buying Banned," *Pittsburgh Press,* August 20, 1972, p.1; "Down but Not Out," *Pittsburgh Press,* July 26, 1972, p. 26. For Morgantown see *Appropriations Hearings—1973,* pp.681, 715, 869–870. Also, see *Transit Option for the Twin Cities Metropolitan Region* (Minneapolis: Twin Cities Area Metropolitan Transit Commission, January 1971), esp. pp.14–25; and "DOT Picks Denver for PRT Test," *Passenger Transport,* October 27, 1972, p.5 For a quick rundown of many of the new approaches to urban mass transportation, see *Transport Technical Trends* (Washington, D.C.: Transportation Association of America, October 1970), pp.48–53; "Klein Points Out PRT Shortcomings," *IRT Digest,* Special Issue, Annual Conference 1973, pp.36–39; and "The Escalating Cost of a People Mover," *Business Week,* March 16, 1974, pp.50–52.

25. See *Final Report, Test and Demonstration of Automatic Train Control for San Francisco Bay Area Rapid Transit District* (San Francisco: Parsons-Brinckerhoff-Tudor-Bechtel, prepared by Westinghouse Electric Corporation as part of CAL-MTD-2 [CA-06-0021], June 1966). One of the best recapitulations of the work done at the BART test track may be found in D. G. Hammond, *The BART Demonstration Programs,* paper presented at the Transportation Demonstration Projects Conference, Washington, D.C., November 19–20, 1969, sponsored by the Technical Council on Urban Transportation, the National Capital Section of the American Society of Civil Engineers, and the U. S. Department of Transportation.

26. In particular, see *SEPACT III Final Report: Operation Reading,* pp. 29, 50.

27. See the Summary sections of *Final Report SEPACT II* and *Final Report SEPACT III.*

28. *Transit Information Aids,* Final Report (Washington, D.C.: Washington Metropolitan Area Transit Commission [INT-MTD-10 (IT-06-0013)], 1971), p.5. Among other things that went wrong with this ill-starred project, the report has an incorrect project number on its cover!

29. Indeed, the major finding of the very first demonstration, an increase of bus service on Detroit's Grand River Avenue (MICH-MTD-1 [MI-06-0006]), was that the three-month demonstration period was too short. Moreover, publicizing a demonstration project as lasting only for a given period is a warning to many potential customers not to rely on a service as a long-range travel possibility.

30. The first of these was a study done in Watts (CAL-MTD-9 [not given]). Others have been conducted in the St. Louis area (MO-MTD-1 [MO-06-0002]) and an over-all look at mobility is being undertaken by M.I.T. (MASS-MTD-3 [not given]). Another interesting study is *Job Accessibility for the Unemployed: An Analysis of Public Transportation in Chicago,* Chicago Committee for Economic and Cultural Development of Chicago, March 1972. This is the final report of ILL-T9-1 (IL-09-0001). Several studies have been conducted in Cleveland as OHIO-MTD-3 (OH-06-0011). These include: *The J. & L. Story: A Manpower/Transportation Demonstration Project* (Cleveland: Cleveland Transportation Action Program [CTAP] CTAP Report No. 1, September 1970); *Downtown Loop Bus Program,* CTAP Report No. 2, October 1970; and *Metro Hospital Bus Service Demonstration Project,* CTAP Report No. 3, November 1970.

31. See also Charles M. Haar, "Transit and the Ghetto," *Nation's Cities* 5, 1 (January 1967), 7–9.

32. No final report is yet available for this study. It has apparently been squelched by UMTA, despite the obvious value to the transit industry if it had been allowed to reach its objectives.

33. For an interesting coverage of what top transit management personnel think should be researched see *Public Transportation Research Needs.*

Chapter Five: The Federal Mass Transportation Programs: What Went Right and What Went Wrong

1. See *Railway Age,* June 14, 1971, pp.26, 27.

2. "269 Grants Went to Improve Transit in '71," *Passenger Transport,* April 14, 1972, pp.1, 5.

3. See "State Departments of Transportation Directory," *IRT Digest,* No. 15 (March/April, 1974), pp.12–20; and Barry A. Brune, "Developing State DOT Organizations," and Thomas D. Larson, "Towards a More Effective State Role in Transportation," in *Proceedings—Thirteenth Annual Meeting, Transportation Research Forum* 13, 1 (1972), published by the Richard G. Cross Co., Oxford, Ind.

4. See George M. Smerk, "An Evaluation of Ten Years of Federal Policy in Urban Mass Transportation," *Transportation Journal* 11, 2 (Winter 1971), p.51. Some of the press releases read as follows: "President Nixon and Secretary Volpe have called on us to write a mass transportation success story for the 1970's, and improved services in cities like Aurora will help us meet that challenge" (News Release UMTA 72–35, for ILL-UTG-21 [IL-03-21]). "This is the kind of improvement that will help us meet the challenge extended by President Nixon in his State-of-the-Union message when he called for us to write a mass transportation success story for the 1970's." (News Release UMTA 72-34, for MASS-UTG-13 [MA-03-0013]). "This is part of President Nixon's program to help upgrade and finance new transit systems across the nation." (News Release UMTA 72-71, for GA-09-0012).

For an interesting statement on the cutbacks in funding see the statement of Michael J. Cafferty in *Urban Mass Transportation: Hearing before the Subcommittee on Housing of the Committee on Banking and Currency,* House of Representatives, 92d Congress, 2d session on *Providing Financial Assistance for the Operating Expenses of Urban Mass Transportation,* February 23, 1972 (Washington, D.C.: U.S. Government Printing Office, 1972), pp.75–78.

5. From a speech and subsequent discussion by Dr. William Ronan, chairman of the board of the Metropolitan Transit Authority of New York, at the annual meeting of the Ohio Public Transit Association, Cincinnati, August 28, 1972.

6. See Chapter 3 for detailed information on the performance of the mass transportation industries.

7. See *Appropriations Hearings—1973,* pp.762–764.

8. William J. Murin, *Mass Transit Policy Planning* (Lexington, Mass.: Heath Lexington Books, 1971), p.11.

9. *Appropriations Hearings—1973,* pp.601, 696, 860.

10. See Chapter 3 for detailed information on commuter railroad patronage.

11. Correspondence between the author and Mr. John E. Pappas, transportation superintendent, Iowa City Transit; Mr. Frank Matone, general

manager, Madison Service Corporation; Mr. Dale Luehring, general manager, Golden Gate Bridge Highway and Transportation District; and Mr. H. P. Ishmael, resident manager, Denver Metro Transit. Local support has also boosted ridership dramatically in Atlanta; Salt Lake City, too, has registered increases. See "MARTA: Setting Atlanta in Motion by Bus and Rail," *Passenger Transport,* January 19, 1973, pp.4, 5; and "Utah Transit Ridership Up," *Passenger Transport,* June 8, 1973, p.5. Also see "Transit Riders Coming Back Coast to Coast," *Passenger Transport,* February 15, 1974, p.1; and "Transit Ridership Continues Dramatic Rise," *Passenger Transport,* March 1, 1974, pp.1, 5.

12. Gilbert C. Thelen, "Mass Transit: Up against the Concrete Wall," *The Nation,* February 21, 1972, p.238.

13. *1972 National Transportation Report: Present Status—Future Alternatives* (Washington, D.C.: U.S. Department of Transportation, July 1972), pp.92–94.

14. Albert R. Karr, "Mass-Transit Groups Say Upsurge Is More Than Token Victory," *Wall Street Journal,* March 21, 1974.

15. The Mitre Corporation, a consultant to UMTA on a regular basis, prepared a series of working papers on the information issue and called for a systematic gathering of data in a number of important areas. Apparently, UMTA chose to ignore Mitre's suggestions, for—at least as of this writing—they have not been carried out, and Mitre was encouraged to direct its thoughts and counsel elsewhere.

16. To the author's knowledge, only the Pennsylvania Department of Transportation has established any standards for mass transportation. These cover such matters as the level of service, marketing, efficiency standards, and information standards. See *Operating Guidelines and Standards for the Mass Transportation Assistance Program* (Harrisburg, Pa.: Bureau of Mass Transit Systems, Pennsylvania Department of Transportation, January 1973).

17. See "Seminar in Research Needs in Transit Operations," in *Public Transportation Research Needs* (Washington, D.C.: Highway Research Board Special Report 137, 1973), pp.37–38.

18. To the author's knowledge, the only follow-up of a technical study-capital grant project was carried out in Iowa City, Iowa. This was not done as an UMTA venture, but as a paper written by several University of Iowa faculty members who had been engaged in the Iowa City technical study. According to their findings, both grants had positive results. See Kenneth J. Dueker and James Stone, *Final Report: Mass Transit Technical Study* (Iowa City: Institute of Urban and Regional Research, September 1971); and *Iowa City Transit Revival* (Iowa City: Institute of Urban and Regional Research, Technical Report No. 3, University of Iowa, January 1972). On a happier note, at the Institute for Rapid Transit 1972 annual meetings in San Francisco, UMTA announced that it was funding an impact study of the Bay Area Rapid Transit District, surely one of the most important tran-

sit events in recent history. Unfortunately, so little thought had apparently been given the project, even though construction of BART has been under way for a decade, that only a short time was available to gather benchmark data before BART opened its first line for service in September 1972.

19. The Department of Transportation attempted to get the Congress to appropriate money for transportation information collection, but the effort went for naught. See Department of Transportation, *Transportation Information, A Report to the Committee on Appropriations, U.S. House of Representatives, from the Secretary of Transportation*, May 1969.

20. *Appropriations Hearings—1973*, pp.837, 857, gives some examples of attempts to build a data base and extend the availability of information. On p.861 there is a brief discussion of the contract with the accounting firm of Arthur Andersen & Co. to develop a uniform financial reporting system for mass transportation. If adopted, such a system could be of great value. Also see *Department of Transportation and Related Agencies Appropriations for 1974, Hearings before a Subcommittee of the Committee on Appropriations, House of Representatives*, 93rd Congress, 1st session (hereinafter called *Appropriations Hearings—1974*), pp.630, 946.

21. For a discussion of this and related issues see "Center City Transportation," *Nation's Cities* 8, 2 (February 1970), 10–32.

22. See, for example, Richard J. Soloman and Joseph S. Silien, *Modes of Transportation* (New York: Urban Transportation Research Council, American Society of Civil Engineers, Sources of Information on Urban Transportation, Report No. 2, August 1968), pp.62–65. Also see *Appropriations Hearings—1973*, p.766.

23. Where monorail and other offbeat systems have been evaluated, they have been brushed aside on economic grounds, as in Manchester, England, and San Francisco. See *Manchester Rapid Transit Study*, commissioned jointly by the Corporation of Manchester, the Ministry of Transport, in association with British Railways, in three volumes: I, September 1967; II, August 1967; III, November 1968; Vol. II is most pertinent. Also see *Rapid Transit* 6, 2 (September/October 1963), (published by the San Francisco Bay Area Rapid Transit District), and Soloman and Silien, *Modes of Transportation*, an extensive discussion of all urban transport modes. Exotic hardware may work well, however, under special conditions. Private capital is planning to construct a monorail or PRT system in Las Vegas. The holiday atmosphere of the place, a high fare, and no incompatible existing rapid transit system may make it a successful venture. Also see *Appropriations Hearings—1974*, pp.653–657, 774–775, 874–877.

24. See, for example, Alan Lupo, Frank Colcord, and Edmund P. Fowler, *Rites of Way: The Politics of Transportation in Boston and the U.S. City* (Boston: Little, Brown, 1971); and Melvin R. Levin and Norman A. Abend, *Bureaucrats in Collision: Case Studies in Area Transportation Planning* (Cambridge, Mass.: M.I.T. Press, 1971).

25. Edward Weiner, "Modal Split Revisited," *Traffic Quarterly* 23, 1 (January 1969), pp.5–28; also M.J. Fertal, E. Weiner, A.J. Balek, and A.F.

Sevin, *Modal Split Documentation of Nine Methods for Estimating Transit Usage* (Washington, D.C.: U.S. Bureau of Public Roads, December 1966).

26. See Request for Proposal No. ROT-UT-30012 for an UMTA Transit Marketing Program, April 24, 1973.

27. The limited cost information available on the PRT systems at Transpo '72 puts the capital cost at about $5 million per mile, including stations and equipment. Operating costs seem to be in the range of from $1.50-$1.70 per vehicle mile. PRT proponents give somewhat lower cost estimates or gloss over the difficulty of economic cost to enjoy the blandishments of exotic hardware. For some of the technical details see *Morgantown PRT Control System* and *Dashaveyor People Mover* (Ann Arbor, Mich.: Transportation Systems Marketing, Bendix Corp., both May 1972).

28. *Appropriations Hearings—1973*, pp.681–685. The "people mover" will probably be given to Morgantown when the demonstration is over; one hopes the city will be able to afford it. Also see *Appropriations Hearings— 1974*, pp.653–657. The Morgantown project was initially expected to cost about $13 million; the reasons for the rise in cost to an estimated $125 million are given in "The Escalating Cost of a People Mover," *Business Week*, March 16, 1974, pp.50–52.

29. Bruce T. Barkley, "Some Public Policy Strategy Considerations," *New Concepts in Urban Transportation*, March 15, 1973, p.320.

30. Some work has been done in these areas. Insight into factors in transportation considered important by consumers may be found in *User Determined Attributes of Ideal Transportation Systems* (College Park: University of Maryland, Department of Business Administration, December 1965); Paine, Nash, Hille, and Bruner, *Consumer Conceived Attributes of Transportation* (College Park: University of Maryland, Department of Business Administration, September 1967). This research was sponsored by the Bureau of Public Roads. In the UMTA sponsored demonstration project in Sacramento (CAL-MTD-10 [CA-06-0028]), one of the subprojects involved some interesting sociological studies of the behavior of riders aboard a bus.

31. *Appropriations Hearings—1973*, p.844.

32. *Appropriations Hearings—1973*, pp.601, 696, 860–861. UMTA has provided some aid to cope with the crime problem. See (CAL-MTD-11 [CA-06-0029]) Robberies and Assaults of Bus Drivers, (DC-RDG-3 [DC-06-0017]) Vandalism and Passenger Security Problems on Transit Vehicles, and (INT-MTD-15 [IT-06-0018]). At the time of this writing the following publications based on these studies are: *Reduction of Robberies and Assaults of Bus Drivers*, Vol. 1, "Summary and Conclusion," (PB 197532); *Reduction of Robberies and Assaults of Bus Drivers—the Scope of the Crime Problem and Its Resolution*, Vol. 2 (PB 198056); *Reduction of Robberies and Assaults of Bus Drivers—Technological and Operational Methods*, Vol. 3 (PB 198057); and *The Scrip System of D.C. Transit System, Washington, D.C.* (PB 194958).

The exact fare plan, whereby bus drivers carry no change and patrons deposit the exact fare in a lock-type farebox, has cut down greatly on bus robberies, but at the cost of making the service less convenient for passengers.

33. This is not to imply that no effort has been made; see *Coordinated Transit for the San Francisco Bay Area—Now to 1975,* final report of Northern California Transit Demonstration Project, prepared by Simpson and Curtin Transportation Engineers, Philadelphia and San Francisco (CAL-MTD-5 [CA-06-0024] and CAL-MTD-6 [CA-06-0025]), October 1967; and *Proposed Regional Transportation Plan* (Berkeley, Cal.: Metropolitan Transportation Commission, June 1, 1973).

34. For some excellent examples of the problems of local coordination of transport effort see Richard Hebert, *Highways to Nowhere* (New York: Bobbs-Merrill, 1972), especially chapters on Dayton and Atlanta.

35. *Capital Grants for Urban Mass Transportation: Information for Applicants* (Washington, D.C.: U.S. Department of Transportation, Urban Mass Transportation Administration, June 1972), esp. pp.18–33.

36. For more information see UMTA projects INT-MTD-1 (IT-06-0007), New Brunswick, NTIS No. PB 174 740; and ILL-MTD-5 (IL-06-0009), Northwest Passage, for which no final report is yet available.

37. *Appropriations Hearings—1973,* pp.897–898, and *Appropriations Hearings—1974,* pp.663, 905–907. An excellent coverage of the shortcomings in transit management may be found in Ray A. Mundy and John C. Spychalski, *Managerial Resources and Personnel Practices in Urban Mass Transportation* (University Park: Pennsylvania State University, Transportation and Traffic Safety Center, November 1973), ch. 1.

38. Daniel P. Moynihan, "Toward a National Urban Policy," chapter in *Toward a National Urban Policy,* ed. Daniel P. Moynihan (New York: Basic, 1970), p.12.

39. See Mitchell Gordon, *Sick Cities* (Baltimore: Penguin, 1965), chs. 12, 13; Daniel R. Mandelker, "Legal Strategy for Urban Development" in *Planning for a Nation of Cities,* ed. Sam Bass Warner (Cambridge: M.I.T. Press, 1966), pp.210–212; and Robert Wood, "Intergovernmental Relationships in an Urbanizing America," in Moynihan, pp.39–49.

40. See *Motor Coach Age,* 24, 8 (August 1972), 12–19, for one of the more dispassionate reflections upon this event.

Chapter Six: Why Do Problems Persist?

1. Much of the problem stems from waning public interest in matters that appear to be dull and overly complicated, and matters so technical that the general public cannot understand them. See Marver H. Bernstein, *Regulating Business by Independent Commission* (Princeton, N.J.: Princeton University Press, 1955), esp. chs. 1, 2, 3; and Robert Fellmeth, *The Interstate Commerce Omission: The Public Interest and the I.C.C.* (New York: Grossman, 1970).

2. *Department of Transportation and Related Appropriations for 1973, Hearings Before a Subcommittee of the Committee on Appropriations,* U.S., House, 92d Congress, 2d session (Washington, D.C.: U.S. Government Printing Office, 1972), p.587 (hereinafter referred to as *Appropriations Hearings—1973*).

3. See, for example, "On the Washington Scene," *Metropolitan* 67, 4 (July/August 1971), 12–13.

4. See *Tomorrow's Transportation: New Systems for the Urban Future* (Washington, D.C.: U.S. Department of Housing and Urban Development, May 1968).

5. *Capital Grants for Urban Mass Transportation: Information for Applicants* (Washington, D.C.: U.S. Department of Transportation, Urban Mass Transportation Administration, June 1972), esp. pp.18–33.

6. Carlos C. Villarreal, "Guidelines: Capital Grant Project Selection," *Passenger Transport,* July 21, 1972, pp.1, 3.

7. "A Commentary: Capital Grant Criteria," *Passenger Transport,* June 2, 1972, p.1. The italics are in the original.

8. *Appropriations Hearings—1973,* pp.618–644, 645, 646. Also see *1972 National Transportation Report: Present Status—Future Alternatives* (Washington, D.C.: U.S. Department of Transportation, July 1972), pp.xi–xiii, 126, 135.

9. See John Burby, *The Great American Motion Sickness* (Boston: Little, Brown, 1971), pp.234–235; and Joe Asher, "Highway Money for Transit: That's What the Man Said," *Railway Age,* April 10, 1972, pp.22–25; and "Editorial," *Metropolitan* 69, 3 (May/June 1972), 36.

10. *Interim Report No. 7, Implementation of Transit Improvements,* prepared by Simpson and Curtin for the Twin Cities Area Metropolitan Transit Commission, St. Paul, Minn. (1971), p.23.

11. See "Nixon Proposes 'Revenue Sharing,'" *IRT Digest* No. 3 (March/April 1971), p.2; and "Nixon Proposes Separate Transit Revenue Sharing," *IRT Digest* No. 4 (May/June 1971), pp.1–4.

12. See "Nixon, Rep. Mills Agree on Revenue Sharing Proposal," *Passenger Transport,* December 10, 1971, pp.1, 7; "Revenue Sharing Checks to Be Mailed Soon," *Passenger Transport,* November 24, 1972, p.1; and Joel Havemann, "Revenue Sharing Report: Problems Snag Nixon Plan as Complaints from Local Areas Mount," *National Journal,* March 17, 1973, pp. 389–390. On the subject as a whole see Paul R. Dommel, *The Politics of Revenue Sharing* (Bloomington: Indiana University Press, 1974).

13. For a detailed discussion of transit management problems and approaches to more enlightened, modern, businesslike practices see George M. Smerk, "Mass Transit Management," *Business Horizons* 14, 6 (December 1971), 5–16. For an excellent discussion of the problems of transit management, see Ray A. Mundy and John C. Spychalski, *Managerial Resources and Personnel Practices in Urban Mass Transportation* (University Park: Pennsylvania State University, Transportation and Traffic Safety Center, November 1973).

14. Some reasonable, modern organizational structures may be found in *Mass Transit Management: A Handbook for Small Cities* (Bloomington: Indiana University, Institute for Urban Transportation, February 1971), ch. 1.

15. Some speculations on the reason that transit management has generally remained outside of the mainstream of modern business thought may be found in Richard J. Solomon and Arthur Saltzman, *History of Transit and Innovative Systems* (Cambridge: M.I.T. Urban Systems Laboratory, USL TR-70-20, March 1971); and Smerk, "Mass Transit Management." Some observations on the present status of marketing in the field of mass transit may be found in Ray A. Mundy, *Marketing Urban Mass Transit— 1973* (University Park: Pennsylvania State University, Transportation and Traffic Safety Center, January 1974).

16. See, for example, the chapter on Indianapolis in Richard Hebert, *Highways to Nowhere* (New York: Bobbs-Merrill, 1972).

17. For a much more detailed coverage of pricing, particularly economic highway pricing, see: George M. Smerk, *Urban Transportation: The Federal Role* (Bloomington: Indiana University Press, 1965), ch. 5; George M. Smerk, *Readings in Urban Transportation* (Bloomington: Indiana University Press, 1968), ch. 4; Richard Hebert, ch. 6; and Martin Wohl, "Public Transport Pricing, Financing, and Subsidy Principles," *Traffic Quarterly* 27, 4 (October 1973), 619–634.

18. Fare cuts in Atlanta have helped boost patronage substantially. A special tax levy helps pay the cost. In San Diego and Iowa City similar fare cuts have had a beneficial effect on ridership, thanks to the willingness of the public officials involved to make money available to pick up the difference between cost of transit operations and farebox receipts. See: "Atlanta Fares Down, Riders Up," *Passenger Transport,* March 27, 1972, pp.1, 6; "Can You Top This? San Diego Story: 53 Miles for 25¢," *Passenger Transport,* November 24, 1972, p.4; and Kenneth J. Dueker and James Stone, *Iowa City Transit Revival* (Iowa City: University of Iowa, Institute of Urban and Regional Research, Technical Report No. 3, January 1972).

The idea of fare cuts helping to boost transit patronage significantly flies in the face of the findings of *An Evaluation of Free Transit Service* (Cambridge, Mass.: Charles Rivers Associates, August 1968—NTIS No. PB179845). This study, performed for DOT, found that price elasticity of demand was very low for cuts in fares and that money would be better spent improving the quality of service—particularly cutting down on the time element—than in making transit free. Improving the quality of service appears to be a good idea, without question. However, because fares have risen to very high levels since the Charles River study was carried out, perhaps a sharp enough cut in fares will cause the curve representing the demand schedule of the public to kink and become relatively price elastic. In short, a 25-cent fare cut to 15 cents may not have anywhere near the impact on ridership of a 45-cent fare cut to 15 cents.

Chapter Seven: What Can Be Done about the Problems?

1. Robert Bartley, "Why An Orderly Transport Growth Makes Toronto's System a Showcase," *Railway Age,* June 11, 1970, p.30.

2. Developing the mobility index concept in a useful, operational fashion is easier to suggest than to do. At the present time studies are being undertaken at Indiana University on this subject under the sponsorship of the University Research Committee.

3. See Wilfred Owen, *The Accessible City* (Washington, D.C.: Brookings Institution, 1972), pp.52–53, and ch. 5.

4. See John Burby, *The Great American Motion Sickness* (Boston: Little, Brown, 1971), pp.113–114. Also see *Hearings Before a Subcommittee of the Committee on Appropriations House of Representatives: Department of Transportation and Related Agencies Appropriations for 1973,* Part 2, pp. 617–646.

5. This section is adapted from George M. Smerk, "Mass Transit Management," *Business Horizons* 14, 6 (December 1971), 5–16. The interested reader should also consult Institute for Urban Transportation, *Mass Transit Management: A Handbook for Small Cities* (Bloomington: Indiana University Graduate School of Business, February 1971), for a more detailed discussion of the necessary marketing ingredients.

6. Along the lines of providing more aid to cities that try to create a better, more helpful operating climate for mass transit, see "Notes and Comments," *Motor Coach Age* 24, 5 (May 1972), 32.

7. The transit management training program at Indiana University is an effort in this direction. All students involved are transportation majors in the School of Business. In addition, they work part-time for the I.U. Campus Bus System, gaining practical experience ranging from vehicle servicing, through driving, clerical work, schedule making, and survey research, to supervision. During summer vacation periods, the students gain perspective by working as interns for major transit firms throughout the country.

8. For an example of making good use of present knowledge and technology, see Joe Asher, "What Does Lindenwold Prove?" *Railway Age,* December 11, 1972, pp.24–25. See also, William J. Vigrass, "The Lindenwold Hi-Speed Transit Line," *Railway Management Review* 72, 2 (Summer 1972), 28–52; and Richard T. Urffer, *The First 22 Minutes* (Philadelphia: Port Authority Transit Corporation, Delaware River Port Authority, 1969).

9. As an example of improving present technology, the testing of a device by which a flywheel beneath a subway car stores the energy otherwise consumed as heat in the braking process is being conducted by the New York City Transit Authority. The stored energy is used to help start the train after a station stop, thus reducing the demand for electric power as well as reducing the level of heat produced by braking. See UMTA Project No. NY-DMG-8 (NY-06-0006).

10. *Appropriations Hearings—1973,* p.762.

11. Ibid.

12. This was prepared under Contract H-782 as part of the bundle of research behind the HUD publication *Tomorrow's Transportation,* cited earlier.

13. See *Transportation Information, A Report to the Committee on Appropriations, U.S., House, from the Secretary of Transportation,* Washington, D.C., May 1969.

14. Ibid., pp.9, 10. See pp.46–48 for a more detailed description of the proposed informational research.

15. "Depending on the level of funding of the program, over the next 24 months (FY '73 and FY '74) the Department's Transportation Information Program calls for the development of:

    1. Complete Commodity Origin-Destination files for all modes with the individual movement as the unit record of observation, on a continuing and current basis.

    2. Complete Person Origin-Destination files for all carrier modes with the individual movement as the unit record of observation, and estimating capability for private auto travel, on a continuing and current basis.

    3. Aggregation and development of a complete national inventory of transportation plant and equipment including rights-of-way, vehicles, and terminals, for all modes, structured as a computer network system, on a continuing and current basis.

    4. A computer file system containing the annual reports of all regulated carriers on a historical archive basis.

    5. Collection and maintenance of a permanent library of significant reports, tables, and materials from other transportation agencies and industry associations with a computerized location, identification, and descriptive system.

    6. Beginning on a labor inventory on an ongoing basis.

    7. Beginning of a Transportation Performance Monitoring system incorporating system performance measure, cost indices, and demand monitoring. A major component of this system will be a rapid reporting system of significant measures reported to the regulatory agencies on a monthly and quarterly basis.

    8. An operating macro-summary display system available throughout the department and other agencies, with interactive capability available within the Office of Systems Analysis and Information."

From a letter by Alan E. Pikarski, Chief, Information Division, Office of Systems Analysis and Information, Office of the Secretary, U.S. Department of Transportation, August 11, 1972.

16. One of the exceptions is the excellent study *The Socioeconomic Impact of the Capital Beltway on Northern Virginia,* prepared by the Bureau of Population and Economic Research, University of Virginia, Charlottesville, in Cooperation with the Virginia Department of Highways and the U.S. Department of Transportation, Bureau of Public Roads, 1968.

17. *Appropriations Hearings—1973*, pp.857–858. Also see *Project FARE (Financial Accounting and Reporting Elements) Task III Report,* Urban Mass Transportation Industry Reporting System Design, Arthur Anderson & Co., Washington, D.C., June 1973; Part I, Task Summary; Part II, Reporting System Instructions; Part III, Reporting System Forms; Part IV, Commuter Rail Reporting; Project No. UMTA-IT-06-0034-73-1.

18. *Appropriations Hearings—1973*, p.865.

19. Based on interviews with affected personnel on both sides. See also Ibid., pp.846, 847.

20. The cavalier treatment of the Congress by the Nixon administration, and the revelations against the administration in the various Watergate investigations might help move the Congress to regain its rightful, constitutional role.

Chapter Eight: Conclusion

1. See, for example, the case studies of Atlanta and Washington, D.C., in Richard Hebert, *Highways to Nowhere* (New York: Bobbs-Merrill, 1972).

2. For extended commentary on the role of transit in relationship to cutting pollution and helping to allay the energy shortage, see *EPA Pollution Regulations and Fuel Shortage: The Impact on Mass Transit,* Hearings before the Subcommittee on Urban Mass Transportation of the Committee on Banking and Currency, U.S., House, 93rd Congress, 1st session, July 26, 30, 31, 1973.